Management Strategies in Athletic Training

Second Edition

ATHLETIC TRAINING EDUCATION SERIES

RICHARD RAY, EdD, ATC
HOPE COLLEGE
HOLLAND, MICHIGAN

DAVID H. PERRIN, PhD, ATC
SERIES EDITOR
UNIVERSITY OF VIRGINIA, CHARLOTTESVILLE

HUMAN KINETICS

Library of Congress Cataloging-in-Publication Data

Ray, Richard, 1957-
    Management strategies in athletic training / Richard Ray. -- 2nd ed.
         p.   cm. -- (Athletic training education series)
    Includes bibliographical references and index.
    ISBN 0-88011-810-5
    1. Athletic trainers.   I. Title.   II. Series.
  RC1210.R38   2000
  617.1'027--dc21   99-27701
                                     CIP

ISBN: 0-88011-810-5

Permission notices for material reprinted in this book from other sources can be found on page xvii.

Acquisitions Editor: Loarn D. Robertson, PhD
Series Editors: Kristine Enderle and Elaine Mustain
Developmental Editor: Joanna Hatzopoulos
Assistant Editors: Susan C. Hagan, Stephan Seyfert, and Mark Zulauf
Copyeditor: Lisa Morgan
Proofreader: Myla Smith
Indexer: Sharon Duffy
Permission Manager: Heather Munson
Graphic Designer: Stuart Cartwright
Graphic Artists: Judy Henderson, Dawn Sills, Angela K. Snyder, and Kathleen Boudreau-Fuoss
Photo Editor: Clark Brooks
Photographer: Tom Roberts
Cover Designer: Stuart Cartwright
Illustrators: Argosy and Angela K. Snyder
Printer: United Graphics
Binder: Dekker & Sons

Printed in the United States of America   10 9 8 7 6 5 4 3 2 1

Human Kinetics
Web site: http://www.humankinetics.com/

United States: Human Kinetics
P.O. Box 5076
Champaign, IL 61825-5076
1-800-747-4457
e-mail: humank@hkusa.com

Canada: Human Kinetics
475 Devonshire Road Unit 100
Windsor, ON N8Y 2L5
1-800-465-7301 (in Canada only)
e-mail: humank@hkcanada.com

Europe: Human Kinetics, P.O. Box IW14
Leeds LS16 6TR, United Kingdom
+44 (0)113-278 1708
e-mail: humank@hkeurope.com

Australia: Human Kinetics
57A Price Avenue
Lower Mitcham, South Australia 5062
(08) 82771555
e-mail: liahka@senet.com.au

New Zealand: Human Kinetics
P.O. Box 105-231, Auckland Central
09-523-3462
e-mail: humank@hknewz.com

This book is dedicated to all my teachers, but especially

To Mom and Dad, my first teachers,
with devotion and thanks.

To Lindsy McLean and Otho Davis,
with respect and pride.

To my students,
with hope for the future.

To Carol,
with love and joy.

CONTENTS

INTRODUCTION TO THE ATHLETIC TRAINING EDUCATION SERIES

The five textbooks of the Athletic Training Education Series—*Introduction to Athletic Training, Assessment of Athletic Injuries, Therapeutic Exercise for Athletic Injuries, Therapeutic Modalities for Athletic Injuries,* and *Management Strategies in Athletic Training,* second edition*—were written for student athletic trainers and as a reference for practicing certified athletic trainers. Many textbooks have been written that in one way or another address the competencies in athletic training. However, absent from these books has been a coordinated approach to the competencies that serves to optimally prepare student athletic trainers for the National Athletic Trainers' Association (NATA) certification examination. If you are a student athletic trainer, you must master the material included in each of the content areas delineated in the NATA publication *Competencies in Athletic Training.* The philosophy of the Athletic Training Education Series is to address these competencies in a comprehensive and sequential manner, while avoiding unnecessary duplication.

The series covers the educational content areas developed by the Education Council of the National Athletic Trainers' Association for accredited curriculum development. These content areas and the text (or in some cases, texts) of the series that primarily addresses each content area are as follows:

- Risk management and injury prevention (*Introduction* and *Management Strategies*)
- Pathology of injury and illnesses (*Introduction, Therapeutic Exercise, Therapeutic Modalities,* and *Assessment*)
- Assessment and evaluation (*Assessment* and *Therapeutic Exercise*)
- Acute care of injury and illness (*Introduction* and *Management Strategies*)
- Pharmacology (*Introduction* and *Therapeutic Modalities*)
- Therapeutic modalities (*Therapeutic Modalities*)
- Therapeutic exercise (*Therapeutic Exercise*)
- General medical conditions and disabilities (*Introduction* and *Assessment*)
- Nutritional aspects of injury and illness (*Introduction*)
- Psychosocial intervention and referral (*Introduction, Therapeutic Modalities,* and *Therapeutic Exercise*)
- Health care administration (*Management Strategies*)
- Professional development and responsibilities (*Introduction* and *Management Strategies*)

The authors for this series—Craig Denegar, Susan Hillman, Peggy Houglum, Richard Ray, Sandy Shultz, and I—are six certified athletic trainers with well over a century of collective experience as clinicians, educators, and leaders in the athletic training profession. The clinical experience of the authors spans virtually every setting in which athletic trainers practice, including the high school, sports medicine clinic, college, professional sport, hospital, and industrial settings. The professional positions of the authors include undergraduate and graduate curriculum director, head athletic trainer, professor, clinic director, and researcher. The authors have chaired or served as members of NATA's most important committees, including the Professional Education Committee, the Education Task Force, Education Council, Research Committee of the Research and Education Foundation, Journal Committee, Appropriate Medical Coverage for Intercollegiate Athletics Task Force, Continuing Education Committee, and many others. The six authors of the series have created the most comprehensive and progressive collection of texts and related instructional materials presently available to athletic training students and educators. These materials, designed to accompany an accredited athletic training curriculum, will also serve to optimally prepare you for successful completion of the certification examination.

You will find several elements common to all the books in the series. These include

- chapter objectives and summaries tied to one another so that students can know and achieve their learning goals,
- chapter opening scenarios that illustrate the importance and relevance of the chapter content,
- cross-referencing among texts for a complete education on the subject, and
- thorough reference lists for further reading and research.

To enhance instruction, the series also includes Microsoft® PowerPoint presentations and instructor guides that comprise features such as course syllabuses, lecture and chapter outlines, case studies, and test banks. Where most appropriate, laboratory manuals accompany texts. Other features vary from book to book, depending on the requirements of the subject matter, but all include various aids for assimilation and review of information, extensive illustrations, and material to help the student apply the facts in the text.

Beyond the introductory text by Hillman, the order in which the books should be used is determined by the philosophy of your curriculum director. In any case, each book can stand alone so that an entire curriculum doesn't need to be revamped to use one or more parts of the series.

When I entered the profession of athletic training nearly 25 years ago, one text—*Prevention and Care of Athletic Injuries* by Klafs and Arnheim—covered nearly all the subject matter necessary to pass the NATA Board of Certification examination and practice as an entry-level athletic trainer. Since that time we have witnessed an amazing expansion of the subject matter necessary to practice athletic training and an equally impressive growth of practice settings in which athletic trainers work. I trust you will find the Athletic Training Education Series an invaluable resource as you prepare for a successful career as a certified athletic trainer and a most useful reference in your professional practice.

David H. Perrin, PhD, ATC
Series Editor

PREFACE

Athletic training has evolved through the years. Our predecessors early in the 20th century were little more than clubhouse helpers for a select population of college and professional athletes. Following the establishment in 1950 of the National Athletic Trainers' Association (NATA), however, credentialing and professional education standards helped create a growing demand for our services. Athletic trainers are now allied health care professionals who provide injury prevention and management services for the public. In this book "athletes" are described in many ways—as physically active people, clients, and patients—and they are presented in real-world settings, including traditional college and high school athletic training programs, sports medicine clinics, hospitals, professional teams, and industrial settings. As athletic trainers' employment settings and clientele have expanded, their need for administrative knowledge and skills has also expanded.

WHY THIS TEXT IS NEEDED

The days when an athletic trainer could get by without some administrative expertise are gone. The financial assets entrusted to the contemporary athletic trainer require prudent, thoughtful management. Athletic trainers can acquire some of the organizational knowledge and skill they need through on-the-job experience, but many entry-level athletic trainers will not get the information they need this way. The primary purpose of this book is to provide a standard for the kinds of knowledge and skills that every athletic trainer entering the field should master. Because entry-level athletic trainers will confront administrative problems that are growing in number and complexity, this book can be used as a reference to help them cope with those problems while they provide high-quality services to their clients.

This text is also intended to enhance the administrative ability of athletic trainers already in practice. It contains a variety of topics and insights that many athletic trainers past the entry level don't consider in managerial or administrative terms. Practicing athletic trainers will learn to apply management theories to the administrative problems they have faced for years and to craft creative solutions to these problems.

This text brings together the body of knowledge about organization and administration and applies it to the profession of athletic training. Credentialing boards of national and state athletic training organizations can use this book as a source of valid questions for credentialing examinations. Currently available sources are either inadequate in focus because they are not intended for athletic trainers or inadequate in scope because they are typically single chapters in books intended for other purposes.

WHO THIS TEXT WILL BENEFIT

The three primary audiences for this text are

- undergraduate students preparing for NATA certification,
- graduate students either preparing for NATA certification or working toward an advanced degree in athletic training, and
- practicing athletic trainers who are already certified but who wish to either develop or update their knowledge and skill in athletic training administration.

HOW THIS TEXT IS ORGANIZED

This book presents theories underlying the management principles that athletic trainers have historically been forced to learn through experience, using anecdotes, practical suggestions, and case studies whenever possible to illustrate how management theory applies to the work of athletic trainers. An opening case precedes each chapter, and the content of the chapter relates to this opening case. Each chapter concludes with two case studies that require students to apply the theories presented in the chapter to real-world situations.

SPECIAL FEATURES

The following pedagogical aids are intended to help instructors and students master the content.

- **Electronic instructor guide.** A comprehensive compendium of useful instructional aids is available for instructors. Included in the instructor guide are case studies, course projects, chapter worksheets, sample examination questions, and a sample course syllabus.

- **Chapter objectives.** Each chapter opens with a list of expected learning outcomes. These objectives are broad enough to form the behavioral objectives for an entire course in athletic training administration.

- **Key words.** Boldfacing highlights key words and important phrases to help readers determine what the most important concepts are at a glance.

- **Glossary.** Readers will find a glossary of important terms at the end of the book. In addition, there is a running glossary that includes the same terms in the margins near the text where the term is used.

- **Sample forms.** There are sample forms for reference in each chapter. Readers can modify these forms for their own use.

- **Case studies.** Each chapter begins with an opening case study and concludes with two more. Each case includes a hypothetical scenario that will help students understand more fully the relationship between the theory and the application of various concepts discussed in the chapter. The cases at the ends of the chapters are accompanied by a series of questions that require students to synthesize the information presented in the chapter and to develop alternative responses to each scenario. The analysis questions are open-ended and encourage students to be creative in developing possible solutions. There is no fixed number of right or wrong answers.

- **Running review statements.** Summaries of the key points of each major section can be found in blue text in the margins to help readers focus on the material that is most important.

- **Chapter summaries.** The most important concepts are summarized at the end of each chapter. Summaries are formatted to parallel the chapter objectives for easier review.

- **Bibliography.** A complete reading list, which includes all the references used to develop the chapters, guides students to sources for additional information on any given topic.

- **Index.** An index of the entire text by author and subject facilitates easy reference.

WHAT'S NEW IN THE SECOND EDITION

The second edition of *Management Strategies in Athletic Training* has been improved significantly. First, this edition is part of the *Athletic Training Education Series,* which is a collection of five textbooks, published by Human Kinetics, that are designed to meet the bulk of the discipline-specific content for an entry-level athletic training curriculum. An improvement to this edition is the inclusion of two new chapters. Helping Athletic Trainers Do the Right Thing: Ethical Considerations in Sports Medicine will stimulate readers to think more carefully and consistently about the ethical soundness of their actions as sports health care professionals. Another new chapter is Special Management Problems for the Athletic Trainer: Administration of Preparticipation Physical Examinations and Drug-Testing Programs. This chapter will help readers do a better job of organizing for these two important functions. Finally, each of the original eight chapters has been updated. New material, which, like the rest of the information from the first edition, flows from the "Health Care Administration" portion of the NATA Role Delineation Study, includes the following:

- A history of management theories
- Discussion of communication theory
- More examples for how to improve administrative practice
- Information on the role of accreditation in health care
- Tips for improving the productivity of a meeting
- Exploration of the role of chart auditing and outcomes studies
- Discussion of informal organizations
- New, up-to-date forms
- Policy and procedure handbook outlines
- Critical assessment of employee application materials
- Exploration of motivation in the workplace
- Information on the Fair Labor Standards Act
- Discussion of needs assessment
- Review of external funding sources
- Discussion of ergonomics in the design of athletic training facilities
- Sample floor plans for a variety of athletic training settings
- Discussion of the Buckley Amendment
- Useful Web sites for athletic trainers
- Updated compilation of list server discussion lists
- Exploration of risk management in athletics
- Discussion of product liability in sports medicine
- Overview of the organizational structure of the NATA

A NOTE TO INSTRUCTORS

If you are an athletic training educator, you might be wondering how this book can be most effectively used as part of a course on athletic training administration. In my experience, this material is learned best when students can apply it to the things they have seen in their short, but interesting, careers. Don't lecture from this book.

Allow students to read the material and develop questions about how the information should or could be applied to real-life problems they've encountered or heard about. Use the questions and exercises in the case studies at the end of the chapter to start class conversations about the material. The instructor's manual that accompanies this book is loaded with extra case studies, class projects, worksheets, and sample examinations. For those who are still uncertain as to how to develop their course, a sample syllabus—the one I use in my course—is provided. Keep in mind that the time you will have with your students in the classroom is very limited and is quite small compared to the amount of time they have on their own. I recommend that you use the time that students have on their own for "first exposure learning." I require my students to read the assigned chapter and complete the chapter worksheet prior to coming to class. When they arrive all I have to do is ask "Any questions?" and an hour later we're finished. We'll typically spend the entire hour talking about, reinforcing, clarifying, and explaining the concepts that they found difficult in their reading. This method has proven to be far more effective than lecturing in this kind of course.

A NOTE TO STUDENTS

If you are a student using *Management Strategies in Athletic Training*, second edition in an athletic training administration course, you might be wondering if you should use this book just as you would all the textbooks you've been assigned in your other courses. I wouldn't recommend it, and here's why: experience. This book was written to help you experience, through reading and doing, what it is like to be an ATC faced with administrative problems. You'll be introduced to fictional ATCs at the beginning of each chapter and their stories will guide you through the material. Ask yourself how the concepts in the book can or should be applied in a real-life setting as you read through the text. How do they apply to the case in the book? How do they apply to the athletic training program at your college or university? As you read each chapter I recommend you use the margin of the book to write notes to yourself. "Why did the ATC in this chapter go over his AD's head? Wasn't that dangerous?" "The book recommends the use of bidding when purchasing supplies. Why doesn't the ATC at our school do this?" Use the questions you develop to guide your participation in class. If you use this approach and aren't afraid to ask questions in class based on your reading, I think you'll find that your athletic training administration class will be one of the most interesting and exciting courses you take on your way to becoming a certified athletic trainer.

A FINAL WORD

Athletic trainers of my generation were forced to learn how to become administrators through the "school of hard knocks." My experience has been similar, I'm sure, to that of many of my colleagues around the country who came of age in the 1970s and early '80s. I wrote this book so ATCs of the new millennium could be better prepared to deal effectively with the many administrative and managerial problems they are likely to face in an increasingly complex health care environment. I hope that after they have read through and experienced the material in this book, they will find themselves prepared for the real world they are about to enter.

ACKNOWLEDGMENTS

I am indebted to many people who gave their time and expertise to help make this book possible. I especially want to thank the professionals at Human Kinetics, who not only offered many suggestions to improve the book but also were kind and patient throughout the process. *Athletic Training Education Series* editor, Dave Perrin, was a fine team leader in helping to organize this work. I am especially thankful for the thoughtful manuscript reviews offered by Rick Zappala, Ken Wright, and Deidre Leaver Dunn. Their insights proved most useful in the editing stage of the project. Finally, I am deeply indebted to the students and my colleagues at Hope College who graciously gave me the time and encouragement to work on this project.

CREDITS

Figure 2.2 Adapted with the permission of The Free Press, a Division of Simon & Schuster, Inc. from *STRATEGIC PLANNING: What every manager must know* by George A. Steiner. Copyright © 1979 by The Free Press.

Figure 2.7 Adapted, by permission, from P. Block, 1987, *The empowered manager: Positive political skills at work* (San Francisco: Jossey-Bass), 133.

Text p. 61 From James A.F. Stoner, *MANAGEMENT*, 2nd ed., © 1982, p. 268, 271. Adapted by permission of Prentice Hall, Englewood Cliffs, New Jersey.

Text p. 63 From James A.F. Stoner, *MANAGEMENT*, 2nd ed., © 1982, p. 274. Adapted by permission of Prentice Hall, Englewood Cliffs, New Jersey.

Figure 3.8 From *The personnel function in educational administration*, 4th ed., by Castetter, © 1986. Reprinted by permission of Prentice-Hall, Inc., Upper Saddle River, NJ.

Figure 3.14 From *Psychology applied to industry* by Dunnette/Kirchner, © 1965. Reprinted by permission of Prentice-Hall, Inc., Upper Saddle River, NJ.

Chapter 4 Brief sections of this chapter appeared previously in *Athletic Business,* 15 (1), copyright 1991 by Richard Ray and *Athletic Business* magazine; and in *College Athletic Management*, 2 (1), copyright 1989 by College Athletic Administrator, Inc. Reprinted by permission.

Figure 4.1 Adapted, by permission, from Standard & Poor's, 1998, *Revenue data for HealthSouth Corporation and Nova Care Corp.* (New York: Standard & Poor's).

Figure 5.1 Adapted, by permission, from R. Muther and J.D. Wheeler, 1977, *Simplified systematic layout planning* (Kansas City, MO: Management & Industrial Research). Extended copyright 1990 by Richard Muther. Adapted courtesy of copyright holder: Richard Muther.

Figure 5.4 Reprinted, by permission, from M.M. Porter and J.W. Porter, 1981, "Electrical safety in the training room," *Journal of Athletic Training* 16: 263–264.

Figure 5.7 Reprinted from Pioneer High School athletic training room blueprint, by permission of Pioneer High School, Ann Arbor, MI.

Figure 5.9 Adapted with permission from Horizon View Development, L.L.C. Designed by Eckert/Wordell Architects, Kalamazoo, MI.

Figure 6.7 Adapted, by permission, from B.J. Miles, 1987, "Injuries on the road: Good information reduces problems," *Journal of Athletic Training* 22 (2): 127.

Figure 6.11 Adapted, by permission, from J.R. Needy, 1974, A sample park and recreation department filing system. In *Filing systems,* edited by J.R. Needy (Arlington, VA: National Recreation and Park Association), 26–29.

Figure 7.3 From *Understanding medical insurance,* 1st ed., by J.C. Rowell. © 1989. Reprinted with permission of Delmar Publishers, a division of Thomson Learning. Fax: 800-730-2215.

Chapter 9 Portions of this chapter were reprinted or adapted, by permission, from P.V. Loubert, 1999, Ethical perspectives in counseling. In *Counseling in sports medicine,* edited by R.R. Ray and D. Wiese-Bjornstal (Champaign, IL: Human Kinetics), 161–175.

Tables 10.2 and **10.3** Reprinted, by permission, from M.C. Koester, 1995, "Refocusing the adolescent preparticipation physical evaluation toward preventive health care," *Journal of Athletic Training* 30: 352–360.

Appendix D Reprinted, by permission, from National Athletic Trainers' Association, 1995, *NATA code of ethics* (Dallas: Author).

CHAPTER ONE

Why Athletic Trainers Organize: The Theoretical Basis of Management

OBJECTIVES

After completing this chapter, you should be able to do the following:

1. Define the concepts of power, authority, and leadership.

2. Understand the historical trends in management and how they might apply to athletic training.

3. Understand the different managerial roles assumed by athletic trainers.

4. Understand the various strategies athletic trainers can employ to improve their managerial effectiveness.

The staff meeting went just about as badly as Sharon Johnson was afraid it might. The athletic trainers she supervises (in the sports medicine clinic of which she is a part owner) are angry. Sharon is also an athletic trainer, brought in by a physician and a physical therapist to help establish sports medicine services in a struggling outpatient physical therapy practice. When Sharon hired her staff of three certified athletic trainers, her partners required that they contribute a percentage of their health insurance premiums. They assured Sharon that this would be a temporary arrangement—three years at most—until they were confident that the expansion into sports medicine was going to pay off. Sharon's athletic trainers were upset because, after three years, they were still being forced to contribute to their health insurance, even though the clinic's physical therapists didn't contribute a penny. Sharon agreed with their position. She felt they ought to be treated like the other professional staff. The problem she faced was that the physical therapist partner wanted to maintain the status quo, whereas the physician was wavering between the two positions.

Sharon finally decided to call a partners' meeting, at which she threatened to pull out of the business unless the issue was resolved in favor of the athletic trainers. The vote was two to one in favor of Sharon's position. Unfortunately, Sharon's cordial working relationship with her two partners was partially eroded in the process. The physical therapist became coldly formal, and the physician was upset that Sharon had used a threat to get what she wanted.

Being powerful is like being a lady. If you have to tell people you are, you ain't.

Jesse Carr

Elements of Sharon's dilemma are commonly experienced by athletic trainers, whatever the employment setting. Most athletic trainers have had to suffer through the tension that results from a power play in their organizations. Though they typically lack formal education or training in management theory, athletic trainers need to be at least conversant with major theories of organizational behavior to make maximum use of the power, authority, and leadership that are normal components of their personal and professional profiles.

FOUNDATIONS OF MANAGEMENT

Athletic trainers can perform their managerial responsibilities best when they exercise leadership with the authority they have been provided by their superiors. Both leadership and authority represent a certain kind of power that all athletic trainers have as a benefit of their position and expertise.

Athletic trainers are often responsible for managing programs with large budgets and staffs. Until recently, intuition and on-the-job experience have been athletic trainers' only tools for attempting to solve administrative problems. Formal study of the principles underlying sound management practice should help athletic trainers perform their jobs better.

The emphasis on the conceptual and theoretical aspects of management is important. Too often, athletic trainers who assume management roles continue to behave like health care providers and forget to behave like managers. This role confusion is understandable. After all, if you have been a practitioner for 10 years or more and are suddenly thrust into a new position with new responsibilities, you have an adjustment to make. Managerial responsibilities are different from patient-care responsibilities. When you take care of a patient, your only responsibility is to the patient. Managerial duties, on the other hand, require you to take a broader view of the needs of not only the patients but also the employees, the department, and the organization. You must consider the needs of various external stakeholder groups. In short, you will need to expand your world view and begin *thinking* like a manager. An understanding of the major theories of management will help athletic trainers make the transition.

POWER

Scholars who devote their careers to the study of power cannot agree on a precise definition, but the definition most inclusive of the research done on the subject was put forth by Bass (1990). Power is the potential to influence.

Why is it important for students of athletic training administration to be able to define, recognize, and use power? Power is the glue that binds persons or groups in a relationship. It is the basis for both authority and leadership. Athletic trainers possess significant power in their relationships with coaches, administrators, clients, and other health care professionals. Sharon's case illustrates an athletic trainer recognizing her potential to influence others and acting on it. Sharon exercised power.

Athletic trainers can exercise power over those above them, below them, and at the same level in an organization. The two primary modalities for the exercise of organizational power are position power and personal power.

Position Power

Athletic trainers, by virtue of their positions, possess resources they can use to influence the behavior of others in their organizations. Someone who supervises student athletic trainers, for example, can influence their behavior through the use of rewards and punishments—grades, financial aid, work-study money, desirable team assignments and internship placements, and the like. In an organization that follows a medical chain of command, the athletic trainer can use the power provided by that policy to change the behavior of a coach who may desire to usurp the athletic trainer's medical authority.

The ability to influence the behavior of a superior has been termed counterpower (Yukl, 1981). Counterpower is a tool that most athletic trainers need because they are typically viewed as support personnel who are less important than other organizational decision makers. Without counterpower, athletic trainers would be little more than technical consultants to more powerful coaches and athletic administrators, unable to influence the actions of these two important groups.

One of the ways athletic trainers can effectively use position power is by controlling the flow of information (Pettigrew, 1972). By controlling information, athletic trainers can influence the perceptions and attitudes of their subordinates. For example, assistant athletic trainers often learn of changes in departmental policy through their head athletic trainers. And student athletic trainers depend to a large degree on instructors and supervisors to inform them of changes in the profession.

Athletic trainers can also make superiors reliant on them for certain types of information. For example, in the draft systems of professional sports, potential draftees are examined by both physicians and athletic trainers. How the results are passed on to decision makers can significantly influence whether an athlete is drafted or not. Ultimately, the athletic trainer exercises influence through providing or withholding information.

Personal Power

The athletic trainer's ability to influence others in the organization often depends more on personal characteristics and personality attributes than on formal authority. Indeed, athletic trainers who use charisma and personal appeal to influence others in their organizations are more likely to receive acceptance and support for their ideas. Coercive power and authoritarian methods, on the other hand, are more likely to produce mere compliance, decreasing satisfaction and performance levels among the staff members these athletic trainers supervise (Yukl, 1981).

power The potential to influence others.

position power The power vested in people by virtue of the roles they play in an organization.

personal power The potential to influence others by virtue of personal characteristics and personality attributes.

counterpower The potential to influence the behavior of a superior.

One of the most effective elements of athletic trainers' personal power is their reputation as experts. People are likely to follow the recommendation of someone they perceive as an expert (French & Raven, 1959). Athletic trainers make judgments based on their expertise in sports medicine every day. Athletes and other physically active patients who follow the treatment plan outlined by an athletic trainer probably have faith in the athletic trainer as an expert. When they fail to follow their treatment and rehabilitation plans, it is often because they have lost faith in the expertise of the athletic trainer supervising their programs. In these cases, the athletic trainer must resort to position power as the basis for achieving compliance. Unfortunately, using the external motivators of position power is rarely as effective as using the internal motivators of personal power.

AUTHORITY

authority   That aspect of power, granted to either groups or individuals, that legitimizes the right of the group or individual to make decisions on behalf of others.

Authority is that aspect of power, granted to either groups or individuals, that legitimizes the right of the group or individual to make decisions on behalf of others. Implicit in this definition is the notion that authority is a subset of the broader construct of power. Although there are authors who disagree with this proposition (Friedrich, 1963; Kahn, 1968), most evidence clearly identifies authority as a type of power (Burns, 1978; Dejnozka, 1983; Good, 1973; Jacobs, 1970; Katz & Kahn, 1966; King, 1987; Lasswell & Kaplan, 1950; Organ & Bateman, 1986). If power is the glue that binds persons or groups together in a relationship, then authority is the applicator through which power is applied. Without authority, athletic trainers would lack position power.

legitimacy   That aspect of power that gives the leader the right to make a request and provides the obligation of the subordinate to comply.

Central to the meaning of authority is the concept of legitimacy. Authority is legitimate by its very nature (Good, 1973; Hollander, 1978; Karelis, 1987; Weber, 1962). **Legitimacy** is a check on the scope of an athletic trainer's authority. Consider Sharon's case at the beginning of this chapter. Although she might have wanted to grant the request of her staff members, she didn't have the authority to do so without the consent of her partners. Any decision made without her partners' consent would have lacked legitimacy.

zone of indifference   A hypothetical boundary of legitimacy, outside of which requests or orders will be met with mere compliance or refusal.

Legitimacy is an especially important concept for athletic trainers who supervise others' work. Barnard (1938) postulated that each person has a **zone of indifference.** People typically accept requests or orders within this zone without conscious questioning because they view them as appropriate given the status of the person making the request. Orders or requests outside the zone, however, lack legitimacy, and people often refuse to comply with them. Athletic trainers who supervise assistants or students should be cautious about asking them to do things outside the zone of indifference. It might be legitimate, for example, to ask a student athletic trainer to wash a whirlpool. Don't expect enthusiastic support if you ask the same student to wash your car!

Another property implicit in this definition of authority is that it involves decision making and is therefore action oriented. Like its parent, power, authority can be observed only when it is exercised. If Sharon had not acted on the vote of her partners in the health insurance case, she would have abrogated her authority in the matter. Athletic trainers are called on to make many administrative decisions during the course of a typical day: Should I order more tape? How should I arrange the team physician's injury clinic schedule? How many athletic trainers will be needed to cover the wrestling tournament? Athletic trainers exercise the authority they have been granted when they answer these questions with action. Indeed, many of their administrative problems stem from hesitation to use their authority.

There is one notable exception to the action orientation normally associated with authority. Some situations call for the athletic trainer to exercise authority by making a conscious decision *not* to act. Let's consider Sharon's dilemma as an example.

Suppose that instead of being neutral, her physician partner was against Sharon's point of view on the health insurance issue and in favor of the physical therapist partner's. In that case, Sharon would know that calling a vote on the matter would likely result in a formal company position against full compensation of health insurance benefits for staff athletic trainers. The only prudent action she could take in this circumstance would be no action at all, other than to continue to try to convince her partners to support her. To request a vote would be counterproductive. The important point is that Sharon's inaction would be goal oriented. She would be letting the issue lie for the moment so she would be able to fight another day.

The athletic trainer's use of her authority can be a powerful tool to prompt task accomplishment. Authority provides a new athletic trainer an immediate power base to help her accomplish tasks. This is sometimes referred to as the **honeymoon effect.** Newly hired people in athletic training programs are often granted more authority to make decisions than they would be six months or a year after arrival. The honeymoon effect is an important factor in rejuvenating programs. Without it, new athletic trainers would have little impact because they wouldn't be able to implement new ideas as easily.

There are several drawbacks to excessive use of authority to accomplish tasks in athletic training programs. Athletic trainers who rely too heavily on their authority are likely to find that their staffs respond with mere compliance and minimal effort (Organ & Bateman, 1986). The athletic trainer who constantly reminds his assistants "who's the boss" might be successful in extracting a minimal amount of work from the assistants, but he is also likely to experience a high rate of turnover. Athletic trainers who rely heavily on authority are also likely to find that their subordinates try to avoid them. The threat, perceived or real, of negative sanctions imposed by an authoritarian supervisor against subordinates is a common theme, even for those athletic trainers with no rational basis for their perceptions.

honeymoon effect
The period of time, usually immediately after arriving in a new position, in which persons are more likely to be granted extra authority to make decisions.

LEADERSHIP

leadership   A subset of power that involves influencing the behavior and attitudes of others to achieve intended outcomes.

Leadership is the process of influencing the behavior and attitudes of others to achieve intended outcomes. Like authority, it is a subset of the broader construct of power (Burns, 1978). There are nearly as many definitions of leadership as there are scholars who have studied the topic—over 130 distinct definitions exist (Burns, 1978). One of the few common denominators among this host of definitions is the assumption that leadership involves an intentional influence process by a leader over followers (Yukl, 1981). In addition, leadership is success oriented. If a "leader" attempts an action and doesn't get the support of followers, has leadership really taken place?

Why is a discussion of leadership important for athletic trainers? The exercise of leadership is the keystone of managerial success. Without the ability to influence attitudes and behaviors toward some predetermined goal, the athletic trainer is an ineffective agent for change in her organization. Unfortunately, we often think of leaders as persons on the national or international stage. Churchill, Ghandi, and Roosevelt were certainly effective leaders. The more common form of leadership is a more local phenomenon, however. We are all surrounded by leaders in our homes, churches, communities, and the sports medicine settings in which we work. Without leadership, the organizations that employ us would stagnate and cease to be effective in providing needed services to their clients.

transactional leadership   The simple exchange between leaders and followers of one thing for another.

To help athletic trainers understand the importance of effective leadership and the effect it can have on their managerial success, it is useful to examine the two types of leadership found in most social structures, including the organizations that employ athletic trainers. Burns (1978) contends that there are two distinct forms of leadership: transactional and transformational. **Transactional leadership** involves the simple exchange of one thing for another in a relationship between two people.

An athletic trainer pays her assistants in exchange for work. An athletic director agrees to send an athletic trainer to a conference in exchange for covering a state high school basketball tournament. Most administrative activities in organizations where athletic trainers work involve the transactional form of leadership. This book is devoted primarily to principles and techniques intended to improve the athletic trainer's ability to be a transactional leader. Transactional leadership is the stuff of management.

Nevertheless, a program or organization in which only transactional leadership takes place will probably not thrive. Organizational renewal and program improvement require transformational leadership. **Transformational leadership** transcends the day-to-day administrative requirements of operating an athletic training program by elevating standards through the creative use of change and conflict. The athletic trainer who can successfully prepare budgets, hire staff, purchase supplies, and schedule personnel is an effective transactional leader. The athletic trainer who recognizes the need to reduce the incidence of eating disorders among her athletes and who implements programs that successfully accomplish this task exhibits transformational leadership.

Transformational leadership almost always involves change in the organization. This change is likely to engender some degree of conflict. Consider the example of setting up an eating disorders program. Such programs cost money. Instructional materials must be developed or purchased. Group facilitators and therapists must be contracted. Funding will either have to come from existing programs or be raised specifically for the project. Decisions like these often bring athletic trainers into conflict with coaches and athletic administrators who are in competition for scarce financial resources. The athletic trainer who is a skilled transformational leader will be able to manage the conflict to meet the needs of coaches, athletic administrators, and athletes with eating disorders. As you can see, the transformational aspect of leadership is both challenging and essential if an athletic training program is to meet the changing needs of its clients.

transformational leadership   That aspect of leadership that uses both change and conflict to elevate the standards of the social system.

A BRIEF HISTORY OF MANAGEMENT

Management is an old concept. Its study and practice have changed over the years. Early 20th century managerial theories include scientific management and human relations management. Management theories developed in the latter half of the century include field theory, MacGregor's Theory X and Theory Y, and Deming's Total Quality Management.

Although basic concepts of organizing the labor of others toward a common goal date back to the ancient past, the study of modern management techniques is a more recent phenomenon. What follows is a brief description of some of the more prominent management ideas that have been developed over the past 100 years.

SCIENTIFIC MANAGEMENT

scientific management A collection of management theories developed in the early 1900s whose emphasis is on the strict control of work in order to maximize production through increases in efficiency.

The **scientific management** movement began in the early 1900s. Widely acknowledged as the father of modern management, Frederick Taylor introduced the idea of division of labor and management whereby workers should be viewed as parts of a large machine whose function was to produce a product. He believed that money was the sole motivating force that would induce workers to perform their jobs well. One of Taylor's major contributions was the time and motion study, whereby a worker's job was broken into discrete tasks, each of which was mathematically analyzed for maximum efficiency. Taylor's contribution to managerial science resulted in more efficient industrial practices in an environment where the self-esteem needs of employees were largely ignored because they were not thought to be important. An efficiently designed athletic training room or sports medicine clinic where the staff can serve the maximum number of athletes or other physically active patients with the least amount of movement between stations is an example of the influence of Taylor's thinking applied to athletic training.

The primary concept driving the development of scientific management was a desire for greater efficiency. Another early theorist in the scientific management movement who helped to define the methods necessary to achieve efficiency was Harrington Emerson. Emerson was an engineer who believed that strict compliance with his "12 principles" would lend greater efficiency not only to specific jobs within a company, but to the entire business itself. Although Emerson's principles were designed with the railroad industry in mind, he was convinced that they had application to any enterprise where the predictability of results was desirable. These principles are summarized below.

Emerson's 12 Principles of Efficiency

1. **Ideals:** Develop clearly defined goals.

2. **Common Sense:** Ensure that goals contribute to the improvement of the enterprise.

3. **Competent Counsel:** Seek advice from those who know more than you do.

4. **Discipline**: Ensure that employees know their jobs and establish a system for recruiting and selecting good employees.

5. **The Fair Deal**: Provide fair wages and good working conditions.

6. **Records**: Document and analyze the work process in order to make good decisions.

7. **Dispatching**: Plan the work schedule for maximum efficiency.

8. **Standards and Schedules**: Establish standards for work through proper placement of employees.

9. **Standardized Conditions:** Optimize the work setting.

10. **Standardized Operations**: Develop a consistent process for the performance of tasks.

11. **Standardized Practice Instructions**: Teach all employees to perform tasks in the same manner.

12. **Efficiency Reward**: Provide financial incentives for excellent performance.

Henri Fayol was another early pioneer in the push for greater efficiency through scientific management. Although many of his ideas were similar to those of Taylor and Emerson, Fayol believed in a principle he called unity of command. Whereas Taylor thought efficiency was enhanced by having the work of an employee directed by several foremen—each with his own area of responsibility—Fayol was convinced that maximum efficiency was possible only when orders were issued by a single boss. If Fayol had been an athletic trainer, he likely would have argued in favor of the appointment of a head athletic trainer who would oversee the entire athletic medicine program—a concept that is in widespread use nearly a century later.

unity of command
A principle of scientific management that requires that the work of an employee be directed by a single superior.

HUMAN RELATIONS MANAGEMENT

The 1920s and '30s saw the rise of the human relations school of managerial theory. The two primary thinkers in this tradition were Mary Parker Follett, a social worker, and Elton Mayo, a Harvard professor. Follett advocated a departure from the strict authoritarianism of Taylor and the other proponents of scientific management. She believed that employees at all levels of an organization should cooperate to develop approaches to accomplishing goals. This democratization of the workplace was a significant departure from the hierarchical structure advocated by scientific management theorists, who thought that the employee's job was simply to implement the orders of his or her superior. Follett taught that cooperation between managers in various departments and between managers and workers was an important motivating element that would lead to greater improvements in meeting organizational goals. In addition, she believed that managers should vary their actions depending on the situation. Managers, she thought, should "take orders" from the situation. The notion of a head athletic trainer who makes all managerial decisions would be anathema to Follet. She would advocate frequent discussions between all members of the sports medicine staff to jointly make policy and solve problems.

Elton Mayo is associated with one of the best-known industrial studies of the modern era. The Hawthorne studies were a series of experiments designed to test the effect of manipulating various working conditions on the production of telephone relay switches. Mayo's experimental design involved informing, and in some cases consulting, the employees being studied regarding the conditions to be manipulated and the variables to be measured. The experiments lasted several years. In most cases, irrespective of the working condition being manipulated, the workers' productivity rose dramatically, even when conditions were adjusted to be less favorable. The three primary lessons to emerge from the Hawthorne studies are as follows:

1. Involvement of employees in workplace decisions can result in improvements in productivity.

2. Factors other than environmental conditions are most important in influencing worker production.

3. Experimental research—especially research involving human behavior—should employ a control group so comparisons between groups can be attributed to the effect of the independent variable.

Hawthorne effect
Also known as the placebo effect. A phenomenon whereby the subjects in an experimental study alter their behavior simply as a result of the process of being studied, even when there is no effect from the independent variable.

The **Hawthorne effect** occurs when subjects in an experiment change their behavior simply because they know they are being studied. Like Follet, Mayo would encourage athletic trainer–managers to involve everyone on the sports medicine staff in collaborating and providing input on the decisions to be made in the operation of the program. Although this seems to be common sense to most of us in the 21st century, it was radical thinking in the early part of the 20th century.

MODERN MANAGEMENT THEORIES

Since the 1950s, there have been many theorists who have devoted their entire careers to the study of management. One such theorist was Kurt Lewin (Gillies, 1994). His Field Theory of Human Behavior posits that employee actions in the workplace are the product of three interacting variables: employee personality, work group structure, and sociotechnical climate. Lewin believed that influencing employees to change their behavior (and thereby improve productivity and efficiency) involved three phases: unfreezing (creating a motivation for a change in behavior, either by applying pressure or reducing threats associated with the change), changing (modifying behavior by either mimicking a role model or learning new behaviors through a discovery process), and refreezing (integrating the new behavior into the workplace with constant reinforcement from others).

Imagine a situation in which a relatively young and inexperienced university athletic trainer repeatedly made the mistake of leaving the athletic training students assigned to him in unsupervised situations. As this athletic trainer's supervisor, it would be your responsibility to ensure that the program's policy requiring student supervision is enforced at all times. Using Lewin's theories, you might employ a three-stage strategy to make sure this happened.

First, you would attempt to "unfreeze" the athletic trainer's behavior. There are several ways to accomplish this, including education and familiarization with NATA Board of Certification (NATABOC) and Commission on Accreditation of Allied Health Education Programs (CAAHEP) rules. Threats of sanctions could also be employed. ("Student supervision is one of your most important jobs. I can't recommend a raise or a favorable performance review if you continue to leave the students unsupervised.")

Contact the NATABOC at **http://www.nataboc.org/**, and the CAAHEP at **http://www.caahep.org/**.

Next, you would attempt to change the athletic trainer's behavior by providing him with a copy of the NATABOC and CAAHEP rules. You might also ask him to shadow you for a day in your work environment so he can learn how you successfully integrate your clinical and educational roles. The final step in the process would be to "refreeze" the appropriate behavior by praising the athletic trainer when you see him providing supervision of student clinical activities. Better yet, you might ask a few of the students to thank him for sharing his time and expertise.

In 1960, Douglas McGregor proposed a new conception of human nature in the workplace with his Theory X and Theory Y. Theory X represented the traditional view of humans at work. Under Theory X, workers were assumed to be inherently lazy, avoiding work whenever possible. Theory X assumes that workers prefer to be directed by others and that their primary concern is financial reward rather than self-improvement. Because of these qualities, Theory X postulates that workers must be coerced to perform their jobs well. Theory Y, on the other hand, holds that work is a natural activity and is as necessary as rest or play. If a person is committed to a task, he will require very little direction to accomplish his goals. The belief that workers naturally learn to seek out and accept responsibility is also a tenet of Theory Y. Finally, Theory Y hypothesizes that most people have the capacity to solve organizational problems and that this quality is not the sole province of managers. Most of us can probably think of supervisors we have worked for who were from either the Theory X or Theory Y school of thought. Athletic trainers who anticipate moving into a management role should contemplate which set of assumptions they resonate most closely with. If your management style is predominantly Theory X and your supervisees are predominantly Theory Y, workplace friction is likely to be a problem. Similarly, if you are new to your supervisory role and your staff was previously led by a supervisor with a contrasting set of assumptions about the nature of work and workers, you should expect a period of transition that may be difficult at times.

Total Quality Management *Also known as continuous quality improvement. A management system that emphasizes continuous improvement in the process by which work is accomplished for the purpose of creating improvements in a product. A continuous focus on the needs and desires of clients is a major focus of TQM.*

The most interesting and important trend in management theory and practice in modern times is the application of Edward Deming's management principles to the industrial workforce in post–World War II Japan. Deming's ideas form the cornerstone of the **Total Quality Management (TQM)** movement, which is still popular in organizations all over the world today. He taught the importance of a clear focus on the mission of an organization and the need for management to continuously demonstrate commitment to this mission and to communicate it to everyone in the organization. He believed that trust and rewarding innovation were two important elements of organizational improvement. Education and self-improvement for people at every level of an organization is fundamental. TQM is a very popular management philosophy in health care organizations. Athletic trainers who work in hospitals are likely to find themselves involved in TQM at an early stage in their careers.

The Japanese took Deming's ideas and, after integrating them with the particular characteristics of their culture, created one of the most powerful, efficient, and productive workforces in history. There are six concepts that are central to the Japanese managerial philosophy (Gillies, 1994). First, the primary trait desired in potential employees is the quality of their character. The training they will need to perform their jobs can be delivered in-house. Second, employees develop a close personal identification with the organization because they are employed for life. Although lifelong employment as a national norm is eroding in Japan, the concept of making an employee feel part of an organizational family is a sound one. Third, the Japanese believe that career progress should be steady but slow. Employees should work in many different departments before moving into managerial positions. Fourth, decision making in Japanese companies is a collective process. Members of the work group all have input into organizational decisions. The group is more valued than the individual. Fifth, a culture of continuous improvement based on the needs of clients is of overriding importance. Finally, the Asian cultural tradition of "saving face" is practiced by supporting and moving unproductive employees around the organization until they become successful.

THREE MANAGEMENT ROLES

Athletic trainers in managerial positions have to assume three roles as part of their jobs: interpersonal, informational, and decisional roles. Each of these roles is complex and has multiple components.

management The element of leadership that involves planning, decision making, and coordination of the activities of a group.

Management is that element of the leadership process that involves planning, decision making, and coordinating the activities of a group of people working toward a common goal. Athletic trainers' regular management activities include scheduling, purchasing, hiring, evaluating, developing programs, accounting, and many others. In his classic text on the science of management, Fayol (1949) defined the following five elements of management: (1) planning, (2) organizing, (3) command, (4) coordination, and (5) control. Gulick and Urwick (1977) added staffing, directing, reporting, and budgeting to Fayol's original list. Dale (1965) felt that innovation and representation were also important management functions.

Mintzberg (1973) described three major roles that all managers, including athletic trainers, assume from time to time:

1. Interpersonal roles
2. Informational roles
3. Decisional roles

INTERPERSONAL ROLES

interpersonal role A managerial role, emanating from the possession of formal authority, that requires the manager to interact and form relationships with others in the organization.

figurehead role An interpersonal role that requires the authority holder to represent the group, usually in a visible public capacity.

liaison role An interpersonal role that requires the leader to interface with others in the group, including superiors, subordinates, and coequals.

Every athletic trainer who manages a department or program will probably be forced to assume three different interpersonal roles at one time or another. The first is the figurehead role. As the person who has been granted formal authority for a particular program, the athletic trainer will be called on to perform certain routine functions such as providing signatures, public speaking, and answering requests for information. The figurehead role is often the most visible managerial task the athletic trainer will undertake. Although it is probably not as vital to the long-term health of the program as other managerial roles, it is important because of the public relations value that it can yield.

The second managerial role the athletic trainer must assume is that of a leader. We have already discussed transactional and transformational leadership.

The third managerial role the athletic trainer must assume is that of liaison. The liaison role is a very important part of the athletic trainer's success or failure as a manager. Athletic trainers must work with a wide variety of people to run a successful athletic training program (see figure 1.1). Although vertical liaison with coworkers above and below him in the organization is commonly understood to be a function of the athletic trainer, horizontal liaison with professional peers is vital to developing and maintaining goodwill between the athletic training program and other departments of the organization and between the program and outside entities. Mintzberg (1973) hypothesized that social equals tend to interact with one another more often than with superiors or subordinates. Thus, athletic trainers need to develop relationships with athletic trainers at other institutions, health professionals in the community, coaches, consulting physicians, and parents. All these people will have an effect on the athletic trainer's managerial success. Chapter 3 discusses the athletic trainer's liaison function in greater detail.

▌Figure 1.1 Liaison relationships of the athletic trainer.

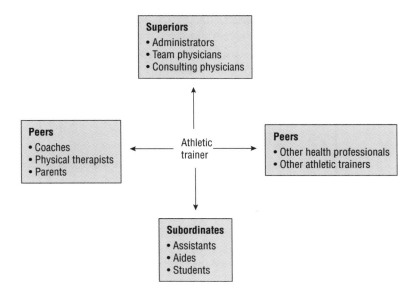

INFORMATIONAL ROLES

informational role Those functions that require the manager to collect, use, and disseminate information.

monitor role An informational role that requires the leader to observe and keep abreast of changes that will affect the group and its activity.

disseminator role An informational role that requires the leader to communicate with members of the group.

The first **informational role** an athletic trainer plays is that of both a **monitor** and a **disseminator** of information. The athletic training program is constantly bombarded with information from a variety of sources on a variety of topics. Journals and trade publications present news of technological advances in preventing and treating athletic injuries. Newsletters and memoranda route organizational news and policy changes. Progress reports and clinical notes arrive in the mail from team and consulting physicians. The first response of the effective athletic trainer–manager is to filter the information. Is it appropriate to share this memo with the staff? Who needs to know about the complications of Rick's knee surgery? Athletic trainers in a variety of employment settings decide these and similar questions daily.

After deciding what information should be passed along and to whom it should be passed, the athletic trainer must decide how to deliver it efficiently and effectively. Some items can be posted on a bulletin board where the staff can scan the information at their leisure. Other items require more explanation and documentation and should therefore be put in writing and delivered individually. This is especially important if the information is confidential or if it is necessary to document that the information was actually passed along. For example, if a staff athletic trainer were not performing up to the standards set by the organization, it would be important to communicate these concerns in writing to keep them confidential and to document that the institution had warned the athletic trainer of dissatisfaction with his work.

Methods for Effective Communication

As a monitor and disseminator of information, you need to use appropriate communication tools. Keep in mind important issues such as efficiency, necessity for documentation, and confidentiality when choosing a method. Some effective methods of communication are:

- Bulletin boards
- Individual meetings
- Newsletters
- Electronic mail
- Staff meetings
- Letters or memos
- Telephone calls

Verbal Communication

In order to be effective in the role of monitor and disseminator of information, the athletic trainer must both understand and be skilled at communicating with everyone in the organization. Verbal communication is one of the primary modes of disseminating information in an organization. There are three elements that influence the process of verbal communication (Drafke, 1994):

1. The meaning of the sender
2. The meaning of the receiver
3. Interference between the sender and receiver

Unfortunately, these three elements often interact in such a way that effective communication is impeded. How often have you said something to someone only to learn that the person was offended either by the way you said it or by the context in which the message was delivered? Sharon's case in the opening scenario is illustrative because it demonstrates the importance of *how* and *where* something is said rather than just *what* is said. Sharon made a statement to her partners in a tension-filled environment where she knew that conflict existed. If she had delivered the same message in a different manner in a different setting, perhaps the outcome would have been more positive. Her verbal tone, along with the potentially hostile mindset of her partners, probably skewed the meaning of most of what she had to say.

interference Anything, including environmental elements or characteristics of the communication medium, that distorts the message sent from the sender to the receiver.

Interference in the communication process is a common problem. Interference can be caused by noisy or distracting work environments. It is also inherent in the methods used to transmit a message from one person to another. For example, because a written message does not usually allow for immediate feedback or clarification, the interference inherent in this method is potentially quite high. Face-to-face communications, on the other hand, allow for greater interaction between the parties and therefore have a much lower potential for interference. Information filtered through a third party is the method most likely to result in corruption of the original message, because it is subject to interference at more than one step of the process. Because of the potential for altered meaning due to interference in various communication methods, Drafke (1994) ranks the following methods in terms of their effectiveness:

1. Face-to-face communication
2. Telecommunication
3. Written communication
4. Communication via a third party

A note on Drafke's ranking is appropriate. As was previously mentioned, written communication serves a very important purpose in helping to document that communication actually occurred. Although there are certain advantages to sitting down with a colleague and discussing an issue in a quiet, calm environment, much of the benefit of this method is lost if the environment becomes noisy or uncomfortable. Written communications also have the advantage of allowing the sender to more carefully consider the words used to convey the message. Sharon's case provides a useful example. She used words in her partners' meeting that were developed and delivered when she was upset. Had she taken the time to compose her thoughts in writing, editing the document carefully over the course of several days while allowing herself to emotionally detach from the issue, she might have been more effective.

Nonverbal Communication

The most important modifiers of an intended message are usually nonverbal elements of that message. Mehrabian (1981) concluded that 55% of any given message is nonverbal. Nonverbal cues can function in a variety of ways to alter a message. Gestures and body position can reinforce a verbal message or they can contradict it. If Sharon had opened the meeting with a cheery "I'm glad to see both of you this morning," while smiling and looking directly at each of her partners, her message would have been quite different than if she had scowled and avoided eye contact. Sharon could have helped control or regulate the meeting by leaning forward, raising her hand, or acting as if she was about to speak as a way of indicating that she had something to say. If Sharon had lost the vote, she would have subverted her actual message ("No problem. I understand and accept your decision.") by staring coldly at her partners for a few moments and then speaking in a flat monotone. See the box below for a list of nonverbal communication cues you should be aware of (Drafke, 1994).

Nonverbal Communication Cues

1. **Clothing and Grooming.** Neat, well-fitting clothes and grooming that conforms to cultural norms often send a message of competence and control.

2. **Territoriality.** Maintain a culturally accepted distance (usually 24–40 in. in the United States) when addressing a colleague. Meetings that take place in the manager's office are often intended to be more formal, serious, or important.

3. **Posture and Facial Expression.** Crossed arms or a body orientation facing away from a person indicates anger, impatience, or boredom. A fixed gaze with a scowl indicates anger or disagreement. Avoiding eye contact often indicates guilt or embarrassment.

4. **Gestures.** Finger tapping expresses boredom. A closed fist or a pointing index finger can indicate anger. A polite handshake indicates receptiveness.

---

spokesperson role
An informational role that requires communication with organizational influencers and members of the organization's public.

internal influencers
Organization decision makers.

The **spokesperson role** is the third informational role that athletic trainers assume. Mintzberg (1973) points out that effective managers must keep two important groups informed. The first group includes the organizational decision makers, also known as **internal influencers.** Internal influencers are people who either are members of, or have close ties to, an organization and who have the power to help shape policy and practice. Table 1.1 shows examples of internal influencers in various settings where sports medicine programs are found.

The second group an athletic trainer should communicate with in his role as spokesperson is the organization's public. Like internal influencers, the members of the sports medicine program's public will vary by setting. Common to each setting are clients (physically active patients, athletes, student-athletes), suppliers, community supporters (members of booster clubs, parents, fans, members of alumni

Table 1.1 Internal Influencers in Common Athletic Training Settings	
Type of Setting	**Influencers**
High school	Coaches, team physicians, athletic directors, principals, central office administrators, board of education members
College and university	Coaches, athletic administrators, other university administrators, team physicians, trustees
Clinic	Clinic owners, hospital administrators, referring physicians, hospital trustees, Supervisors
Professional athletics	Coaches, general managers, other club administrators, owners, team physicians

groups), consulting health professionals, and the news media. The athletic trainer will be expected to communicate with each of these groups from time to time, taking on the role of the organization's expert in sports medicine. The expert spokesperson role is a source of considerable personal power for the athletic trainer.

DECISIONAL ROLES

decisional role   That portion of a manager's work that requires her to use authority to make decisions.

The last group of roles athletic trainers must assume as part of their managerial responsibilities is probably the most important; it is made up of **decisional roles.** Decisional roles require the athletic trainer to use both personal and position power by exercising authority. The effective athletic trainer–manager will also use decisional roles to exercise transformational leadership by planning strategies to serve clients better.

entrepreneurial role A type of decisional role in which the leader initiates and designs controlled change within an organization.

The first decision-making role assumed by the athletic trainer is **entrepreneurial.** Although most of us envision an entrepreneur as someone who creates new businesses, the term refers here to an athletic trainer who designs and initiates changes for her programs and organizations. If the athletic trainer fails in this entrepreneurial role, the sports medicine program will probably stop improving. One of the ways athletic trainers can become entrepreneurs for the sports medicine program is by focusing on small, solvable problems and on new opportunities, and initiating improvements in both areas. All athletic trainers could probably come up with a list of 10 to 15 concrete steps that would improve their programs. Athletic trainers could also improve their programs by taking advantage of some of the opportunities they face. The key is the ability to make decisions about which changes to implement on the basis of what is feasible.

disturbance handler role   A type of decisional role in which the leader manages conflict.

The second decision-making role involves the athletic trainer as **disturbance handler.** Disturbances requiring the attention and intervention of the athletic trainer almost always revolve around conflict. The role of conflict manager is often a difficult and uncomfortable one for athletic trainers for several reasons. First, conflict almost always involves change. Indeed, some scholars have defined the term *conflict* as change (Burns, 1978). Controlled change is a necessary ingredient for healthy program and organizational growth. Unfortunately, such change often occurs with some human costs attached.

Blake and Mouton (1984) have identified eight traditional methods managers should consider to resolve a conflict. Each is most effective under specific circumstances, and many cases may require a combination of two or more approaches.

1. **Cooperation by Edict.** This is the most frequently attempted and least frequently successful method. It requires that the athletic trainer have a high degree of control over subordinates, and its effects diminish rapidly. "My way or the highway" is a poor conflict management technique for most complex situations. By walking into the meeting, banging the table with her fist, and demanding that the benefits policy be changed Sharon got her way but she might have also permanently fractured the relationship with her partners.

2. **Negotiation.** Negotiation between the two parties may resolve surface issues, but deep-seated conflict often remains unresolved because neither side gets everything desired. Negotiation often ends up destroying old precedents and establishing new ones, so it should be used with caution. If Sharon had used a negotiation strategy, she might have suggested that the extra money needed to pay the full cost of the athletic trainers' medical insurance be raised by eliminating or reducing a benefit that all employees now receive, such as continuing education funding. Although the athletic trainers' insurance needs

might have been met through this solution, it is unlikely that anyone would have felt good about the loss of continuing education funding.

3. **Leadership Replacement.** Leadership replacement is a common technique when conflict resolution fails at one level and rises to the next level of the organization. Although new leaders can bring fresh perspectives to a problem, they lack a sense of the history and culture of the organization. In essence, this is the strategy that Sharon proposed to resolve the issue in the opening case. "If you don't respect me enough to take my advice on this matter, then find someone else."

4. **Personnel Rotation.** Although this may be an effective conflict resolution method for a small staff, it is unlikely to change large-group norms. Changes due to personnel rotation are usually temporary in large groups. The other two partners in Sharon's practice might have decided to bring in a new partner had Sharon resigned. This wouldn't have resolved the conflict between the athletic trainers and the partners, but it would have demonstrated the partners' resolve to stick to their position and eased inter-partner conflict.

5. **Organizational Structural Changes.** Such changes are often attempted to ameliorate conflict. Unfortunately, if the nature of the work remains the same, so does the conflict. If the two partners had decided to allow Sharon to purchase that part of the practice involving the athletic trainers and lease their services back to the parent company, they would have been applying this strategy. Sharon could then have implemented the personnel policies she desired without continued conflict with her partners.

6. **Liaison Persons.** Liaison persons are often appointed or elected to represent the parties in a conflict. Although this can be beneficial, it can slow communication by adding another layer to the organizational structure. If the relationship between Sharon and her physical therapist partner were strained to the point that an impasse was unavoidable, Sharon might have been wise to ask one of the physical therapist employees who agreed with her position to speak with the partner and act as a go-between.

7. **Flexible Reporting Relationships.** Using flexible reporting relationships can be an effective way to manage interpersonal conflict, especially if the conflict is between the program head and one of the subordinate staff. Having the staff member report to another staff member instead of the program head can often insulate the two players from each other. For example, if a clinic employee who reports to Sharon is acknowledged by all to be a good and capable professional, but this employee has a problem with Sharon's management style, it might be wise to rearrange the reporting relationship so the employee reports to one of the other partners.

8. **Mediation and Arbitration.** These conflict resolution techniques are the last resort because they involve bringing in a third party from outside the organization to impose binding solutions that both parties may accept, but that neither party is likely to desire or feel ownership in. If Sharon and her partners cannot agree on the medical benefits issue, they might submit to a mediation process whereby a third party, perhaps an attorney or another mediation specialist, would be brought into the case. The mediator would listen to all the facts and attempt to lay out a strategy that all the parties could agree to.

Thomas and Kilmann (1974) described five more general approaches to conflict resolution. To help resolve conflicts in the sports medicine unit, athletic trainers could choose one of the following methods.

1. **Competition.** Competing resolves conflict between two or more members of the sports medicine unit through confrontation. Central to the concept of competition is the notion that one athletic trainer's position power will be imposed, to the exclusion of the others'. This is very similar to cooperation by edict. In Sharon's case, she was the "winner" and her two partners were the "losers." Sharon was able to exert her will over that of her partners. Unfortunately, the relationship she enjoyed with them was then damaged.

2. **Accommodation.** Accommodating involves conceding to the other party in the conflict. The physical therapist and physician in the opening case accommodated Sharon by conceding to her wishes in the matter.

3. **Avoidance.** Avoiding involves bypassing a conflict to prevent the unpleasant consequences normally associated with confrontation. Unfortunately, this method resolves nothing and conflict is almost certain to reappear at some point. Avoidance is one of the most frequent methods employed by managers in all kinds of settings. If Sharon had failed to confront her partners she would have been practicing avoidance. The medical insurance question would still continue to hound her, but she would maintain the relationship with her partners.

4. **Collaboration.** Collaborating is the method most likely to result in lasting conflict resolution. It involves both parties to a conflict attempting to solve the problem together by investigating various possible alternatives. Collaboration requires creative solutions that typically meet the needs of both parties. It would have been ideal if Sharon could have collaborated with her partners to find a creative solution in the opening case. Collaboration becomes very difficult, however, once emotions are interjected into a dispute and positions become hardened. After Sharon demanded that her partners change the benefits policy, it would have been surprising if the three partners were able to truly collaborate on that issue anymore.

5. **Compromise.** Compromise is similar to collaboration in that it attempts to meet the needs of both parties. The major difference is that compromising resolves the conflict by defining a position somewhere in between those of the two parties, whereas collaboration develops new positions previously not considered by either party. Compromise is the result of negotiation. The medical-benefits-for-continuing-education swap mentioned earlier is a good example of the kind of compromise that results from negotiation.

allocator of resources role A decisional role in which the leader exercises authority to determine how organizational assets will be deployed.

The third decision-making role played by an athletic trainer is **allocator of resources.** The athletic trainer generally has the formal authority to determine how time, money, supplies, equipment, and personnel should be deployed. If the athletic trainer–manager does not have this authority, frustration and managerial apathy are likely to result. Sharon's case at the beginning of this chapter is a good example. Although she wanted to allocate company funds toward full compensation of the athletic trainers' health insurance costs, she was unable to do so without being granted the formal authority of her partners. This frustrated not only Sharon but also the staff athletic trainers.

negotiator role A decisional role in which the leader uses authority to bargain with members of the internal or external audience.

The final managerial role an athletic trainer assumes is that of **negotiator.** The athletic trainer negotiates on behalf of the organization he represents. Thus, the negotiator role is actually a combination of several different roles, including the figurehead, resource allocator, and spokesperson (Mintzberg, 1973). Although most arrangements the athletic trainer negotiates on behalf of the organization must eventually be ratified by someone closer to the top of the organizational structure, the athletic trainer must be granted a limited amount of authority to enter into meaningful discussions with another party. Typical arrangements negotiated by athletic trainers include prices for supplies and services, sponsorship for various activities, and grants for specific programs.

IMPROVING MANAGERIAL EFFECTIVENESS

Successful athletic trainer–managers will be able to elicit commitment from their subordinates and coworkers if they are courteous, confident, and open-minded. Athletic trainers must also use simple language, make reasonable requests, and explain their requests. Finally, they must use their authority regularly, especially to confirm task accomplishment.

Leaders usually, but not always, exercise authority by making legitimate requests. In response, staff might commit, comply, or resist. Athletic trainers can use many methods to decrease the likelihood of resistance and increase the possibility of commitment (Yukl, 1981).

When making requests of subordinates, athletic trainers should take the following positive steps to ensure commitment.

- **Be courteous and respectful.** Avoid emphasizing differences in status, intelligence, financial responsibility, and other factors related to rank. If Sharon was having trouble with one of her employees, she would be unlikely to gain that employee's commitment by saying "I'm the boss. You work for me. Do it or else." The employee might comply, but that's the best Sharon could hope for.

- **Radiate confidence.** If the leader communicates doubt through verbal or nonverbal cues, the staff is unlikely to comply with enthusiasm. The athletic trainers who came to Sharon for redress of their medical benefits complaint would probably feel better about the situation if Sharon approached the issue with confidence, saying "Don't worry. I'll get this mess straightened out."

- **Use simple language.** When instructions must necessarily be complicated, check to be sure that subordinates understand them. If Sharon is communicating a complex treatment plan to a new staff member, she would do well to use the simplest language possible, ask the staff member to restate the instructions, and check back to make sure the instructions are being carried out. Inexperienced leaders often make the mistake of using overly technical jargon as a way of demonstrating their position power.

- **Make reasonable requests.** Test requests for legitimacy by consulting with coworkers above you or at the same level in the organization. Referring to formally approved policies, rules, and negotiated agreements can help legitimize requests. Sharon might have strengthened her position with her partners in the opening case if she had taken the time to get some advice on the reasonableness of her position. If she could have referred to formal company documents, such as the employee handbook, she might have been able to make a stronger case.

- **Provide rationale.** Providing reasons for your request will help reduce the perceived status gap between you and your staff. If Sharon circulates a memo to all clinic staff that informs them that employee parking fees are about to double, she had better explain the reasons for the price increase. If she doesn't, the employees are free to attribute any false motive they can think of to account for the increase. If she does explain the increase, the employees still won't like it, but they have a better chance of understanding it and complying.

- **Use the chain of command.** Following established lines of communication decreases the possibility of message distortion. Make requests in writing whenever possible. If one of the clinic's employees bypasses her supervisor and brings her concern directly to Sharon, all three parties will be put in a difficult position. Sharon and the employee now have information that the supervisor doesn't have. This lack of information will doubtless lead to trouble at some point in the future.

- **Use authority regularly.** If you make legitimate requests regularly, your staff will be less likely to resist. If Sharon continuously backs away from issues that require her to make decisions based on her authority as a partner in the company, her employees will grow used to that mode of decision making. When the day comes that Sharon does exercise her authority, the employees are likely to resent her for it.

- **Exercise authority to confirm task accomplishment.** If you do not demand compliance for legitimate requests, future noncompliance is more likely. If Sharon asks one of her employees to do something, the employee doesn't do it, and Sharon doesn't do anything about it, it won't take long for all the employees to figure out that Sharon is a pushover and a weak leader.

- **Be open-minded.** Staff members who consider their leader to be a heartless automaton with no concern for their ideas or feelings are unlikely to respond to requests with enthusiasm. If Sharon listens to her employees' concerns with genuine interest and acts on those concerns whenever possible, she is much more likely to gain the trust and respect of those employees.

APPLICATIONS TO ATHLETIC TRAINING: THEORY INTO PRACTICE

The following two case studies will help you apply the concepts in this chapter to situations you may face in actual practice. The questions at the end of the case studies are open ended; there are many possible correct solutions. A working knowledge of the injury evaluation skills you learned from the Athletic Training Education Series text *Therapeutic Exercise for Athletic Injuries* is especially useful for case study 1.

Case Study 1

During the second half of an NCAA Division III tournament soccer game, the goalkeeper of the host team was involved in a collision and fell to the ground in pain. Julie Raferty, the school's athletic trainer, evaluated the injury on the field and determined that the goalkeeper, who was unable to run or cut and could walk only with a pronounced limp, had suffered a Grade 2 ankle sprain. Julie decided to remove the player from the game based on three factors: the athlete could not perform without significant dysfunction, the team had another game in a few days and the athletic trainer wanted to begin immediate treatment in preparation, and the team was winning the game by two goals and appeared to be in control.

As Julie helped the goalkeeper from the field, the coach jogged out to meet them and asked the athlete how he felt. When he replied that his ankle was injured but not too badly, the coach said it was the athlete's decision whether to keep playing. Julie interjected, telling the coach that she felt further play would jeopardize a rapid recovery. The coach looked again at the athlete and said the decision was his. The athlete replied that he would try to continue. Julie tried again to express her opposition, but the athlete was already walking back to the goal and the coach was leaving the field.

Julie was confused, upset, and incensed that the coach would usurp her authority in the matter. The athletic department had a medical chain of command procedure that clearly authorized the team physician, or the athletic trainer in the physician's absence, to make decisions about playing status for injured athletes. Julie wasn't sure what she could have done to change the outcome.

Questions for Analysis

1. How do the concepts of power and authority apply to this case? Who had power, and how was it used? What was the basis for this power? Who had authority, and how was it used?

2. What might Julie have done differently (either before or during the incident) to avoid the situation?

3. What should Julie do now? Which conflict resolution methods are most appropriate for this case? Is there only one correct solution, or do several possibilities exist?

Case Study 2

After interviewing for a job in a large Texas high school, Jim Hoopes, a certified athletic trainer with 17 years of experience, decided he would accept a job offer there. His primary reason for accepting the job was that he was burned out in NCAA Division I athletics. He thought the high school position would give him the contact with athletes he enjoyed without the headaches of running a major university sports medicine program.

Jim arrived in Texas in June to allow plenty of time to organize his new program before the athletes came back in August. During the first week on the job, Jim began to realize that there were a few questions he should have asked during his interview. Even though the sports medicine program had an adequate budget, Jim was not allowed to order any equipment or supplies without the written permission of his athletic director. When Jim presented a list of supplies needed for the next year, the AD approved only half the items. In addition, he told Jim he would have to purchase them from the local sporting goods dealer. Jim complained that he needed all the items on the list and that if he purchased everything from the local vendor, the sports medicine budget would be spent before Christmas.

Another problem Jim faced during the first few weeks concerned a drug and alcohol education program he proposed for student-athletes. Jim wanted to involve all the coaches and team captains in a preliminary workshop and then develop programs for individual teams. When he presented his plan, the AD smiled and said, "That kind of thing has been tried before and it didn't work then. I don't see why it would work now. Besides, we don't have any serious problems like that in our school."

When the athletes arrived in August, Jim quickly gained a reputation as a caring and competent athletic trainer. Injured athletes came to know him as someone who would take good care of them and who could help them return to action as soon as possible. The coaches also appreciated Jim's talents and expertise. They liked the way he communicated with them and appreciated his hard work in keeping their teams healthy.

Questions for Analysis

1. In what ways did the honeymoon effect work for Jim in his new job? In what ways didn't it work?

2. Which of Jim's early leadership actions were transactional? Which were transformational?

3. Which management roles did Jim assume during his first few months on the job? Which were most important in helping him establish relationships with the various groups at his new school?

4. Jim is obviously having trouble working with his new athletic director. Which conflict management strategies should he consider in attempting to work out his differences? Given the personality style of the AD, what are some likely outcomes of Jim's conflict management attempts?

5. If you were in Jim's position, would you have handled anything differently? What alternative actions would you have taken?

SUMMARY

1. *Define the concepts of power, authority, and leadership.*

   Power is the potential to influence. Athletic trainers possess two forms of power: personal and position. Authority is that aspect of power, granted to either groups or individuals, that legitimizes the right of the individual or group to make decisions on behalf of others. Leadership is the process of influencing the behavior and attitudes of others to achieve intended outcomes. There are two forms of leadership: transactional and transformational. Transactional leadership involves the exchange of one thing for another between two people in a relationship. It makes up the majority of managerial tasks that athletic trainers perform. Transformational leadership raises the standards of the program or organization through the creative use of conflict and change. It is essential for the ongoing health and development of a sports medicine program.

2. *Understand the historical trends in management and how they might apply to athletic training.*

   There have been at least three distinct trends in management theory in the 20th century. The primary goal of scientific management was to increase productivity. The human relations school of management thought emphasized involving individuals in every level of an organization in decision making for goal accomplishment. Modern management theories include Field Theory, McGregor's Theory X and Theory Y, and Deming's Total Quality Management.

3. *Understand the different managerial roles assumed by athletic trainers.*

   Management is that element of the leadership process that involves planning, decision making, and coordinating the activities of a group of people working toward a common goal. Athletic trainers play many managerial roles, which can be generalized into three groups: interpersonal, informational (which includes elements of both verbal and nonverbal communication), and decisional roles.

4. *Understand the various strategies athletic trainers can employ to improve their managerial effectiveness.*

   Athletic trainers can improve their managerial effectiveness by using nine techniques: making polite requests, making requests in a confident tone, making clear requests, making legitimate requests, explaining the reasons for the request, using proper channels, exercising authority regularly, insisting on compliance, and being responsive to subordinate concerns.

CHAPTER TWO

What Athletic Trainers Do: Program Management

OBJECTIVES

After reading this chapter, you should be able to do the following:

1. Understand and develop vision and mission statements for a sports medicine program.

2. Understand the principles underlying sports medicine strategic planning.

3. Develop and link sports medicine policies, processes, and procedures.

4. Communicate and develop ownership in a sports medicine program among inside and outside stakeholders.

5. Understand the principles of effective meeting planning and management.

6. Understand the principles of effective sports medicine program evaluation.

Janet Horton arrived at work one morning to find a note from the director of rehabilitation services on her desk requesting her presence at a meeting later that morning. She wasn't sure why the director would want to meet with her. She had been doing a good job since arriving at the hospital two years before. Still, she was apprehensive as she walked down the hallway to the meeting.

"Janet," the smiling director said, "you have been doing a fine job here at Memorial Hospital. As the only certified athletic trainer in the department, you are playing an important role in helping us establish our niche in the sports medicine market. Our physically active patients appreciate having an athletic trainer on staff who can work with them during their rehabilitation. I want you to take on a very important project. The hospital administration and I think we need to be more aggressive in marketing our sports medicine program. We want you to begin an outreach program to the three Ashton County high schools to help attract patients to our hospital. School doesn't start for a few months, so you have plenty of time to get organized. Thanks a lot and keep up the good work."

Janet had mixed emotions about the new assignment. On one hand, she was pleased that the director trusted her with this new responsibility. On the other hand, she had no experience with community outreach programs. She didn't know where to begin.

The best is the enemy of the good.

Voltaire

The predicament Janet finds herself in is a common one, because all organizations change over time. Whether you are employed in a high school, college, professional, or clinical setting, you are bound to face organizational changes at some point in your career. These changes force us to examine our sports medicine programs from time to time to see if they are still consistent with both the needs of our clients and the mission of the institution that employs us. The concepts discussed in this chapter are intended to help athletic trainers plan, implement, and evaluate sports medicine programs.

VISION STATEMENTS

A vision statement is the first step in planning for the existence of a new sports medicine program or the improvement of an existing one.

vision statement
A concise statement that describes the ideal state to which an organization aspires.

The first step an athletic trainer must take when planning sports medicine programming is to develop a brief, succinct description of what the program should eventually become—a **vision statement.** The vision statement should be both ambitious and compelling (Block, 1987). It should spell out the athletic trainer's hopes and aspirations for the program. Janet might consider a vision statement for her community outreach program that looks like this:

> *The Memorial Hospital Sports Medicine Outreach Program shall provide injury prevention, care, and rehabilitation services of recognized excellence to the high school students of Ashton County. Memorial Hospital is committed to becoming the leader in sports medicine services in the Ashton County area.*

The vision statement contains four distinct elements. First, the statement identifies the provider of the service: Memorial Hospital. Second, it identifies the actual service to be provided: injury prevention, care, and rehabilitation. Third, it identifies the target clients: the high school students of Ashton County. Finally, the statement includes a quality declaration that identifies aspirations for how the program will be received by internal and external audiences. Although these elements might seem self-evident, they are important because of the way they function in the next step—the mission statement. The vision statement should become the ultimate standard by which the program is judged. Without a clearly articulated vision statement, developing the program mission and evaluating the effectiveness of the program become much more difficult.

The Four Elements of the Sports Medicine Program Vision Statement

1. Name of the service provider
2. Description of the service to be provided
3. Identification of the target clients
4. Quality declaration

MISSION STATEMENTS

The sports medicine program's mission statement should serve as a blueprint for every program activity and service. It should be comprehensive enough to describe the program, but simple enough that everyone knows it well.

mission statement
A written expression of an organization's philosophy, purposes, and characteristics.

After the athletic trainer has explored and identified her vision for the sports medicine program, she should expand upon this vision and create a mission statement. Pearce (1982) has defined the **mission statement** as "a broadly defined but enduring statement of purpose that distinguishes a business from other firms of its type and identifies the scope of its operations in product and market terms." Gibson, Newton, and Cochran (1990) have suggested the following component parts of a mission statement. Adapted for a sports medicine program, they include

- the particular services to be offered, the primary market for those services, and the technology to be used in delivery of the services;
- the goals of the program;
- the philosophy of the program and the code of behavior that applies to its operation;
- the "self-concept" of the program based on evaluation of strengths and weaknesses; and
- the desired program image based on feedback from internal and external stakeholders.

The mission statement for a sports medicine program should help an athletic trainer accomplish three things (Gibson, Newton, & Cochran, 1990). First, the mission statement should help the athletic trainer direct resources toward accomplishing specific tasks. This is especially important, because athletic trainers are often called on to perform a broad variety of tasks for a divergent group of supervisors. Athletic trainers need a framework within which they can make decisions about the relative importance of one task versus another.

The second function of the successful mission statement is that it should inspire athletic trainers to do a good job. The mission statement should communicate that the work they do is important and needed. The athletic trainer should believe in the precepts described in the mission statement. Want (1986) has suggested that successful mission statements help employees, including athletic trainers, understand the values and beliefs of the organization and thereby help establish employee commitment.

Finally, the mission statement should be action oriented and should stimulate a change in behavior. It should be written to require the formation of program goals and objectives. It should ideally challenge the athletic trainer to periodically evaluate the effectiveness of the sports medicine program.

Based on these principles, the mission statement for the Memorial Hospital Sports Medicine Outreach Program might read as follows:

The Memorial Hospital Sports Medicine Outreach Program delivers traditional athletic training and sports medicine services to the student-athletes of the three high schools located in Ashton County. The services to be delivered can be broken down into three primary types: injury prevention (taping, bracing, padding, orthotics construction), management of athletic injuries, and rehabilitation of athletic injuries. In addition, whenever possible, we will strive to integrate education about athletic injuries so that our clients can be empowered to lead healthier, injury-free lives. We are committed to using whatever technology is available and affordable in the delivery of these services. We will remain committed to the continuous upgrading of the equipment used in the delivery of sports medicine services so our clients will receive the most modern care available in the area.

The purpose of the program is fourfold. First, we hope to allow easy access to sports medicine services for high school student-athletes. Second, we hope to encourage a philosophy of sport that places a high value on health and wellness. Third, we hope to enable injured student-athletes to return to their sports as soon as is medically safe. Finally, we hope to be able to substantially reduce the risk of athletic injury for those high school students in our service area.

The underlying philosophy for the outreach program is the same as for all the other programs of Memorial Hospital; that is, the needs of the patient shall always be the first consideration for all members of the hospital staff. Furthermore, we expect the athletic trainer(s) who will be providing these services to maintain the highest standards of quality consistent with the National Athletic Trainers Association Code of Professional Practice and the credentialing statutes of this state.

We are committed to ongoing evaluation of our outreach program so our clients can be assured of the highest quality in sports medicine care. Furthermore, we are committed to addressing problems and concerns in a timely manner so the needs of our clients and employees can continue to be met.

Finally, the Memorial Hospital Sports Medicine Outreach Program aspires to be a program of recognized excellence. It is our intention to support the program with the human and financial resources necessary to accomplish the stated goals of the program. It is our desire to establish Memorial Hospital as the primary and most outstanding outlet for the delivery of sports medicine services in the area.

PLANNING

Athletic trainers must do two kinds of planning in order to help their programs fulfill their missions: strategic and operational. Both are essential if a sports medicine program is to be successful.

planning A type of decision-making process in which a course of action is determined in order to bring about a future state of affairs.

The athletic trainer has long been thought of as a jack-of-all-trades. Although athletic trainers' roles have become more specialized since sports medicine clinics began in the late 1970s, most athletic trainers still handle a broad variety of job-related activities (see figure 2.1). Because the athletic trainer's job has so many aspects, he or she must develop planning skills.

Planning is an athletic trainer's best hope for accomplishing sports medicine program goals. Without planning, he or she leaves the ultimate success or failure of the sports medicine program to chance (Castetter, 1986). Ackoff (1970) has defined the planning process as a special type of decision making with three characteristics: It takes place before any action occurs; it is needed to produce a future state that would be unlikely to occur without action; and the desired future state results from multiple, interdependent decisions.

The Memorial Hospital case illustrates the need for careful sports medicine program planning. The hospital administration has placed the bulk of the planning re-

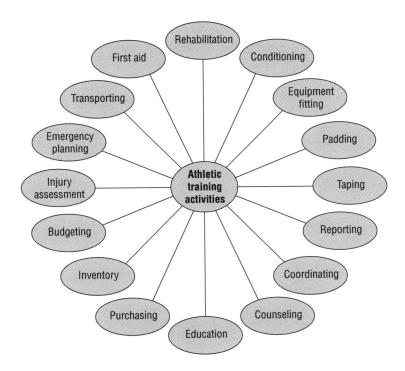

Figure 2.1 Job-related activities of the athletic trainer.

sponsibility in Janet's lap. The plan she develops, if adopted by the hospital administration, will eventually determine whether the program succeeds or fails. To plan effectively, Janet should break the task into its two component parts: strategic planning and operational planning.

STRATEGIC PLANNING

Strategic planning is a process that identifies a course of action to be taken to bring about a future state of affairs. Although it is normally conducted at the top of an organizational structure, strategic planning at the program level can have many benefits.

First, strategic planning requires an athletic trainer to critically examine the sports medicine program and to ask two questions: Why does this program exist? What should the business of this program be? These questions are fundamentally important. Because all organizations and their programs change, they must be asked and answered on a regular basis, or athletic trainers might find that their sports medicine programs no longer serve the purposes for which they are most needed.

The second reason for ongoing strategic planning at the sports medicine program level is to determine whether the program is consistent with the overall mission of the institution or organization. This is especially important in institutions or organizations subject to rapid change. Sports medicine clinics based in hospitals are especially vulnerable to the shifting missions of their institutions. The mission of a professional athletic team often changes dramatically when a new coach is hired. If the sports medicine program isn't periodically reviewed for mission congruence, problems will arise, because the administration might view the purpose of the sports medicine program differently than the athletic trainer does.

The third reason for strategic planning at the sports medicine program level is that it helps build support for the program. Strategic planning is, by definition, a process that involves persons at all levels of the organization. By asking students, staff athletic trainers, coaches, and administrators to take part in the strategic planning process, an athletic trainer will be forging important allies with an increased sense of ownership in the sports medicine program.

Finally, strategic planning should be a tool for improvement, helping to determine the relative strengths and weaknesses of the program and to transform it positively. In addition, the strategic planning process will help direct more action-oriented operational plans.

Many conceptual models could be used to develop a strategic plan for the sports medicine program. The model presented in figure 2.2 adapts the process developed by Steiner (1979), but athletic trainers should further modify the methodology to meet the needs of their institutions. In most cases, the combination of institutional mission, needs, and goals will help determine the most appropriate planning methods.

*strategic planning
A type of planning that involves critical self-examination in order to bring about organizational improvement.*

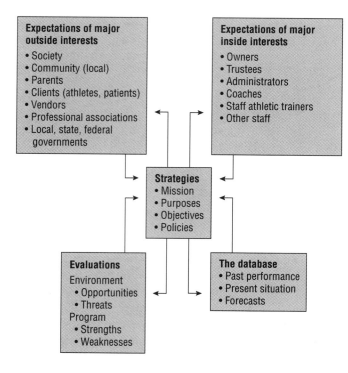

Expectations of major outside interests
- Society
- Community (local)
- Parents
- Clients (athletes, patients)
- Vendors
- Professional associations
- Local, state, federal governments

Expectations of major inside interests
- Owners
- Trustees
- Administrators
- Coaches
- Staff athletic trainers
- Other staff

Strategies
- Mission
- Purposes
- Objectives
- Policies

Evaluations
Environment
- Opportunities
- Threats
Program
- Strengths
- Weaknesses

The database
- Past performance
- Present situation
- Forecasts

▌**Figure 2.2** A model for strategic planning in sports medicine.

Adapted from Steiner 1979.

Major Outside Interests

The first groups whose interests must be considered when developing a strategic plan are those outside the institution or organization. Of these groups, the interests of clients should take precedence. In addition, the interests of parents; the local community; vendors; professional associations like the National Athletic Trainers' Association (NATA) and the National Collegiate Athletic Association (NCAA); and local, state, and federal governments are important. Professionals who manage athletic training education programs must be familiar with the NATA Board of Certification (NATABOC) requirements and the Commission on Accreditation of Allied Health Education Programs (CAAHEP) requirements for athletic training education program accreditation. In some cases, an athletic trainer will need only simple information from one of these groups. For example, if a program is in a state that monitors the credentials of athletic trainers, it doesn't require much planning to know that it must be staffed by athletic trainers with the necessary credentials required by law. Conversely, some of the information the athletic trainer will need to develop the strategic plan might be more difficult to gather. For example, as important vendors of medical services, local physicians might have a substantial interest in how the sports medicine program is planned. Only by meeting with these physicians and involving them in the planning process can an athletic trainer be assured of their enthusiastic endorsement of the program being planned.

Contact the National Athletic Trainers' Association Board of Certification at **http://www.nataboc.org/**.

Contact the Joint Review Committee on Educational Programs in Athletic Training at 7108-C Alton Way, Englewood, CO 80112-2106 or **http://www.cewl.com/**.

The most important group whose interests must be considered is the program's client base. Without patients, athletic trainers and sports medicine programs would be unnecessary. The athletic trainer can incorporate clients' perceptions into the strategic planning process in several ways, including written questionnaires, telephone surveys, and suggestion boxes.

Methods for Gathering Feedback From Clients on Sports Medicine Services

- Written questionnaires
- Telephone surveys
- Suggestion boxes
- Involvement on planning committees
- Focus groups

If the athletic trainer needs more detailed insight, it might be necessary to involve clients as members of planning committees. Another method for securing detailed feedback from clients on the quality of services and their desire for future services is to use the focus group technique. This technique involves gathering a group of approximately 10 clients who are representative of the total population of clients. A trained facilitator meets with the group and asks a series of open-ended questions about program quality and the clients' desires for the future. This process is generally repeated with several different groups as a reliability check. The information is then collated and used to help build the strategic plan.

Gathering valid and reliable information from clients is not a task for the untrained. The literature is full of poorly written and poorly analyzed client-based questionnaires. Sampling methods and statistical analysis of the data must meet modern scientific norms. Athletic trainers can turn to several sources of assistance for this phase of the strategic plan. Most colleges and universities have faculty members with expertise in social science research who are willing to consult. Many of the larger educational institutions have full-time planners available to assist with projects like these. Most large hospitals either have full-time planners or contracts with management consultants to help in the development of the strategic plan.

Major professional associations and the government are two important sources of information for assessing what outside interests are necessary to develop the strategic plan for the sports medicine program. Professional associations such as the NATA, the NCAA, the American Physical Therapy Association, and the National Federation of State High School Athletic Associations (NFSHSAA) are important, because they are often the source of professional credentials that act as "gatekeepers" for practitioners in sports medicine and they mandate quality standards for sports medicine programs. The NCAA and the NFSHSAA set the rules for each sport, including safety rules that impact athletic trainers and sports medicine programs. Both of these organizations have rules for administering physical examinations that have a marked effect on sports medicine programs.

Accreditation

accreditation Formal recognition provided to an organization or one of its programs indicating that it meets certain prescribed quality standards.

One of the most important outside interests a sports medicine program must consider are standards-setting groups that provide health care organizations or their programs with **accreditation.** Accreditation is a statement by a standards-setting organization that the sports medicine program meets certain performance standards. Although athletic training programs associated with high schools, colleges, and universities are generally not accredited (except as part of their institution's overall accreditation by one of the regional educational accrediting agencies), sports medicine programs housed in clinics and hospitals will be subject to the scrutiny of the accreditation process typically associated with those settings. Accreditation is almost always voluntary, but there are often strong motivations for a health care organization to become accredited. In some cases, the state license an organization needs to operate is dependent on its accreditation status. Access to third-party reimbursement and managed care contracts is often made easier if a health care organization is accredited by an appropriate standards-setting body.

Although the process for obtaining accreditation is similar for most standards-setting bodies (see the section on program evaluation), the important element to remember during the strategic planning process is to build the sports medicine program's goals, programs, and practices with accreditation standards in mind. It is also important to remember that accreditation standards are usually minimalist in design. In other words, a particular standard usually describes the absolute minimum level of performance the sports medicine unit must achieve in order to satisfy the requirements of the standard. The danger in building a program around the accreditation standards is that the program might do things well, but at a minimally acceptable level. If outstanding performance is the goal, athletic trainers will have to look well beyond the minimal requirements of most accreditation standards. There are two important accrediting agencies that clinic- and hospital-based sports medicine programs should consult as they plan their programs: the Joint Commission on

Accreditation of Healthcare Organizations (JCAHO) and the Commission on Accreditation of Rehabilitation Facilities (CARF).

The **JCAHO** is the oldest and largest health care standards-setting body in the nation. It accredits approximately 15 000 health care organizations in the United States. It has offered accreditation for ambulatory care facilities, including hospital-based and independent rehabilitation clinics, since 1975. Advantages of JCAHO accreditation include the following:

Joint Commission on Accreditation of Healthcare Organizations (JCAHO)
The oldest and largest health care standards organization in the country. JCAHO accredits ambulatory health care facilities.

1. Provides objective evaluation of the program's performance
2. Stimulates quality improvement
3. Enhances community confidence
4. Helps meet Medicare certification requirements
5. Enhances access to third-party reimbursement
6. Helps meet facility licensing requirements

For more information about JCAHO programs, write to The Joint Commission on Accreditation of Healthcare Organizations, One Renaissance Blvd., Oakbrook Terrace, IL 60181, 630-792-5000. The JCAHO Web site address is **http://www.jcaho.org/**.

Commission on Accreditation of Rehabilitation Facilities (CARF)
A nonprofit agency that sets quality standards for rehabilitation services and facilities.

Another accreditation agency that athletic trainers who work in clinics and hospitals should consider as they plan their programs is the Commission on Accreditation of Rehabilitation Facilities. **CARF** is a nonprofit agency that establishes standards of quality for rehabilitation services. Established in 1966, CARF accredits approximately 11 000 programs. CARF accreditation is intended to

1. offer consumer protection and enhance consumer confidence,
2. involve consumers in developing standards for rehabilitation,
3. promulgate common performance standards for rehabilitation programs,
4. identify rehabilitation programs that have met national performance standards,
5. improve government relations with the rehabilitation industry by offering evidence of effective use of public money for rehabilitation purposes, and
6. provide rehabilitation facilities with tools for improvement.

For more information, write to the Commission on Accreditation of Rehabilitation Facilities, 4891 East Grant Rd., Tucson, AZ, 520-325-1044. CARF's Web site address is **http://www.carf.org/**.

CARF offers accreditation for organizations that typically house sports medicine programs through its Medical Rehabilitation Division. CARF and JCAHO began to integrate their accreditation processes for rehabilitation hospitals in 1997 and are working on expanding this joint process to other rehabilitation facilities in the future.

Major Inside Interests

Athletic trainers are not typically found (but are becoming more common) among the top management of an institution or organization. Top managers, including team owners, university administrators and trustees, and boards of education have certain expectations for the sports medicine program, so it is important that the athletic trainer involve a representative sample of these persons as part of the planning team. Without the active support of these groups, the strategic plan for the sports medicine program is likely to fail. Consider the Memorial Hospital case as an example. Janet was left to plan the sports medicine outreach program by herself. She knows two things: First, at least a few, and possibly more, hospital administrators support the program; and second, she isn't sure which direction the program should take. The next logical step for Janet is to identify those administrators who support the concept and include them in the planning process. This will have two likely effects: It will strengthen ownership for the program among the people who will have to eventually approve or disapprove it, and it will provide Janet with some fresh ideas about the type of program the hospital wants.

Another major inside group is made up of the coaches. It is wise to include coaches in the planning effort, because they have a legitimate need to be involved in, or at least informed about, the health care of their athletes. The success of the team and their success as coaches often depends on the overall health of their athletes. In addition, coaches have a powerful impact on the attitudes and behaviors of the athletes on their teams. If the coaches in the three Ashton County high schools don't have confidence in the expertise and care patterns that Janet will offer them through the outreach program, they are unlikely to be receptive to the advice she offers, and Memorial Hospital is unlikely to receive many referrals. Janet is the hospital's primary marketing tool to these schools, and most of her contacts will be with students and coaches. The final reason coaches should be involved in the planning process is that they are an important power base in any athletic program. A successful coach can sometimes become one of the most powerful people in the entire organization. It makes sense to try to use such power to build alliances with the sports medicine program.

The most important inside group to tap in developing the strategic plan is the institution's athletic trainers. They are the professionals inside the organization with the most sports medicine expertise. As such, they are the best sources of information about how the program should be developed. However, the athletic trainers must be involved in the proper manner. Too often, meetings intended to develop strategic directions for sports medicine programs can become complaining sessions about problems with working conditions, salary, and professional standing in the institution. These issues are important, but if they become the focus of the athletic trainers' roles in the strategic planning process, the resultant plan will be little more than a shopping list of their demands, which is unlikely to foster administration support or improved care for injured athletes and other physically active patients. Athletic trainers must constantly ask themselves during the planning process "How can we improve the quality of service to our patients?" Questions that deviate significantly from this are unlikely to have strategic value.

The Database

This portion of the strategic planning model helps athletic trainers devise alternative action plans and estimate their potential value for meeting the goals of the sports medicine program. First, the past performance of the program is analyzed, and trends in patient loads, injury rates, clinic profits or losses, and athletic trainer performance evaluations are considered, along with other information. Next, the program's present situation is analyzed. Data about staffing levels, budget, client population size, number of sports to be served, demands and expectations of outside and inside interests, and any applicable laws that affect the program will be needed. Finally, a forecast for the future is developed. Ammer and Ammer (1984) have defined the term **forecast** as a process of predicting future conditions on the basis of various statistics and indicators that describe the past and present situations. Forecasts are highly informed and educated guesses that should always be backed up with documented evidence. Athletic trainers should consider the predicted rise in the cost of medical goods and

forecast A prediction of future conditions based on various statistics and indicators that describe an athletic program's past and present situations.

services and the future availability of professional staff, support employees, and consulting medical personnel when preparing the forecast. In addition, they should consider advances in technology, because the available technology often drives the practice of sports medicine.

WOTS UP Analysis

WOTS UP analysis
A data collection and appraisal technique designed to determine an organization's strengths, weaknesses, opportunities, and threats in order to facilitate planning.

The last data-collection procedure to be accomplished in the strategic planning process is often referred to as a **WOTS UP analysis** (Steiner, 1979). WOTS UP is an acronym for "**w**eaknesses, **o**pportunities, **t**hreats, and **s**trengths **u**nderlying **p**lanning." Because the WOTS UP analysis identifies strengths and weaknesses already present in the sports medicine program, it is most appropriate for programs that are already established (see appendix A). It is very important that the WOTS UP analysis be conducted by a broad spectrum of participants. Interpretation of the data is subject to the biases of the interpreter, so only the involvement of a representative group of both outside and inside interests will yield useful results.

The WOTS UP analysis often reveals important sources of both opportunities and threats for the sports medicine program. In the Memorial Hospital case, a WOTS UP analysis would probably help Janet identify allies she might not have previously considered; many will have a vested interest in seeing the program succeed. She would also undoubtedly identify sources of opposition to the program that she would need to develop plans to deal with. Many of the techniques used in this strategic planning process can be interchanged with those used in the process of program evaluation. See the section on program evaluation (pp. 44–51) for more information.

OPERATIONAL PLANNING

operational plan
A type of plan that defines organizational activities in the short term, usually no longer than two years.

Once an athletic trainer has developed a strategic direction for the sports medicine program, the strategies must be translated into practice through the use of **operational plans.** Whereas strategic plans are meant to provide program direction over a long period of time, say five years, operational plans define the activities of the program for a much shorter period of time, usually no more than one or two years. The importance of functioning operational plans for the sports medicine program should not be underestimated. One of the most common pitfalls in every type of organization that undertakes strategic planning is the failure to effectively translate the strategic vision for the program into workable, useful operational plans (Garofalo, 1989). Three often-misunderstood types of operational plans are policies, processes, and procedures.

Policies

policy   A type of plan that expresses an organization's intended behavior relative to a specific program subfunction.

Castetter (1986) has defined **policy** as a plan for expressing the organization's intended behavior relative to a specific program subfunction. By definition, policies are broad statements of intended action promulgated by boards empowered with the authority to govern the operation of the organization.

Policies are not intended to answer detailed questions about how the sports medicine program operates. They are intended as road maps to guide an athletic trainer in developing and operating a sports medicine program in accordance with the desires of the policy board. Athletic trainers will rarely be empowered to dictate policies, because they usually do not sit on the governing boards of institutions. They should, however, be consulted in the development or modification of institutional policies that affect the sports medicine program. A well-managed organization with a sports medicine program should have policies in place that express the intended behaviors of the program. The athletic trainer is obviously a crucial ingredient in advising those in authority on the development and implementation of these policies. An example of a policy statement for the Memorial Hospital Sports Medicine Outreach Program might look like the following:

Sample Policy Statement

Memorial Hospital acknowledges its role in the following activities:

- Reducing the incidence of injury among high school student-athletes

- Making competent medical care readily and easily available to the student-athletes of Ashton County

In addition, Memorial Hospital recognizes that a program delivering sports medicine services to the three high schools of Ashton County will help it fulfill its mission to be the leader in sports medicine in the Ashton County area. Consequently, the Board of Trustees of Memorial Hospital has established the following policies:

1.0 Provide sports medicine services at the site of athletic practice and competition for the three Ashton County high schools.

1.1 Provide sports medicine coverage using only personnel who have been trained and credentialed as experts in sports medicine, including certified athletic trainers.

1.2 Maintain an injury database to determine the risk of injury to athletic participants.

1.3 Provide hospital-based management of injuries requiring follow-up care.

1.4 Provide education on the prevention of injuries and the development of healthy lifestyles to the students of the three Ashton County high schools.

1.5 Assist in the prevention of athletic injuries by providing physical examinations and screening services for the students of the three Ashton County high schools.

Processes

process   A collection of incremental and mutually dependent steps designed to direct the most important tasks of an organization.

Processes are the next step down from policies on the hierarchy of operational plans. **Processes** are the incremental and mutually dependent steps that direct the most important tasks of the sports medicine program. Each process should be related to at least one, and possibly many, of the policies that govern the program. Each policy will undoubtedly have several supporting processes.

Processes of the Sports Medicine Program

- Injury prevention
- Injury recognition
- Injury management

- Injury rehabilitation
- Organization and administration
- Education and counseling

Procedures

procedure   A type of operational plan that provides specific directions for members of an organization to follow.

Procedures provide specific interpretations of processes for athletic trainers and other members of the sports medicine team. They are not abstract. They should be written in clear and simple language so they will be interpreted the same way by different people. Procedures are the lowest level of the planning hierarchy. An example of how policies, processes, and procedures are linked for the Memorial Hospital program might look like this:

Policy 1.0
It is the policy of Memorial Hospital to provide sports medicine services at the site of athletic practice and competition for the three Ashton County high schools.

Process for the Injury Rehabilitation Subfunction
The sports medicine team, including the physician, athletic trainer, and physical therapist, shall work together to provide student athletes with a rehabilitation program appropriate for their injuries. Consideration will be given to the location of the rehabilitation program (home, school, or hospital), the equipment required

to attain the desired rehabilitative effect, the insurance coverage provided by the student's family, and the insurance coverage provided by the school.

Procedure for Discharge From Rehabilitation

Physical therapists or athletic trainers shall discharge student athletes from rehabilitation only after consulting with the attending physician. Discharge shall occur when the critical long-term goals, established when the student-athlete was admitted, have been met. All discharged student-athletes shall be given verbal and written instructions in the long-term care of their injuries. The names of all discharged student-athletes shall be placed on the mailing list for the Memorial Hospital Sports Medicine Newsletter. All discharged student-athletes shall be called both at six months and one year post-discharge by an athletic trainer to check on the status of their injuries.

Practices

practice The action that actually takes place in response to administrative problems.

Even the most well-considered procedure often leaves room for an athletic trainer to make professional judgments about how to handle particular administrative tasks. The ways that administrative tasks are actually accomplished are known as **practices**. Practices should never contradict the directions provided for in the procedure they are intended to support. For example, a sports medicine clinic might have a written procedure requiring that all electrical modalities be calibrated and safety-inspected once per year. This is clearly a sound procedure that is consistent with professional standards. The athletic trainer–administrator still has several decisions to make. Which vendor will she contact to service the equipment? What time of the year will she choose to have the equipment serviced? Should she send all of the equipment out at once, send half of the inventory at one time, or stagger the schedule for each piece of equipment? The decisions she makes are examples of practices. Practices are important because they allow the athletic trainer to make decisions based on changing conditions, without violating the letter or the spirit of the policies and procedures manual.

Policies, processes, and procedures are usually communicated to employees in the form of a policies and procedures handbook. This is a very important document. Not only does it educate employees regarding the procedures they are to follow, it also serves as a legal foundation for action if they do not. Poorly written or incomplete procedure handbooks are frequently the basis for employee action against employers, since they are often viewed as a kind of contract.

Large organizations, such as hospitals and universities, commonly have more than one handbook. One contains all of the organization's policies (remember that policies are statements passed by the board in control of the organization). Another contains procedures that are intended to apply to all employees of the organization, regardless of which department employs them. Human resources procedures are typically codified in procedure manuals of this type (see figure 2.3). The last kind of manual contains procedures specific to a certain sub-unit or department of an organization. It typically contains procedures that apply only to the kinds of activities that take place in that department. See figure 2.4 for an example of such a manual for a hospital-owned orthopedic and sports medicine clinic. The boxes on p. 35 and p. 37 contain examples of procedures drawn from two different settings: a dress code from a university sports medicine program, and a 10-hour workshift procedure from a sports medicine clinic.

Other Types of Operational Plans

Policies, processes, and procedures are types of operational plans common to almost every organization. They should be reviewed and modified as appropriate at least

Figure 2.3 Table of contents for a human resources procedures manual for a midsize not-for-profit hospital.

Adapted, by permission, from *Human Resources Procedures Manual*, Holland Community Hospital, Holland, MI.

Contents

Procedure Title

Absences, Excused
Absences/Tardiness, Unscheduled
Adoption Assistance
Awards Dinner
Benefit Accrual Hours
Bereavement
Bulletin Boards
Cardiopulmonary Resuscitation (CPR)
Certification
Call-In Compensation, Standby
    and Emergency
Confidential Information
Confidentiality of Information on
    Computer Systems
Counseling, Corrective Action
Credit Union
Death in Family
Disability Insurance
Dismissal
Dress Code/Personal Appearance
Dual Relationships between Hospital
    Employees and Patients
Educational Assistance
Employee Assistance Program
Equal Opportunity
Family and Medical Leave, Unpaid
Fair Treatment
Flexible Staffing
Floating Holiday Time
Gifts and Tips
Health Requirements and Services
    for Employees
Holidays
Insurance, Life
Insurance, Supplemental Life

Introductory Employees
Job Posting
Jury Duty
Laser Image Identification Badges
Lay-Off Procedure
Leave of Absence
New Employee Orientation
Overtime, Rest and Meal Periods
Paid Time Off
Part-Time Employees
Patient Care, Staff Requests Not to
    Participate in Aspects of
Pay, Shift and Weekend Premium
Payroll Check Distribution
Payroll Deductions
Performance Reviews
Preemployment Alcohol/Drug Screening
Promotion Guidelines
Recruitment Cash Bonus
Relatives, Employment of
Resignations
Retirement
Seniority
Sexual Harassment
Social Security
Solicitation and Distribution of Literature
Staffing, Supplemental
Time Clocks
Vacation
Weapons
Work Schedule
Workers' Compensation
Workers' Compensation Supplement

Dress Code Procedure

All members of the university sports medicine staff shall be professionally attired at all times during their work shift. Staff members and students shall wear a university-approved name badge at all times when on duty. The first badge shall be provided at university expense. The cost of replacement badges is the responsibility of the staff member. Athletic trainers (staff and students) shall wear a uniform shirt approved by the Head Athletic Trainer while on duty. Each staff member will receive two uniform shirts per year. Additional uniform shirts are the responsibility of the staff member. All staff members shall wear a uniform jacket when covering outdoor events during cool weather. The jackets are the property of the university and may be checked out from the clothing locker in the main athletic training room storage room. The following clothing is prohibited at all times, regardless of setting:

- blue jeans
- sweatshirts
- unkempt clothing
- clothing with holes

Questions regarding this procedure should be directed to the Head Athletic Trainer.

Contents

AUTHORIZATION AND INTAKE

Medical supervision of rehabilitation services
Receiving and processing referrals for rehabilitation services
Prior authorization
Reimbursement
Intake process

DOCUMENTATION AND COMMUNICATION

Communicating the status of the hospital outpatient
Communicating the physical therapy ambulatory and transfer needs of the hospital patient with nursing and other ancillary services
Communicating the status of patients seen under contract

RECORD KEEPING

Patient records—The patient folder
Department records

PATIENT CARE

Assignment of patients
Outpatient registration
Patient scheduling
Priority of care for hospital patients
Dispensing of crutches, braces, and other patient care items
Broken appointments and cancellations
Discharge planning for rehabilitation patients
Quality assurance
Home visit program
Participation of the patient/family in the treatment plan
Assessments of patients
Orientation
Initial assessment
Case management—Neurorehabilitation
Initial team meeting
Individual program plan
Therapeutic progress report
Client referral
Follow-up
Waiting list
Physical aggressive behavior and self-injurious behavior
Recipient rights
Peer review
Input from persons served
Outcomes
Accessibility
Education of clients/care givers regarding universal precautions/infection control
Nonvoluntary discharge

DEPARTMENT MANAGEMENT

Hours of operation
Charging for services
Preventative maintenance
Approval process for new and revised procedures
Pricing for patient charge items
Ordering supplies and equipment
Authorizing/training of vehicle operators
Maintenance/inspection of van
Handling vehicle incidents/accidents
Access to outpatient rehabilitation
Utility management
Robbery emergency plan
Hostage crisis plan

PERSONNEL

Flexible staffing
Dress code
Time, mileage, and productivity logging
Orientation
Continuing education
Comp time for professional salaried exempt employees
Vacations and leaves of absence
Ten-hour shift option
Rehabilitation department staffing
Therapist staffing pool
Verification of credentials

SAFETY

Handling incidents
Handling patient arrests
General safety rules
Emergency plan
Power failure

INFECTION CONTROL

Personnel policies—General information
Contract personnel policies
Three-minute surgical scrub
Debridement
Linen disposal
Wound cultures
Dressing removal
Burn patient management
Special handling of physical therapy equipment
Isolation patients receiving whirlpool
Reusable sterile supplies, Care and storage of
Disposable sterile supplies, Care and storage of
Disinfection of whirlpool tanks
Departmental routine cleaning
Routine cleaning by Environmental Services
Disinfection of bandage scissors
Disinfection of hyperbaric extremity chamber
Treatment protocol for hyperbaric chamber
Management of catheterized hydrotherapy patients
Fluidotherapy

PHYSICAL THERAPY

BAPS
Biofeedback
Compression—Jobst pump
Compression—Wright linear pump
Conditioning—Treadmill
Contrast bath
CPM
Cryotherapy—Cold packs
Diathermy
Electrical stimulation—High voltage
Electrical stimulation—Low voltage
Electrical stimulation—Medium frequency
Electrical stimulation—MENS
Electrical stimulation—TENS
Fluoromethane spray
Gait training
Hot packs
Hydrotherapy—Hubbard tank and whirlpool
Hyperbaric oxygen unit
Hyperstimulation analgesia with pulsed IR laser
Isokinetic testing
Massage
Myofascial release
Paraffin bath
Phonophoresis
ROM splint fitting
Traction—Cervical, manual
Traction—Cervical, motorized
Tilt table
Ultrasound

Figure 2.4 Table of contents for procedures manual for a hospital-owned orthopedic and sports medicine clinic.

Adapted, by permission, from *Rehabilitation Services Procedure Manual*, Holland Community Hospital, Holland, MI.

Ten-Hour Work Shift Procedure

Memorial Hospital offers its employees the option of working either five 8-hour shifts per week or four 10-hour shifts per week. Since each department can accommodate only a certain percentage of its employees on a 10-hour shift, each employee is required to apply for this privilege with his or her supervisor. Interested employees should complete the "Request for 10-Hour Shift" form and submit it to his or her supervisor. The supervisor shall make every reasonable effort to accommodate the employee's request, consistent with the need to keep the department adequately staffed at all times. The supervisor shall respond in writing to the employee's request within 10 days. Supervisors are instructed to consider the following elements when deciding if an employee should be granted 10-hour shift status:

• The minimum number of employees required to service patients during peak, minimal, and average loads.

• The minimum number of employees required to implement the department's emergency plan.

• The degree to which the employee requires supervision consistent with hospital policy and state law.

• The number of employees already granted ten-hour work shift status. The number of such employees should not normally exceed 25%.

Employees who have questions regarding this procedure should consult with their supervisors.

once every three years. Other types of operational plans have fixed life spans. Budgets are a type of operational plan that are usually one year in length. (See chapter 4 for an expanded discussion of budgets.) Two additional planning techniques that result in fixed-term operational plans are Program Evaluation and Review Technique (PERT) and Gannt charts.

PERT

PERT (Program Evaluation and Review Technique) A method of graphically depicting the time line for and interrelationships of the different stages of a program.

PERT (Penton/IPC Education Division, 1982), an acronym for "**program evaluation and review technique,**" is a useful tool for helping athletic trainers develop plans for implementing programs. It is also useful for evaluating actual outcomes against expected outcomes. PERT is essentially a method of graphically depicting the time line for and interrelationships of different stages of a program. Users depict events as circles and activities as lines or arrows connecting two or more events. One of the advantages of using the PERT planning technique is that it allows athletic trainers to visually display events that occur simultaneously. PERT is most often used with large, complicated projects in business and industry, but it can also be applied to the smaller projects that athletic trainers are often called upon to develop and administer (see figure 2.5).

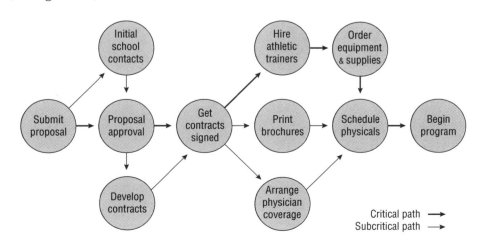

Figure 2.5 PERT diagram for a hospital-based sports medicine outreach program.

Gannt Charts

A **Gannt chart** is a graphic planning and control method (Stoner, 1982). It has many potential applications in sports medicine, because it takes discrete tasks and maps them on a calendar (see figure 2.6). Athletic trainers can use a Gannt chart to demonstrate to their superiors the progress being made on particular projects (Randolph & Posner, 1988). When used in this way, it becomes a powerful tool for communicating sports medicine plans to crucial members of the internal and external audience. For example, in the opening case of this chapter, Janet could use a Gannt chart not only to plan the implementation of the sports medicine outreach program, but also to provide her superiors with concise, easy-to-understand progress updates.

Both PERT and Gannt charts are challenging for the untrained to construct. Depending on the complexity of the project, the final result, graphically illustrating the milestones and critical path of a project, can appear somewhat bizarre. The first few times an athletic trainer attempts these methods, he or she should use pencil and paper. As expertise is gained, computer software can be used to help create either chart. Many easy-to-use programs, designed specifically for this purpose, are available.

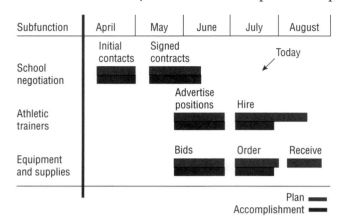

■ **Figure 2.6** Gannt chart for a new hospital sports medicine outreach program.

COMMUNICATING AND DEVELOPING SUPPORT FOR THE PLAN

Unfortunately, all the effort an athletic trainer expends developing the sports medicine program plan will be wasted unless other people inside and outside the organization accept it. One of the most difficult aspects of planning for the delivery of sports medicine services is developing a sense of ownership in the people who make up the major organizational power bases. Plans developed without such ownership are unlikely to remain politically viable for very long. The ability to translate plans into action and develop support for the program is the ultimate measure of political skill.

Block (1987) has developed a support-building strategy that could be useful to athletic trainers as they attempt to develop ownership for their sports medicine programs. The strategy is based on the **agreement-trust matrix** (see figure 2.7). The first step in the process is to identify those people who will have an impact on the eventual success or failure of the sports medicine program. After these people have been identified, they are labeled as follows.

■ **Figure 2.7** Agreement-trust matrix.
Adapted from Block 1987.

Allies

The **allies** of the athletic trainer exhibit a high level of agreement with the plans for the sports medicine program. In addition, they are people the athletic trainer trusts. They not only are supporters of the sports medicine program but also have an established record of honesty and truthfulness. The director of rehabilitation services at Janet's hospital in the opening scenario is a good example of an ally. He has expressed his support for Janet and her work, and his request to have her develop the outreach program demonstrates trust in her judgment.

Opponents

opponents Persons who support a particular program but dispute the implementation of a plan related to that program.

Opponents of the athletic trainer should not be viewed as enemies. They are persons whom the athletic trainer trusts to give an honest opinion of the sports medicine program or its components, but who have opposing views to those of the athletic trainer. Opponents can often serve a useful purpose—their challenge can lead to more critical examination of the sports medicine program, resulting in stronger strategic and operational plans.

One possible opponent from the opening case might be an orthopedic surgeon who serves as an unofficial team physician for one of the Ashton County high schools. Although he might be a trustworthy person with whom Janet has had good relations in the past, he might harbor disagreement with her proposal, since it could potentially funnel away a significant number of surgical cases from his practice if Janet or her staff begin acting as gatekeepers for injured high school athletes.

Bedfellows

bedfellows Persons who exhibit support for a particular plan but who have a history of untrustworthy behavior and vacillation.

Bedfellows are those who agree with the plans of the athletic trainer for the sports medicine program but have a history of untrustworthy behavior. Bedfellows are generally quick to ally themselves with the sports medicine program, but they tend to be manipulative and to operate "behind the back."

The vice president for finance at the hospital in the opening case is a good example of a bedfellow. He might be an enthusiastic supporter of the outreach program during the conceptual phase of planning. When the contracts are signed with the high schools and he has to find money in the budget for additional athletic trainers to support the program, however, he might prove to be a less enthusiastic member of the team. Bedfellows are often quick to support ideas in the conceptual stage, but they often fail to deliver when they are asked to make a contribution to get a program up and running.

Adversaries

adversaries Persons who are unsupportive of both a program and a particular plan related to the program.

People with whom the athletic trainer has attempted negotiation that has been fruitless are known as **adversaries.** Not only do they disagree with the athletic trainer's plan for the sports medicine program, they are untrustworthy and dishonest as well. It is important to be able to distinguish between adversaries and opponents. A common pitfall occurs when opponents who are honest, trustworthy persons of differing viewpoints are labeled as adversaries. Opponents can make the sports medicine program stronger. Adversaries are often strengthened through confrontation because that tends to legitimize the alternative vision they have for the sports medicine program. Negotiation will not alter their vision of how the program should function. If an athletic trainer has done a good job of including a wide spectrum of people in the planning effort, the number of adversaries should be relatively small.

The likeliest adversaries Janet will confront are the other sports medicine service providers in the Ashton County area. If there are clinics that now provide some services to the three county high schools, they will undoubtedly oppose Janet's plans to create a sports medicine monopoly at the hospital. The clinics and the hospital were in competition before this issue, and the new proposal will only serve to enhance that sense of competition.

Block (1987) suggests specific strategies for developing support among the four types of organizational players:

Allies

- Confirm the fact that the person agrees with the sports medicine plan.
- Profess appreciation for the quality of the relationship.

- Admit any faults and shortcomings of the sports medicine plan.
- Request the support and continued counsel of the ally.

Janet might use the following language in a conversation with the director of rehabilitation services in order to develop his support:

Thanks for showing your support for the outreach program at the staff meeting this morning. I appreciate your confidence in me and your support for the program. I know the plan is not complete yet, but I hope to have the holes patched up by next week. As the plan continues to take shape I'll need your support more than ever. Thanks again.

Opponents

- Profess appreciation for the quality of the relationship. Emphasize the trust and honesty that have characterized the relationship.
- Explain the plan for the sports medicine program along with any supporting arguments for why it should be implemented.
- Define your interpretation of the opponent's views in a nonthreatening manner.
- Attempt to engage the opponent in a problem-solving process to find common points.

Janet might use the following language in a conversation with the orthopedic surgeon in order to develop his support:

Dr. Jones, I want you to know how much I've enjoyed working with you since I arrived at the hospital two years ago. You're one of the best surgeons I've ever worked with and you've really taught me a lot. You've read about the outreach program we're planning. Let me take a few minutes to explain why I think it's so important for the high school students of our county. . . . I know you may think that our program might take away some of the business you've developed at the high school. We certainly don't want that to happen. Can you suggest some strategies we might consider as we implement our outreach program that would help us accomplish our goals while helping you maintain what you've worked so hard to establish?

Bedfellows

- Confirm the fact that the person agrees with the sports medicine plan.
- Convey your concern about the person's willingness to be open and honest. Express a willingness to share a portion of the blame and to find a way to improve the trust relationship so the program can move ahead.
- Clearly state your expectations for the person's behavior toward the sports medicine program. What is it that you want the person to do?
- Ask the person what expectations he or she has for you in order to improve the relationship.
- Attempt to establish a consensus for future working relationships with bedfellows.

Janet might use the following language in a conversation with the vice president for finance in order to develop his support:

Jim, your support of the outreach program at the senior staff meeting last week was just great. I'm glad that you agree with what we are trying to accomplish with the program. However, I'm concerned that as we continue to move ahead with the plan, the financial realities of adding staff are going to confront us in a very real way. If your support breaks down at that point the program will be in big trouble. I know that you and I have had a few disagreements in the past. I'm sorry we haven't always been the best of colleagues—I'll accept some of the blame for that. But this program is too big and too important to allow our past differences to get in the way. When the budget request comes across your desk in a few weeks, Jim, I really hope you'll be able to approve it. I appreciate the time you've given me to talk to you about this and hope that we'll be able to do this in the future when we have issues we need to confront together.

Adversaries

- Explain the plan for the sports medicine program with any supporting arguments for why it should be implemented.
- Define your interpretation of the adversary's views in a nonthreatening manner.
- Explain any actions you have taken or will take to implement the sports medicine plan so that everything is "out in the open."
- Avoid making demands that are unlikely to be met.

Janet might use the following language in a conversation with the owner of a competing clinic:

Sally, I wanted you to know that we plan to institute an outreach program for the Ashton County high schools beginning next month. I didn't want this to hit you "out of left field." We think there are many potential benefits for our county's high school athletes under this plan. I know that you will be concerned that this program will cut into your business. It isn't our intention to hurt your business. We simply have identified a need in the community that we feel a responsibility to meet. Our program will provide the following services: . . .

MEETINGS

Meetings are a necessary and often-lamented part of the athletic trainer's managerial life. Athletic trainers can experience more success in their meetings if they organize well, divide the meeting into three parts, control their own meeting behavior, avoid new business and reports, look to the future, and make high-quality decisions.

One of the most common methods for developing and communicating organizational plans is the meeting. Meetings in sports medicine settings can take many forms. The most common is the staff meeting, where personnel from a work group unit (e.g., the athletic trainers employed by the university athletic department or the rehabilitation professionals employed in an outpatient clinic) gather to discuss issues critical to the function of the unit. Athletic trainers can also be involved in other kinds of meetings. For example, Janet, the athletic trainer in the opening scenario, will undoubtedly have to meet—probably more than once—with the staff from the Ashton County schools in order to organize the hospital's outreach program. Irrespective of the type or setting, meetings are often viewed as exercises in frustration. Many of us have participated in meetings where nothing was accomplished. We often walk away afterward fuming "Did anything useful just happen in there? What a waste of time!" (See figure 2.8)

Although dull, unproductive meetings might be the norm, they are not inevitable. Tropman's (1996) research with meeting experts throughout North America revealed that successful meetings were characterized by four qualities:

1. The group was able to reach decisions in the meetings.
2. The group rarely needed to meet to "undo" or revise decisions they had already made; they made high-quality decisions the first time.

■ **Figure 2.8**   Meetings are often viewed as unproductive time wasters.

DILBERT reprinted by permission of United Feature Syndicate, Inc.

3. The decisions made were important and meaningful to the organization.

4. The meetings were enjoyable and the members felt they had spent their time well.

The meetings that Janet must organize with the Ashton County schools will be more successful if she can implement the following seven principles of effective meeting management (Tropman, 1996).

ORGANIZE FOR THE MEETING

Although it sounds obvious, many meetings fail because nobody prepares for them. Meetings are like a play—they need a script, actors, props, and practice. The script is the agenda (see figure 2.9). The actors are the meeting participants. Some will have more noticeable roles than others, but all are necessary if the meeting is to be successful. The props are the materials needed to conduct business during the meeting. These will almost always include various documents, and might include equipment, such as a blackboard, flip chart, or overhead projector. The last element—practice— is something that most meeting managers disregard. All of us in athletics know the importance of practice. Practice helps eliminate mistakes and random elements from interfering with performance. Practice in the context of a meeting might include checking with several of the key members of the meeting group to get their "read" on important issues to be discussed or decided during the meeting. It certainly involves each participant preparing for the meeting by becoming familiar with each item on the agenda.

DIVIDE THE MEETING INTO THREE PARTS

Too often, participants in a meeting have a role to play that requires them to speak only once. For example, when Janet meets with the department to report on the progress she has made with the outreach program, she'll probably stand up, deliver her report, answer a few questions, and sit down. That might be all she does in this department meeting. Although her involvement was not unimportant, she could probably fall asleep after speaking (which happens a lot at meetings) and not be missed. One method that can be used to organize a meeting and maximize the participants' time and input is to divide the meeting into three parts:

AGENDA

Sports Medicine Outreach Program Planning Committee Meeting

February 5, 2001

Third-Floor Conference Room

Item	**Facilitator**
1. Announcements	
a. High school contract negotiations	Janet
b. New supply bid procedures	Bill
2. Decisions	
a. Budget allocations	Tom
b. Staff travel reimbursement	Bill
c. Comp time for ATCs covering night events	Janet
3. Discussion	
a. Which physicians should we recruit?	Janet
b. How should we market the program?	Tom and Janet

▌Figure 2.9 Sample meeting agenda.

1. Announcements
2. Decisions
3. Discussion

If this formula is rigidly adhered to, all of the meeting participants will be able to give appropriate input at the right times. Meeting managers who deviate from this formula run the risk of allowing the meeting to stray from its original purpose.

CONTROL YOUR MEETING BEHAVIOR

Most people who hate meetings (which is most people) are particularly annoyed because of the behavior of the other meeting participants. We are very quick to see the faults in others but slow to recognize our own shortcomings. This is an important issue for athletic trainers who participate in meetings. Behavior in a group setting is infectious. Optimism or pessimism can sweep through a meeting room if the climate is right. You should carefully analyze your own meeting behavior as a first step toward trying to improve the meeting behavior of others.

AVOID NEW BUSINESS

A common item on most meeting agendas is "new business." The intent of "new business" is to allow meeting participants to bring issues or concerns to the table for discussion. The problem with this time-honored practice is that nobody in the room, with the exception of the person who introduced the issue, is prepared to address the topic with any intelligence. New business, therefore, violates the first principle—organize for the meeting. People can't organize for something they don't know anything about. A good rule to follow when conducting a meeting is "discuss everything on the agenda and don't discuss anything not on the agenda."

AVOID REPORTS

Too often, staff members' valuable time is wasted listening to reports in a meeting when the information could more effectively be delivered and analyzed in writing beforehand. Written reports can be referred to in the "decisions" or "discussion" section of the meeting. If they receive written reports in advance of the meeting, participants have the opportunity to digest the information and formulate well-considered questions at their own pace rather than making snap judgments on a tight time schedule. Written reports should be brief and should contain only the most important elements of an issue or proposal. Participants can be referred to more inclusive reports if they want more information, but short executive summaries will encourage them to read and prepare for the meeting.

LOOK TO THE FUTURE

One of the most frustrating aspects of most meetings is the sense of hurried decision making. Most meeting groups are exposed to issues too late in the decision cycle. Athletic trainers who are involved in planning meetings can avoid this problem by carving out some time—during either the announcements or the discussion period—for consideration of future issues. This preview helps those in the group prepare their thinking when the issue is finally presented to them in a formal way. Facilitating informal discussion of issues is a difficult technique to master. The meeting chairperson must be well versed in the organization's issues and be able to package the information for the group so members can process it at an appropriate level.

MAKE HIGH-QUALITY DECISIONS

Making high-quality decisions is difficult. Most meeting groups fail because they cannot make decisions at all—of any quality. They simply fail to decide. Those who do make decisions often have to go back and undo or revise their decisions. The important elements involved in making high-quality decisions in a group setting include gathering and communicating all the pertinent information, processing the likely outcomes of various alternatives, developing a list of pros and cons for the alternatives, considering the perspectives of all the stakeholders, and deciding to decide. The chairperson of the meeting is critical in this regard. Decisions do have to be delayed when the preceding elements are not satisfied. If the chair can orchestrate all of these elements, however, the time has arrived to make a decision. It is important to go back and revisit the decision after its implementation to evaluate its effectiveness and to learn new lessons for the future, but this process should not interfere with making a decision in the first place.

PROGRAM EVALUATION

Sports medicine program evaluation is a critical, but often ignored, part of the athletic trainer's managerial responsibilities. Program evaluations can be either formative or summative, and goals, objectives, criteria, and outcomes, based on patient charts and other data sources, are frequently used.

Athletic trainers are called upon to assess various aspects of a sports medicine program on a regular basis. How is Bill's knee rehabilitation coming along? Is he on schedule? Was the drug education seminar we hosted last week effective? Will the behavior of the athletes change as a result? Questions like these help determine the quality of the program. Unfortunately, even the most thorough and well-conceived strategic and operational plans don't always produce the desired results. To maximize the value of a sports medicine program, athletic trainers must engage in **program evaluation** regularly.

Worthen and Sanders (1973) have defined *evaluation* as "the determination of the worth of a thing. It includes obtaining information for use in judging the worth of a program, product, procedure, or objective, or the potential utility of alternative approaches designed to attain specified objectives " (p. 19). The athletic trainer should

program evaluation
A systematic and comprehensive assessment of the worth of a particular program.

answer two underlying and related questions when evaluating a sports medicine program: What would the likely effects be if the sports medicine program ceased to exist? and, How are the persons who have access to the program better off than those who do not have access to the program? Each of these questions is crucial—the answers will ultimately help the organization determine if it is committing an appropriate amount of human and financial resources to sports medicine. These questions, and indeed every area of the program evaluation, should be supported by documented evidence.

Types of Evidence to Support Sports Medicine Program Effectiveness

- Patient files
- Injury summaries and statistics
- Treatment summaries and statistics
- Client testimonials
- Student athletic trainer graduation and certification statistics

- Critical incident reports
- Staff accomplishments
- Client surveys
- Alumni surveys
- Surveys of employers of alumni

Evidence of sports medicine program quality can and should be derived from several sources. Reviews of patient files, injury and treatment summary statistics, and client testimonials are examples of data that should be used. Educational programs should evaluate student graduation and certification rates. Surveys of client and alumni satisfaction can provide valuable evidence of perceived program quality, because they allow respondents to reflect for a period of time prior to providing feedback. None of this evidence is sufficient in isolation. Considered together, however, it can help provide an overall assessment of the effectiveness of the sports medicine program. Although the athletic trainer will certainly be required to render judgments based on professional experience, others who will judge the program will need tangible proof that the sports medicine program is accomplishing its mission.

CHART AUDITING

Patient chart auditing is one of the most common methods for evaluating the effectiveness of a sports medicine program. The patient chart should contain a detailed history of the patient's problems, treatment goals, specific interventions, and the patient's reaction to those interventions (see chapter 6). As such, it provides an excellent data source from which to draw conclusions regarding the effectiveness of the sports health care being provided by the program. Although many chart auditing techniques exist, internal and external techniques are most common.

internal chart audit
A patient records review technique performed by the sports medicine staff as part of a quality-assurance program.

An **internal chart auditing** procedure is typically performed by the members of the sports medicine staff and it serves as an important component of a total quality management process for the sports medicine program (see chapter 1). It is intended to be an internal check to ensure that certain quality standards are being upheld in the treatment of injured patients. Any number of factors might be examined. For example, the director of a sports medicine clinic might be concerned that a large number of ACL patients are having a portion of their reimbursement requests denied because the allowable number of visits is being exceeded. One way to find out why this is happening is to pull the charts of all ACL patients for the preceding year and look for common elements. Was there a common surgeon? Were most of the patients who had their insurance claims denied seen by one or two clinicians? Were the patients mostly older industrial workers or younger physically active people?

Once a pattern has been identified, a plan to address the causes of the problem can be developed and implemented.

Computerized patient databases make internal chart audits fairly painless. Searching for every patient with an ACL injury, for example, and discovering common elements between patients is a simple task with a computer. When records are not computerized, the process must be performed by hand, which can be very time consuming.

A second kind of chart auditing process is known as **external chart auditing.** External chart auditing is used by accreditation agencies to ensure that commonly held standards of practice in patient care are being upheld by a sports medicine program (see the sections on external evaluators and accreditation). Third-party reimbursement agencies also use external chart audits to determine the appropriateness of claims for reimbursement. One of the most common instances of external chart auditing occurs when practitioners bill Medicare for the services they provide to qualifying patients. These claims are evaluated by either a **carrier** or an **intermediary** and must be extensively documented in order to qualify for reimbursement (Esposto, 1993). When an intermediary or a carrier evaluates a Medicare claim, it looks for a record of the patient's progress and a rationale for reimbursement. The chart must contain information sufficient to document that the services were directly related to a treatment plan established by the physician or other health care provider. It must also document that the services provided were reasonable and necessary. The Medicare guidelines for determining what is reasonable and necessary include the following:

- The treatment must be accepted as standard for the effective remediation of the patient's condition.

- The patient's condition must be such that only the services of the particular health care provider could be used to provide the care.

- There must be a reasonable expectation that the patient's condition will improve in a specific period of time.

- The treatment plan must be reasonable with respect to the amount, duration, and frequency of treatment.

SUMMATIVE VERSUS FORMATIVE EVALUATION

Two types of program evaluations athletic trainers might be called on to perform are **summative** and **formative** (Fitz-Gibbon & Morris, 1987). The summative evaluation includes

- a summary statement of program effectiveness,
- a description of the program,
- a statement of documented achievement of program goals,
- unanticipated outcomes of the program, and
- comparisons with other similar sports medicine programs.

The formative evaluation includes

- identification of potential problems in the sports medicine program,
- discussion of areas that need strengthening,
- recognition of program strengths, and
- ongoing assessment of program objectives.

---

external chart audit A patient records review technique, performed by an accreditation agency or a payer, intended to ensure that patient care is appropriate and meets certain minimum standards.

carrier Charge-based providers contracted by the federal government charged with reviewing Medicare claims made by physician or other health care providers.

intermediary Cost-based providers contracted by the federal government charged with reviewing Medicare claims made by hospitals.

summative evaluation An assessment designed primarily to describe the effectiveness or accomplishments of a program.

formative evaluation An assessment designed primarily for improvement of a program.

Good program evaluation is expensive in terms of both overt and covert costs. Ideally, athletic trainers should use rigid experimental research designs incorporating control or nontreatment groups for every program evaluation. This is the best way to determine whether a sports medicine program is having the intended effect. Unfortunately, only those athletic trainers with graduate school training will have the research and statistical skills necessary to carry out such experimental designs. In addition, the athletic trainers often find it impossible to carry out evaluation projects of this scope and complexity because they take too much time away from the other duties they must be accountable for. The athletic trainer should strive to include as much comparative information as possible in the program evaluation; this will help other stakeholders appreciate the quality of the program compared to other programs of its type.

One way athletic trainers can provide evidence of comparative quality with sports medicine programs at other similar institutions is by using other athletic trainers as **external evaluators.** Similarly, the Joint Review Committee on Educational Programs in Athletic Training uses athletic trainers trained in program evaluation to judge the quality of athletic training education programs for schools requesting accreditation. External evaluators can also be useful for reducing bias. It can be difficult, or even impossible, for athletic trainers to be objective about their own programs. Asking expert third parties, who have little to lose or gain, to assess the program helps lend credibility to the evaluation results (Joint Committee on Standards for Educational Evaluation, 1981).

external evaluators Experts not affiliated with an organization who are retained to assess the various programs within the organization.

Before the external evaluator arrives, the institution must commit itself to allowing reasonable access to the people and information the evaluator will need to make accurate judgments and to generate useful suggestions for improvement. A competent external evaluator will want to have access to all the evidence. In addition, a good external evaluator will interview the athletic trainers, team physicians, athletic administrators, coaches, student athletic trainers, athletes, and other physically active patients to gain a broad-based perspective of the quality of the sports medicine program. After the site visit, the evaluator should prepare a report that lists perceived strengths and weaknesses of the sports medicine program and specific steps that could be taken to improve the program.

GOALS, OBJECTIVES, AND CRITERIA

Program evaluation should be based on an analysis of the athletic training program's goals and objectives. These goals and objectives should be evaluated using measurable criteria established in advance of the evaluation. **Goals** are derived from the mission statement. They are general statements of program intent. Each goal is supported by two or more objectives. **Objectives** are more specific in nature and describe how the program intends to achieve a particular goal. **Criteria** are highly specific—and typically quantifiable—statements that provide the "yardstick" for determining whether a particular objective has been accomplished. Examples of a goal with supporting objectives and criteria from the Memorial Hospital case at the beginning of the chapter might include the following:

goals General statements of program intent.

objectives Specific statements of how a program intends to accomplish a particular goal.

criteria Quantifiable measures used to determine whether a particular objective has been accomplished.

- **Goal:** The Memorial Hospital Sports Medicine Outreach Program shall provide easy access to sports medicine services for high school student-athletes.

- **Objective #1:** High school student-athletes will have access to Outreach Program staff within 24 hours of the onset of injury.

- **Criterion for Objective #1:** Eighty percent of those high school student-athletes responding to the Outreach Program annual patient satisfaction survey will indicate that they were seen within 24 hours of the onset of their injuries.

• **Objective #2:** High school student-athletes will incur minimal travel in accessing the services of the Outreach Program staff.

• **Criterion for Objective #2:** Ninety percent of those high school student-athletes responding to the Outreach Program annual patient satisfaction survey will indicate that they traveled less than five miles from their homes to be seen by an Outreach Program staff member.

Frequency of Program Evaluation

How often should a sports medicine program be evaluated? Although there is no universal answer, some guidelines apply regardless of the setting in which the sports medicine clinic is housed:

• Collect and collate evaluation evidence continuously. If data is collected only immediately preceding the evaluation, there might not be sufficient time to complete the task. Gathering the evidence is the most time-consuming aspect of program evaluation.

• Perform a mini-evaluation once every year. There are two advantages to this approach: It will force the athletic trainer to compile evidence of program effectiveness for a reasonable time frame, and it will identify program weaknesses that require immediate attention.

• Conduct a complete evaluation of the sports medicine program every three to five years. This schedule will allow the athletic trainer to examine strategic issues, such as mission congruence and program goals and objectives, which shouldn't change very often.

Program Self-Study

Part of the mission statement for the Memorial Hospital Sports Medicine Outreach Program specified that the program would be evaluated on an ongoing basis to ensure quality care for the high school student-athletes being served. One of the ways Janet could evaluate the effectiveness of the program would be to design and implement a self-study process every three to five years (see figure 2.10). The self-study should critically examine all the major elements of the program. It should result in a report to the primary stakeholders of the sports medicine program (Morris & Fitz-Gibbon, 1978). Reports from external evaluators and condensed transcripts of documentary evidence should be included as appendixes.

OUTCOMES

*outcomes assessment
An evaluation method
used in health care that
seeks objective evidence
that a patient's
functional ability was
enhanced through the
care provided by the
athletic trainer.*

One of the major thrusts related to program evaluation that has developed since the late 1980s is objective measurement of patients' functional abilities through the use of **outcomes assessment.** Outcomes assessment is a type of evaluation process designed to provide objective, measurable evidence that the care provided by the athletic trainer was effective in improving the patient's functional ability. Outcomes assessment is likely to play an increasingly important role in health care in general and for athletic trainers specifically. As the available dollars for health care continue to shrink at the same time that athletic trainers are actively seeking access to third-party reimbursement, quality assurance processes and utilization reviews will become critical factors in determining who will get paid and who will not (Stewart, 1993). Health care professions that cannot demonstrate that their interventions are effective and medically necessary will find themselves without access to third-party reimbursement in the increasingly competitive managed care market. In addition, organizations that cannot document that their interventions are cost effective will be bypassed in favor of those that can.

SPORTS MEDICINE OUTREACH PROGRAM SELF-STUDY

Instructions

The self-study for the sports medicine program shall consists of four areas: general considerations, patients, staff, and program. The athletic trainer in charge of the program shall answer the questions below and prepare a report with supporting evidence to be submitted to the Director of Rehabilitation Services and the Vice President for Patient Services. In addition, the Director of Rehabilitation Services, in consultation with the athletic trainer, shall select an appropriate external evaluator. The external evaluator's report shall be included in the self-study as an appendix.

General considerations

1. What is the mission of the program? Is the mission statement consistent with the mission of Memorial Hospital? Is the mission statement consistent with national standards for the delivery of sports medicine services?

2. Does the program work well in the context of the Department of Rehabilitation Services? How does the program take advantage of available resources? Do the program's staff members work well together? Do they work well with the rest of the hospital staff?

3. Who provides leadership for the program? Are the program leaders effective?

4. What are the priorities of the program? Are they appropriate? Do they mesh well with the priorities of Memorial Hospital? Do the priorities of individual staff members mesh well with the priorities of the sports medicine program?

Patients

1. Do patients achieve the short- and long-term goals established at the beginning of their treatment programs? Do patients have easy and quick access to evaluation and treatment services? Do the students of the Ashton County high schools use the program? If not, why not? Are the program's patient loads consistent with national averages?

2. Does the program help reduce the incidence of injury in the Ashton County high schools? If not, what factors account for this? In what ways can the program be improved so as to reduce the incidence of injury?

3. Are the students of the Ashton County high schools better educated with respect to healthy lifestyles than students elsewhere? What efforts have been made to educate students regarding healthy lifestyles? What additional efforts should be/could be made in this area?

Staff

1. How effective are staff members as providers of sports medicine services? Are some staff members ineffective? What can be done to resolve the problem?

2. Do staff members possess the standard credentials for delivery of sports medicine services? Do they engage in programs of continuing education?

3. Are staff members considered experts in their fields? Can they boast of professional accomplishments consistent with experts of regional or national reputation?

4. Are staff members performing in a manner consistent with their position descriptions and codes of professional conduct?

5. Is the size of the staff appropriate for the tasks it must accomplish? Could the same job be done with the same quality with fewer staff members?

Program

1. Is each component of the sports medicine program effective? Which components are the strongest? Which are the weakest? How could the weak components be strengthened?

2. Is each component of the sports medicine program necessary? If not, should some components be eliminated? Are there additional components that should be added to the program? Who would they serve? What is the desired effect of any new component?

3. Is the sports medicine program cost effective? Does the income it generates support its budget? Is it efficient? How could it become more efficient?

■ **Figure 2.10** Self-study form for a hospital-based sports medicine clinic.

The focus on outcomes assessment is particularly important for athletic trainers employed in clinics and hospitals. These organizations remain financially sound only if they can be reimbursed for their services, either through government programs like Medicare and Medicaid, or through private insurers. As the private insurance market continues to make the transition from a traditional fee for service to a managed care model, it will be more important than ever for these organizations to be able to document that they improve their patients' function in an efficient and cost-effective manner. Hospitals and clinics that cannot produce documentary evidence to demonstrate the effectiveness of their patients' functional outcomes will have a difficult time getting the contracts from managed care organizations that will, to an increasing degree, be their lifelines.

Outcomes assessment is important for athletic trainers who work in professional, collegiate, and high school settings, as well. Although outcomes have not traditionally been systematically assessed in these settings, the increasing pressure that most athletic trainers are under from cost-conscious administrators makes it important to be able to document that athletic trainers not only provide an excellent service but that they do so in an economical fashion. Outcomes data could potentially serve a very useful purpose in justifying new staff or in defending against an athletic director who wants to contract all sports medicine services to an outside agency.

There are many methods for conducting outcomes assessments. The three most common models, however, are patient chart documentation, randomized clinical trials, and patient surveys. Each has strengths and weaknesses (see table 2.1). All three are important sources of outcomes data. The usefulness of each of these methods, however, is dependent on the degree to which standard research protocols that reduce the likelihood of drawing spurious conclusions are employed. Outcomes studies that do not employ control groups, randomize patient selection and therapeutic methods, or blind the researchers and the subjects often provide results that are suspect.

Table 2.1 Strengths and Weaknesses of Different Outcomes Assessment Models

Model	Strengths	Weaknesses
Patient chart documentation	1. Provides outcomes for specific patients 2. Required for Medicare reimbursement	1. Labor intensive 2. Dependent on charting skills of practitioner 3. Does not systematically control for situational variables
Randomized clinical trials	1. Uses rigid controls to reduce confounding factors 2. Controls variance 3. Useful for examining very specific problems	1. Requires the use of a control group 2. Poor focus on broad or multiple issues 3. Time intensive
Patient surveys	1. Easy to administer 2. Useful for examining a broad range of issues 3. Useful for assessing patient satisfaction	1. Instruments must be subjected to a validation process 2. Lack of patient specificity 3. Self-reported data are often unreliable

One of the most visible ways in which outcomes assessment has been performed in athletic training has been the NATA Reimbursement Advisory Group's three-year outcomes study. The study used an instrument called the Athletic Training Outcomes Assessment (ATOA) to link specific treatments with outcomes and to assess athletic training procedures for efficacy and efficiency (Keirns, Knudsen, & Webster, 1997). The ATOA is designed to consider a number of factors, including type of injury, body part, type of treatment, affective variables, comorbidities, and patient outcome expectations (see figure 2.11). Bear in mind that this outcomes study has many of the weaknesses of other outcomes studies that use self-reported patient surveys, including the lack of a control or comparison group. Campbell (1999) reports that data from the three-year study yielded the following results:

1. Athletic training methods produce excellent overall outcomes, with the best results in functional outcomes and physical outcomes.

2. Athletic training techniques are effective in treating injuries at all body locations, especially in the lower extremities and spine.

3. Industrial patients treated with work-hardening techniques by athletic trainers had excellent outcomes.

4. The total number of treatments provided is a positive factor in determining positive outcomes.

5. A high degree of patient satisfaction with athletic trainers and their services exists.

6. Athletic training outcomes are consistent across site types, referring sources, and payer groups.

7. As the number of days increased between an injury and the onset of treatment provided by a certified athletic trainer, the patients' favorable perceptions of their outcomes decreased.

ATHLETIC TRAINING OUTCOMES ASSESSMENT©

TO BE COMPLETED AT INITIAL ENCOUNTER

Site-Athletic Trainer Code _____ Patient Name_____ Age _____ Sex _____

(for site use only)

Site Type _____

1. Sports Medicine Clinic
2. Clinic—High School/College
3. High School Training Room
4. College/University Training Room
5. Professional Training Room
6. Industrial Setting

Referring Source _____

1. Self
2. Coach/Supervisor
3. Insurer
4. Primary Care Physician/Generalist
5. Orthopedic Physician/Specialist

Payer _____

1. Medicaid
2. Medicare
3. Managed Care
4. Workers' Compensation
5. CHAMPUS (government/military)
6. Private Insurance
7. Institution
8. Patient

TO BE COMPLETED BY ATHLETIC TRAINER AT INITIAL EVALUATION

Duration Between Injury/Surgery and Beginning of Athletic Training Treatments _____days
(Put 0 if treatments begin on the same day as the injury/surgery.)

Location of Injury/Surgery _____
(Give only the <u>one</u> most primary location. If another injury, identify as a comorbid factor.)

1. toe(s)	4. lower leg	7. hip	10. abdomen	13. cervical	16. arm	19. wrist
2. foot	5. knee	8. pelvis	11. lumbar	14. head	17. elbow	20. hand
3. ankle	6. thigh	9. groin	12. thorax	15. shoulder	18. forearm	21. finger(s)

Type of Injury _____
(Give only the <u>one</u> most primary injury. If another injury, identify as a comorbid factor.)

1. joint dysfunction	9. strain; grade III	17. skin/wound infection	25. fracture
2. joint degeneration	10. sprain; grade I	18. bursitis	26. avulsion
3. joint hypomobility	11. sprain; grade II	19. musculotendonous injury	27. neurologic disease

TO BE COMPLETED BY PATIENT AT INTAKE AND DISCHARGE

Patient—Your responses to this questionnaire will help your athletic trainer and this clinic determine rehabilitation outcomes for specific medical conditions in response to specific treatments. This will help us optimize our treatment services to you and other patients. Your responses will be kept confidential and will not affect your care in any way. Thanks for your assistance.

AT INTAKE   **AT DISCHARGE**

CRITICAL PROBLEM	SEVERE PROBLEM	MODERATE PROBLEM	MINOR PROBLEM	NO PROBLEM		CRITICAL PROBLEM	SEVERE PROBLEM	MODERATE PROBLEM	MINOR PROBLEM	NO PROBLEM
					Instructions—Please rate your current capacities specific to the injury for which you will receive, or have received, treatments. Please answer all questions as best you can, even if some of the questions seem somewhat irrelevant to you. Circle the appropriate response according to the (0 1 2 3 4) scale; 0 - critical problem, 1 - severe problem, 2 - moderate problem, 3 - minor problem, 4 - no problem.					
0	1	2	3	4	**Work Activities**—lifting/lowering, holding/handling, carrying, pushing/pulling, bending over, squatting/stooping, kneeling, crawling, reaching, turning/pivoting, gripping/pinching, fingering	0	1	2	3	4
0	1	2	3	4	**Sports/Recreation/Wellness Activities**—running, jumping, throwing, catching, kicking, swinging, withstanding impacts, weightlifting, specific sport/recreation/wellness activities	0	1	2	3	4
0	1	2	3	4	**Movement**—getting into desired positions, range of motion, speed of motion, bilateral differences (e.g., limping), need for support device	0	1	2	3	4

▌**Figure 2.11** Excerpt from Athletic Training Outcomes Assessment forms.
Reprinted with permission from BIO* Analysis Systems.

APPLICATIONS TO ATHLETIC TRAINING: THEORY INTO PRACTICE

The following two case studies will help you apply this chapter's concepts to real-life situations. The questions at the end of the case studies have many possible correct solutions. Use these studies as homework or exam questions or to stimulate class discussion.

Case Study 1

The chairperson of the Department of Physical Education and Athletics met Susan Quigly, the college's athletic trainer, in the hallway. After exchanging the news of the day, the chairperson said, "By the way, I've been working on the NCAA self-study, and one of the sections deals with drug education programs and policies. I know we are just a small college that doesn't have many problems with drugs, but I can't send this thing over to the president without addressing the issue, especially in light of the emphasis the NCAA places on it. Would you be willing to organize a program so we can at least meet the NCAA guidelines?"

"What would you want such a program to include?" asked Susan. "This could potentially be a huge project."

"You're the expert," replied the chairperson. "Let me know what you come up with."

Susan had strong opinions on the use and abuse of alcohol and other drugs. Several of her family members had been negatively affected by their use. She had plenty of examples of how alcohol had impacted her students. She decided that if she was going to take on this program, she wasn't going to allow any half-measures. She knew that for a problem as complex as drug and alcohol use among college students, she was going to have to develop a comprehensive program to be successful.

After checking with several other athletic trainers who had developed programs for their schools, Susan began writing a proposal for the program. She decided to include the following elements:

- A standards-setting workshop led by a trained facilitator to help the coaches and team captains develop their own rules and sanctions for alcohol and other drug use

- A policy statement that addressed the college's concern over the drug and alcohol issue with procedures to provide an action plan to deal with the problem

- A series of educational seminars and workshops for the student-athletes that would form the bulk of the drug and alcohol education program

- A research study to find out the extent of the problem on campus and to determine the effectiveness of the program

The entire program would cost approximately $3,000 for the first 18 months. Because the department wouldn't allocate any funds for the project, Susan wrote a grant proposal to a local community foundation that covered the cost. Susan was pleased and confident. After six months of planning, the program was finally ready to go.

Questions for Analysis

1. Based on what you know of Susan's planning effort, how successful is the drug and alcohol education program likely to be? How would you have planned for this program?

2. Who are the inside interests in this case? Who are the outside interests? How are they likely to be affected by this program? How should they be involved in planning it?

3. How much support do you think Susan will be able to develop for the program? What strategies should she use to develop support?

4. How should Susan evaluate the effectiveness of the program? What elements should be included in the evaluation plan?

5. How should the policy that Susan wants to see adopted be written? Develop an example of a process and a procedure that might support such a policy.

6. If you were in Susan's position, would you have handled anything differently? What alternative actions would you have taken?

Case Study 2

Dan Wu was halfway through his first year as the chairperson of the Department of Athletic Training Studies at a midsize university. The department he led offered a CAAHEP-accredited undergraduate major in athletic training. The department was housed in the College of Allied Health and had graduated an average of 10 students per year for the past eight years. The department was staffed by two full-time faculty members and three adjunct members who had release time from the athletic department.

Dan received a memo from the dean of Allied Health informing him that it was his department's turn for a departmental review. In keeping with the new policy of allowing greater administrative freedom to department chairpersons, Dan would be al-

lowed to collect and present the evidence he thought the provost and the dean's council should use to judge the effectiveness of the department. Dan was told he would have to submit his report in five months.

A few days later Dan was having lunch in the faculty cafeteria when the dean of Allied Health walked over. "Dan," the dean said, "you should know that the dean's council has been given instructions to reduce our budget by 10% next year. After discussing the problem, we all agreed that the only way to do it without weakening all the programs is to eliminate one of them. I wanted you to know that, unofficially, your department is one that is being considered in the cutback. No decision will be made until after the departmental reviews come in."

Questions for Analysis

1. What evidence should Dan present when preparing the report for the departmental review? What plan for collecting the evidence would you develop if you were in Dan's position?

2. Which aspects of the evidence should Dan highlight, considering the uncertain future of his department? How could he best feature this evidence for maximum impact?

3. Would an external evaluator be useful in this situation? What qualities of the external evaluator would help lend credibility to the report?

4. Besides the departmental self-study, what other steps could Dan take to safeguard the future of the department? What are the likely effects of these actions? Could any of these actions have negative consequences?

SUMMARY

1. *Understand and develop vision and mission statements for a sports medicine program.*

   Change is a pervasive aspect of organizational life that affects sports medicine programs. The development of vision and mission statements can help a sports medicine program develop a philosophical infrastructure that will allow it to adapt appropriately to change. A vision statement should identify the service provider, the service to be provided, the recipients of the service, and the expected quality of the service. The mission statement is a broadly defined, enduring statement of purpose that defines the scope of operations of the sports medicine program. The mission statement should direct the athletic trainer toward accomplishing specific tasks, motivate and inspire, and guide the development of goals and objectives.

2. *Understand the principles underlying sports medicine strategic planning.*

   Planning is a set of activities the athletic trainer should use to bring about a desired future state for the sports medicine program. Strategic plans are broadly written guides for developing specific program goals and objectives. The development of a strategic plan involves identifying the needs of both outside and inside interests; gathering information that identifies the historical and present status of the program; and analyzing the strengths and weaknesses of, the threats to, and the opportunities for the sports medicine program.

3. *Develop and link sports medicine policies, processes, and procedures.*

   Operational plans are explicit steps that guide the actions of the athletic trainer so specific tasks can be accomplished. A policy is an operational plan for expressing the organization's intended behavior relative to a specific program subfunction. Policies require the approval of persons in legal authority, such as boards of trustees or owners. Processes are a collection of incremental and mutually dependent steps designed to direct the most important tasks of the sports medicine program. Procedures provide athletic trainers with specific direction for various processes.

4. *Communicate and develop ownership in a sports medicine program among inside and outside stakeholders.*

   Planning will be ineffective unless the athletic trainer can elicit support for the plan by identifying and influencing allies, opponents, bedfellows, and adversaries. The agreement-trust matrix can be a useful tool in this process. Athletic trainers should employ specific strategies with each of these groups to more effectively gain support for their programs and ideas.

5. *Understand the principles of effective meeting planning and management.*

   Meetings are viewed by most people as a necessary evil, but if properly organized they can be productive engines of decision making. Meetings are generally most effective if athletic trainers organize in advance, divide the meeting into parts, control their own behavior, avoid new business and reports whenever possible, and have a future-oriented perspective.

6. *Understand the principles of effective sports medicine program evaluation.*

   Athletic trainers should evaluate the effectiveness of their sports medicine programs to ensure that the programs will continue to improve and to document program quality. Formative program evaluation identifies strengths and weaknesses and provides alternatives for improvement. Summative evaluation judges the quality of the program. Program evaluation is most valid when it compares program clients with persons without access to the program using the scientific method. This is often difficult, expensive, and impractical. As much comparative data as possible should be used to evaluate the program. The use of an external auditor, along with chart auditing and outcomes studies, can facilitate unbiased assessments. A periodic self-study process that involves collecting evidence of program quality and answering questions crucial to program development is recommended.

CHAPTER THREE

Who Athletic Trainers Work With: Human Resource Management

OBJECTIVES

After reading this chapter, you should be able to do the following:

1. Understand the different forms of organizational culture that can exist in a sports medicine program.

2. Formally define the relationships of the persons working in a sports medicine program by developing an organizational chart.

3. Understand the components of staff selection.

4. Develop a position description and a position vacancy notice.

5. Understand the recruitment and hiring process, especially as affected by discrimination and bias based on race, gender, disability, religion, or national origin.

6. Understand the differences between the three major supervisory models.

7. Understand the purposes, methods, and standards for the evaluation of athletic trainer performance.

David Lewis had just completed his 10th year as the head athletic trainer at a major NCAA Division I university. David liked his job, and the feedback he received from most of the coaches and athletic administrators was positive. In short, David was content.

David was concerned about one aspect of the job, however: Problems had developed with Judy Armstrong, one of his assistants. Although the coaches and athletes she worked with thought she was doing a good job, Judy seemed to have difficulty working with the other athletic trainers on the staff. She was perceived as argumentative, inflexible, and arrogant. David decided on a face-to-face meeting to confront the problem.

David was not prepared for Judy's assessment of her problems with the rest of the staff. "David," she began, "I'm not the problem around here—you are! I'm no different in most respects from any of the other staff athletic trainers except that I'm not willing to keep my mouth shut and put up with all the garbage that goes on around here. For instance, none of us knows where our job responsibilities begin and end. Oh sure, we know what sports we're supposed to work with, but beyond that who is responsible for the duties that overlap from team to team? Where is it spelled out? There are eight assistant athletic trainers here at the university, not counting graduate assistants. We are constantly stepping on each other's toes because we don't know what our own jobs are, let alone what the other person's is. And another thing. Where do I stand relative to the other athletic trainers? I've been here three years and my performance has never been evaluated! I might be able to put up with the lousy hours and the miserable pay if I just got some positive reinforcement for the good things I do from time to time. Think about it, Dave. The average employment length for assistant athletic trainers since you came is about two years. Why do you think everybody leaves so fast if this is such a great place? Don't pin this on me, because I'm not the problem!"

Although the meeting with Judy had put David in an angry and defensive mood, he sensed a kernel of truth in her arguments. He was not a strong personnel administrator and he knew it. In fact, he hated most of the administrative duties that his position required of him. The assistant athletic trainer turnover problem had nagged at him for years. Suddenly, the contentment that David had with his job had vanished. He was frustrated.

By working faithfully eight hours a day, you may eventually get to be a boss and work twelve hours a day.

Robert Frost

The problems with personnel administration that led to David and Judy's confrontation are typical of many sports medicine programs. Athletic trainers are professionals who are, in general, oriented toward providing clinical services. Most have never had any training in how to manage human resources. Some athletic trainers excel at this aspect of administration without any formal understanding of human resource systems, but they are the exceptions. The most complicated tools the athletic trainer will ever work with are people. Without a system for managing these assets, a sports medicine program is unlikely to accomplish its mission. This chapter focuses on the human resource function of a sports medicine program and the skills athletic trainers need to be successful in this area.

ORGANIZATIONAL CULTURE

Sports medicine programs typically exist in organizations that exhibit one of three kinds of organizational culture: collegial, personalistic, and formalistic. Each is typified by certain values, beliefs, assumptions, and behavior norms.

organizational culture The values, beliefs, assumptions, and norms that form the infrastructure of the organizational ethos.

collegial culture A type of organizational culture characterized by consensus, teamwork, and participatory decision making.

The first decision the athletic trainer in charge of a staff makes, consciously or unconsciously, is what kind of organizational culture the program will have. **Organizational culture includes the basic values, behavioral norms, assumptions, and beliefs present in an organization (Owens, 1987). A sports medicine program's organizational culture defines, to a large extent, what it means to be an athletic trainer in that setting. It influences the levels of commitment and loyalty of the athletic trainers working in the program.

Bennis and Nanus (1985) have described three general categories of organizational cultures (which they refer to as *social architecture*) that the athletic trainer should consider as part of sports medicine human resource management: collegial, personalistic, and formalistic.

THE COLLEGIAL CULTURE

The **collegial** sports medicine program is one in which the emphasis is on consensus, teamwork, and participation in most decisions by all members of the staff, who tend to view each other as peers. The head of the department allows and encourages everyone to offer input so that the decision-making process is consensual. Although this type of organizational culture appears ideal, it is inappropriate in some settings. For example, when quick decisions are required, the consensus-oriented style of the collegial culture is inappropriate, because formal authority is watered down among the members of the staff. If the staff is small, on the other hand, the collegial culture is probably both appropriate and useful.

THE PERSONALISTIC CULTURE

personalistic culture A type of organizational culture characterized by autonomy in decision making and problem solving.

The sports medicine program that Dave "leads" has a **personalistic culture**. It places little emphasis on policy and procedure. Each member of the staff makes her or his own decisions. Teamwork and group consensus are not high priorities. Although program leaders might be available for advice and counsel, the staff athletic trainers' problems are perceived to be *their* problems, not the program's. The personalistic organizational culture is a form of controlled anarchy.

THE FORMALISTIC CULTURE

formalistic culture A type of organizational culture characterized by a clear chain of command and well-defined lines of formal authority.

The sports medicine program with a clear chain of command and well-defined lines of authority operates in a **formalistic culture**. The formalistic culture is typical of bureaucratic programs in which there is a heavy emphasis on policy, procedure, and rules. It discourages risk taking and deviation from the established source of authority. Although this might seem undesirable for a sports medicine program, there are certain advantages to the formalistic style. First, decisions can be made more rapidly, because various members of the staff have formal authority. Second, established policies and procedures can provide direction to staff athletic trainers and continuity in quality of service for clients. Finally, programs with large staffs might benefit from a formalistic culture, because it divides and defines responsibilities and thereby enhances internal organization.

ORGANIZATIONAL STRUCTURES

Every sports medicine organization has a structure. The **organizational structure** of the sports medicine program plays an important role in how well staff members accomplish the program's mission. Each athletic trainer in the program has a different job to perform. Although there might be overlapping duties and similarities from one athletic trainer to another, each is responsible for distinct duties. The only

Organizational structure—the formal relationship that each person has to another within an organization—is best described in one of three types of organizational chart: function oriented, service oriented, or matrix.

organizational structure   A model that defines the relationships among the members of an organization.

span of control   The number of subordinates supervised by a particular individual in an organizational setting.

organizational chart   A graphic representation of an organization's structure, usually arranged by function, service, or in a matrix format.

exception to this rule, of course, is the sports medicine program staffed by only one athletic trainer, which is not uncommon at most high schools and many small colleges. Organizational structure need not be a concern for athletic trainers in these environments.

When designing the organizational structure of a sports medicine program, athletic trainers must consider the desired span of control. **Span of control** refers to the number of subordinates who report to a given supervisor. Although management researchers disagree on the precise formula for establishing a span of control, most agree that supervision of employees, including athletic trainers, is easier and more effective if supervisors are directly involved with three to six subordinates (Ouchi & Dowling, 1974). Organizational structures are typically depicted in organizational charts.

The **organizational chart** is a graphic illustration that shows the formal relationship between the various athletic trainers and other health care workers in a sports medicine program. Organizational charts are useful because they show staff members their roles in relation to the overall program. In the opening case, Judy would probably have better understood the role David expected her to play if he had taken the time to develop an organizational chart for the university's sports medicine program. This task is especially important for newly hired athletic trainers, because they lack a historical perspective for "how things are done around here."

Although there are many ways to graphically depict a sports medicine program's organizational structure, most are charted according to function, service, or in a matrix form.

FUNCTION-ORIENTED ORGANIZATIONAL CHART

The organizational chart based on function is probably the most common in sports medicine settings. It makes supervision easier because it requires supervisors to specialize along lines of expertise (see figure 3. 1). Functional organizational structures are especially well suited to sports medicine clinics or universities with large staffs, because they facilitate allocation of staff members to projects for which they have special skills and knowledge.

Functional organizational structures also have several disadvantages. They can make it difficult to make rapid decisions, because requests often have to make their way up the chain of command. They can also make it difficult to establish accountability for particular areas of responsibility. Consider the struc-

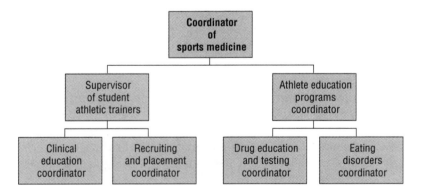

∎ Figure 3.1 Sports medicine organizational chart: division by function.

ture depicted in figure 3.1. If student athletic trainers are consistently failing the NATA certification examination, who should be held accountable? Is the athletic trainer in charge of clinical education at fault, or is the recruiting and placement coordinator guilty of bringing poor students into the program? Finally, the functional approach to organizing a sports medicine program can isolate staff members, because it places little emphasis on sharing ideas or teamwork to accomplish program goals.

SERVICE-ORIENTED ORGANIZATIONAL CHART

Another way to define the structure of a sports medicine program is to organize the staff according to the services they provide. Figure 3.2 provides an example from a

Advantages and Disadvantages of a Functional Structure

Advantages

- Suited to a stable environment
- Fosters development of expertise
- Allows specialization
- Requires minimal internal coordination
- Requires fewer interpersonal skills

Adapted from Stoner 1982.

Disadvantages

- Slow response time in large programs
- Bottlenecks due to sequential task performance
- Less innovative; narrow perspective
- Might create conflicts over program priorities and staff responsibilities
- Little emphasis on sharing ideas and teamwork

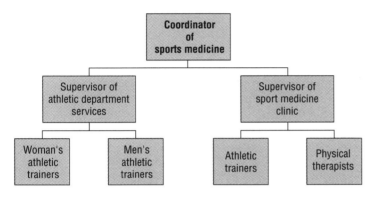

Figure 3.2 Sports medicine organizational chart: division by service.

large university that operates a sports medicine clinic in addition to the traditional sports medicine services provided by athletic department athletic trainers. Except for the box for the coordinator's position, the boxes in this chart represent athletic trainers who have responsibilities to certain client groups. This type of organizational chart is especially appropriate for programs that serve a diverse clientele.

Like its function-oriented counterpart, the service-oriented organizational chart has both advantages and disadvantages. One of the advantages of this system is that it facilitates coordination of services to any one client group because of the relatively strict division of responsibility. Accountability is easier to obtain, because athletic trainers work with well-defined client groups. Finally, the chief decision maker can usually act more quickly and easily because intermediate supervisors have more authority to make their own decisions.

Among the disadvantages of this system are problems balancing power and authority. When service groups are tightly defined, the athletic trainers working with a particular client group might tend to place the interests of that unit over the mission of the total program. This can result in power struggles between the members of the various program units. Another disadvantage with the service-oriented organizational structure is that it sometimes inflates personnel costs. Strictly delimiting service groups means that the expertise of an athletic trainer working in one unit is often unavailable to an athletic trainer working in another. Consequently, additional

Advantages and Disadvantages of Service-Oriented Organizational Structures

Advantages

- Suited to fast change
- Allows for high service visibility
- Allows full-time concentration on tasks
- Clearly defines responsibilities
- Permits parallel processing of multiple tasks

Adapted from Stoner 1982.

Disadvantages

- Fosters politics in resource allocation
- Inhibits coordination of activities
- Restricts problem solving to task needs
- Permits in-depth competencies to decline
- Creates conflicts between tasks and priorities
- Can inflate personnel costs

athletic trainers are required to balance the expertise between units. Supervisory expenses go up proportionally.

MATRIX ORGANIZATION CHART

matrix structure
A type of chart that describes an organizational structure in terms of both functions and services.

Many athletic trainers will be tempted to structure their sports medicine programs in terms of function or service. Unfortunately, most traditional sports medicine programs will not match these models. Athletic trainers should consider an alternative to function or service paradigms: the matrix structure. The **matrix structure** combines the strongest features of the service and function models (Kolodny, 1979).

In matrix structures, athletic trainers and other members of the sports medicine team report to two or more "bosses," depending on the project they are working on. The organizational chart for a matrix organization has both horizontal and vertical elements. If David accepts Judy's advice and develops an organizational chart for the university's sports medicine program, he might design a structure similar to the one in figure 3.3. The vertical elements show the chain of command in the program. The horizontal elements depict project teams that take advantage of the athletic trainers' specialization in certain areas. Not everyone has to be placed on a project team. Some athletic trainers will lack expertise in some areas. Others will be new to the organization and might need time to become acclimated. In educational settings like David's, some of the athletic trainers might have release time to teach sports medicine courses, making it difficult for them to be assigned to project teams.

The advantages of the matrix system as a model for deploying athletic trainers include the ability to efficiently use the staff's expertise. In addition, the matrix structure reduces coordination problems and enhances economic efficiency by assigning only the necessary number of athletic trainers to any given project.

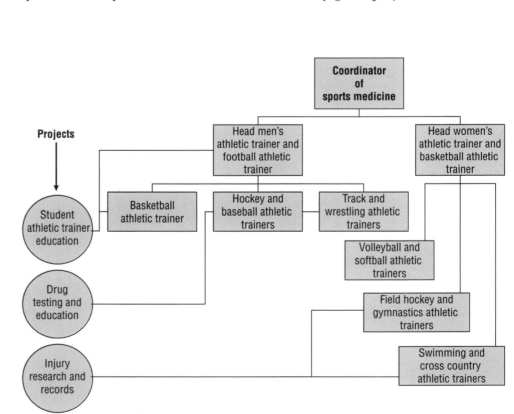

▌Figure 3.3   A matrix organization structure.

Advantages and Disadvantages of the Matrix Organizational Structure

Advantages

- Gives flexibility to the organization
- Stimulates interdisciplinary cooperation
- Involves, motivates, and challenges people
- Develops athletic trainers' skills
- Frees program coordinator for planning

Disadvantages

- Can create a feeling of anarchy
- Encourages power struggles
- Might lead to more discussion than action
- Requires high level of interpersonal skill
- Can be time consuming to implement

Adapted from Stoner 1982.

There are also disadvantages to the matrix model. Athletic trainers need a high level of interpersonal communication skill to work effectively with various coworkers on different tasks. For example, in the opening case study, Judy finds that, like most athletic trainers, she must accomplish a number of tasks with other staff members. Because her interpersonal skills were not highly developed, she was unable to get along with her fellow athletic trainers. Another disadvantage of the matrix system is that athletic trainers can become frustrated and morale can suffer when people are switched between projects or when one project ends and another begins. Because many projects have a finite life span, this is a common problem.

INFORMAL ORGANIZATIONS

Relationships between people in an organization often have nothing to do with the formal organizational structure. People form relationships in organizations for at least 11 reasons: social contact, satisfaction of needs, power, peer pressure, problem solving, goal congruency, shared understanding, information and communication, knowledge and expertise, formal organizational support, and physical proximity.

Organizational structures, with their accompanying charts, are a useful starting point in helping athletic trainers and those with whom they work understand their roles in a sports medicine unit. Unfortunately, these devices rarely tell the whole story about how a sports medicine unit really functions. The formal organization, as defined by the officially approved organizational chart, is almost always accompanied by the informal organization. Although the formal organization represents the theoretical relationships between the various members of the sports medicine unit, the informal organization represents the actual relationships as they exist and change from day to day. Whether athletic trainers are managers or employees, only those who understand both the formal and informal organizations will succeed in any given setting.

Why do athletic trainers and others join informal organization groups? There are many reasons, but Drafke (1994) believes these are the most common:

- Social contact. The informal organization allows people to join small groups and form relationships, thus filling an important human need. People develop friendships at work. The informal organization allows this to occur.

- Satisfaction of needs. The relationships developed at work can provide for many of the psychological needs that most people have. Self-esteem is often bolstered via the informal organization, because it allows people to exercise power and assume leadership in a small group even when they have no formal authority to do so.

- Power. Many people join groups in the informal organization because they sense that their power will be enhanced by doing so. A group is often able to influence the outcome of a decision, whereas an individual might not.

• Peer pressure. Athletic trainers frequently join a group in the informal organization as a result of peer pressure to do so. A person who doesn't ally him- or herself with a group might be shunned.

• Problem solving. Most people in the informal organization look to their peers as the first source in obtaining advice on how to solve work-related problems. This is frequently a less intimidating method than seeking the advice of one's superior on the formal organizational chart.

• Goal congruency. Informal organization groups often form as a result of commonly shared beliefs or goals. These goals might or might not be limited to work-related functions. Athletic trainers might choose to join a group based on the common interests of the other members of the group.

• Understanding. Often an individual joins a group in the informal organization because the group members encounter similar kinds of problems at work. Athletic trainers are more likely to ally themselves with other groups of athletic trainers because of this shared experience and desire for understanding.

• Information and communication. The informal organization is potentially a tremendous information source. Athletic trainers often choose which groups to join based on how much information the group is privy to. Athletic trainers who share information about organizational issues—whether officially sanctioned or not—will find others flocking to their group to "hear the latest news." Knowing when to pass on unofficial information and when not to is an important survival skill.

• Knowledge. The person who occupies the manager's role in the formal organization does not always have the most knowledge on a given subject. Athletic trainers will frequently seek out others in the informal organization for answers to their questions rather than going directly to their supervisors.

• Formal organization support. The power structure of the informal organization commonly functions to keep the department or institution going when the formal organization is flawed or temporarily incomplete. The "take action now and apologize later" strategy, as opposed to asking permission, is common in both health care and athletic organizations. This strategy often works because the informal organization influences day-to-day operations more than the formal organization does.

• Physical proximity. Many people join groups in the informal organization because they work with the group members every day. Indeed, it is difficult to join a group when contact is infrequent.

STAFF SELECTION

Staff selection is commonly assumed to be limited to just that—selection of employees. Staff selection is actually a much broader construct, and includes any procedure used to make employment decisions.

The basis for human resource management in sports medicine is **staff selection.** Although the term *staff selection* might imply only identifying and hiring new athletic trainers, it has a much broader meaning in law. The Equal Employment Opportunity Commission's *Uniform Guidelines on Employee Selection Procedures* (1979) defines *staff selection* as any procedure used as a basis for any employment decision. Athletic trainer hiring, promotion, demotion, retention, and performance evaluation are all considered selection activities by law (see figure 3.4). To comply with the *Uniform Guidelines,* athletic trainers must be sure their employment practices do not adversely impact any group protected under the law. The only exception to these rules occurs when an organization can prove that it discriminates as a result of "business necessity." The following sections provide practical suggestions for athletic trainers with staff-selection responsibilities.

staff selection The procedures used as the basis for any employment decision, including recruitment, hiring, promotion, demotion, retention, and performance evaluation.

position description A formal document that describes the qualifications, work content, accountability, and scope of a job.

job specification A written description of the requirements or qualifications a person should possess in order to fill a particular role in an organization.

person specification A specific delineation, based on the job specification of the qualities, skills, and characteristics a person must have in order to fill a particular role.

job description A written description of the specific responsibilities a position holder will be accountable for in an organization.

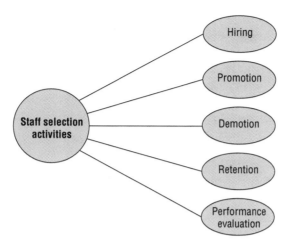

Figure 3.4 Staff selection activities in sports medicine.

POSITION DESCRIPTION

A formal document that contains information about the required qualifications for, and the work content, accountability, and scope of, a job is known as a **position description**. The position description is an important communication link between the athletic trainer and the supervisor that creates a common understanding of the role the athletic trainer should play in the program. Although many supervisors assume their staffs agree with them about the duties for which they are responsible, Myers (1985) concluded that fewer than 50% of the employees he surveyed agreed with their supervisors on the standards and responsibilities of their jobs. When position descriptions are poorly written or are absent altogether, athletic trainers are unlikely to be able to meet the undefined expectations of their supervisors. Unfortunately, many athletic trainers do not have position descriptions (Ray, 1991a) (see figure 3.5). In addition, many athletic trainers' position descriptions are poorly written, couched in trait-oriented language, or lacking weights for various job descriptors.

The athletic trainer's position description should be divided into two sections: the job specification and the job description (see figure 3.6). The **job specification** describes the qualifications an athletic trainer should have to fill the role (Haddad, 1985). An element that helps clarify the job specification is the **person specification**. The person specification translates the job specification into meaningful qualities the person must have to be successful in the role. It also helps operationalize and define what those qualities must be for this particular job. The **job description** lists the responsibilities for which the athletic trainer will be held accountable (U.S. Small Business Administration, 1980). Each responsibility should be assigned a weight so

Figure 3.5
Position description frequency among athletic trainers.

Data from Ray 1991.

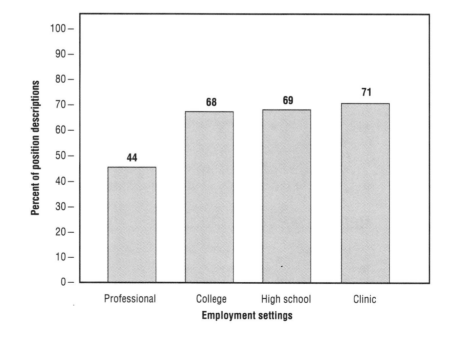

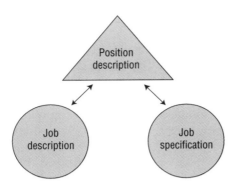

■ **Figure 3.6**
Position description
components.

that the athletic trainer will understand which duties are considered the most important (Fowler & Bushardt, 1986). The weights assigned to various responsibilities can be determined in a variety of ways. One method is to determine what percentage of the athletic trainer's time will be devoted to a particular responsibility. This method would place more weight on "taping ankles" or "wound care" than on "performing CPR." An alternative would be to assign weights according to how critical the job responsibility is. Using this method, "performing CPR" would clearly be weighted more heavily than "taping ankles" or "wound care." No matter which method is used, the weights must reflect the values of the organization. The casual observer should be able to see the organization's mission clearly reflected in the weighting of job responsibilities. Another important element in successful weighting of job responsibilities is to be sure that the weights are realistic. If every job responsibility is weighted as a "5" on a 1 to 5 scale of importance, the position description will not be of much value in helping the athletic trainer understand what is most important and what is less critical.

Athletic trainers who write position descriptions struggle with several important questions. Should the items be specific or general? Should the document describe what ought to be or what is? Although no definitive answers to these questions would meet the needs of every situation, general guidelines do exist. It is generally useful to be as specific as possible when delineating the duties and responsibilities of the athletic trainer. This is important because it provides clear direction for the athletic trainer. To avoid allowing employees to perform only minimal job responsibilities, Sikula (1976) suggests adding a general concluding statement near the end, such as "and any other duties related to the performance of this job as assigned by the Coordinator of Sports Medicine."

The question of whether the job description should be normative or descriptive is not easy to answer. Ideally, the athletic trainer should have some input into the design of her own position description. She probably knows the most about the job and its responsibilities (Aldrich, 1985). Unfortunately, when incumbents write their own job descriptions, they tend to be narrowly focused and to ignore tasks the incumbent does not enjoy, no matter how important they are to accomplishing the mission of the sports medicine program. For this reason, the program head should perform a final check on all position descriptions. The combination of input from the supervisor and from the subordinate into the position description will be more likely to result in a balance between the needs of the employee and those of the sports medicine program. Position descriptions for new athletic trainers should be written as normatively as possible so the new employee can begin to adapt to the new work setting. In any case, the position description should only reflect the characteristics of the job, not ambiguous personal characteristics like loyalty, initiative, and trust.

Finally, no matter which approach is used, the position description should be reviewed and modified as needed, but at least once a year, to reflect changes in the athletic trainer's qualifications or the work environment (Bruce, 1986). For an example of what Judy's position description might look like, see figure 3.7.

RECRUITMENT AND HIRING

recruitment The process of planning for human resource needs and identifying potential candidates to meet those needs.

Attracting and retaining qualified, competent staff members is crucial to the overall success of a sports medicine program. **Recruitment** of athletic trainers and other allied health care professionals should be viewed from two perspectives: the long-range need for human resources within the sports medicine program (see figure 3.8) and the immediate staffing needs.

POSITION DESCRIPTION

Job title: Assistant Athletic Trainer
Department: Intercollegiate Athletics
Incumbent: Judy Armstrong

Date: July 1, 2001
Status: Salaried Nonfaculty
Supervisor: Linda Black, Head Women's AthleticTrainer

Written by: David Lewis, Coordinator of Sports Medicine, and Judy Armstrong
Approved by: James Wilson, Director of Intercollegiate Athletics

JOB SPECIFICATION

Factor	Job Specification	Person Specification
Education	Requires minimum of bachelor's degree.	Must have a bachelor's degree.
Certification	Requires credentials consistent with Ohio law and recognized national standards.	Must be NATA certified, hold a valid Ohio license, and be certified in CPR.
Working conditions	Requires travel over weekends and holidays, 50–70 hours of work per week, and exposure to all kinds of weather.	Must have flexible schedule and be in good physical condition.
Physical demands	Requires lifting of injured athletes, manual dexterity, and administration of CPR.	Must be able to lift heavy weights and have functional use of all four extremities.

JOB DESCRIPTION

Job Responsibilities	Relative Importance (1 = low 5 = high)
Coordinates and delivers athletic training services to members of the field hockey and gymnastics teams including, but not limited to, coordination of physical exams, evaluation and treatment of injuries at practices and games, design and supervision of rehabilitation programs, counseling within the limits of expertise, and prepractice/game taping	5
Refers injured athletes to appropriate physicians according to guidelines in the *Standard Operating Procedures*	5
Submits injured athlete status reports to coaches by 11:00 a.m. of the day following the injury	4
Maintains computerized injury/treatment database according to guidelines in the *Standard Operating Procedures*	3
Coordinates NCAA Injury Surveillance program by conducting in-service training for student athletic trainers, collecting and checking the accuracy of individual and weekly injury report forms, and mailing completed forms to the NCAA by Monday of each week	3
Prepares annual injury and treatment report for all sports by June 1	3
Exhibits behaviors in strict compliance with the NATA *Code of Professional Practice*	5
Performs other duties not specifically stated herein but deemed essential to the operation of the sports medicine program as assigned by the Coordinator of Sports Medicine or the Head Women's Athletic Trainer	Varies

❚ **Figure 3.7** Sample position description.

For more information on recruitment and hiring, see chapter 1 (Athletic Training: The Profession and Its History) of Hillman's *Introduction to Athletic Training* in the Athletic Training Education Series.

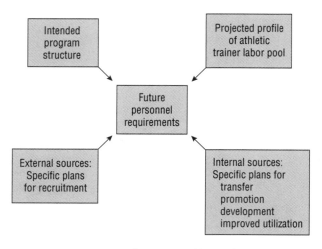

Figure 3.8 Long-range recruiting considerations.

Reprinted from Castetter 1986.

Figure 3.9 Factors influencing immediate recruitment needs.

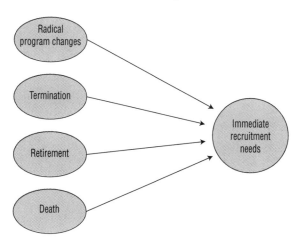

The long-term staffing plan depends, to a significant degree, on the strategic plan of the sports medicine program. How is our client base likely to change? How will the accomplishment of our goals and objectives affect our need for staffing? The long-range recruiting plan should consider a number of factors, including the likelihood of promotion or transfer of present staff members, upcoming retirement plans, and the projected availability of athletic trainers and other allied health care workers in the labor pool. All these factors are important. For example, if the program structure will support an additional athletic trainer but the pool of qualified applicants is inadequate, the human resources plan for the sports medicine unit might need to be revised. Each of these factors should be evaluated annually so future staffing needs can be met.

The other perspective in the recruitment process is the immediate need for staffing the sports medicine program. Immediate staffing needs typically arise as a result of four changes in the makeup of the present staff: radical program changes, termination (for either personal or professional reasons), retirement, and death. Each of these actions can result in the immediate need to fill a vacant position (see figure 3.9).

Neither the long-term nor the immediate staffing needs of the sports medicine unit can be accomplished unless those needs are successfully integrated into the overall institutional or departmental staffing plan. Athletic trainers are often frustrated when their staffing requests are denied or otherwise put on hold. Too often, the response to this negative outcome is "Athletic training always gets shortchanged around here. Our needs are always considered last priority." Frequently the reason for these decisions is not that athletic training and its needs are low priorities, but rather, that athletic training managers have not carefully cultivated institutional decision makers, who are faced with pressures from many competing interests. The athletic training manager must place a strong emphasis on ensuring that the staffing needs of the sports medicine program are communicated to institutional decision makers in such a way that they will be frequently reminded how important those needs are to the operation of the program.

Many institutions that employ athletic trainers have specific procedures in place for recruiting and hiring all personnel. In these institutions, the athletic trainer in charge of staffing the sports medicine program has little choice but to become well informed about the policies and procedures and to scrupulously adhere to them. Most institutional recruitment and hiring policies and procedures are designed to prevent the more blatant forms of discrimination based on race and gender. In many cases, the athletic trainer will be required to document every step of the recruitment and hiring process to ensure that all qualified applicants are afforded equal opportunity in the hiring process. McCarthy (1983) has suggested that employers ask the following questions of their recruitment and hiring practices to determine if they could be discriminatory:

- Are hiring restrictions based on sex, national origin, age, or religion bona fide occupational qualifications?

- Are the prerequisites listed in the job specifications valid indicators of success as an athletic trainer?

- Is there a legitimate necessity for policies and procedures that adversely affect any given class of employee?

- Are the questions asked in the hiring interview directly related to the prospective employee's ability to perform the job responsibilities?

- Have reasonable accommodations been made to enable handicapped persons or persons of various religious beliefs to perform the job?

- What precautions have been taken to ensure that present recruitment and hiring policies and procedures do not perpetuate past discriminatory practices?

Validity and Reliability in Hiring

validity (in staff selection) The employment of criteria that predict how well a candidate will perform in a role.

In addition to ensuring that racial and gender bias is systematically purged from the hiring process, it is also important that the methods used are employed consistently and that hiring criteria are predictive of success in the position. **Validity** in staff selection criteria is important for several reasons. First, the use of valid hiring criteria is more likely to produce an athletic training staff that functions well in its role. Second, using valid hiring criteria enhances efficiency in the staff selection process, because productive employees are less likely to leave the organization, which would create gaps that must be filled. Finally, valid hiring criteria can help demonstrate that the hiring process was fair and free from bias.

Establishing validity in hiring criteria is a difficult process that often takes years to accomplish. A significant amount of trial and error might be involved in validating the process. In general, athletic training managers ought to scrutinize every established criterion for a particular position and ask themselves two questions:

1. Could a person who did not meet this criterion be reasonably expected to succeed in this position?

2. How likely is a person who meets this criterion to succeed in this position?

If the answer to the first question is "yes," the criterion is not valid and should be discarded. The answer to the second question is a bit more tricky. It requires the athletic training manager to predict a probability value on the basis of his knowledge of the position and his past experience. If the answer to the second question is "quite likely," then the criterion is probably valid. If, on the other hand, the athletic training manager cannot predict how successful candidates would be, even if they met the criterion, the criterion is probably not valid. I use the modifier "probably" because the only way that a manager can definitively assess the validity of employment criteria is by collecting data over time and correlating the relationship between various employment criteria and success or failure in the position.

reliability (in staff selection) Consistency of staff selection procedures.

Reliability in staff selection is the degree to which employment standards and practices are applied with consistency to all candidates. Like validity, reliable procedures are important to ensure that bias is reduced to a minimum. Reliable procedures also help produce the same information when applied to different candidates. For example, suppose that all candidates for an athletic training position with a large urban police or fire department were required to submit to a drug-screening procedure. If the procedure resulted in an unacceptably high rate of false positive or false negative results, it would be an unreliable staff selection criterion because its use provides different information for candidates with similar characteristics.

Reliability can be enhanced by ensuring that all candidates go through an identical screening process, including the questions asked during the interview.

Hiring practices vary greatly from organization to organization. Some sports medicine programs employ a very informal process, whereas others adhere to rigid procedures. Most will use a system that resembles the following 10-step process.

Common Steps for Recruiting and Hiring Sports Medicine Personnel

1. Request for position
2. Position request approval
3. Position vacancy notice
4. Application collection
5. Telephone interviews

6. Reference checks
7. On-site interview
8. Recommendation and approval for hiring
9. Offer of contract
10. Hiring

Step 1: Request for Position

Athletic administrators, general managers, principals, and clinic administrators will not consider filling a vacancy or adding a new position unless the athletic trainer makes a specific request. Some organizations require that a specific form be completed as part of the request process. Others require a position description. Obviously, requests for additional personnel are generally screened more cautiously than requests for position replacements. Such requests should be detailed enough to document need, based on both present and forecasted program conditions. There are many potential sources of information the athletic trainer manager could use to justify the position. Outcomes data, patient load, revenue statements, and student-faculty ratios are just a few examples of the kind of justification most administrators will require before they approve a position.

Step 2: Position Request Approval

After the athletic trainer in charge has submitted the request to the appropriate administrative officer, the request will probably be approved, denied, or held up pending further study. Athletic trainers should try to anticipate the data administrators will need in order to make a decision.

Step 3: Position Vacancy Notice

Once the request for position is approved, the athletic trainer might be required to advertise the position vacancy to satisfy collective bargaining agreements and state and federal guidelines. Position vacancies should be posted both internally, so present sports medicine staff who wish to apply for the positions may do so, and externally. Position vacancy notices may be posted externally in any of the following locations:

- Local newspapers
- National Athletic Trainers' Association Placement Vacancy Notice Service
- NCAA News
- ATHTRN-L
- *Chronicle of Higher Education*

See the NATA Web site at **http://www.nata.org/**.

- Publications of the American Alliance for Health, Physical Education, Recreation and Dance
- Publications of the American Physical Therapy Association
- Publications of the American College of Sports Medicine

Position vacancy notices are frequently posted on ATHTRN-L, an Internet discussion group for athletic trainers. To subscribe, contact **listserv@indiana.edu**.

Finally, many athletic trainers find it useful to send a copy of the position vacancy notice to program directors of Commission on Accreditation of Allied Health Education Programs (CAAHEP)-approved athletic training education programs and to the head athletic trainers of schools that offer internships for their student athletic trainers.

Beginning in 2004, only graduates of CAAHEP-accredited programs will be eligible for NATABOC certification.

The position vacancy notice should not be a carbon copy of the position description, but it should include a summary of the major responsibilities, a list of prerequisite qualifications, and a brief description of the major attributes of the institution or organization. In addition, the position vacancy notice should have the name, address, and telephone number of the person responsible for coordinating the hiring effort for the sports medicine program along with a list of required application documents. Typical application documents include a resume or curriculum vitae, letter of application, letters of reference, and transcripts. Many institutions require notice of nondiscrimination near the bottom of all position vacancy notices (see figure 3.10).

Although the position vacancy notice is an important step in the hiring process, athletic trainers who wish to attract the very best candidates to their programs must rely on their networking skills to do so. For example, assume that David Lewis in the opening case has a position vacancy in his program. He has been in the business for many years and has been careful to get to know many athletic trainers around the country. There are two or three highly qualified athletic trainers with whom he is familiar that he knows would be a good match for the position in his program. If he wants to attract them to this position, he will have to take an active role in informing them about the position and encouraging them to apply. He should send them a copy of the position vacancy notice, but he should also speak with them personally to express his interest in attracting them to his institution. Athletic trainer–managers responsible for staff selection should maintain a file on people they think would be excellent candidates for future positions in their organizations. When openings occur, these people should be contacted directly and encouraged to apply.

A word of caution regarding this technique is appropriate. Athletic trainers who actively recruit from the ranks of other sports medicine programs run the risk of being accused of "stealing" another organization's employees. This can often lead to bad feelings and damaged institutional relationships. Although there is no foolproof method for avoiding this unpleasant side effect of network-based employee recruiting, it is generally best to work with the candidate to develop a strategy to minimize the consequences and preserve the relationship. In most cases candidates will not want their employers to know they are considering another position until they are reasonably certain they will, in fact, be hired by the new organization.

Nowhere is network-based recruiting more important than in the effort to identify, recruit, screen, and hire members of minority groups. Athletic trainers who wish

---

POSITION VACANCY
Ohio Technological University
Assistant Athletic Trainer

OTU is seeking applications for the position of assistant athletic trainer in the Department of Intercollegiate Athletics. Primary responsibilities include the delivery of athletic training services for the field hockey and gymanstics teams, although occasional work with other teams will be required. This position also includes responsibility for coordinating the sports medicine program's injury research and records program, including maintenance of the computer database and coordination of student athletic trainers involved in NCAA injury surveillance data collection.

Minimum qualifications include a bachelor's degree, NATA certification, an Ohio athletic training license, and current American Red Cross CPR certification.

Salary is negotiable and will be commensurate with experience. This position is a 10-month, renewable-term, salaried nonfaculty contract.

Ohio Technological University has an enrollment of 25 000 students and is located in an urban center of over 250 000. OTU offers 41 undergraduate majors and 15 graduate degree programs. The university is a member of the NCAA Division I and offers eight sports for men and eight for women. OTU is an equal opportunity, affirmative action employer. Women and members of minority groups are encouraged to apply.

Interested persons should send a letter of application, resume, three letters of reference, and undergraduate transcript by June 1 to

David Lewis
Coordinator of Sports Medicine
Ohio Technological University
Urban Center, OH 40000
(217) 555-5555

▌ Figure 3.10 Sample position vacancy notice.

to enhance the racial diversity in their programs are faced with a difficult challenge, because the number of ethnic minority certified athletic trainers is quite small. In order to encourage members of minority groups to apply for their positions, athletic trainers will probably have to employ at least four strategies. First, the position vacancy notice should be mailed to the athletic trainers at all of the historically black colleges and universities. Second, the position vacancy notice should be mailed to the program directors at universities that offer CAAHEP-accredited athletic training education programs. Third, the position vacancy notice, along with a personal letter, should be sent to certified athletic trainers who identify themselves as members of a minority group. Finally, the athletic trainer will probably need to directly contact minority athletic trainers with whom he or she is familiar and personally invite them to apply for the position. Even if all four of these strategies are used, it might take quite a long time to successfully recruit minorities to a program.

A list of minority athletic trainers is available from the NATA Ethnic Minority Advisory Council, 2952 Stemmons, Dallas, TX 75247.

Step 4: Application Collection

The next step in the process is to receive and screen applications for the position. A common practice is to appoint a committee of interested persons with a legitimate stake in hiring the athletic trainer to screen applications. The operation of search committees varies widely. Some operate on consensus, whereas others follow strict parliamentary procedure and vote on the suitability of various candidates for the position.

In any case, incoming applications should be sorted into three groups: unqualified applicants, qualified applicants with complete application files, and apparently qualified applicants with incomplete application files. As the application deadline approaches, the committee should send a letter to apparently qualified applicants with incomplete files requesting an immediate response if they wish to remain under consideration for the position. A copy of all correspondence with applicants should be kept on file as evidence of good-faith hiring practices on the part of the institution or organization.

What process should be used to critically assess a candidate's credentials? No foolproof method exists, but there are "red flags" of which athletic trainers should be aware as they evaluate the materials submitted as part of the application package.

Application Letter

Athletic trainers should ask themselves the following questions as they read an application letter (see figure 3.11 for a sample letter).

- Is the letter personalized? An application letter addressed "To Whom It May Concern" indicates a gross lack of preparation on the part of this candidate.

- Is the letter well written? The application letter demonstrates the writing skills of this potential employee. A candidate whose application letter is poorly written and full of grammatical errors is likely to write poorly after he or she is hired.

- Does the letter briefly describe the candidate's experiences and qualities without duplicating the contents of the resume?

- Does the letter describe why the candidate thinks he or she is qualified for this particular position? Letters that do not contain this information are often "form letters" that candidates routinely include with all job application packets.

Resume

Athletic trainers should ask themselves the following questions as they read an applicant's resume (see figure 3.12 for a sample resume).

- Is the resume professionally prepared? A poorly formatted resume often shows that the applicant has poor organizational skills.

- Does the resume contain all the usual categories of information? Common categories include personal information, educational background, professional experience, honors and awards, and references. Other categories that might be appropriate include publications, presentations, grants, and volunteer and community service.

- Does the resume reflect a continuous time line from the date the candidate entered school until the present? Gaps in the record are not necessarily bad, but they should be investigated if the candidate is chosen for a telephone interview.

- Does the candidate's experience reflect the kind of position for which she is applying? If the candidate has never worked in a setting similar to the one for which she is applying, it will be difficult to predict how well she is likely to perform based on past experience.

- Do the previous professional experiences listed on the resume reflect stability? A resume filled with many previous jobs of short duration raises questions about the employability of the candidate.

February 5, 2001

David Lewis, ATC
Coordinator of Sports Medicine
Ohio Technological University
Urban Center, OH 40000

Dear Mr. Lewis:

The purpose of this letter is to request that I be considered as a candidate for the assistant athletic trainer position at Ohio Technological University. I have been a high school athletic trainer for the past five years and am very interested in furthering my career at the university level. I am particularly interested in the position at OTU because it would allow me to build on the skills I have developed since finishing my master's degree. On a personal note, I am also interested in this position because it would allow me to move back to a region of the country where my parents and most of my family reside.

As you can see from my resume, two of the sports with which I have experience are gymnastics and field hockey. I have enjoyed working with these sports at the high school level, and I am anxious and excited to have the chance to work with college-level gymnasts and field hockey players. I have asked the coaches of the teams I have worked with in my present position to write to you in support of my application. I am confident that they will be able to help you gain a better sense of my athletic training skills in these two sports. I believe that my experiences as a college-level gymnast would also help qualify me for your position.

Thank you very much for considering my application. Enclosed you will find a resume and a list of references. I would be grateful for the opportunity to interview with you and your staff at any time you think would be appropriate. If you have any questions regarding my background or application, please do not hesitate to contact me.

Sincerely yours,

Amy Hays

Amy Hays, MS, ATC

▌ **Figure 3.11**   Sample application letter.

- Are the references listed on the resume well-known, reputable members of the profession? References with whom the athletic trainer is personally acquainted are more likely to provide an honest appraisal of the candidate's qualities—both good and bad.

- Does the resume reflect the candidate's experiences without exaggeration? Many candidates will attempt to make their experiences more glamorous than they really were. For example, if a candidate indicates that he was an assistant athletic trainer at a Division I university and you deduce that this all took place while he was a junior in college, he has probably inflated his experience as a student athletic trainer at that university.

Letters of Reference

An athletic trainer should ask him- or herself the following questions when reading the letters of reference:

- Does the writer recommend the candidate for the position? Although it is rare, some people are actually honest enough to indicate that, in their opinion, a candidate is not well suited for a particular position.

Amy Hays, MS, ATC
1234 South Armstrong St.
Way-Out-West, CA 90000
(999) 555-2000
amyhays@network.com

Professional Goals

I would like to use the experience I have gained as a certified athletic trainer in the high school setting in a more competitive and athletically challenging environment. I would especially like to secure a position in a Division I university.

Educational Background

1997	Master of Science in Athletic Training, Big State University
1995	Bachelor of Science, Regional University (Major—Athletic Training Minor—Biology)
1993	Associate of Arts, Wiley County Junior College

Professional Experience

1997–Present   **Way-Out-West High School**   I serve as the head athletic trainer in a high school comprising 2000 students and 20 sports, including

Boys' Sports	Girls' Sports
Football	*Field Hockey*
Cross Country	*Cross Country*
Soccer	*Soccer*
Basketball	*Basketball*
Swimming	*Swimming*
Gymnastics	*Gymnastics*
Volleyball	*Volleyball*
Track	*Track*
Baseball	*Softball*
Tennis	*Tennis*

In addition, I coordinate the school's drug and alcohol prevention program. My responsibilities also include maintenance of injury and treatment records.

1999–Present   **Western County Triathlon**   I serve as the medical director for this event, which draws over 1000 participants from all over the state.

1999–Present   **Summertown Gymnastics Club**   I teach gymnastics at this club during the summer.

Certifications

1995–Present	Certified Athletic Trainer, National Athletic Trainers' Association Board of Certification
1996–Present	Certified Basic Life Support Instructor, American Red Cross

Memberships

1993–Present	National Athletic Trainers' Association
1997–Present	Far West Athletic Trainers' Association
1997–Present	California Athletic Trainers' Association

(continued)

▌**Figure 3.12**   Sample resume.

Honors and Awards

1997   Athletic Training Scholarship, Big State University

1994   Most Valuable Gymnast, Regional University

Publications

Hays, A. (1999). Scaphoid non-union in a gymnast: A case study. *California Sports Medicine,* 2(3):14–16.

References

These people have given their permission to be contacted for additional background on my experiences and qualifications:

Ms. Renee Bigelow
Athletic Director and Gymnastics Coach
Way-Out-West High School
1245 Western Dr.
Way-Out-West, CA 90000
(999) 555-8903

Ms. Lillie Thompson
Field Hockey Coach
Way-Out-West High School
1245 Western Dr.
Way-Out-West, CA 90000
(999) 555-8903

Dr. Martin Dykstra, ATC
Program Director
Graduate Athletic Training Program
Big State University
Bigville, OH 40001
(444) 555-1111

■ **Figure 3.12**   *(continued)*

- Does the writer balance the candidate's strengths and weaknesses? Every candidate has both, and the useful letter of reference will mention them.

- Does the information in the letter confirm what appears on the resume? Inconsistencies should be verified through a telephone call to the person who wrote the letter of reference.

- Is the letter of reference excessively short or vague in its assertions? People who don't really want to recommend a candidate will often write a very short letter confirming the candidate's employment and little else. Another common technique is to use language that is so bland and nondescriptive that it becomes difficult to determine whether the writer actually recommends the candidate or not.

- Does the letter include references to actual job performance? A strong letter of reference will focus on the quality of the candidate's performance. Weak letters often focus on personality traits that, while valuable and desirable, might not reflect on the quality of the candidate's work.

Step 5: Telephone Interviews

After the qualified applicants have been identified, members of the search committee should interview especially promising candidates by telephone. Telephone interviews prior to on-site interviews are important to weed out unsuitable applicants and to provide additional information not readily communicated in application letters or resumes. Telephone interviewers should be friendly and informative, but they should avoid making statements the candidate might interpret as promises or verbal contracts that might be binding upon the institution. Questions asked in the telephone interview should elicit additional information unavailable in the application documents. Each candidate should be asked the same questions in the same order to ensure reliability. Questions should always focus on candidates' job-related behavior and should not focus on personal characteristics (Drake, 1982). Table 3.1 contains some examples of legal and illegal questions that athletic trainers should be aware of when conducting interviews (Falcone, 1997; Fry, 1993).

Step 6: Reference Checks

After the applicant pool has been further narrowed as a result of the telephone interviewing, the search committee should begin checking references. This is an important aspect of the recruitment and hiring process, because it allows the athletic trainer to validate the information supplied by the candidate. Some application materials need not be checked. Notarized transcripts, diplomas, and certificates are usually, but not always, valid. Expiration dates and signatures should be checked.

The most valuable information source is usually the applicant's previous employers or, for entry-level applicants, internship supervisors. An applicant's performance in similar employment settings is the best predictive factor of how the person will perform the new job. Notes from all conversations should be kept in the applicant's file for future reference by other members of the search committee.

Step 7: On-Site Interview

On-site interviews are costly and time consuming. Only those applicants who are obviously well qualified for the job should be interviewed on-site. Candidates about whom the search committee has serious reservations should not be interviewed. The on-site interview is important for both the candidate and the organization. It

Table 3.1   Examples of Legal and Illegal Interview Questions

Illegal question	Legal question
Are you a U.S. citizen?	Could you, after employment, submit verification of your legal right to work in the United States?
Do your religious beliefs allow you to work on Sundays?	Weekend and holiday work is a condition of this position. Is that acceptable to you?
Are you married? Do you have children?	Weekend and overtime work is a condition of this position. Is that acceptable to you?
Do you have any illnesses or disabilities?	Can you perform the essential job functions of this position with or without accommodation?
Did you serve in the military? What kind of discharge did you receive?	Did you serve in the military? Were any of the jobs you performed similar to those in this position?
Where did you learn to speak Spanish?	Do you speak any languages other than English that would be useful in this position?

allows the candidate to become familiar with the work setting and it allows the search committee to see the candidate in the work setting.

The on-site visit can be organized in many ways. Most visits should include a number of interviews with institutional stakeholders such as coaches, athletes and other physically active patients, athletic administrators, owners, team physicians, and other athletic trainers. Time should be set aside for the candidate to ask questions about the job. Candidates should have an opportunity to tour the facilities and inspect their potential worksites. The visit should typically be one or two days in length, depending on the level of responsibility of the position and the number of people who need to be involved in the interview process. If David Lewis, the athletic trainer in the opening case, was conducting an on-site interview for a candidate in the Ohio Technological University sports medicine program, the visit might be structured like the one in figure 3.13.

The people that the candidate will work closely with should be allowed the largest amount of interview time with him or her. Interviews with people the candidate will have limited contact with or those with only a tangential interest can be more limited in time and scope.

One of the important aspects of the on-site interview that many managers fail to recognize is the need to "sell" the job to the candidate. Too often, we assume that the mere offer of a job will be enough to induce a candidate to accept. This is frequently not the case. A significant part of the interview process should be devoted to highlighting the benefits of the job, organization, and community.

Reliability in the on-site interview is just as important as it was in the telephone interview. Irrespective of how the interview process is organized, the selection process will be made more reliable if a structured interview process is employed. In a structured interview, each candidate is asked the same questions in the same order, preferably by the same people. This process helps improve the chances that the search committee members will have the information they need to be able to make distinctions between the candidates.

Step 8: Recommendation and Approval for Hiring

After the candidates have been interviewed on-site, the search committee must make a recommendation for hiring to the appropriate person in the organization with formal authority to approve such an act. The recommendation for hiring should be accompanied by supporting documentation, including the candidate's resume, transcripts, letters of recommendation, and interview notes, so the decision maker has the necessary information to make a final choice. Search committee members should be sure they make a final recommendation for hiring based solely on the qualifications of the candidate and not on personal characteristics unrelated to the job, such as race, marital status, national origin, or creed.

Step 9: Offer of Contract

After the most outstanding candidate has been selected, whoever is authorized to negotiate a contract with the candidate should call and verbally extend an offer of employment. If terms of employment can be agreed to over the telephone, the authorized institutional representative should prepare a formal employment contract consistent with institutional rules, collective bargaining agreements, and state and federal laws. The contract should include the starting date for the job, length of employment, salary and benefits, position title, and job responsibilities as specified in the position description. In addition, a clause stating that the athletic trainer agrees to abide by the terms and conditions delineated in the institution's employee handbook should be included. Two copies of the signed contract should be sent to the athletic trainer with instructions to sign and return one of the copies by a given date,

Itinerary for the visit of

John Olmstead
Candidate for the position of head men's athletic trainer

Monday, June 11

10:00 A.M.	Arrive at Urban Center Airport, met by David Lewis.
10:30 A.M.	Meet with Linda Black, head women's athletic trainer, Fieldhouse athletic training room.
11:45 A.M.	Lunch with Student Athletic Trainers Club representatives Jim Gleason and Elaine Williams.
1:30 P.M.	Meet with James Wilson, director of intercollegiate athletics, central administration building.
2:45 P.M.	Meet with Dr. Reid Chesterfield, team physician, Student Health Service.
3:30 P.M.	Meet with Greg Campbell, head football coach, Memorial Stadium.
4:15 P.M.	Meet with Lucy Sneller, director of human resources, central administration building.
5:00 P.M.	Check into Campus Inn.
6:30 P.M.	Dinner with David Lewis, coordinator of sports medicine, and Rick Ellis, assistant athletic trainer, Campus Inn Grill.

Tuesday, June 12

7:30 A.M.	Breakfast with Tom Hernandez, head men's basketball coach, University Club.
8:30 A.M.	Meet with members of the search committee, Fieldhouse conference room.
11:00 A.M.	Fly home. Jim Gleason will accompany to the airport.
11:00 A.M.	Search committee meeting, Fieldhouse conference room.

■ **Figure 3.13** Sample on-site interview itinerary.

usually within 10 to 14 days. There are certainly less formal ways to handle the offer of contract, but the less formal the process, the greater the chances for misunderstanding and trouble later.

Step 10: Hiring

Once a written employment contract has been signed, a letter should be sent to the other applicants thanking them for their interest in the position and informing them that the position has been filled. This is an important courtesy that too many institutions, unfortunately, ignore. Another step that some institutions take at the end of the hiring process is to distribute a press release to the media announcing the addition of the new athletic trainer to the sports medicine staff. This is a valuable public relations tool for the sports medicine program, and it makes the new athletic trainer's induction into a relatively unfamiliar work setting more comfortable.

STAFF SUPERVISION

The concept of management as defined in chapter 1 includes the notion that managers coordinate the activities of a group of people toward a common goal. They accomplish this partly through the use of supervision. **Supervision** is a process whereby

Athletic trainers might be required to supervise other employees for the purpose of improving their work outcomes or professional development. The three kinds of supervisory models include inspection-production, clinical, and developmental.

supervision A process whereby authority holders observe the work activities of an employee in order to improve the outcomes of the employee's work or to improve the employee's professional development.

authority holders observe the work activities of an employee to improve the outcomes of the employee's work or the professional development of the employee. Supervision is different from summative evaluation. The purpose of summative evaluation is to place a value on the quality of an employee for the purpose of determining appropriate employment actions including retention, promotion, demotion, transfer, discharge, and compensation level. In the opening case, Judy was upset that David had never evaluated her performance during the three years she had worked for him. Judy lacked both summative evaluation and supervision. She didn't know if she was meeting the expectations of the program. She became frustrated because David didn't appear to care about her, her work, or her development as a professional.

Supervision is one of the most difficult managerial functions for an athletic trainer to master for several reasons. First, unless the employees the athletic trainer supervises are perfect in every way, supervision requires some degree of confrontation. Second, almost every supervisory problem is unique in some way. Responding to the employment-related problems of athletic trainers requires creativity and emotional investment in the staff and their development. Finally, effective supervision requires the athletic trainer to consider the opinions and perspectives of others. Athletic trainer–supervisors should develop strategies to reduce the level of bias they bring to situations so the needs of both the sports medicine program and its employees can be met. Athletic trainers can use many different supervisory models. Tanner and Tanner (1987) have described four: inspection, production, clinical, and developmental. This discussion will combine the inspection and production models because their differences are minor.

MOTIVATION

Before the various supervisory models are introduced, it would be helpful to consider the role that supervisors play in motivating employees. Motivation of workers is generally acknowledged to be an important supervisory function, yet it remains one of the most poorly understood and applied management concepts in most work settings. The supervisory models described in this section differ in many ways from each other, in part because of the different assumptions each makes about the nature of motivation in the workplace. The inspection-production model, for example, has its roots in the scientific management movement of the early 1900s (see chapter 1, pp. 6–7). One of the most important assumptions underlying that theory is that people are motivated in their work only by financial reward. We now know that motivation in the workplace is a much more complex phenomenon that is influenced by many more factors than the promise of financial gain.

Motivation is a complex concept. Three basic questions must be answered in order to fully understand the role that motivation plays in the supervisory roles that athletic training managers must assume (Steers & Porter, 1987).

1. What energizes human behavior?
2. What directs or channels human behavior?
3. How can human behavior be maintained or sustained?

Each of these questions lies at the heart of the broader question "How do I motivate the athletic trainers under my supervision to do the very best job possible?" There are no easy answers to any of these questions, and that is the primary reason this book does not contain a table entitled "How to Motivate Athletic Trainers." We have learned quite a bit about motivation, however, and it seems that the concept can be broken down into four basic components (see figure 3.14):

■ **Figure 3.14**
A basic model of
motivation.

Reprinted from
Dunnette and Kirchner
1965.

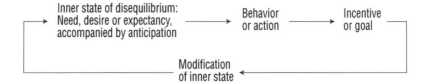

1. Needs or expectations of the employee
2. Employee behavior
3. Employee goals
4. Feedback from the supervisor or other sources

Although this model does a good job of explaining workplace motivation at its simplest level, it is a poor predictor of employee behavior in actual job settings. There are at least four confounding factors that complicate this model:

• *Motives can only be inferred, not seen.* It is often very difficult to know why employees act the way they do at work. Although their behavior might be observable, the motivation for that behavior is often not. For example, if Judy from the opening case puts in extra time in the training room by volunteering to cover special events and other similar functions, we would know only that she is a hard worker. We wouldn't know what her motivation was for consistently volunteering. Perhaps she wants the extra money. Maybe she has a very limited social life and her affiliation needs are met solely through her work. Maybe she wants David's job and she sees this as a way to demonstrate that she is capable and worthy of being promoted.

• *Motives conflict with each other and are subject to change.* Most of us deal with conflicting motivations in many segments of our lives. These motives are usually not static, but rather, they change as do the other situational variables in our lives. For example, Judy's behavior might be the result of conflicting motivations. If she has young children at home, the motivation to get ahead at work might conflict with her desire to fulfill her role as a parent. If she is the primary breadwinner, she might see the extra work as an opportunity to supplement the family finances. As her children get older, their needs (and hers) will change, resulting in a different set of motivating factors.

• *Individual differences exist with regard to motives.* If everyone responded to the presence of motivators in the same way, supervision would be a very easy thing. Unfortunately, what motivates one person is often insufficient to motivate another. Judy is motivated (by something) to work extra hours in the training room. David might not be. He might be the last to arrive and the first to leave every day. He could receive extra pay by covering special events, but he chooses not to. Same motivator (extra pay), different behavior.

• *Goal attainment modifies behavior in different ways.* In addition to the fact that people are motivated by different things, they often respond differently to achievement of the same goals. Take the example of Judy and David. After David was appointed head athletic trainer, he "coasted," rarely volunteering for extra work, even if it meant extra pay. Assume that Judy would like to be head of the program one day. Will she also "coast" once she has achieved that goal? Will she continue to volunteer for extra duties? Or will she work even harder in the hopes that she might be promoted to a position on the athletic director's staff?

As you can see, although motivation seems to be a fairly straightforward concept, its application is very complex and difficult to predict. As you read the following sections, keep in mind the assumptions that each supervisory model makes for the nature of human behavior at work. When you are eventually placed in a position where you have to supervise athletic trainers and other health care professionals, you will be forced to choose a supervisory style that will mesh with your basic assumptions of what motivates different people.

INSPECTION-PRODUCTION SUPERVISION

inspection-production   A supervisory model that emphasizes the use of formal authority and managerial prerogatives in order to improve employee efficiency and efficacy.

The primary characteristic of the **inspection-production** model of supervision is an emphasis on authoritative managerial efficiency. Athletic trainers who prefer this approach to supervision insist on strict observance of program policies and procedures. This model views services of the sports medicine program as products and the athletic trainer employees as the raw materials used to develop those products. In the inspection-production mode, supervising athletic trainers require all employees of a sports medicine program to develop a comprehensive list of goals for the year. Then they carefully check progress toward accomplishing these goals during the course of the year. This model's overriding emphasis is on accomplishment of program goals and objectives and on attainment of the program mission.

The advantage of the inspection-production model is that it can be effective in helping a sports medicine program accomplish its goals. It sets well-defined limits on job-related behavior for all employees and consequently enhances common understanding of the athletic trainers' roles. This approach to supervision is usually associated with formalistic bureaucratic organizations that have many levels of supervisory management.

There are several disadvantages to using the inspection-production system of supervision in service-oriented enterprises, including sports medicine programs. This model was originally developed and implemented in industrial settings where inputs and outputs could easily be measured. Inputs and outputs are not easily measured in most sports medicine settings. Although some measures of program success or failure should be developed, interpretation of them will vary widely depending on the audience.

Another problem with this model is the nature of the work that athletic trainers do. Most athletic trainers perform a wide variety of jobs, and not all of them are easily observed or quantified. For example, if David Lewis wanted to be sure Judy Armstrong was meeting the program standard for taping effectiveness and efficiency, he could simply observe her as she prepared a team for a practice or game. But how would David inspect the effectiveness and efficiency of Judy's counseling skills? Her rehabilitation skills?

Finally, the inspection-production method of supervision can cause professional employees, such as athletic trainers, to feel unappreciated and unfulfilled. Since the dominant ethos is program goal accomplishment and not professional development, athletic trainers will rarely appreciate what little developmental feedback they receive. They will tend to view such feedback in negative terms.

CLINICAL SUPERVISION

clinical supervision   The process of direct observation of an employee's work, with emphasis on measurement of specific behaviors, and the subsequent development of plans to remediate deficiencies in performance.

Clinical supervision is the process, borrowed from education, of direct observation of an athletic trainer at work and the subsequent development of plans to remediate deficiencies in performance (Acheson & Gall, 1987). It requires the supervisor to observe a sample of the athletic trainer's performance, to analyze the strengths and weaknesses of the performance, and to collaboratively develop a structure for helping the athletic trainer overcome such weaknesses. This type of supervision can be particularly appropriate for student interns, although it is useful for professional staff as well. Among the many supervisory techniques that can be applied within the clinical supervision model, one of the most promising for athletic trainers is work sampling (Hagerty, Chang, & Spengler, 1985). Work sampling identifies the type of work athletic trainers do and the amount of time they spend doing it. Hence, it can be an effective tool for both clinical supervision and job analysis. Work sampling consists of logging the activities of athletic trainers at randomly selected times and analyzing the data to judge the nature and quality of the work being performed. Appropriate activities facilitate the goals and objectives of the sports medicine program. Inappropriate activities duplicate efforts, are extraneous to the purposes of the program, fulfill purely personal or social wants, or allocate too much time to tasks that are not suited to the athletic trainer's qualifications.

Among the advantages of clinical supervision is its emphasis on collegial working relationships and cooperative planning. The clinical model of supervision promotes the professional status of the athletic trainer and involves the athletic trainer in as much of the supervisory process as possible. The role of the supervising athletic trainer is consultative rather than authoritative.

The primary disadvantage of the clinical system of supervision is that the supervising athletic trainer must devote large blocks of time to supervising individual employees. Because clinical supervision requires direct observation of an athletic trainer's performance and most supervising athletic trainers have significant responsibilities in the treatment of injured clients, it becomes very difficult to find the time to implement a truly clinical system of supervision. Another problem with clinical supervision is that it requires training to properly interpret observed supervision data.

DEVELOPMENTAL SUPERVISION

developmental supervision   A supervisory model that emphasizes collaboration between supervisors and supervisees in order to help them solve problems and develop professionally.

Developmental supervision involves collaboration between a supervising athletic trainer and employees. The emphasis is on helping employees develop professionally while meeting the needs of the sports medicine program. The overriding theme of developmental supervision is participative management—employees discuss common problems and suggest and implement creative solutions. The system is intended to improve both the sports medicine program and its employees by increasing employee involvement in problem solving. It acknowledges the interdependence of the goals of the program and those of the athletic trainers.

The primary advantage of the developmental model is its emphasis on personal growth and its integration of athletic trainer and sports medicine program goals. The developmental system tends to build an organizational culture that places a high level of importance on meeting the needs of athletic trainers to improve program quality. Athletic trainers working in organizations with this focus are generally happy and content with their professional development.

Unfortunately, well-developed, happy employees are not a guarantee of overall program success. Collegiality and collaboration are desirable only when they bring different perspectives and new ways of thinking to difficult problems. Heavy emphasis on collaboration can actually delay problem solving because of the need to preserve the collegial organizational climate.

Which supervisory model is best? Is one model more appropriate for a university setting? For a sports medicine clinic setting? These are difficult questions to answer, because the three supervisory models have never been empirically investigated in sports medicine settings. We can intuitively draw a few tentative conclusions, however. First, most sports medicine programs should probably integrate elements of each model into their supervisory plans. Whenever collaborative problem solving can be used, it should be, because athletic trainers have a greater sense of ownership in the resulting solutions. When questions arise about the effectiveness of an athletic trainer, direct observation of her work and suggestions for improvement by the supervising athletic trainer would probably be useful. There will be times, however, when the supervisor will have to take other actions. If an employee has not responded well to attempts at collaborative problem solving or suggestions from the supervisor, there might be no alternative but for the supervising athletic trainer to impose a solution to correct the actions of the employee.

PERFORMANCE EVALUATION

Performance evaluation is an underused and generally poorly performed human resource tool in athletic training. Performance evaluation systems and methods should meet established standards so that they are legal and fair, useful, accurate, and practical.

performance evaluation
The process of placing a value on the quality of an employee's work.

Performance evaluation is the process of placing a value on the quality of an athletic trainer's work. Performance evaluation is important for at least two reasons. First, it can help a supervising athletic trainer make valid and reliable distinctions between athletic trainers who are performing at or above program expectations and those whose work is unsatisfactory. Second, a properly implemented system of performance evaluation helps the athletic trainers being evaluated identify areas of weakness and eliminate or reduce them.

Figures 3.15 (p. 85) and 3.16 (p. 90) provide examples of performance evaluation instruments based on the opening scenario. Remember, however, that any performance evaluation instrument not based on a specific athletic trainer's weighted job description and not designed for a particular purpose is useless. Performance evaluation is *not* the annual completion of a form. Performance evaluation is a process done throughout the entire year that involves mutually establishing goals, creating performance standards for accomplishing those goals, measuring the level of accomplishment, mutually understanding how well the athletic trainer met his goals, and mutually developing plans to remediate performance deficiencies and continue professional development. Measuring performance often requires the input of the athletic trainer being evaluated, the athletic trainer's peers, the supervisor, the clients, and the consulting physicians. Any performance evaluation instrument not built on these principles would be so riddled with caveats as to render it meaningless.

STATUS OF PERFORMANCE EVALUATION IN ATHLETIC TRAINING

Of the few printed resources for athletic trainers on performance evaluation, most are outdated and advocate a trait-oriented approach (Parks, 1977; Penman & Adams, 1980). Trait-oriented evaluation systems place a value on athletic trainers' performance by assessing human qualities. For example, if David Lewis were to evaluate Judy Armstrong's performance using a trait-oriented approach, he would be likely to label her "aggressive," "unfriendly," and "difficult to get along with." Unfortunately, none of these terms refers to the quality of her work. Although trait-oriented systems are the easiest to implement, they usually lack validity and reliability (Dobbins & Russell, 1986; Huber, Podsakoff, & Todor, 1986). For example, Cascio and Bernardin (1981) reported a survey of 47 administrators that identified 75 different definitions of *dependability*.

Unfortunately, the performance of athletic trainers in many settings is not formally evaluated annually (see figure 3.17 on p. 92). For example, in Ray's 1991 study of performance evaluation in all athletic training settings, only 35% of athletic trainers employed in the professional athletics setting reported being evaluated on an annual basis. Of those athletic trainers who were evaluated regularly, most perceived their performance evaluations differently from their supervisors. For example, athletic trainers and their supervisors had different perceptions on whether the NATA's *Competencies in Athletic Training* and *Standards of Practice for Athletic Training* were used as a basis for evaluating athletic trainer job performance. One of the most likely reasons for this discrepancy is that a significant number of athletic trainers are evaluated by nonmedical supervisors who are not very familiar with the athletic trainer's

Ohio Technological University
Department of Intercollegiate Athletics

Annual Performance Evaluation Instrument

Employee being evaluated: <u>Judy Armstrong</u>   Evaluation: <u>July 1, 1999–June 30, 2000</u>

Supervisor conducting evaluation: <u>David Lewis</u>   Date of feedback conference: <u>July 10, 2000</u>

This information may be shared only with: <u>Judy Armstrong, Linda Black, David Lewis, James Wilson</u>

Data sources used in the performance evaluation: <u>Supervisor's direct observations and feedback from team physicians and athletic trainer coworkers as provided on the "Ancillary Data Source" form.</u>

Purpose:

The purposes of the annual performance evaluation include (1) assisting employees to identify strengths and weaknesses of their performance in job-related responsibilities so they can work with their supervisors to improve performance, and (2) collecting job-related performance information that may be used for the following staff selection activities: promotion, demotion, retention, dismissal, and compensation. Only job-related performance may be used as the basis for this evaluation.

Role-Specific Ratings:

<u>Instructions to evaluator</u>: Assess the performance of the employee for each specific job responsibility. Rate only those responsibilities included on this employee's position description. Provide performance quality ratings using a 1 to 5 scale. Provide performance frequency ratings using a 1 to 5 scale. Multiply performance quality ratings by performance frequency ratings by relative importance points (from position description) for overall performance ratings. Provide rationale for each rating.

Performance Quality Ratings

1–Job responsibility is performed at an unacceptable level of quality (significant improvement is expected).

2–Job responsibility is performed at a below-average level of quality (significant improvement is expected).

3–Job responsibility is performed at an average level of quality (most other employees perform at this level).

4–Job responsibility is performed at an above-average level of quality (some improvement is possible).

5–Job responsibility is performed at an outstanding level of quality (no improvement is possible).

Performance Frequency Ratings

1–Job responsibility is performed 0–20% of the time.

2–Job responsibility is performed 21–40% of the time.

3–Job responsibility is performed 41–60% of the time.

4–Job responsibility is performed 61–80% of the time.

5–Job responsibility is performed 81–100% of the time.

(continued)

■ **Figure 3.15**   Performance evaluation instrument based on the opening case.

Job Responsibilities for Judy Armstrong					
Responsibility	Performance Quality Rating	Performance Frequency Rating	Relative Importance Points	Total Possible	Total Achieved
Coordinates and delivers athletic training services to members of the field hockey and gymnastics teams including, but not limited to, coordination of physical exams, evaluation and treatment of injuries at practices and games, design and supervision of rehabilitation programs, counseling within the limits of expertise, and prepractice/game taping.	Rationale:	Rationale:	5	125	
Refers injured athletes to appropriate physicians according to the guidelines in the *Standard Operating Procedures.*	Rationale:	Rationale:	5	125	

▌ **Figure 3.15** *(continued)*

Job Responsibilities for Judy Armstrong					
Responsibility	Performance Quality Rating	Performance Frequency Rating	Relative Importance Points	Total Possible	Total Achieved
Submits injured athlete status reports to coaches by 11:00 A.M. of the day following the injury.			4	100	
	Rationale:	Rationale:			
Maintains computerized injury/treatment database according to guidelines in the *Standard Operating Procedures*.			3	75	
	Rationale:	Rationale:			
Coordinates NCAA Injury Surveillance Program by conducting in-service training for student athletic trainers, collecting and checking the accuracy of individual and weekly injury report forms, and mailing completed forms to the NCAA by Monday of each week.			3	75	
	Rationale:	Rationale:			
					(continued)

▮ Figure 3.15

Job Responsibilities for Judy Armstrong					
Responsibility	Performance Quality Rating	Performance Frequency Rating	Relative Importance Points	Total Possible	Total Achieved
Prepares annual injury and treatment report for all sports by June 1.			3	75	
	Rationale:	Rationale:			
Exhibits behaviors in strict compliance with the NATA *Code of Professional Practice.*			5	125	
	Rationale:	Rationale:			
				700	

■ **Figure 3.15** *(continued)*

Working Conditions:

Instructions: Describe any unusual working conditions beyond the control of the employee that may have affected his or her ability to perform the assigned duties.

Critical Incidents:

Instructions: Describe any critical incidents that occurred during the evaluation period that are consistent with the strengths and weaknesses of the employee's job-related performance.

Performance Improvement Plan:

Instructions: List below the steps the employee should take in order to improve his/her job-related performance.

Employee Response:

Instructions: Describe below any points of agreement or disagreement with your supervisor's evaluation of your job-related performance.

▌Figure 3.15

Ohio Technological University
Department of Intercollegiate Athletics

Annual Performance Evaluation
Ancillary Data Source Instrument

Employee being evaluated: Judy Armstrong   Evaluation: July 1, 1999–June 30, 2000

Supervisor conducting evaluation: David Lewis

This information may be shared only with: Judy Armstrong, Linda Black, David Lewis, James Wilson

Purpose:

The purpose of this instrument is to help supervisors provide employees with valid and reliable feedback regarding their performance by allowing them to collect information from peers and coworkers. The information may also be used to make employee selection decisions regarding promotion, demotion, retention, dismissal, and compensation.

Instructions: Use the specific job responsibilities below from the employee's position description to guide your assessments. *Assess only the employee's performance on these responsibilities. Assess only those responsibilities that you directly observed.*

Job Responsibilities of Judy Armstrong	
Responsibilities	Comments
Coordinates and delivers athletic training services to members of the field hockey and gymnastics teams including, but not limited to, coordination of physical exams, evaluation and treatment of injuries at practices and games, design and supervision of rehabilitation programs, counseling within the limits of expertise, and prepractice/ game taping.	
Refers injured athletes to appropriate physicians according to the guide-lines in the *Standard Operating Procedures*.	

▌**Figure 3.16** Performance evaluation ancillary data source form based on the opening case.

Job Responsibilities of Judy Armstrong	
Responsibilities	Comments
Submits injured athlete status reports to coaches by 11:00 A.M. of the day following the injury.	
Maintains computerized injury/ treatment database according to guidelines in the *Standardized Operating Procedures.*	
Coordinates NCAA Injury Surveillance program by conducting in-service training for student athletic trainers, collecting and checking the accuracy of individual and weekly injury report forms, and mailing completed forms to the NCAA by Monday of each week.	
Prepares annual injury and treatment report for all sports by June 1.	
Exhibits behaviors in strict compliance with the NATA *Code of Professional Practice.*	

_____   _____   _____
Signature   Position   Date

■ **Figure 3.16** *(continued)*

job responsibilities. In addition, only about half of these supervisors have had any formal training in how to conduct a performance evaluation or interpret the data derived from the evaluation (see figure 3.18).

Another reason that athletic trainers and their supervisors have differing opinions on the nature of performance evaluation is that many athletic trainers, even if they are formally evaluated, never receive feedback regarding their performance from their supervisors (see figure 3.19). This lack of communication is an important reason for the lack of understanding between athletic trainers and their supervisors.

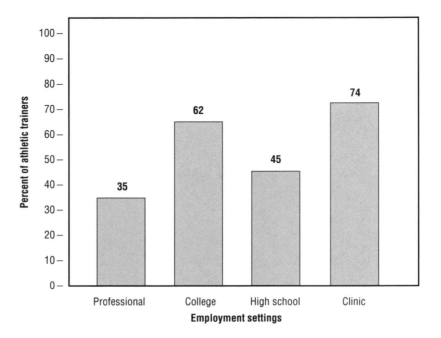

▌Figure 3.17
Incidence of athletic trainer performance evaluation by employment setting.

Data from Ray 1991.

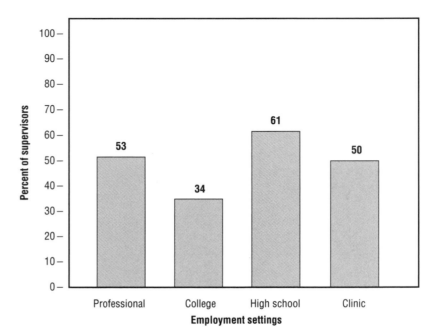

▌Figure 3.18
Percentage of supervisors of athletic trainers who have been formally trained in performance evaluation.

Data from Ray 1991.

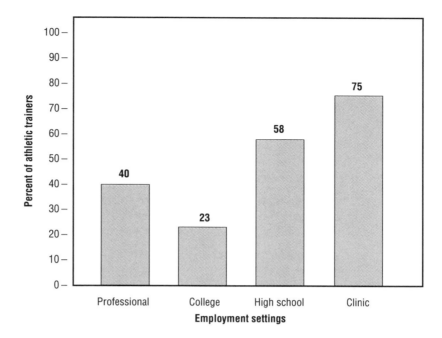

■ **Figure 3.19**
Percentage of athletic trainers who receive feedback regarding their performance from their supervisors.

Data from Ray 1991.

PERFORMANCE EVALUATION METHODS

Practitioners of performance evaluation disagree about which methods are most effective for rating employee job performance (Reinhardt, 1985). The performance evaluation methods used should be appropriate for the purposes and defined uses of the evaluation (Schneier, Beatty, & Baird, 1986). No single method of performance evaluation matches every setting or meets the needs of every organization. Table 3.2 contains a summary of the strengths and weaknesses of the most common performance evaluation methods.

Seven performance evaluation methods are used most often: management by objectives, written essays, critical incident reports, graphic rating scales, forced choice rating, ranking, and behaviorally anchored rating scales. Fowler and Bushardt (1986) developed a method called the task-oriented performance evaluation system (TOPES) that they alleged to be a simple, job-specific method of measuring performance-related behavior. Unfortunately, it has not been field tested extensively or validated for different settings or uses. Work sampling, as described previously, can also be used as a form of performance evaluation. Keaveny and McGann (1980), in their research into the performance appraisal format and its influence on role clarity and evaluation criteria, determined that behaviorally anchored rating scales were superior to graphic rating scales to help professionals understand the performance area being rated, the perceived performance level for each rating area, and the behavior changes that would be necessary to improve ratings for each performance area.

PERFORMANCE EVALUATION STANDARDS

The Personnel Evaluation Standards (Joint Committee on Standards for Educational Evaluation, 1988) have significantly influenced the practice of performance evaluation in a variety of settings. This publication provides widely accepted evaluation principles that educational professionals can use to improve their personnel evaluation systems. These standards have been adopted by many policy boards as the official standards for judging performance evaluation systems. Although *The Personnel Evaluation Standards* were written for educational settings, they are rooted in valid and reliable evaluation principles and could be applied in noneducational settings.

Table 3.2 Strengths and Weaknesses of the Most Commonly Used Performance Evaluation Methods

Method	Weaknesses	Strengths
Management by objectives	Tends to emphasize job characteristics that can be measured over those that cannot.	Employee is able to have input into the standards by which he or she is evaluated.
Written essay	Dependent on subjective data; validity dependent on writer's skill and judgment.	Evaluator can write a detailed profile of the employee's work.
Critical incident report	Can be subject to writer bias; often based on subjective data; negative incidents usually receive more notice than positive.	More detail regarding the employee's work can be provided.
Graphic rating scale	Scale elements often not valid or job related.	Simple to administer; low cost.
Forced choice rating	Fails to provide specific feedback; not useful in human resource planning; does not relate job performance to selection criteria.	Simple to administer; low cost.
Ranking	Difficult to discriminate performance levels on multitask jobs; discourages cooperation among work-group members.	Simplifies the task of allocating rewards.
Behaviorally anchored rating scales	Most useful for employees with identical job responsibilities; expensive and time consuming to develop; difficult to update as job responsibilites change.	Evaluates behaviors rather than traits; specific to single job category.

Athletic trainers employed in professional athletics, sports medicine clinics, and industry can benefit from the application of these standards, because validity and reliability of performance evaluation is important in their job settings as well.

Performance evaluation systems for athletic trainers should be

- legal and fair,
- useful,
- practical, and
- accurate.

The Joint Committee on Standards for Educational Evaluation (1988) has identified 21 standards in four broad categories: propriety, utility, feasibility, and accuracy. What follows is a description of each standard and an example of how it could be applied in an athletic training setting. Although the list seems long, keep in mind that performance evaluation is a very important part of the athletic trainer–manager's responsibilities. Even small deviations from the ideal can result in potentially damaging consequences for the employee, the supervisor, and the institution.

Propriety Standards

The following five **propriety standards** help ensure that performance evaluation is legal and fair.

propriety standards
Performance evaluation standards intended to help ensure that the process is legal and fair.

Service Orientation

Performance evaluation systems for athletic trainers should meet the needs of the persons they are intended to help, including athletic trainers, their clients, and their employing institutions. If any of these groups is neglected, the system should be reconfigured accordingly. Assume, for example, that David institutes a performance evaluation system in response to Judy's complaints. If David configures the system so that all that it consists of is a 15-minute feedback conference once a year, Judy's needs are unlikely to be met. The system would fail to serve those it was intended to help.

Formal Evaluation Guidelines

The procedures by which the athletic trainer's performance is evaluated should be recorded as written institutional policy and made available to athletic trainers so they are aware of the process. Each step of David's new performance evaluation system should be published in the department handbook so Judy and her fellow athletic trainers are aware of and understand the system.

Conflict of Interest

Evaluation procedures should ensure that conflicts of interest are eliminated. For example, if Judy Armstrong and her supervisor, Linda Black, were both candidates for the same job promotion, Linda would have a conflict of interest when evaluating Judy's performance. Formal evaluation procedures should specify how to avoid such conflicts.

Access to Personnel Evaluation Reports

Only those persons who have a legitimate need to know should be allowed access to an athletic trainer's performance evaluation records. Each athletic trainer should be informed of who has access to the information and under what circumstances such access will be granted. Judy's performance evaluation might legitimately be shared with Linda Black, David Lewis, and the athletic director, but nobody else should have access to it.

Interactions With Evaluatees

Athletic trainers should be treated with respect and dignity when being evaluated. When supervisors are judgmental, they are less likely to enhance trust in the performance evaluation system. They can promote trust by taking a counseling attitude (Dorfman, Stephan, & Loveland, 1986). If David simply calls Judy into his office and assaults her with critical and threatening language during her feedback conference, the system is unlikely to achieve its goals.

Utility Standards

utility standards Performance evaluation standards intended to help ensure that employee appraisal is useful to workers, employers, and others who need to use the information.

The following five **utility standards** ensure that an athletic trainer's performance evaluation is useful (Joint Committee on Standards for Educational Evaluation, 1988).

Constructive Orientation

If performance evaluation is to be useful, both athletic trainers and their supervisors must perceive that evaluation procedures actually result in improvements in professional development and accountability. If either perceives evaluation as a meaningless waste of time, the information obtained is unlikely to be useful. Performance evaluation should help athletic trainers improve their performance. David and Judy should together develop strategies designed to help Judy improve. If David does nothing but point out Judy's shortcomings, little will be accomplished.

Defined Uses

Performance evaluation data should be used only for the purposes for which it was collected. Athletic trainers should be informed of these uses prior to data collection; the data might not be valid if used for other purposes. Athletic trainers are likely to lose trust in the system if the information is used for unstated purposes. For example, assume that David stated, in the written description of the system in the department handbook, that the purpose of the performance evaluation process was to "improve athletic trainer performance for the purpose of improving the quality of health care being provided to injured athletes." He would be violating the "defined uses" standard if he then used the information he gathered during the process to decide if Judy should be promoted when Linda Black resigned. The information was gathered for one purpose and used for another.

Evaluator Credibility

The persons who evaluate an athletic trainer's performance should have institutional authority and be knowledgeable about athletic training duties. In addition, they should be trained in the theory and practice of performance evaluation methods. Team physician and peer athletic trainer input can improve the credibility of evaluation, because these people are often more knowledgeable about athletic training job responsibilities than coaches or athletic administrators. If David works closely enough with Judy to understand her job responsibilities, and if he knows how to implement a valid and reliable performance evaluation system, he should have enough credibility to satisfy this standard.

Functional Reporting

If performance evaluation is to be perceived as useful, athletic trainers should receive both formal and informal feedback on job performance. This feedback should be job related and timely, and it should contain specific suggestions for improving performance. If David evaluates Judy's performance in June, but doesn't meet with her to discuss the results until October, the usefulness of the information is decreased. Similarly, if David has no suggestions for helping Judy improve, it is left to her to try to figure it out on her own.

Follow-Up and Impact

All recommendations from the performance evaluation should be implemented so professional development can occur. An important component of the follow-up process involves forming a plan for professional improvement that focuses on identified weaknesses in an athletic trainer's performance. This plan should be developed jointly by the athletic trainer and his or her supervisor. In order for this standard to be met, David must monitor whether or not Judy is actually improving her performance by implementing the plan that they developed together. If she isn't, and David does nothing about it, the system is simply a waste of time and money.

Feasibility Standards

feasibility standards Performance evaluation standards intended to help foster practicality in the employee appraisal process.

The following three **feasibility standards** foster practicality in performance evaluation (Joint Committee on Standards for Educational Evaluation, 1988).

Practical Procedures

Performance evaluation procedures should intrude as little as possible into an athletic trainer's normal job-related activities. Athletic trainers will view evaluation procedures that require them to redirect significant amounts of energy and attention away from clients as impractical. If David developed a system that required Linda to follow Judy around for a week to monitor her work activities, he would probably learn a great deal about her performance, but it wouldn't be a very practical or efficient way to collect the information.

Political Viability

All the users of the athletic trainer performance evaluation system should have input into its development so it will be accepted and used as intended. Evaluation systems designed without input from athletic trainers are unlikely to be effective for professional development—they might be viewed as bureaucratic tools that interfere with the athletic trainers' jobs. If David tried to impose a performance evaluation system on the members of the sports medicine staff without their input, they would probably resent it, and its usefulness would be greatly decreased.

Fiscal Viability

Institutions should recognize that effective athletic trainer performance evaluation systems require outlays of both time and money. Administrators who develop budgets should build the costs of evaluating performance into the overall institutional budget. It would be quite expensive if Linda were to follow Judy around for a week so she could observe her work. Although she would learn quite a bit about Judy's performance, someone else would have to do Linda's work during this time, which is costly. This system would not be fiscally viable.

Accuracy Standards

accuracy standards
Performance evaluation standards intended to improve the validity and reliability of the employee appraisal process.

The following eight standards are intended to improve the validity and reliability of a performance evaluation and thereby lend **accuracy** to the system (Joint Committee on Standards for Educational Evaluation, 1988).

Defined Role

Athletic trainers should be evaluated using criteria that are directly related to the specific roles they are responsible for. This standard is especially important because of the wide variety of roles athletic trainers often assume. If evaluation data are collected and interpreted without regard to role definition, it is likely to lack validity for evaluating job-related performance behaviors. Developing a weighted position description is an important first step in defining the athletic trainer's role. Judy's position description (see figure 3.7 on p. 67) is critical in helping both David and Judy understand the roles for which she will be evaluated. If David strayed from the roles described in her position description when evaluating her performance, he would be unfairly holding her to a standard she could not have reasonably anticipated.

Work Environment

Specific aspects of the athletic trainer's work environment should be recorded during the performance evaluation process so individual differences in working conditions can be considered in the final evaluation. For example, if Judy Armstrong were working with a new coach, that would be taken into consideration during her performance evaluation, because it is a factor beyond her control and might drastically alter the nature of her job.

Documentation of Procedures

The procedures that are actually followed during the evaluation process should be recorded so athletic trainers and other users of the information can compare actual with intended evaluation procedures. As David evaluates Judy's performance, he must be careful to record each step in the process. If David and Judy have a dispute that results from her performance evaluation, a third party should be able to examine the record to determine if there were any procedural flaws on David's part.

Valid Measurement

Procedures developed or adopted for evaluating an athletic trainer's performance should measure the job-related behaviors they are intended to measure so that accurate conclusions about performance can be drawn. Institutions should be able to defend the accuracy of the procedures. One potentially useful source of information regarding Judy's performance could come from the outcomes studies conducted in her department. If David could link specific patient outcomes with the care Judy provided, he would have objective data he could use to develop judgments regarding her effectiveness.

Reliable Measurement

Institutions should ensure that methods used to evaluate performance are consistent across time and for different evaluators. Using multiple evaluators trained to follow specific evaluation procedures is a good way to build reliability into the evaluation system. David must be very careful to apply the same evaluation techniques and methods when evaluating Judy's performance that he uses with every other member of the department. If he gathers information regarding Judy's performance from Linda Black, the team physician, and other members of the department, his assessment is more likely to be reliable.

Systematic Data Control

Information collected during performance evaluation should be recorded and stored so it can easily be retrieved in the future and so that future interpretations are similar to those conclusions drawn immediately after the athletic trainer's performance evaluation. If data are misplaced or lost, future evaluators might draw erroneous conclusions because they will lack a complete perspective. For example, the performance evaluation information David develops for Judy this year must be stored in such a way that when he evaluates her next year he can use this year's information. The alternative is to hope that he can remember the recommendations for improving Judy's performance when he evaluates her in the future.

Bias Control

All possible biasing factors should be eliminated from athletic trainer performance evaluation so accurate conclusions can be reached. Using multiple evaluators is an effective technique to help reduce bias. Evaluating only job-related behaviors also controls bias. Personal traits unrelated to the actual job performance expected of athletic trainers should not be considered in the performance evaluation. Rigorous adherence to the other accuracy standards will help reduce performance evaluation bias. If Judy performs all of the functions on her position description with a high degree of competence, but David gives her low performance ratings because he simply doesn't like her, he is guilty of violating this standard. If he were to use other evaluators, like Linda Black, as part of the process, it would help reduce the possibility for bias.

Monitoring Evaluation Systems

Because the circumstances related to an athletic trainer's job might change over time, the systems used to evaluate performance should be modified as well. Institutional policies should require evaluation and modification of athletic trainer performance evaluation systems from time to time. David and the rest of the staff should periodically meet to decide if the performance evaluation system is working well and to discuss how it might be modified.

THE FAIR LABOR STANDARDS ACT AND ATHLETIC TRAINING

The FLSA is a law intended to ensure that employees are justly compensated for the work they do that exceeds the boundaries of the normal work week. Athletic trainers might or might not be exempt from the provisions of the FLSA depending on how their jobs are structured.

The culture of athletic training has traditionally been one that prescribed long hours at modest pay in order to meet the needs of injured athletes whose schedules rarely conform to the typical 40-hour workweek. Coaches, athletic directors, and athletes have come to expect that athletic trainers will stay in the athletic training room until the last person has been attended to, even if doing so requires 60–70 hours per week. This culture is now being challenged by many in the profession who desire a higher quality of life, both in terms of a more reasonable workweek and a compensation package befitting the level of education required for practice in athletic training. One of the primary issues of concern to athletic trainers is whether or not they are exempt under the Fair Labor Standards Act (FLSA).

The Fair Labor Standards Act was passed by Congress in 1938 and has been amended several times since then. It generally requires that employees be paid overtime (usually time and a half) or receive compensated time (1.5 times the hours worked in excess of 40) for work beyond 40 hours per week. Not all employees are covered by the FLSA. Executives, administrators, and professionals are generally exempt from the provisions of the law. All other employees are considered nonexempt.

For a good summary of the FLSA as it applies to athletic trainers working in educational settings, visit the Web site of the Texas Classroom Teachers Association at **http://www.tcta.org/**.

Athletic trainers in several states have challenged their exempt status and won the right to overtime by being classified nonexempt. Athletic trainers in Kansas, with some exceptions, are considered nonexempt employees as the result of a case involving the athletic training staff at the University of Kansas. A similar situation exists in the state of Washington. High school athletic trainers in Texas, on the other hand, lost the right to be classified nonexempt in a 1999 case.

If athletic trainers are professionals, how can they be classified as nonexempt employees under the FLSA? The first point that must be made is that the word *professional* is used in different ways. Athletic trainers call themselves professionals because of their education, specialized knowledge, and practice standards. The FLSA, however, defines a professional as a person whose primary duties consist of either

1. *the performance of a learned or educational profession entailing work which requires the exercise of discretion and judgment; or*

2. *the performance of work requiring invention, imagination, or talent in a recognized field of artistic endeavor. (48A Am Jur 2d, Labor and Labor Relations § 3967, p. 813)*

The two important elements in the preceding tests are "learned profession" and "exercise of discretion and judgment." A learned profession is one that requires an advanced kind of knowledge, usually beyond the high school level, in the field of science or education that was obtained by prolonged and specialized instruction. Specific academic training as a prerequisite for entering a profession is usually required.

The "exercise of discretion and judgment" element is much less well defined and is often problematic when the issue of whether or not athletic trainers should be classified as professionals (and therefore be exempt from the FLSA) is addressed. For example, in some states the provisions of a credentialing act require athletic trainers to be supervised by physicians. Some athletic trainers in the aforementioned cases have argued that because they do their work under the direction of a physician, they are not exercising discretion and judgment. In institutions without team physicians, athletic trainers might, in fact, be forced to exercise discretion and judgment, even though the work they perform is the same as that performed by nonexempt athletic trainers at a similar institution. Athletic trainers who teach at least 50% of the time are generally exempt and are not entitled to overtime, because teachers are considered professionals under the FLSA. Athletic trainers who spend more than 50% of their time in management or administrative roles might also be exempt.

APPLICATIONS TO ATHLETIC TRAINING: THEORY INTO PRACTICE

Use the following two case studies to help you apply the concepts in this chapter to real-life situations. The questions at the conclusion of the studies are open ended, with many possible solutions.

Case Study 1

The new manager of the Wellness Center, a physician-owned sports medicine and rehabilitation clinic, instituted a policy requiring all supervisors to evaluate their employees and recommend salary increases. This new program was an attempt to implement a merit-pay system at the center. In the past, everyone had received an across-the-board increase without regard to how they had performed during the past year.

Sandra Hotchkiss supervised the center's six certified athletic trainers. Upon receiving the memo mandating the new policy, Sandra decided she would simply write a narrative describing each of the athletic trainers. She felt such a narrative would be a useful guide for the new manager in awarding pay increases since it would provide her with in-depth analysis of the strengths and weaknesses of each athletic trainer. The following are examples of the evaluations she submitted.

Brian Robinson

Brian Robinson is one of the best athletic trainers employed by the center. He is thoughtful, works well with the patients, has a cheerful personality, and gets along great with the staff. Brian has received positive feedback from the athletic director at South High School, where he is assigned during the fall and spring. The athletes and parents seem to like him and there haven't been any problems that I am aware of, although I have only been out there a couple of times. My recommendation is that Brian be given a 5% salary increase.

Juan Diaz

Although I think Juan is basically a pretty good athletic trainer, he has had several problems over the past year. Juan seemed to be in the middle of a couple of controversies at Martin Luther King High. I know King is an inner-city school and Juan has a lot of tough problems to overcome down there, but I just wish he could deal more effectively with them so we wouldn't have to spend time on them at the Center. Juan hasn't been very effective in getting many referrals to the Center from his high school. As I mentioned earlier, although I think Juan does a good job as an athletic trainer, I can't recommend anything higher than a 3% increase for him this year.

Sandra was surprised when, three weeks later, on the day after the salary increases were announced, Juan stormed into her office and informed her that he was going to sue both her and the Center for discrimination based on negligent evaluation.

Questions for Analysis

1. What were the strengths and weaknesses of the performance evaluation system initiated by Sandra Hotchkiss?

2. How could the Center's new manager have approached the problem more constructively and effectively? How would this have affected Sandra? How would it have affected Brian, Juan, and the other athletic trainers?

3. Describe the performance evaluation system you would implement if you were in Sandra's position. What concerns, if any, would you express to the new manager regarding the new policy?

Case Study 2

John Freeman had just bought the local professional football franchise. He had made his fortune in the fast-food restaurant business, starting off with one small fried chicken restaurant and building it into a multimillion-dollar chain with restaurants all over the world. At his first meeting with the club's staff, John announced that he was bringing in a consultant to do a management audit of every department. He explained that sound management was the cornerstone of his success in business and in life. He expected each member of the staff to adopt that philosophy. Sound management, in his opinion, was the key to success in any business and professional football was a business!

A few weeks later, Rick Condelato and the rest of the sports medicine staff spent the better part of two days answering questions and explaining the club's sports medicine operation to the management consultant. The consultant asked about policies and procedures. He examined the recordkeeping system. He investigated the supply and equipment purchasing routines. He became familiar with how Rick selected student athletic trainers for summer training camp. As far as Rick could tell, no stone was left unturned.

About a month later, the management consultant and John Freeman, the new owner, walked into the athletic training room and told Rick they wanted to discuss the results of the recent management audit with him. "Rick," the consultant began, "for the most part, you are managing this part of the club's operations fairly effectively. You buy only what you need and you don't pay more than you have to. The procedures you have implemented are consistent with club policy, and they seem to be efficient and effective. But in talking with your assistants, the assistant coaches, and some of the players, I have determined that you don't do a very good job of utilizing your staff to its fullest potential. The information they provided leads me to believe that you don't delegate authority enough. You try to do too much by yourself. Take a look at the organizational chart I developed of your operation as it presently exists" (see figure 3.20).

"Rick," said John Freeman, "I want you to reorganize your staff so you can work more efficiently. From what everybody tells me, you're a good man and although I expect maximum effort, I don't want you to get burned out simply because you haven't organized your staff well enough. I expect to see your reorganization report on my desk by Monday of next week."

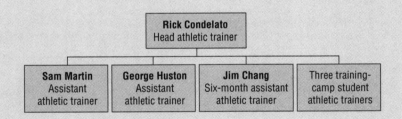

■ **Figure 3.20**   Organizational chart for Rick's sports medicine program.

Questions for Analysis

1. What is wrong with the current organizational structure in Rick's program? What problems are likely to arise based on the present structure?

2. How could Rick reorganize to reduce the amount of work he is responsible for and still accomplish everything that needs to be done?

3. If you were in Rick's position, what organizational structure would you devise to meet the mandate of the new club owner?

4. What strategies should Rick employ to make sure that his assistants develop ownership in the new organizational structure?

SUMMARY

1. *Understand the different forms of organizational culture that can exist in a sports medicine program.*

   Organizational culture includes the basic values, behavioral norms, assumptions, and beliefs of a sports medicine program. The type of organizational culture will have an effect on human resource management. The three major types of organizational cultures are the collegial, personalistic, and formalistic cultures.

2. *Formally define the relationships of the persons working in a sports medicine program by developing an organizational chart.*

   The relationships between the various members of a sports medicine program are best illustrated by an organizational chart. Athletic trainers can describe these relationships in one of three ways: by function, by service, or in a matrix format.

3. *Understand the components of staff selection.*

   Staff selection is a commonly misunderstood term. It is defined by the *Uniform Guidelines on Employee Selection Procedures* as any procedure used as the basis for an employment decision. Hiring, promotion, demotion, performance evaluation, retention, and discharge are all examples of selection activities as defined by federal law.

4. *Develop a position description and a position vacancy notice.*

   A position description is a formal document that describes the qualification requirements, work content, accountability, and scope of a person's job. The weighted position description is an important first step in helping athletic trainers understand the expectations of their employers. The position description generally comprises two sections: the job specification and the job description.

5. *Understand the recruitment and hiring process, especially as affected by discrimination and bias based on race, gender, disability, religion, or national origin.*

   Recruitment and hiring are two of the most visible, expensive, and time-consuming aspects of the human resources function in sports medicine. Recruitment activities should be viewed in terms of long- and short-term needs. The prime directive in recruiting and hiring is that all qualified applicants should receive equal consideration. Athletic trainers and other sports medicine personnel must be hired on the basis of their qualifications and not on the basis of race, gender, religion, or national origin. The recruitment and hiring process usually follows these 10 steps: request for position, position request approval, position vacancy notice, application collection, telephone interviews, reference checks, on-site interview, recommendation and approval for hiring, offer of contract, and hiring.

6. *Understand the differences between the three major supervisory models.*

   The three major types of supervisory models are inspection-production, clinical, and developmental. The inspection-production model emphasizes authoritative managerial efficiency. Clinical supervision is the process, borrowed from education, of direct observation of an athletic trainer at work and the subsequent development of plans to remediate deficiencies in performance. The overriding theme of developmental supervision is participative management.

7. *Understand the purposes, methods, and standards for the evaluation of athletic trainer performance.*

Performance evaluation is the process of placing a value on the quality of an athletic trainer's work. In some settings, athletic trainers are not formally evaluated and lack position descriptions. Much of the performance evaluation literature intended for athletic trainers is based on a trait-oriented approach. Trait-oriented evaluation is usually biased and is rarely useful for improving performance. Athletic trainers should acquaint themselves with the 21 performance evaluation standards developed by the Joint Committee on Standards for Educational Evaluation. They are intended to guide the development of performance evaluation systems and to offer improvements in four major areas: propriety, accuracy, utility, and feasibility.

CHAPTER FOUR

What Athletic Trainers Use: Financial Resource Management

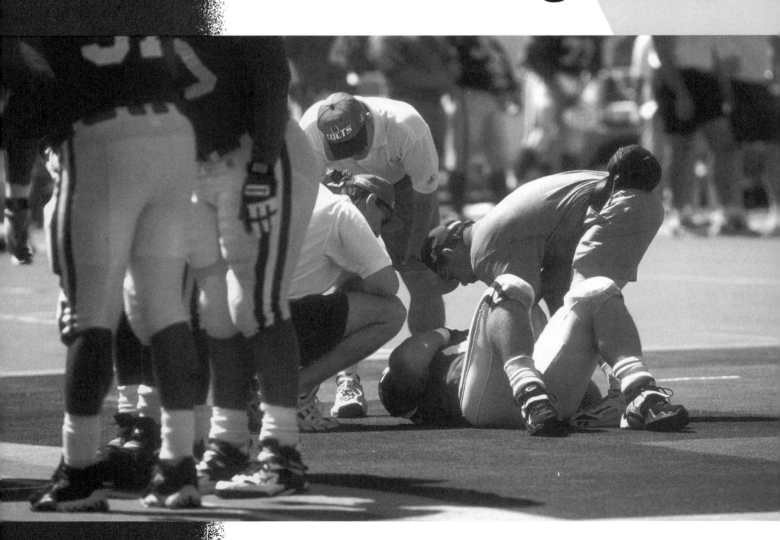

Brief sections of this chapter appeared previously in *Athletic Business* 1991 and in *College Athletic Management* 1990. See credits on page xvii for more information.

OBJECTIVES

After reading this chapter, you should be able to do the following:

1. Understand the different kinds of budgeting processes and apply them to an athletic training setting.

2. Coordinate the purchasing of athletic training equipment, supplies, and services so as to maximize the use of program funds.

3. Manage an athletic training program's inventory of equipment and supplies.

Stan Curtis was a certified athletic trainer for a large metropolitan school system in Grant, California. Stan's job was to provide athletic training services for school district athletes in a centralized athletic training room. The athletic training room was located in a municipal stadium, where the schools of the district played football, soccer, baseball, and softball, and ran track meets. In addition, Stan supervised the certified athletic trainers who worked in the district's six high schools. Every aspect of running the district's sports medicine program, from budgeting and purchasing, to maintaining an inventory for each school, was Stan's responsibility.

One day in early June, Stan received a phone call from his boss, the director of cocurricular activities. "Stan, I'm not going to be able to approve those purchase orders you sent over the other day," she said. "The recent defeat of our tax referendum has really screwed up the district's finances. I don't think any of your athletic trainers are going to lose their jobs because they're all tenured and have been in the system for quite a while, but your supply budget is definitely going to feel the pinch. Not only are you going to have to reduce it by 30% immediately, but from now on you're going to have to justify every line item. I'm sorry about all this, Stan, but I've got my orders and there isn't anything I can do about it. I'll send those POs back to you today."

Stan was troubled. He didn't know how he was going to be able to cut 30% of his budget and still provide the same services at the same level of quality. In the past, the budgeting process had been fairly simple. He had checked with the athletic trainers at the schools to find out what they would need for the upcoming year. If it sounded reasonable and the whole thing fit within the amount he had to work with, he ordered the supplies and that was that. He knew his athletic trainers were going to be furious about this. Budgeting was about to become a whole new ball game.

We haven't got the money, so we've got to think!

Ernest Rutherford

The common denominator in almost every management problem is money or the lack of it. Money is the engine that drives athletic enterprises, regardless of the level of competition. Sports medicine programs associated with athletic programs are subject to all the economic pressures those programs experience, whether the setting is a high school, college, university, professional team, or hospital. For athletic trainers working in independent sports medicine clinics, the need for sound financial management practices is even more acute, because these operations are usually affected more rapidly during an economic downturn. The effects of poor financial management are generally compounded when the resource pool is shallow. The amount of money an athletic trainer will have to operate a sports medicine program in an educational setting varies greatly depending on the level of competition engaged in by the institution's teams (Rankin, 1992). The economics of the health care industry at any given time also impacts how athletic trainers manage financial resources. The move away from traditional third-party reimbursement toward managed care models has drastically altered the financial landscape in which most sports medicine clinics operate. Small, independent clinics are being gobbled up by enormously profitable, publicly traded health care corporations at a phenomenal rate (see figure 4.1). Most sports medicine clinics have been forced to expand their services to include nontraditional activities such as performance enhancement and nutritional counseling.

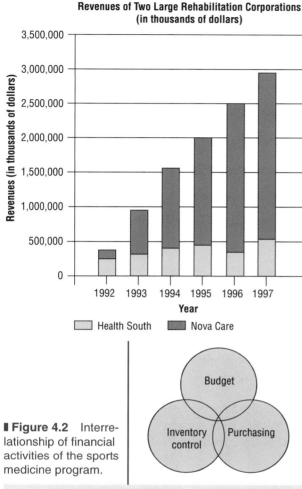

Revenues of Two Large Rehabilitation Corporations (in thousands of dollars)

▮ **Figure 4.1**   Revenues of the two largest private-sector employers of athletic trainers.

Adapted from Standard & Poor's 1998.

Traditional rehabilitation is being transformed so that athletic trainers might see a patient only a few times, with the bulk of the rehabilitation consisting of liberal doses of advice and a home program of exercise. These changes have a significant effect on the health care professionals—including athletic trainers—who operate, own, manage, and work in these environments.

The purpose of this chapter is to help athletic trainers become more astute stewards of their institutions' financial resources by presenting the theory and application of various techniques for budgeting, purchasing, and inventory control. These three topics are presented as distinct and separate processes, but in reality they are closely related to each other in a financial planning network (see figure 4.2). Although the ideas discussed in this chapter are applicable to almost any setting, athletic trainers should realize that certain types of sports medicine clinics, as small businesses, require more financial planning than this book can suggest. Athletic trainers who manage independently owned and operated sports medicine clinics should seek the counsel of experienced management consultants, attorneys, and accountants. In addition, the U.S. Small Business Administration publishes a management series that can help these athletic trainers become more familiar with the wide variety of issues facing owners of all types of small businesses.

▮ **Figure 4.2**   Interrelationship of financial activities of the sports medicine program.

The Small Business Administration's management series is available from the Superintendent of Documents, U.S. Government Printing Office, Washington, DC 20402.

BUDGETING

Budgeting is the method athletic trainers use to put a sports medicine program's mission into financial terms. There are several different budgeting methods, but none will be effective unless the athletic trainer properly plans for the budget process by developing a well-conceived needs assessment and by periodically evaluating the budget.

budget   A type of operational plan for the coordination of resources and expenditures.

Budgeting financial resources is a process organizational leaders ask program heads to accomplish. Athletic trainers and others responsible for planning and delivering sports medicine services must develop skills in planning and implementing budgets so that needed services are delivered in an effective, timely manner and allocation of financial resources is consistent with the strategic plans of both the institution and the sports medicine program.

A **budget** is a plan for the coordination of resources and expenditures (Horine, 1991). A budget also serves as a tool for estimating receipts and disbursements over a period of time (Mayo, 1978). Beyond its practical uses as a restraint on resource waste and as a predictive tool for the financial health of a sports medicine program, a budget is a quantitative expression of the athletic trainer's management plan. As such, it is both a strategic plan for how the sports medicine unit will function over a given period of time and an operational plan for how it will accomplish its goals.

Although many practitioners think of budgeting as a task that begins and ends in a narrow time frame during a particular part of the year, the wise athletic trainer should see budgeting as a continuous process of prioritizing, planning, documenting, and evaluating the goals of the sports medicine unit and translating these goals into concrete plans for how to expend available resources. Because athletic seasons stretch over all 12 months and new programs of all types are added to the athletic trainer's responsibilities, the budgeting process requires constant attention to fund status and ongoing evaluation for the next budget cycle.

Jones and Trentin (1971) have suggested that budgets should be used as the primary tools for planning and controlling a program. This helps athletic trainers differentiate between the concepts of budgeting and forecasting. As mentioned in chapter 2, forecasting is the process of predicting future conditions on the basis of various statistics and indicators that describe the past and present situations. Forecasting is typically accomplished by only a few people near the top of the organizational chart. Because budgeting is a type of planning, however, it requires input from the grass roots of the sports medicine program. An effective budget will consider the input of all employees about using the financial resources to meet documented program needs as opposed to simply allocating funds according to past traditions.

TYPES OF BUDGETS

Most sports medicine budget planning is based on one of six budgeting models (Ray, 1990). The six most common budgeting methods include zero-based, fixed, variable, lump-sum, line-item, and performance budgeting. Each of these methods can be an effective way to help athletic trainers plan the financial activity of their programs, depending on the particular circumstances and nature of the programs they direct. Depending on the financial health of the program and its parent institution, each budgeting method will normally be coupled with either permission to increase spending or a mandate to reduce spending.

The **spending ceiling model,** also known as the *incremental model* (Wildavsky, 1975), is the budgeting circumstance most often desired by sports medicine program directors. This is the model Stan used to determine his budget in the opening case. This method requires justification only for expenditures that exceed those of the previous budget cycle. Budget increases are most often linked to the inflation rate, which presents problems for sports medicine programs because prices for medical goods and services have risen faster than inflation (see figure 4.3). Athletic trainers who use this method are usually able to balance financial resources and expenditures for two to three years, but often fall behind after that because of the difference between the inflation rate and the cost of medical goods and services.

Sports medicine programs in financial crisis are often forced to combine their primary budgeting method with the **spending reduction model.** This is the model that Stan will be forced to adopt as a result of the financial problems in his school district. Under the spending reduction model, department heads, including directors of sports medicine programs, are required to reduce their budgets to preserve institutional funds. This budget method requires the most imagination and creativity of all the budget models for obvious reasons. Because financial resources tend to be reduced periodically in most sports medicine settings, the wise

spending ceiling model A type of expenditure budgeting that requires justification only for those expenses that exceed those of the previous budget cycle. Also known as the incremental model.

spending reduction model A type of budgeting used during periods of financial retrenchment that requires reallocation of institutional funds, resulting in reduced spending levels for some programs.

▌Figure 4.3 Health care costs as a percentage of gross domestic product.

From the Health Care Financing Agency.

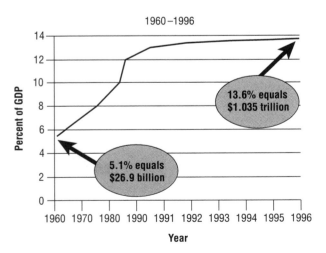

1960–1996

athletic trainer should identify those goods and services that could be cut without seriously affecting the program. If a financial crisis does arise, the athletic trainer will be prepared.

Each of the following budgeting methods can be used in either a spending ceiling or spending reduction mode:

Zero-Based Budgeting

zero-based budgeting
A model that requires justification for every budget line item without reference to previous spending patterns.

Zero-based budgeting is an administrative method that requires unit directors to justify every expense without reference to previous spending patterns. This method requires close attention to documentation of actual program needs. Stan is being forced to adopt a combination of the spending reduction and zero-based methods in the opening case. Although it requires more effort on the part of the athletic trainer, zero-based budgeting can be an excellent tool for developing priorities in a sports medicine program. Zero-based budgeting requires athletic trainers to evaluate each subfunction of the sports medicine program and to rank it according to how important it is to the accomplishment of the overall mission. The director should include a rationale for each item included in the budget request, explaining why the expense is necessary and what alternatives there are to funding it.

Fixed Budgeting

fixed budgeting
A method in which expenditures and revenues are projected on a monthly basis, thereby providing an estimate of cash flow.

Fixed budgeting is a process that is appropriate for sports medicine programs in financially stable environments. It requires an athletic trainer to project both expenditures and program income, if any, on a month-by-month basis to determine total program costs and revenues for the fiscal year. This is useful because it can help the athletic trainer determine what the cash flow of the operation is likely to be at various points in the year. This type of budgeting is probably most appropriate for large, well-established sports medicine clinics during periods of relative economic certainty. It is rarely used in school sports medicine programs because most of these programs are not income oriented.

Variable Budgeting

variable budgeting
A method requiring that monthly expenditures be adjusted so they do not exceed revenues.

Unfortunately, the athletic trainer who coordinates the activities of a sports medicine clinic will rarely be able to predict the monthly balance of expenditures to revenues with perfect accuracy. The **variable budgeting** system requires that expenditures for any given time period be adjusted according to revenues for the same time period. For example, assume that the clinic director budgeted $25,000 for expenses in June, anticipating that revenues would be approximately $50,000. Under the variable budgeting system, if the actual revenues were only $40,000, the clinic director would be required to reduce expenditures by 20% for that month. As with fixed budgeting, this method is rarely used in school-based programs.

Lump-Sum Budgeting

lump-sum budgeting
A method that allocates a fixed amount of money for an entire program without specifying how the money will be spent.

When a parent organization provides an athletic trainer with a fixed sum of money and the authority to spend that money any way the athletic trainer sees fit, the sports medicine program is operating under **lump-sum budgeting.** Most athletic trainers who use lump-sum budgeting like it, because it gives them the freedom to spend money where they think it is needed the most. Lump-sum budgeting requires that athletic trainers be held accountable after the fact.

Line-Item Budgeting

line-item budgeting A method that allocates a fixed amount of money for each subfunction of a program.

Line-item budgeting requires that athletic trainers list anticipated expenditures for specific categories of program subfunctions. Typical line items for a sports medicine program include expendable supplies, equipment repair, team physician services, and insurance (see figure 4.4). Line-item budgeting allows a parent organization to

Budget Comparison Report					
Acct. No.: 213702		Dept.: Sports Medicine		Responsible person: Stan Curtis	
Object code	Account description	99/00 Expense	00/01 Budget	01/02 Request	Percent change
3110	Travel	229.25	300.00	300.00	0
3205	Supplies	7,632.32	9,000.00	9,475.75	5.3
3305	Printing	89.29	100.00	100.00	0
3315	Speakers	0	1,500.00	1,500.00	0
3320	Stipends	5,997.96	6,300.00	6,300.00	0
3360	Postage	257.65	300.00	300.00	0
3530	Repairs	313.15	500.00	500.00	0
3650	Phone	428.89	475.00	500.00	5.0
3720	Uniforms	430.00	500.00	500.00	0
3850	Periodicals	150.00	150.00	150.00	0
4035	Insurance	200.00	250.00	300.00	16.7
4100	Dues	90.00	100.00	100.00	0
Department total		$15,818.51	$19,475.00	$20,025.75	2.8

❙ Figure 4.4 Sample line-item budget for a school-based sports medicine program.

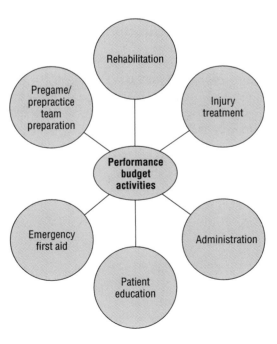

❙ Figure 4.5 Performance budget activities.

retain a higher level of control over the sports medicine program, because money budgeted for one line cannot usually be spent on another line without permission. The advantage of a line-item budget is that it is easy to understand and prepare. The disadvantage of this method is that the athletic trainer has limited flexibility in responding to midyear financial crises, because funds dedicated to one use cannot be easily transferred to another use.

Performance Budgeting

Performance budgeting breaks the functions of a sports medicine program into discrete activities and appropriates the funds necessary to accomplish these activities. Examples of activities typically associated with a school sports medicine program include prepractice and pregame team preparation, rehabilitation, injury treatment, administration, patient education, and emergency first aid (see figure 4.5). Expenses for each of these activities can be calculated and used to determine the overall budget. This method is similar to line-item budgeting in that "mini-budgets" are developed for separate categories of expenditures. Performance budgeting is not commonly used in sports medicine programs because of the expense and difficulty of analyzing specific activity costs.

*performance
budgeting
A method that allocates
funds for discrete
activities.*

PLANNING THE BUDGET

The process of budget planning varies depending on institutional budgeting cycles and rules and the type of budgeting system being used. Before Stan faced a budget crisis, he probably used a spending ceiling or incremental budget model similar to the one that follows.

Needs Assessment

The first step in any budget cycle involves a careful assessment of program needs. Witkin and Altschuld (1995, p.4) define **needs assessment** as, "A systematic set of procedures undertaken for the purpose of setting priorities and making decisions about program or organizational improvement and allocation of resources. The priorities are based on identified needs."

*needs assessment
A systematic set of
procedures undertaken
to set organizational or
programmatic priorities
based on identified
needs.*

*need The discrepancy
between the present
program status and the
desired future state of
one or more aspects of
the program.*

A **need** is the gap between a present state of being and the desired state to which a program should aspire (Kauffman, Rojas, & Mayer, 1993). Needs are commonly confused with solutions. For example, suppose that Stan, the athletic trainer in the opening case, was concerned that too many of the student-athletes under his care were being referred to outside clinics for their rehabilitation rather than completing their recovery in his facility. Underlying his concern was the fact that these services were driving up the cost of the school district's insurance policy. In addition, Stan was also troubled that he and his team physician were "out of the loop" when return-to-play decisions were made for many of these athletes. The need in this case would be Stan's desire to have all (or, in any case, most) of the injured athletes complete their rehabilitation in-house.

This need should not be confused with the many possible solutions to help meet the need. Stan could develop a closer working relationship with the physicians who are referring the athletes to the outside clinics. He could do a better job of educating the parents about the rehabilitation services and capabilities of his staff. He could improve the rehabilitation facilities in the school where he works. He could hire another staff member whose sole function would be rehabilitation. He might even encourage the school administration to refuse payment for rehabilitation services performed outside the school unless they are approved in advance by Stan or the team physician. Some of these solutions will have budgetary consequences and some won't. The important thing to recognize for the purpose of the needs assessment, however, is that none of these options is a need. Each is a potential solution that might help eliminate the need in this case. Stan does not *need* a new rehabilitation facility, but the program does need to keep more of its patients in-house.

Needs assessment as it relates to budget planning should generally include the following three phases:

Phase 1: Exploration
During this phase, an athletic trainer should

- identify the needs of the sports medicine program,
- decide what information to collect for each of the identified needs, and
- decide where and how to collect the information.

Phase 2: Information Gathering
During this phase, an athletic trainer should

- collect as much information as possible for each of the identified needs,
- prioritize needs, and
- determine causes for each of the needs.

Phase 3: Decision Making

During this phase, an athletic trainer should

- develop alternative solutions for each need,
- determine budgetary implications for each solution,
- prioritize solutions, and
- integrate solutions into the program budget.

Funding Source Decisions

The next step in planning a budget for a sports medicine program is for the athletic trainer and the division head (e.g., athletic director, chair of the physical education department, general manager, or principal) to agree which fund will provide the various items the athletic trainer needs. This discussion should cover all of the program's projected expenses. Too often, athletic trainers focus only on the costs associated with supplies and equipment during the budget planning process, to the exclusion of other items important for running the program, including services, telephone, photocopying, and so on. Once all program costs have been identified, each should be allocated to a particular budget. Protective pads, for instance, might fall into the sports medicine or equipment budgets. Costs associated with physical examinations might be covered by the health services budget. Expenditures for travel to professional meetings might be included in the parent department's travel budget instead of the sports medicine budget. These decisions will depend on both the working relationship and the financial philosophies of the individuals involved.

Which fund these expenditures fall under will affect who controls the funds. If Stan's travel to professional conferences is covered under the director of cocurricular activity's overall travel budget, Stan will probably be required to justify each meeting he wishes to attend. In addition, he will likely be subject to all the restrictions on travel that apply to other district employees who report to the same director.

Another important decision that must be made involves whether the purchase of certain injury-protection equipment should be covered by the sports medicine budget or by the budget of the team that will be using the equipment. If an item is clearly intended for use by one team, it makes sense to include that item in the team's budget rather than that of the sports medicine program. If such items are placed in the budget of the sports medicine program, other teams might develop false expectations of the sports medicine staff.

For example, if Stan purchases lateral knee braces to be used specifically by injured football players, then other coaches might expect Stan to purchase knee braces or similar devices for their athletes. This is probably an expense the sports medicine program will not be able to continue to support. A more rational approach would be for the football coaches to include the expense of the knee braces in their own budgets. Only in this way will Stan be able to avoid setting a precedent he won't be able to afford for long.

Improved Budget Planning

The first year a budget is planned for the sports medicine unit is often the most difficult because of the lack of a precedent on which to base financial plans. The process of budgeting for the first year of operation most closely approximates the zero-based budgeting model, because a rationale for each purchase must be developed without reference to established spending patterns. The presence of such spending patterns facilitates subsequent budget planning, which then approximates the spending ceiling or incremental model. Athletic trainers can enhance their budget planning for sports medicine goods and services by following these guidelines:

- Keep a running inventory of all consumable and nonconsumable supplies.
- When budget submission time comes, calculate the amount of each type of consumable supply that has been used. Project and estimate how much more of the supply will be needed to complete the fiscal year, taking into account the different needs of the sports seasons yet to come.
- Based on estimates of how much of each type of supply will be needed to complete the fiscal year, and taking into account any changes that will take place during the next fiscal year (e.g., new varsity sports, longer seasons, and so on), estimate the amount of each type of supply that will be needed for the next fiscal year.
- Consult with several vendors to obtain estimates of how much prices are expected to rise for the next fiscal year. With this information, develop anticipated prices for all the consumable supplies that will be needed for the next fiscal year.

CAPITAL EQUIPMENT AND IMPROVEMENTS

Budget planning for nonconsumable capital equipment and capital improvements is often more difficult than for consumable supplies that are typically reordered every year. Therapeutic modalities, ice machines, and rehabilitation equipment are examples of nonconsumable capital equipment. They are very expensive, and many sports medicine directors are not able to include them in their annual supply budgets. Planning for acquisition, repair, and replacement of such items requires careful coordination between directors of sports medicine units and higher-level decision makers. Renovations, additions, or modifications to existing facilities are known as *capital improvements*. Because the capital budget is often unrecoverable once spent, it is essential that purchases and projects of this type be screened by multiple levels of authority and that such expenditures are consistent with the accomplishment of the sports medicine program's mission (Jones & Trentin, 1971). The following suggestions will help budget planners meet the needs of the sports medicine program in this area:

- Treat equipment repair as a consumable supply and include it as a line item in the annual operating budget. If the institution will agree to "roll over" the unused balance of this account from year to year, it can serve as a fund for capital equipment purchases.
- Develop priority lists for capital equipment and improvement requests complete with documentation of need. Suggest possible funding alternatives to decision makers.
- Make institutional fund-raisers aware of the priority list and the documentation of need so they can keep these needs in mind when soliciting funds from contributors.
- Consider answering grant requests from funding agencies or engaging in research projects funded by industry. For example, Hope College became a testing site for a new analgesic cream, which brought the sports medicine unit over $25,000. This money is now used to fund capital equipment purchases for the sports medicine program.

BUDGET EVALUATION

Most directors of sports medicine units either ignore budget evaluation completely or perform it reluctantly. Evaluation of the budget is, however, very important in the overall budgeting process, because it allows administrators to reach informed judgments on how well the financial resources of the institution are being expended. The following three relatively simple steps can help athletic trainers evaluate how well the budget process is working.

- **Maintain dual accounting systems.** In addition to the accounting done in the sports medicine unit, request computer printouts from the institution's business office to make sure expenditures are being charged to the proper funds.

- **Evaluate service contracts.** Service contracts, such as for ambulance service, insurance, team physicians, and student athletic trainers, should be evaluated each year to make sure that pay rates are competitive for the amount of work being done. Keep a running log of all activities of each contractor, including the number of hours worked and the type of work actually performed.

- **Compile statistical information.** Periodic statistical reports of how consumable and nonconsumable supplies and equipment are being used can help an athletic trainer justify financial resource deployment. For example, treatment records are an excellent source of information about how often and on whom therapeutic modalities are being used. Many computer software packages can help develop statistical reports.

PURCHASING

Athletic trainers implement the budget when they purchase equipment, supplies, and services for the sports medicine program. Although bidding is usually the most cost-effective purchasing method for consumable supplies, other purchasing options can be more effective for capital equipment and services.

purchasing
The process of acquiring goods and services.

request for quotation (RFQ) A document that provides vendors with the specifications for bidding on the sale of goods and services.

bidding A process whereby vendors provide cost quotations for goods and services they wish to sell.

negotiations The process of bargaining.

Once the sports medicine budget has been approved, the process of budget implementation can begin. **Purchasing** is the process that athletic trainers use to implement the budget plan. Methods of purchasing supplies, equipment, and services are critical to the cost-effective operation of the sports medicine program. Creative purchasing strategies have been shown to reduce expenditures for sports medicine supplies by up to 40% (Ray, 1991b). The six basic steps in purchasing (Wright, 1983) include request for quotation, negotiation, requisition, purchase order, receiving, and accounts payable.

The Six Basic Steps in the Purchasing Process

1. Request for quotation
2. Negotiation
3. Requisition
4. Purchase order
5. Receiving
6. Accounts payable

REQUEST FOR QUOTATION

The first step in the purchasing process involves sending a request for quotation to a variety of vendors. A **request for quotation (RFQ)** is a document that accompanies a bid sheet and provides instructions for vendors to bid on the supplies, equipment, and services needed by a sports medicine program (see figure 4.6). The use of RFQs is known as **bidding,** and it is the most effective way to reduce costs for expendable sports medicine supplies (see figure 4.7). Certain questions should be considered before supply bid sheets are distributed to vendors (see table 4.1 on p. 117).

NEGOTIATIONS

Negotiations are an important part of the purchasing process, because their effective use can help safeguard the interests of a sports medicine program. Athletic trainers should negotiate in the following three categories of purchases.

Grant Public Schools   Department of Sports Medicine

Request for Quotation
(This is not an order)

Submit Bid To: Stan Curtis, Head Athletic Trainer
                  Grant Public Schools
                  Municipal Stadium
                  Grant, CA 98201

If additional information is required, contact Stan Curtis at (415) 555-7708.

Date Mailed: April 11, 2001   Closing Date: May 2, 2001

Goods must be able to be delivered before: August 1, 2001   Billing not before: July 1, 2001

In order to receive consideration, one copy of the "Request for Quotation," with your bid properly filled in, must be signed and returned by the specified closing date.

All prices and conditions, including freight charges, must be shown. Additions or conditions not shown on this bid will not be allowed.

Contracts or purchase orders resulting from this quotation may not be assigned without the consent of the Head Athletic Trainer, Grant Public Schools.

The seller agrees to protect the purchaser from all damages arising out of alleged infringements of patents.

Unless otherwise specified, the right is reserved to accept or reject all or any part of your proposal.

Delivered F.O.B. to specific address in Grant, California 98201. Seller assumes all freight and delivery expenses.

If given an order for item(s) specified on the attached "Grant Public Schools Sports Medicine Bid Request," bidder agrees to furnish the items at the price(s) specified and under the conditions indicated.

Bidder to complete:

Bidder's name and address:	Prices will be good for _____ days.
_____	Delivery will be made _____ days after receipt of order.
_____	
_____	Signed by _____
Telephone Number:	Printed name _____
1-800- _____ and/or	Title _____ Date _____
Area Code (_____) _____	

■ **Figure 4.6**   Sample request for quotation form to accompany bid sheet.

Capital Equipment

This is the expensive, durable equipment that often makes up the bulk of the reha-bilitation and therapeutic modality inventory for a sports medicine program. Purchases are infrequent and costly.

Medium-Priced Annual Rebuys

These are usually purchases of services that require annual renegotiation. Examples include salaries, physician consulting fees, ambulance services, and athletic medical insurance.

Grant Public Schools Sports Medicine Bid Request

Please complete and return within three weeks of receipt to Stan Curtis, Head Athletic Trainer, Grant Public Schools, Grant, CA 98201.
Phone (415) 555-7708 or fax (415) 555-7922

All bid prices should include the following factors:
  —Cost of shipping to Grant, CA
  —Billing no sooner than 7/1/01

*If listing a substitute item, please specify brand name, packaging quantities, and product codes. If no brand is specified in the *Item* column, please specify the brand you are bidding in the *Substitute* column.

Item	*Substitute	Quantity	Bid price/unit	Total
1.5-inch J & J Coach Tape (no substitute)		110 cases		
3-inch elastic tape (Elastikon or substitute)		10 cases		
2-inch elastic tape (Conform or substitute)		10 cases		
3-inch underwrap		5 cases		
6-inch elastic wraps (irregular if available)		20 dozen		
3-inch elastic wraps (irregular if available)		4 dozen		
1/8-inch adhesive felt (6" x 36")		20 pieces		
1/8-inch adhesive foam (5" x 72")		10 pieces		

▌Figure 4.7   Sample bid sheet to accompany request for quotation.

Types of Services Commonly Purchased by Athletic Trainers

- Team physician
- Consulting physician
- Ambulance
- Liability and malpractice insurance
- Athletic accident insurance
- Drug screening
- Laboratory and radiology
- Equipment service contracts

Lower-Cost Consumable Supplies

These items constitute the bulk of the sports medicine supply budget. Although some supplies will have to be reordered throughout the year, careful planning will allow the athletic trainer to place only one major supply order for the entire year. This will

Table 4.1 Factors to Consider in the Bidding Process	
Question	**Consideration**
Will brand names be specified or are generic products acceptable?	Products for which a brand name is required should have a "no substitute" notation clearly marked on the bid sheet.
How many and which vendors will be invited to bid?	The suggested minimum is three. Vendors who have a reputation for excellent service should be considered over those who do not.
Will the institution or the vendor be responsible for paying shipping costs?	Most suppliers of consumable products are willing to pay shipping if specified on the bid.
What types of products will be purchased via bidding?	Consumable supplies and some types of durable equipment are good candidates for bidding. Most services should be bid only with great cautionbecause the quality of service may be reflected in lower prices.
When should RFQs be sent to vendors?	This depends on the institution's purchasing process. If athletic trainers are required to purchase supplies through a central purchasing department, a minimum of three months from RFQ to delivery should be allowed.

help the athletic trainer's negotiating position because of the discounts normally associated with quantity purchasing.

Negotiable Points in Sports Medicine Purchasing

The following five elements can be negotiated for purchases in each of the three categories (Barlow, 1982):

1. Price
2. Supply
3. Quality
4. Shipping
5. Technical support

Price

Price is the most obvious point for negotiation in purchasing sports medicine goods and services. The use of the RFQ is the first step in price negotiation for consumable supplies, but it isn't the only option available. Vendors are often willing to negotiate price reductions after submitting the RFQ. However, if athletic trainers use excessive price negotiation after vendors have returned the RFQ, a poor working relationship and higher prices in subsequent years are likely to result. Athletic trainers have an ethical responsibility to avoid the practice of playing one vendor against another for the purpose of achieving the lowest possible price. Most vendors understand that they will be most competitive if they keep their prices low. In addition, they understand that athletic trainers will use bidding to try to keep their costs as low as possible. But playing one vendor against another after the bids have been returned is frowned upon and is sure to damage your relationship with vendors. Price negotiation is usually the most effective when purchasing services, for which bidding is less common.

Supply

Among the most common points for negotiation between athletic trainers and vendors are delivery and payment schedules for purchased goods. Because many educational institutions have fiscal years that begin on July 1, it has become common practice for athletic trainers to order supplies for the next school year in May, take possession in June, and defer billing until after July 1. This allows athletic trainers time to restock and prepare for their fall seasons during one fiscal year and pay for the supplies during the subsequent year. Negotiation over delivery and billing is even more important for sports medicine clinics, where fluctuations of cash flow have a greater impact.

Quality

Athletic trainers typically negotiate for the quality of the goods they purchase by specifying brand names or generics on the bid sheet. Another item of negotiation that is particularly applicable to large capital improvement items is the warranty. Although every product should be accompanied by an **implied warranty**, the athletic trainer is free to negotiate an **express warranty** that affirms the performance characteristics of the product. See figure 4.8 for an example of an express warranty.

Shipping

The two primary points for negotiation about shipping purchased goods are payment of shipping costs and the freight-on-board (f.o.b.) point. The wise athletic trainer will include a statement in the RFQ stipulating that the vendor will assume all costs associated with shipping and handling the product. This is a common practice that clarifies the cost of supplies for athletic trainers by allowing vendors to factor the costs of shipping into their bids. The f.o.b. point specifies the place at which title for the sports medicine supplies will pass from the vendor to the purchaser. Generally, athletic trainers should specify their institutions or clinics as the f.o.b. point to provide greater protection against loss or damage during shipping.

implied warranty
An unstated understanding that a vendor will "make good" if a product is faulty.

express warranty
An explicit statement specifying the conditions, circumstances, and terms under which a vendor will replace or repair a product if found to be faulty.

f.o.b. point *Freight-on-board point. The point at which the title for shipped goods passes from vendor to purchaser.*

For the period of:	We will replace at no cost to you:
One year from the date of the original purchase	Any part of the ultrasound unit that fails due to a defect in materials or workmanship. During this one-year period we will also provide, free of charge, any necessary labor to replace or repair the defective component.
Five years from the date of the original purchase	Any part of the generator or crystal that fails due to a defect in materials or workmanship. During this five-year period we will also provide, free of charge, any necessary labor to replace or repair the defective component.
Seven years from the date of the original purchase	Any part of the plastic housing that fails due to a defect in materials or workmanship. During this seven-year period we will also provide, free of charge, any necessary labor to replace or repair the defective component.
What this warranty does not cover:	

- Improper installation
- Failure of the product if it is abused, misused, or used for a purpose other than that for which it was intended
- Damage to the unit caused by flood, fire, or natural disasters
- Damage to circuit breakers or electrical systems
- Incidental damage caused by failure of this unit
- Routine maintenance or calibration

▌**Figure 4.8** Example of an express warranty for an ultrasound unit.

Support

Negotiation for technical support is especially important for high-technology capital improvement items. Computers and isokinetic testing and rehabilitation devices are two examples of the type of equipment for which athletic trainers might require technical support. The cost of this support is often negotiable and will become an important factor in the overall cost during the life of the equipment.

REQUISITION

requisition A type of formal or informal communication, usually written, used for requesting authorization to purchase goods or services.

The next step in the purchasing process is completing and submitting a **requisition** for needed supplies, equipment, or services (Wright, 1983). This step can either be formal or informal depending on the authority level of the athletic trainer in the overall institutional bureaucracy. The requisition is simply a written request to expend institutional funds for needed resources (see figure 4.9).

PURCHASE ORDER

purchase order A document that formalizes the terms of a purchase and transmits the intentions of the buyer to purchase goods or services from a vendor.

Once an athletic trainer has approved requisitions in hand, purchase orders can be produced and sent to vendors. A **purchase order** is a document that formalizes the terms of the purchase and transmits the intentions of the buyer to purchase goods or services from the vendor (see figure 4.10). It should be completed and transmitted only after the RFQs have been received from the vendors. An important decision is

Grant Public Schools				Purchase requisition	
Suggested vendor		Previous supplier? Yes ❑ No ❑	Date		
Ship to:	Attn:		Date needed		
Quantity	Description			Unit	Total
Requested by:	Requested for:		Acct. no.	Approved by:	
For purchasing department use only					
Date ordered	P.O. No.	Ordered from:		Ship via:	

▮ **Figure 4.9** Sample purchase requisition form.

Vendor's copy

Grant Public Schools

Purchase order no.

To:

This number must appear on all invoices ↑

↓ Ship to Grant Public Schools, Grant, CA

❏ Memorial Stadium, 225 Stadium Dr.

❏ Central Administration, 321 Pine St.

❏ Physical Plant, 5436 Elm Ave.

Bill to: Grant Public Schools
          Grant, CA 98201

Account number:	Order date:	Ship via:	
Quantity	Description	Unit price	Amount
Please send duplicate invoices.	Approved by:		

Figure 4.10   Sample purchase order form.

whether to award purchase orders to vendors based on the low bid for the entire supply order or to make the award based on the low bid for each individual item. Athletic trainers will save the most money if they make the award based on each item. There are drawbacks to this method, however. Most vendors have a minimum-order policy. A vendor awarded a purchase order for $4.95 out of a possible $10,000 RFQ will be unlikely to negotiate favorable terms in the future. One possible solution is to award purchase orders only for amounts over a certain critical level, usually around $200. This breaks the total supply order into packages that will save the athletic trainer money and ensure a reasonable profit margin for the most competitive vendors.

RECEIVING

receiving   The process of accepting delivery of goods purchased from a vendor.

Receiving is the process of accepting delivery of goods purchased from vendors. When goods are received, they should immediately be checked to make sure that the packing slip matches the contents of the shipping container and to determine whether all the goods specified in the purchase order have been received. All goods should be inspected for damage. If any damage is discovered, it should be reported

For more of the best sports resources...

Don't Delay! Return this card for more information on our wide range of books, videos and software.

To ensure we send you the most appropriate information, please tell us your specific areas of interest using the section to the right of this card. Please also tell us in which Human Kinetics product you found this card.

Now simply fill in your details below and return FREEPOST* to Human Kinetics – the premier publisher for sports and fitness.

Name _____

Address _____

_____

Postcode _____

Telephone _____ **Facsimile** _____

E-mail _____

If you do not wish to receive regular updates from Human Kinetics please indicate by ticking here ○

✓ **Please indicate your interests below:**

○ Adapted PE
○ Aquatics
○ Biomechanics of Exercise & Sport
○ Coaching
○ Motor Behaviour & Development
○ Nutrition
○ Personal Training
○ PE/Children & Sport
○ Physiology of Exercise & Sport
○ Physiotherapy & Massage
○ Recreation & Outdoor Sports
○ Research & Measurement
○ Socio-cultural Issues in Sport
○ Sport Psychology
○ Strength & Conditioning
○ Sports Management
○ Specific Sports (please state)

Other Specific Areas
_____
_____

Human Kinetics Europe Limited

FREEPOST NEA9109

LEEDS

GREAT BRITAIN

LS16 6YY

to the vendor immediately. Most vendors have a policy of replacing damaged goods only if reported within a given time period.

ACCOUNTS PAYABLE

Payment for sports medicine supplies and equipment is usually due within a specified time period after the receipt of the goods or the invoice, whichever arrives last. Athletic trainers who work in educational, professional, or industrial settings should submit invoices to their respective business offices as soon as they receive them to take advantage of early payment discounts offered by most vendors. Those athletic trainers who work in independent sports medicine clinics should evaluate the terms of the early payment discount. If the finance charge is lower than the current cost of money, it would make sense to stretch the payments as far as possible into the payment term. For example, assume you are in charge of an independent sports medicine clinic that needs to borrow money from a bank to cover supply purchases during certain times of the year when cash flow is predictably slow. If a particular vendor charged .5% per month (6% annual percentage rate) on the unpaid balance of your account, and the bank was charging you an annual rate of 8%, it would make sense to pay off your account with the vendor over the maximum time allowed and spend the 2% you will save on another program need.

ALTERNATIVE PURCHASING STRATEGIES

Besides the traditional method of bidding for sports medicine supply purchases and paying for them with institutional funds, athletic trainers should consider three other potential sources of cost savings: pooled buying consortia, alumni and booster organizations, and external funding organizations and programs.

Pooled Buying Consortia

pooled buying consortium A group of similar institutions that merge resources to purchase goods in large quantities for the purpose of receiving volume discounts.

A **pooled buying consortium** can be an effective method for purchasing certain types of sports medicine supplies. Schools that are members of an athletic conference should consider pooling their adhesive tape orders, for example, to receive a quantity discount. This method can be effective for many different types of supplies including bandages, ice bags, paper cups, elastic wraps, and crutches, among others. Pooled buying consortia have been used for many years by coaches and athletic directors to purchase balls and other athletic equipment for less than it would cost to purchase such supplies individually.

Alumni or Booster Organizations

Alumni and booster organizations can be very helpful in offsetting the costs of large capital expenses that would usually lie outside the normal budget of the sports medicine program. Treatment and rehabilitation devices are expensive items that booster clubs are often willing to purchase for the sports medicine program. Athletic trainers are cautioned, however, to work in conjunction with the institutional development officer when making such requests of booster clubs. Many institutions have policies designed to ensure that all philanthropy is channeled through the development office to maximize the ability of the institution to obtain such gifts.

External Funding Organizations and Programs

There are many private and public sources of funds that athletic trainers can access for certain narrowly defined purposes (The Foundation Center, 1997). These organizations and agencies provide money to help offset the costs of research and education for a wide variety of problems related to sports medicine. Grants from organizations are generally used to pay for expenses associated with specific projects and are not

External Funding Sources

Contact the following sources for information on external funding:

Organization or Agency	World Wide Web Address
National Athletic Trainers' Association Research and Education Foundation	http://www.nata.org/
American College of Sports Medicine	http://www.acsm.org/
Gatorade Sports Science Institute	http://www.gssiweb.com/
National Institutes of Health	http://www.nih.gov/
National Science Foundation	http://www.nsf.gov/

intended to fund the routine expenses associated with operating a sports medicine program. For example, a college with a Commission on Accreditation of Allied Health Education Programs (CAAHEP)-accredited athletic training education program that wanted to begin a lecture series might consider applying to a funding agency to help offset the cost of the series for a specific period of time. An athletic trainer who needed a particular piece of equipment to conduct a research project might also consider applying for a grant. Drug and alcohol education programs are often initiated with the use of external funding.

The Foundation Center is an outstanding source of information for persons interested in applying for financial support from one of the thousands of public or private funding sources. See its Web site at **http://www.fdncenter.org/** for complete online information about how to get started, how to develop a proposal, where to apply, and so on.

Athletic trainers interested in obtaining a grant from a funding agency will have to prepare a comprehensive grant application according to the exact specifications outlined in the application instructions. Most grant programs are competitive, and only the most worthy projects are normally funded. It is important for an athletic trainer to select a funding agency whose goals are in congruence with the project for which he or she is seeking support. Some organizations and agencies have funding programs that are national in scope. Many states, cities, and local school districts also have either public or private foundations that support worthy projects. Some businesses will offer grants of either cash or products for sports medicine–related projects (Margolin, 1983). Most universities have an office dedicated to assisting their employees identify potential sources of external funding for specific projects.

Reasons Grant Proposals Fail

Anyone who has ever written a grant proposal knows that the proposal may be rejected. There are many reasons why grant proposals are not funded (Locke, Spirduso, and Silverman, 1993). If the application is late or incomplete it will probably be rejected. Similarly, if the proposal is not written to the granting agency's specifications, or if it is poorly written, it may be rejected. Even well-written proposals that are submitted on time may be denied if the project is of insufficient importance in advancing the field. If the budget is unrealistic or the proposed methods are inappropriate the granting agency is unlikely to fund the request. Finally, the grant application may fail if the project is of a low priority for the granting agency.

CAPITAL EQUIPMENT—BUY OR LEASE?

Once a decision has been made to acquire an expensive piece of equipment, the athletic trainer and the organization's business manager must decide whether to purchase the equipment or lease it. Many expensive rehabilitation devices and other therapeutic modalities can be leased rather than purchased. Obviously, there are advantages and disadvantages to both methods. The primary advantage of purchasing over leasing is cost. This is especially true if the equipment is being purchased outright as opposed to being financed. The other advantage of purchasing is that the sports medicine program owns the equipment. This can become a disadvantage, however, if the equipment is based on high technology that becomes obsolete before the equipment is fully depreciated (Kess & Westlin, 1987). One of the advantages of leasing is that it allows an institution to use its capital in other ways than encumbering large amounts in equipment purchases. There can also be some tax advantages for sports medicine clinics when they lease their equipment as opposed to buying it.

Relative Merits of Leasing

Advantages	Disadvantages
• Possible tax advantages	• Higher overall costs
• Decreased risk of obsolescence	• No ownership
• Lower initial costs	• Higher effective interest rate than traditional financing

PURCHASING SERVICES

Purchasing services is different in several ways from purchasing supplies or equipment. The first, and most obvious, difference is that the quality of a service can be more difficult to assess than that of a product.

For example, assume that a large university sports medicine program contracts with a local radiology clinic for all its X-ray, MRI, CT, and nuclear medicine needs. It will probably be more difficult for the athletic trainers at that university to determine the quality of these diagnostic services than it would be, for example, for them to determine the quality of the athletic tape they purchase. This is true, in part, because they are forced to rely on the professional judgment of another person in the case of the radiology services. They don't have the expertise, in this example, to make an informed judgment on the quality of every aspect of the service. This problem can be compounded if there is only one radiology service available in the community. The athletic trainers cannot compare the service they receive from one radiology practice with what another might be able to offer. Athletic tape, on the other hand, is easier to evaluate. Many different brands and styles are available from many different vendors. It is a straightforward exercise to determine which brand is best for the money.

Nevertheless, there are methods athletic trainers can employ to take some of the uncertainty out of purchasing services:

• *Try to get the service free of charge.* Most team physicians volunteer their time. Many ambulance companies are willing to park at the site of an athletic contest free of charge. Some service providers are willing to donate their time in exchange for an advertisement in the game program.

- *If you can't get the service for free, try to employ cost sharing whenever possible.* For example, your team physician might not be willing to see injured athletes in his office for free, but he might be willing to accept only what the athlete's insurance will pay.

- *When more than one provider is available for a particular service, be sure to evaluate, in advance, what each is willing to provide and at what price.* For example, if there are two ambulance services in your community, speak with each to find out how much they charge for event standby and transport. Find out which hospitals they are willing to transport patients to. Ask them about their mean response time. Will they participate in your emergency-plan drills?

- *Investigate the service provider's reputation with other athletic trainers.* If you are searching for an orthopedic surgeon to service your athletes, ask other athletic trainers whom they use and why.

- *Develop a contract or memorandum of understanding that specifies your expectations of the service provider.* This can help improve communication between the sports medicine program and the service provider and prevent problems in the future. The contract should specify a period of time, usually no more than two years, for which the contract will be in effect.

- *Develop a database for each service provider.* How many injured or ill athletes did your team physician see last year? How long do your athletes have to wait to be seen by the orthopedic consultant? What is the rate of false-positive drug screens reported by the laboratory you employ? Only by answering these kind of questions and comparing those answers with the cost of retaining the services of these providers will you be able to judge the value of this aspect of your program.

INVENTORY MANAGEMENT

Athletic trainers have a financial responsibility to maintain control over the inventory of sports medicine equipment and supplies. This can usually be accomplished by inventorying regularly, centralizing storage of supplies, automating the inventory process, restricting access to storage areas, and implementing reminder systems.

inventory management
The process of controlling equipment and supply stocks so that services can be provided without interruption while the use of institutional resources is maximized.

The U.S. Small Business Administration publication *Business Basics: Inventory Management* (1980) defines **inventory management** as follows:

- *Acquiring an adequate supply and variety of inventory to meet production and sales needs*

- *Providing safety stocks to meet unexpected demand or delays in inventory replenishment*

- *Investing in inventory wisely so that excessive capital is not tied up, excessive space is not required, and unnecessary borrowing and interest expense is not required*

- *Maintaining accurate and up-to-date records to help identify and prevent shortages and to serve as a database for decisions* (pp. 2–3)

Inventory management is one of the most important aspects of increased efficiency in a sports medicine program. It is equally important for large and small operations. Large operations, such as professional athletic teams and universities with NCAA Division I football programs, have big investments in sports medicine supplies that should be managed wisely and prudently. Larger programs are more likely to operate multiple facilities, making the control and distribution of sports medicine supplies more difficult and requiring more attention to inventory techniques.

Inventory control is important for small programs as well, because errors in inventory and supply management result in more financial hardship for programs with smaller budgets. Another problem faced by athletic trainers in smaller programs is that coaches, athletic administrators, and physical education teachers often have access to the athletic training room and the sports medicine supplies in it.

The following suggestions should help athletic trainers improve their ability to track the location and rate of use of their supplies.

• **Inventory regularly.** Compile a complete inventory of expendable supplies at least once a month. Institutions that operate multiple athletic training rooms should inventory the stock in each facility every week. The inventory reports for these satellites should be compiled in the primary training room and used to develop the monthly inventory report.

• **Centralize storage.** Wherever possible, centralize the storage of sports medicine supplies to make them easier to manage. If supplies need to be stockpiled in several locations, send the smallest amount that will suffice for a reasonable time period, preferably one week. This system requires athletic trainers to be more attentive to inventory levels and helps prevent sudden or unexpected shortages.

• **Automate the inventory process.** Develop and implement a continuous monitoring system that allows for a quick check of inventory levels at any time. One effective method utilizes a computerized inventory record based on standard spreadsheet software. When supplies are removed from the central storage site, the athletic trainer fills out a small form indicating the date, type, and amount of supply being taken and the amount remaining after the withdrawal (see figure 4.11). At the end of each day, a student athletic trainer or secretary enters the information on the forms into the computer record. This allows the athletic trainer to track the status of the inventory on a daily basis.

• **Restrict access.** Unauthorized access to the athletic training room and the supply room where sports medicine supplies are kept is the primary cause of inventory control breakdown. Institutions should develop policies and procedures that specify who has access to the sports medicine facility and under what circumstances. I strongly recommend that as few people as possible have keys to the facility—access

Figure 4.11
Sample inventory control form.

Sports Medicine Supply Checkout Form

Date _____

Supply type _____

Quantity _____

Supply destination _____

Amount remaining in storage _____

Person taking the supplies _____

Person recording the withdrawal into the computer _____

should be limited to only those persons who are responsible for and have a legitimate need to use it. Policies should clearly state the responsibilities of anyone issued keys to the facility.

• **Keep a reminder system.** Each type of supply should be marked with a sign that reads "Reorder when *X* amount remains" to remind athletic trainers to reorder supplies when they reach a critically low level.

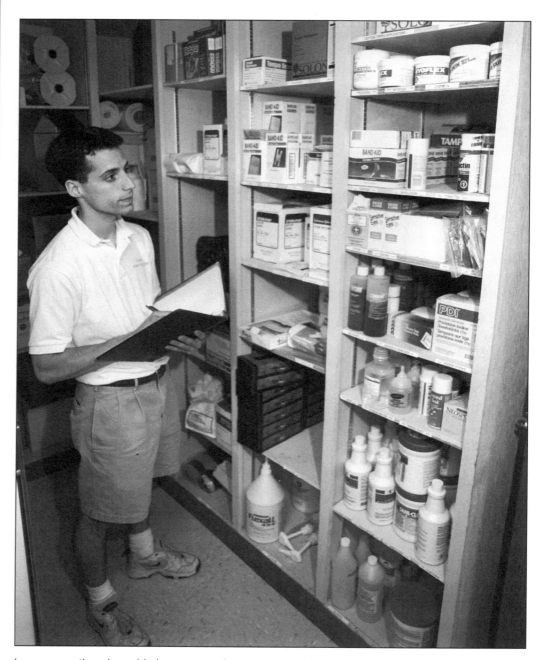

Large operations have big investments in sports medicine supplies that should be managed wisely and prudently. It is important to take inventory on a regular basis.

APPLICATIONS TO ATHLETIC TRAINING: THEORY INTO PRACTICE

Apply the concepts discussed in this chapter to the following two case studies to help you prepare for situations you might face in actual practice. The questions at the end of the studies are open ended—many possible correct solutions exist.

Case Study 1

Tammy Jenkins had just arrived at Los Ranchos College after being appointed the school's first certified athletic trainer. It was mid-June and Tammy knew she had quite a bit to do to get ready for the arrival of the fall sports athletes in August. She decided to start by approaching the athletic director.

"Coach," Tammy began, "I need to order the sports medicine supplies as soon as possible if we expect to be ready to go in August. I need to know a few things. First, how much money do I have to work with? Second, are there any specific purchasing procedures I need to follow? I'd really like to get busy with this today if I could."

The athletic director informed Tammy that she didn't have a specific budget for sports medicine supplies. In the past, sports medicine supplies were paid for out of the general athletics budget, which he controlled. "You just put your list together and I'll take a look at it," he told her. "Oh, I almost forgot," the athletic director continued, "I wanted to make sure we at least had the tape here in time, so I went ahead and ordered it. It should be delivered some time in July."

Although Tammy was uncomfortable about not having a specific budget, she knew she wouldn't be able to change everything right away. She spent the rest of the day compiling an inventory of the supplies on hand. That evening she put together a list of the supplies she thought she would need to get through the first year, along with an estimate of each item's cost.

When she presented it to the athletic director the next day, he told her she would need to cut the proposal by 25%. "I think this list is fairly modest," Tammy said. "I'm not sure I can cut that much out of it." After further discussion, the athletic director told Tammy that the cost of the tape, when added to the total cost of her supply list, was just more than he could afford. When Tammy asked how much he had paid for the tape, she was astonished to find out that it was 100% higher than the price she paid at the school where she used to work. "Where did you order the tape from?" asked Tammy. "We get all our supplies from Acme Sporting Goods downtown. We always have. Anything you need, just call them and they'll take good care of you. The owner is a big supporter of the college," replied the athletic director. Tammy suddenly realized that she had her work cut out for her!

Questions for Analysis

1. What budgeting system does the Los Ranchos College sports medicine program use? Is it optimal for the conditions? What system would you implement? Why?

2. Why was Tammy so distressed when she found out how the tape had been purchased? What is the likely effect of this purchasing system on Tammy's program? How should the purchasing system be altered?

3. If Tammy changed from direct purchasing at Acme Sporting Goods to a system of competitive bidding, what would be the likely result?

4. What can Tammy do to lower her costs for sports medicine supplies while maintaining the supportive relationship the college enjoys with the owner of Acme Sporting Goods?

5. If you were in Tammy's position, would you have taken the same approach to purchasing supplies? If not, what would you have done differently? Why?

Case Study 2

Diversified Physical Therapy Services is a large rehabilitation services corporation that operates a string of clinics in a 10-county area in eastern Iowa. In addition to the clinics, DPTS also supplies rehabilitation professionals to 12 hospitals. DPTS recently acquired contracts at 15 high schools to supply sports medicine services. The contracts provide an athletic trainer for each school for 1000 hours per year. As an additional service, DPTS purchases all the sports medicine supplies for the schools up to a maximum of $2,500 per school.

At a recent meeting of the DPTS partners, one of the owners expressed concern over the plan to provide the schools with sports medicine supplies. Although he liked the idea in general, he was concerned about waste and cost-effectiveness. He also pointed out to the other partners that if each school used less than the $2,500 allotment, the company would be coming out ahead.

The DPTS partners decided to create a central storage site for all 15 high schools. The athletic trainers would be allowed to take what they needed for a two-week period. When those supplies were exhausted, they would have to come to the central storage site, which was housed in a clinic in the geographic center of the schools' service area, and check out enough for another two weeks. The business manager in the clinic where the supplies were stored would be responsible for auditing supply requisitions to ensure that each school remained below the $2,500 limit.

Questions For Analysis

1. What are the strengths of the central supply plan adopted by DPTS? What are the weaknesses?

2. What alternatives are there to the central supply plan? Would they be superior? If so, why?

3. What are the strengths and weaknesses of the plan to provide up to $2,500 in supplies to each school? Is this a service that most schools would want? Why or why not?

SUMMARY

1. *Understand the different kinds of budgeting processes and apply them to an athletic training setting.*

   A budget is a plan for the coordination of resources and expenditures. It helps ensure that needed services are delivered effectively and on time and that financial resources are expended in accordance with the institutional mission. There are at least six different types of budgeting systems: zero-based, fixed, variable, lump-sum, line-item, and performance. Each can be used in either a spending ceiling (or incremental) or spending reduction mode. Careful consideration of which funds will support the various activities of the sports medicine program enhances budget development. Budgeting for the first year of the sports medicine program is the most difficult because of a lack of previous spending patterns. Budgeting for capital improvements is more difficult than for consumable supplies because of the expense involved. Budget evaluation is an important but often neglected activity that will help athletic trainers make more informed decisions on how to expend program resources.

2. *Coordinate the purchasing of athletic training equipment, supplies, and services so as to maximize the use of program funds.*

   Purchasing is the process of budget implementation. The six most common steps in the purchase of sports medicine supplies include request for quotation, negotiation, requisition, purchase order, receiving, and accounts payable. Athletic trainers should attempt to negotiate with vendors over price, supply, quality, shipping, and technical support. Alternatives to purchasing via bidding include pooled buying consortia and the use of alumni and booster organizations. Athletic trainers should consider the relative merits of leasing over buying when shopping for expensive capital equipment.

3. *Manage an athletic training program's inventory of equipment and supplies.*

   Inventory management is an important aspect of administration for athletic trainers. Mistakes in inventory management can have drastic consequences for both large and small programs. Athletic trainers should be aware at all times of the status of their supply inventory so they are able to deliver sports medicine services in a timely manner.

CHAPTER FIVE

Where Athletic Trainers Work: Facility Design and Planning

OBJECTIVES

After reading this chapter, you should be able to do the following:

1. Understand and defend the importance of the design phase in planning and constructing new sports medicine facilities.

2. Understand the facility design and construction process in sports medicine settings.

3. Understand the common design elements found in a well-planned sports medicine facility.

4. Describe the sports medicine facility in terms of its specialized function areas.

After meeting with the university president, the whole staff was excited about beginning the planning for a new athletic building. The president informed everyone that the board of trustees had approved the project. The athletic director, the chair of the physical education department, and the vice president for finance were appointed to the planning committee for the new building. After the meeting, the athletic director asked Kelly McCarthy, the director of sports medicine, to submit his ideas for the sports medicine facility in the new complex. Although Kelly was enthusiastic about the prospect of a new facility, he was a little nervous about having to design the new sports medicine center because he had never done anything like this before.

Kelly spent a few weeks toying with some ideas for the new sports medicine center before he finally drew a rough sketch and submitted it to the athletic director. The athletic director thanked him and filed the sketch away in a drawer labeled "New Building." Kelly didn't hear from the athletic director about the new sports medicine center again, so he assumed his ideas had been accepted.

Six months later construction began. Four months after the groundbreaking, Kelly and the rest of the athletic department staff were given a "hard-hat tour" of the site to view the progress on the project. When they reached the area that was to contain the new sports medicine facility, Kelly was astonished at how small it seemed in comparison to the sketch he had submitted. When he asked the construction manager about its size, he was told that the planning committee had had to shave off a few feet to accommodate the conference and media area in the adjacent basketball coaches' dressing room. Kelly was assured that the sports medicine facility would look much bigger after the "finish work" was completed.

When the building finally opened, Kelly and his staff moved into a sports medicine facility that, although brighter and newer than the old facility had been, was neither bigger nor more functional. He had essentially traded one undersized facility for another.

No architecture is so haughty as that which is simple.

John Ruskin

Kelly McCarthy's experience with planning a new athletic building is common among athletic trainers. The opportunity to be involved in the planning, design, and construction of a sports medicine facility usually comes only once during the careers of most athletic trainers, who typically have little or no experience in facility planning. Most buildings are designed and constructed to provide service for decades, so decisions made during the planning, design, and construction phase of the sports medicine facility are, for all practical purposes, permanent. Hence, it is understandable but very unfortunate when expensive and uncorrectable mistakes are made. This chapter will help athletic trainers understand the basic processes of planning, designing, and constructing a sports medicine center.

CONCEPTUAL DEVELOPMENT

The most important phase in constructing a new sports medicine center is developing an appropriate concept for its design. Whether the facility is intended to serve a school or a professional or private sports medicine clinic, the conceptual development process is essentially the same despite the important differences in layout and funding strategy between these facilities.

The design process is a critical time for athletic trainers to influence the final form of the sports medicine facility. Elements of the process include needs assessment, institutional approval, selecting a construction process, selecting an architect, developing schematics, securing funding, bidding construction, bid analysis, and beginning and monitoring construction.

At least two arguments support paying careful attention to the conceptual development of the design of the sports medicine center. First, this is the only stage of the project that involves review by those people who will actually use the facility. After the project has begun, there will be many reviews, but they will primarily be carried out by construction professionals and municipal employees such as plumbing and electrical inspectors. The athletic trainer is empowered during the design phase of a facility construction project.

In the opening scenario, Kelly McCarthy made a poor decision by assuming that because he did not receive any feedback from the planning committee his recommendations would be implemented as submitted. Obviously, Kelly should have checked often to be sure that his ideas were being implemented. The construction of a new building is a political act that involves making choices about how limited resources will be used. The time for athletic trainers to exercise their influence is during the design phase.

The second argument for paying attention to design development relates to permanency and cost. Buildings are intended to last a very long time. Once the foundation is poured and bricks and mortar are in place, changes based on new thinking about the way the sports medicine facility should be designed become very expensive to implement. Although the owners of private sports medicine clinics can always sell the building in the future if they become dissatisfied with its design, school and university officials generally do not have this option, because most campus-based sports medicine centers are part of large, multipurpose buildings.

THE DESIGN PROCESS

Most athletic trainers will never be involved in the selection of an architect. As mentioned before, however, many will be responsible at some point in their careers for input into the design of new sports medicine centers. Understanding the processes normally used by institutions during the design and construction phases of a new building can help athletic trainers to avoid the kinds of mistakes made by Kelly McCarthy in the opening case. The steps described in the following paragraphs are not the only way to design, plan, and construct a new facility. They do represent, however, the most common elements of the construction process.

Phases of Design and Construction of a Sports Medicine Center

1. Conduct a needs assessment.
2. Seek approval for the project.
3. Select a construction process model.
4. Select an architect.
5. Develop schematics.
6. Secure the required funding.
7. Bid the construction.
8. Analyze bids and take action.
9. Begin construction.
10. Monitor construction.

The Planning Committee

*planning committee
A group of institutional employees who work with an architect to develop the design of a building.*

The **planning committee** is a group of individuals appointed to work with the architect to develop the design of a new building. Planning committees should include people representing the various activities that will take place in the building. Fletcher and Ranck (1991) suggest that the members of the planning committee be appointed by the chief executive officer of the institution and include employees who will be responsible for operating, maintaining, and using the building. They also recommend that in school and university settings at least one person from administration, the business office, and the physical plant be assigned to the planning committee.

primary decision makers Institutional members who have formal authority over large units or sub-units of an organization.

secondary decision makers Professional staff members primarily responsible for delivering a program within an organization.

definers People who use or receive the services of a program.

program statement A document, prepared by the users, the architect, or both, that specifies the anticipated space requirements based on known work patterns provided by the users.

Theunissen (1978) suggests that the most appropriate person to act as chair of the planning committee is the person who leads the department or discipline most responsible for the use of the new facility. In many, if not most, cases this person will not be an athletic trainer. Hence, athletic trainers must effectively communicate their needs so they can be incorporated into the overall design.

The planning committee should reflect a balance between primary decision makers, secondary decision makers, and definers (Dougherty & Bonanno, 1985). Among the **primary decision makers** are institutional members with formal authority over large units or sub-units of an organization—the people in a position to see "the big picture." **Secondary decision makers** are typically professional staff members who deliver a program. In a school sports medicine setting, they include athletic trainers, team physicians, and selected faculty members. **Definers** are the people who will actually use the facility. In a sports medicine setting, definers would be patients, students, and athletes. Athletic trainers from other institutions might also act as definers by giving advice and asking questions that might not have occurred to the primary and secondary decision makers.

Step 1: Conduct a Needs Assessment

The first step in designing a new sports medicine facility is a comprehensive assessment of future program needs. Information from the needs assessment (see chapter 4, pp. 111-112), combined with a statement of present operating status, is called the **program statement.** The program statement is an important document, because it helps the architect determine space requirements for the new facility (Dibner, 1982). The process of needs assessment might seem tedious, but without it a competent job of planning for future space needs cannot be accomplished. One of the many mistakes Kelly McCarthy made in the opening case was that he sketched out a design for the new sports medicine center without taking into account future growth patterns. The needs assessment is usually conducted at the departmental or program level and involves asking and answering a series of questions (see table 5.1). If the administrator of a sports medicine program has been doing a good job of programmatic self-study, the needs assessment will be much easier to complete (see figure 2.10 on p. 49).

Step 2: Seek Approval for the Project

Once the needs assessment has been completed, assuming it justifies the need for a new sports medicine facility, the people with financial control of the institution must be convinced that the project is necessary. This step is important whether the sports medicine program is in a school, professional, or private clinic setting. Every organi-

Table 5.1 Sports Medicine Facility Needs Assessment Concerns

Question	Where to look for answers
What is the present clinic caseload? How is it likely to change?	Annual reports, interviews with staff and administrators
Is the present facility adequate? Why or why not?	Building codes, national design standards, literature review, peer consultation
Is the present facility suitable for implementing the strategic plan?	Program and institutional facility strategic plans
Which program problems are related to facilities?	Critical incident reports, interviews with staff, accreditation reports

zation has a person or a group of people who must ultimately decide whether to spend the vast sums required for new construction. An athletic trainer must be willing to document the need for such facilities in great detail. Even after such documentation is presented, however, the athletic trainer should not be too disappointed if it takes months, or more realistically, years for such a project to be approved.

Step 3: Select a Construction Process Model

lump-sum bidding A process whereby general contractors provide cost quotations for the right to construct or renovate a building.

There are three common ways to proceed when constructing new facilities. **Lump-sum bidding** is the most traditional method, often used for governmental units like public schools and colleges. In lump-sum bidding, the architect submits schematic drawings to several general contractors. The contractors study the plans and quote a cost based on the instructions provided by the architect. Because some contractors might intentionally underbid a project to secure a contract, it is wise to screen the contractors in advance and send bids only to those with proven records. The importance of this step can't be overemphasized. The temptation to simply accept the lowest bid without regard for the reputation of the contractor is very powerful. The differences in the bids can amount to many thousands of dollars. This is money you might have to eventually spend, however, if the workmanship is shoddy or if corners have been cut. It is prudent to visit at least one building constructed by each of the contractors to determine the quality of their work. Be sure to spend some time alone with the owners so you will feel free to ask questions about the experiences they had with the contractor. Although negative responses to some of the following questions would not necessarily reflect on the contractor's skill, it would be wise to find out if

- the contractor worked well with the architect,
- the project was completed on time,
- the project stayed within the budget,
- all the building systems functioned properly when the project was finished,
- the construction was of high quality,
- the contractor was willing to require subcontractors to correct any mistakes,
- the owners would make any changes to the building if given the chance, and
- the owners would hire this contractor again.

Advantages and Disadvantages of Lump-Sum Bidding

Advantages	Disadvantages
• Results in lowest possible price	• Contractors might underbid
• Ensures fairness	• Less control for owner
• Complies with state and federal statutes	• Contractor might cut corners

construction management A method that involves the general contractor as part of the design team from the beginning of the building process.

Another construction model that may be used is termed **construction management**. The construction-management approach utilizes the general contractor as part of the design team; that is, the contractor is on board from the beginning of the project, rather than coming in near the end of the design phase. The construction manager can then advise on building materials, schedules, cost analysis, and necessary subcontractors. A drawback to using the construction-management approach is the manager's fee, which can approach 5% of the total project cost. In addition, the manager will not exert direct authority over the work of the subcontractors, because the subcontractors are hired by the owner (Snider, 1982).

Advantages and Disadvantages of Construction Management

Advantages
- Construction manager is part of design team
- More advice on materials, costs, and schedules

Disadvantages
- Construction manager's fee
- No direct control over subcontractors

design/build A method that uses only one firm to both design and construct a new building.

The third construction process method is known as **design/build.** This system uses only one firm to both design and build a sports medicine center. As with the other construction models, there are advantages and disadvantages to the design/build concept. The obvious advantage is that the owners have only one firm with which to communicate. They can take any problems that arise to a single source for redress, allowing for more rapid, and potentially cost-saving, approaches to solving problems that arise during the construction phase of the project.

The streamlined approach used in design/build is also its weakness, however. It involves fewer checks and balances among the various firms normally involved in a construction project. The integrity of the entire project rests on the abilities of one firm—specifically on the abilities of a few people in one firm. This is a good reason to screen design/build proposals even more carefully than a more traditional construction process model.

Advantages and Disadvantages of Design/Build

Advantages
- Easier communication
- Ability to "fast track" problems

Disadvantages
- Fewer checks and balances
- Greatest potential for major problems

Step 4: Select an Architect

An architect is retained by the owner of a clinic or the chief executive officer of an institution to create building designs. In addition, the architect should be available to provide advice and guidance from the very beginning of a project until the keys to the new facility are handed over to the users. Although the selection of an architect is listed as the fourth step in this text, it frequently comes earlier in the process. In fact, an architect can help with many of the previous steps.

Several methods can be used for selecting an architect (Dibner, 1982). The first and easiest way is to contract with a firm recommended by friends or colleagues. For obvious reasons, this might not serve a sports medicine program well. A better method is to develop a list of architectural firms with a variety of attributes—big and small, local and distant, and so on. Interview each firm to determine whether it would be suitable for and interested in taking on the project. A site visit to at least one project each firm has completed is recommended. A third method for selecting an architect is to commission a design competition. This method is typically used only on very large projects, because it is costly in terms of money and time.

> ### Three Methods for Selecting an Architect
>
> 1. Ask friends and colleagues.
> 2. Screen several architectural firms.
> 3. Commission a design competition.

Whichever method is used, a good match between the client and the architect must be obtained. Forseth (1986) recommends that architects for sports medicine facilities be selected on the basis of their openness to suggestions and their previous experience in designing similar facilities. *Athletic Business* (Directory of Architects, 1998) magazine publishes a directory of architects that have experience in designing athletic facilities. Many of these architects have designed sports medicine facilities as a part of these larger projects.

Step 5: Develop Schematics

schematic drawings
A graphic representation, derived from the program statement, that illustrates the relationships among the principal functions of a building.

Once the program statement mentioned previously has been developed, the architect will develop **schematic drawings** that describe the relationships among the principal functions of the sports medicine center. One of Kelly McCarthy's errors in the opening case was that he never met with the architect to develop the schematic drawings that were eventually submitted. Had he done so, the architect probably would have been able to help him think in detail about traffic patterns and space requirements—two of the major elements that should be addressed in the schematic drawings.

Determining Space Needs

Several authors have suggested methods to help athletic trainers determine how much space will be needed when planning for a new sports medicine center. Penman (1977) has suggested that the minimum amount of space required for a "barebones" athletic training room stocked with only one treatment table, one taping table, some counter space and miscellaneous equipment is 300 sq ft. Secor (1984) has expanded on Penman's idea by creating a formula athletic trainers can use to plan for space requirements based on the number of athletes and other physically active patients they expect to serve during peak caseloads:

$$\text{(Number of patients at peak / 20 per table per day)} \times 100 \text{ sq ft}$$
$$= \text{Total square footage}$$

Although the base estimate of 100 sq ft per treatment and taping table provides a useful starting point for determining space needs, athletic trainers charged with the design of a new sports medicine center must take into account that varied functions will take place in the sports medicine center and each of these functions will have different space requirements.

Another factor that influences the overall space requirements of a sports medicine center is the proportion of work that will be done in each of the various sections. The type of client served by the sports medicine center will largely determine this factor. For example, a hospital-based sports medicine center will probably dedicate a greater proportion of its space to rehabilitation. In contrast, the typical college and high school sports medicine facility requires a larger taping and bandaging section than private or hospital-based sports medicine clinics. Finally, the anticipated growth of the program must be factored into the size estimates for the schematic drawings (Cohen & Cohen, 1979). Growth is one of the most difficult forecasts to make, but it is very important—especially considering the exploding demand for access to sports medicine services.

In summary, the following factors influence the space requirements of a sports medicine facility:

- Number of clients to be served
- Type of clients to be served
- Amount and kinds of equipment needed
- Number and qualifications of staff
- Projected growth of the program

Traffic Patterns

traffic patterns
The anticipated flow of people from one area of a building to another.

When working with the architect to develop the schematic drawings, it is essential to determine anticipated **traffic patterns** based on the relationship of the subfunctions of the sports medicine center to each other. This is a crucial step in the design phase. Attractive, functional sports medicine facilities are characterized by smooth traffic flow among all of the different parts of the facility. If the actual traffic patterns that develop once the facility is built are not anticipated at this stage, the result is likely to be a sports medicine center that seems noisy, congested, crowded, or all three. Muther and Wheeler (1973) suggest that the best way to ensure smooth traffic flow is to identify each of the subfunctions of the sports medicine center and to justify the space they will occupy by placing them on a **relationship chart** (see figure 5.1). This is a task that is usually completed by the architect in consultation with the athletic trainer. The relationship chart can seem a bit confusing at first glance, but it's actually quite simple. The chart is constructed so that the row for each special area intersects the rows for all of the other areas. The athletic trainer's task is to decide how close each area should be to any other area and to justify her reasoning for each decision. For example, it is generally undesirable for the hydrotherapy area to be in proximity to the storage area, because moisture could easily damage sports medicine supplies that require a cool, dry environment for maximum shelf life. The intersection of the rows for these two areas would be coded with an "X" and a "7," indicating that these areas should be kept apart for climate control purposes. Conversely, the hydrotherapy area should be close to the office so patients can be directly observed at all times. The intersection of these two rows would be coded with an "A" and a "1." Once charted, the physical relationship of subfunctions to each other become less conceptual and more concrete.

relationship chart
A table used to justify the placement of various rooms within a building.

Once the space relationships have been established, coded, and justified on the relationship chart, the next step is constructing a **bubble diagram**. The bubble diagram illustrates the spatial relationships among the subfunctions of a sports medicine center based on the "closeness" factors established in the relationship chart. Although the bubble diagram is by no means a floor plan, it is the first step toward being able to visually understand how all the parts of the sports medicine center will be laid out (see figure 5.2).

bubble diagram
An abstract, graphic representation of the relationship of one function of a building to another based on the "closeness" factors established by the relationship chart.

Step 6: Secure the Required Funding

Obviously, all construction projects require a source of funding. A wide variety of funding options are available for sports medicine center construction depending on the type of institution. Private sports medicine clinics generally have fewer options, however, than public-sector institutions like high schools, colleges, and universities. Even professional athletic teams have greater flexibility in financing sports medicine facilities than private clinics do, because many of the stadiums that house them are constructed at least in part with public tax dollars. The owners of most private sports medicine clinics will be forced to secure loans from a bank for new construction.

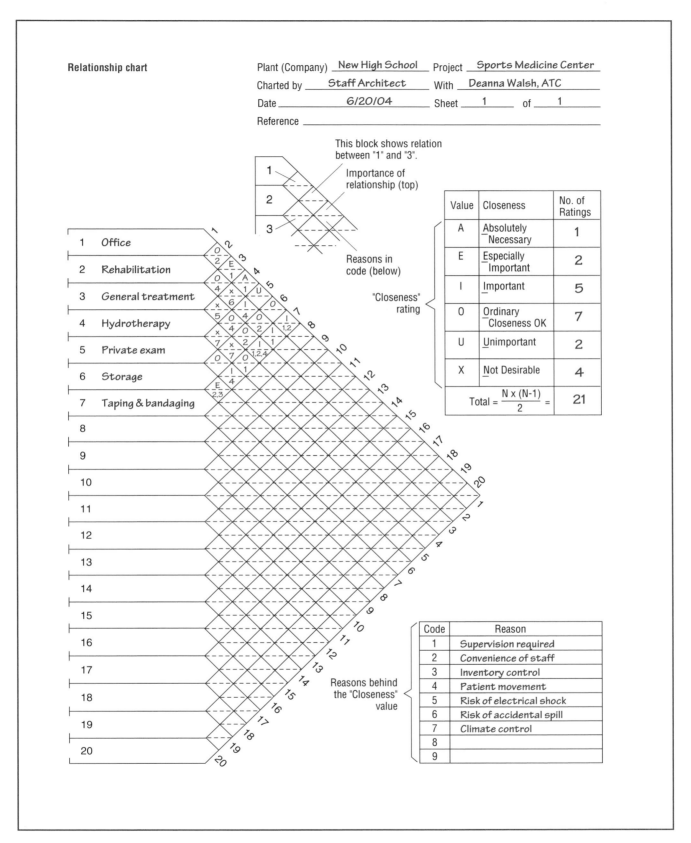

Figure 5.1 Sample relationship chart used to justify the placement of various spaces in a sports medicine facility.

Adapted from Muther and Wheeler 1977.

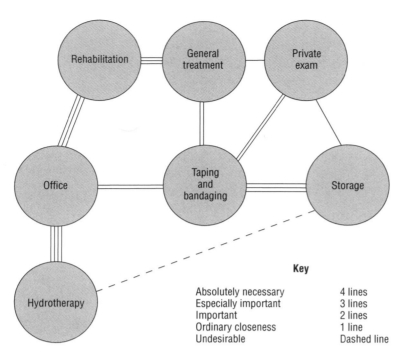

I Figure 5.2 Bubble diagram showing accessibility needs within a sports medicine facility.

Key

Absolutely necessary	4 lines
Especially important	3 lines
Important	2 lines
Ordinary closeness	1 line
Undesirable	Dashed line

Athletic trainers who approach a financial institution for a loan should remember that banks are more likely to make loans for the construction of multipurpose buildings. For example, the athletic trainer who wishes to build a sports medicine clinic as part of a larger medical arts building will probably have a better chance of securing a loan than the person who wants to build a health club that offers sports medicine services. The medical arts building can be used for many purposes, whereas the health club would probably require extensive remodeling prior to resale should the bank need to foreclose. In general, medical practitioners are perceived by bankers to be good risks.

At least two things are usually required of an athletic trainer who applies for a **commercial loan** from a bank for new construction of a private sports medicine facility: an assignment of life insurance (this protects the bank against loss in the event the athletic trainer dies before paying off the debt) and a **business plan.** The business plan is essential, because it contains information the bank will need to project whether the clinic is likely to succeed or not. A business plan for a sports medicine clinic would include the following items:

- A statement of the activities the clinic will engage in
- A **market analysis** detailing the clinic's competitive advantages, analysis of the competition, pricing structure, and marketing plan
- The credentials of the principal owners and operators of the clinic
- Historical and projected financial statements of both cash flow and income
- A breakdown of costs associated with the project based on the schematics developed by the architect
- The amount of personal equity being committed by the athletic trainer
- The amount of the loan being requested

Sports medicine facilities in the public sector, including private educational institutions that receive state and federal assistance, can be funded in at least three ways other than by a commercial loan.

Methods for Funding Public-Sector Sports Medicine Facilities

- Capital campaigns
- Bond sales
- Borrowing from endowment
- Commercial loans

One of the most common fund-raising methods is the **capital campaign.** A capital campaign is a major institutional response to several needs intended to be remedied over three to five years. Capital campaigns are usually authorized and directed

commercial loan
An amount of money, borrowed from a lending institution, for the purpose of establishing, improving, or maintaining a business.

business plan
Used by commercial loan officers to assess the viability of a business. Includes a written description of the activities the business will engage in, a market analysis, historical and projected financial statements, and other associated information.

market analysis
Includes a written description of the competitive advantages of a business, analysis of the competition, pricing structure, and marketing plan.

capital campaign
A program, usually of fixed length, designed to raise funds for program creation, development, and improvement.

by the persons at the very top of the institutional hierarchy. They are intended to secure pledges of financial support from a broad institutional constituency including alumni, faculty and staff, foundations, affiliated institutions such as churches, and friends. Funds for a new sports medicine center will almost always be a small fraction of the overall goal for a capital campaign. Nevertheless, an athletic trainer might be heavily involved in helping secure pledges under the direction and supervision of the institutional development officer.

Another way public-sector institutions and some hospitals secure funding for the construction of sports medicine facilities is through the sale of **tax-exempt bonds.** The sale of such bonds is usually authorized either by public vote (as in the case of elementary and high school construction) or by a bonding authority established by the states. Bonds are usually sold in one of two ways: publicly, usually to friends of the institution, or privately to a bank or other financial institution as part of its investment portfolio. A common practice is for similar institutions to pool their projects and sell bonds together under one issue. This is a useful practice, because it lowers the overhead costs associated with conducting a bond issue.

The third common method institutions use to finance new sports medicine facilities is to borrow internally from their **endowments.** An institution's endowment is the sum of its assets in cash and investments. Institutions usually hesitate to borrow from endowments, because the interest earned from an endowment can account for a significant percentage of the annual operating budget. If the endowment is quite large, however, and the sports medicine building project is relatively modest in relation to it, this is probably the easiest method of financing such a project.

Step 7: Bid the Construction

If an athletic trainer is using the lump-sum bidding model, this is the time to bid the construction. Before the actual bids are sent to the contractors who will compete for the job, the architect will develop the **construction documents** (Dibner, 1982). The construction documents are highly detailed technical drawings that the contractors will need to determine a realistic estimate of construction costs. The construction documents are the drawings that will be used to guide construction of the new sports medicine center.

The architect will then prepare and send a packet of **bidding documents** to acceptable contractors. The bidding documents include an invitation to bid, the bid form, and special instructions from the architect. The bidders must submit their bids within a specified amount of time, and all bids are opened at the same time. Normally, administrators hire the contractor who submits the lowest bid. In many states, public institutions are required by law to allow all qualified contractors to bid for new construction projects. In addition, a certain percentage of the construction budget might have to be reserved for contractors of historically underrepresented minority groups.

Step 8: Analyze Bids and Take Action

Once the sealed bids have been opened, the planning team must carefully analyze each one. First, the athletic trainer–architect team must make sure that the information on the returned bids is consistent with the project as described in the bidding documents. If a contractor changes any item of the project, producing a lower bid, and the change goes unnoticed, legal problems could result. Another reason to carefully screen the bids is to ensure that there is some consistency in the costs quoted by the various contractors. If one contractor's quotation is significantly lower than all the others, the athletic trainer and architect should ask for an explanation. Obviously, the quality of the finished facility will suffer if the contractor cuts corners to secure the contract.

tax-exempt bonds Bonds authorized and sold by governmental agencies to provide funding for construction projects.

endowment That portion of an institution's assets in cash and investments not normally used for operational purposes.

construction documents The highly detailed technical drawings a contractor will use to determine building costs and to guide construction.

bidding documents The package of materials prepared by the architect and sent to contractors, including the invitation to bid, the bid form, and special bidding instructions.

If the returned bids exceed the available funding, four possible courses of action can be pursued (Biehle, 1982). The first is to delay the project while additional funding is raised. If it takes excessive time to raise the funds, the total project cost will probably rise as a result of inflation. The second option is to negotiate a lower price with the contractor. This almost always involves eliminating certain features that were part of the original design or using less-expensive building materials. The third option is to ask the architect to develop an alternative design. This is costly in terms of both time and money. Finally, the project can be abandoned. If this happens, the athletic trainer should realize that there are termination fees written into most architects' contracts in excess of the compensation the architect will be owed for the time and energy already spent on the project. In addition, the architect might retain the rights to the drawings. If the athletic trainer plans to use them for a future project, the right to do so should be negotiated prior to signing the architect's contract.

Step 9: Begin Construction

This step is fairly self-explanatory. Once the contractor's bid has been accepted, the architect works with the athletic trainer's (or the institution's) attorney to draw up the construction contract. The architect will have access to several standardized contract forms for this purpose.

Step 10: Monitor Construction

Several people play important monitoring roles during construction. The first is the **general contractor,** who is responsible for coordinating the work of the various **subcontractors** and for ensuring the quality of their workmanship. It is the architect, however, who represents the athletic trainer or the institution and ensures that the building is being constructed according to the standards developed by the architect. If the workmanship does not comply with the standards enumerated in the contract and construction documents, the architect has the authority to reject the work (Dibner, 1982).

The athletic trainer and the planning committee have important roles to play during the construction phase. They should be present on the job site as often as possible to make sure the design features agreed upon are being implemented. The frequent presence of the athletic trainer at the construction site can ensure that the "little details" are implemented as planned. The athletic trainer should know the sports medicine facility better than anyone else.

If the athletic trainer suspects that the contractor or subcontractor is not properly implementing the architect's design, she or he should quickly inquire into the situation. It is very important, however, that the athletic trainer address all concerns to the architect and not to the contractor or subcontractors. As the agent of the athletic trainer or the institution, the architect will investigate and mediate a solution to the problem.

general contractor
The company responsible for coordinating the actual construction of a building.

subcontractor   A company hired by the general contractor to complete a particular portion of the building project. The subcontractor's work is usually devoted to a particular skilled trade, such as plumbing, electrical work, or landscaping.

ELEMENTS OF SPORTS MEDICINE FACILITY DESIGN

In order to realize a fully functional space for a sports medicine program, an athletic trainer should plan for the following elements: size, location, ergonomics, electrical systems, plumbing systems, ventilation systems, lighting, and specialized function areas.

An athletic trainer must consider at least eight elements when working with an architect to design a new sports medicine facility: size, location, ergonomics, electrical systems, plumbing systems, ventilation systems, lighting, and specialized function areas (see figure 5.3). Size and space estimates have been discussed in the section on developing schematics. Now I'll address the other seven design elements.

LOCATION

A sports medicine center that is intended to serve the general population should be located near other health care providers. Patients will appreciate, for example, not

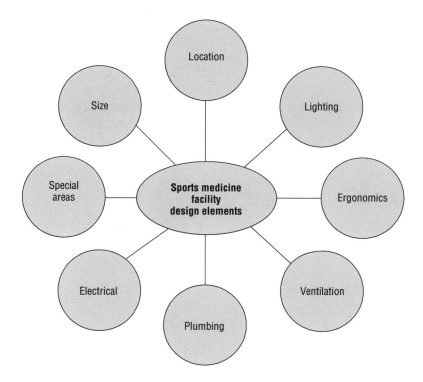

▌ **Figure 5.3**
Elements in the design of sports medicine facilities.

having to travel far for X-ray or laboratory services. And proximity to referring physicians is a practical feature. The ideal location for a private sports medicine clinic is in a medical office building that houses those other health services—physicians, laboratory, and X-ray.

Having athletic facilities nearby is useful for observing a rehabilitating patient's functional capacity in running or other sports skills. If the clinic sees a lot of student-athletes, a location close to the school makes travel convenient for students.

As mentioned earlier, school-based sports medicine centers for student-athletes are usually housed in large multipurpose athletic, physical education, or recreation buildings. The placement of the sports medicine center within the facility is an important decision. Most experts agree that it should be as close as possible to both the men's and women's locker rooms (Fahey, 1986). Although it has been suggested that each locker room have direct access to the sports medicine center, problems of security and privacy might intervene. Athletes and other physically active patients should not have to cross through another activity area to reach the sports medicine center.

Another consideration is the position of the sports medicine center relative to outside entrances. An injured athlete should have to walk or be carried through as few doors as possible—ideally, a door should lead directly from the outside playing fields into the sports medicine center. Wherever the center is located, it should have extra-wide doors that will accommodate two people assisting a nonambulating athlete. (Such wide doors will also be able to accommodate a stretcher, spine board, or gurney.)

In a multistory building, a ground-floor location is most accessible to clients who ambulate with difficulty. If the sports medicine center cannot be located on the ground floor, it should be close to an elevator.

Having an institution's facilities for health services and sports medicine services adjacent has several advantages. First, cooperation can be enhanced if athletic trainers and other health professionals work together daily. Second, placing these two facilities next to each other means that certain operations can be shared, often resulting in savings of time or money. For example, if health services and sports medicine services are adjacent, medical records can be stored in a single location (the health service file room). Assuming that procedures protecting student confidentiality are upheld, medical records are thus more conveniently available and more complete.

The referral process is also enhanced by proximity among facilities. A student-athlete who reports to the athletic trainer with an illness can be referred without delay to the health service (and the likelihood of compliance is increased). Likewise, if a student who is not an athlete comes to the health service with an orthopedic injury, the athletic training staff is readily available to be consulted. Perhaps the ultimate argument for this arrangement, however, is financial—costs can be lowered because facilities, supplies, and services need not be duplicated. If the health service contains private examination rooms, they don't have to be included in the sports medicine center. Secretarial services can be shared, as well as certain types of equipment and supplies, such as cast saws and suture kits. Having health services adjacent to the sports medicine center also eliminates the need for athletic trainers to store or dispense medications; this can more properly be handled by health service personnel.

Although this concept generally functions well on small campuses, larger schools might find it difficult to implement, because athletic facilities are typically located on the periphery of the campus, whereas student health services are more centrally located. But a combined facility should be considered whenever possible in light of the many advantages.

ERGONOMICS

Although ergonomic considerations in the design of a sports medicine facility are partially covered in other sections of this chapter (see the sections on lighting and ventilation, for example), there are a few ergonomic design issues that do not fit neatly into other sections and so are included here.

ergonomics
The scientific study of human work.

Ergonomics is the scientific study of human work. It is a multidisciplinary field that originated when engineers, anatomists, physiologists, psychologists, and health care professionals came together to design optimal working environments for military uses (Reilly, 1981). Ergonomics has a much wider application today and is considered essential in the design of products and work processes and environments, although it has been slow to catch on in health care environments (Scholey & Hair, 1989). It has been defined by Pheasant (1991, p. 4) as "the science of matching the job to the worker and the product to the user." The purpose of considering ergonomics in the design of a sports medicine center is so that athletic trainers can work more productively, safely, and comfortably. Not all the work that athletic trainers do is performed in the sports medicine facility, of course. Athletic trainers perform a wide variety of tasks requiring a sound ergonomic basis on the field, in the gym, and in the office. Athletic trainers employed in industrial settings are frequently called on to suggest workstation design changes based on ergonomic problems. This section is especially important for industrial settings. There are many ergonomic considerations that are beyond the scope of this text.

For more information on this topic, see chapter 1 (Athletic Training: The Profession and Its History) of Hillman's *Introduction to Athletic Training* in the Athletic Training Education Series.

One of the prime tenets of ergonomic design is that people, including athletic trainers, come in different shapes and sizes. It is important, therefore, in a new sports medicine facility to design spaces, furniture, and fixtures that are as adaptable as possible. Pheasant (1991) has identified four errors in design thinking that athletic trainers would do well to avoid as they plan their facilities.

Four Ergonomic Errors in Design Thinking

As you plan the design of the sports medicine facility, be sure to keep the following improper assumptions about ergonomic elements in mind.

1. This design works for me so it will work for everyone.
2. This design works well for the average person, so it will work well for everyone.
3. Because there is so much variability in the population, we can't worry about designing the facility for everyone—people will just have to adapt.
4. Style and appearance are more important than ergonomic function.

Tables

Treatment and taping tables typically come in one height, even though the stature of the athletic trainers using the tables is highly variable. Consider installing taping tables of several different heights. If a taping counter is planned, plan for three sections ranging in height from 32–40 inches. The ideal treatment table, from an ergonomic standpoint, would be adjustable so it could be raised or lowered depending on the task to be accomplished (just as a dentist's chair can be raised or lowered depending on the height of the patient and the procedure to be performed).

Shelves and Cupboards

Equipment should be stored on shelves or in cupboards that are easy to reach. It should not be stored on the floor where the athletic trainer will have to stoop to lift it. Some equipment can be hung on pegs fixed to the wall. Step stools should be available near the equipment storage area so short athletic trainers can access the equipment without having to reach too far overhead.

Stools

Stools whose height can be adjusted should be available at every treatment station so that athletic trainers can administer treatments in a sitting position if necessary. This is especially important when treatment tables are not adjustable—as most are not—and the athletic trainer is tall.

Carts and Dollies

Rolling carts, dollies, and laundry bins should be available so that equipment and supplies can be moved from one place to another with a minimum of effort.

ELECTRICAL SYSTEMS

Electrical system design is one of the few elements that, if improperly done, could cause injury or death. Three-pronged hospital grade plugs and electrical outlets (characterized by a green dot), along with circuit breakers, are useful in preventing damage to electrical equipment, but because electrical shock can cause severe burns or cardiac arrest (see figure 5.4), all electrical outlets in a sports medicine center should also be equipped with a **ground fault interrupter (gfi)**, designed to interrupt the flow of electricity if a surge of five milliamps or more is detected (Porter & Porter, 1981). Gfis can be installed either as part of the electrical outlet or as part of the circuit breaker, and they are required equipment in rooms in public and private buildings where water is present.

Another issue in electrical design is the location of electrical outlets. Secor (1984) recommends that electrical outlets be spaced every 4 ft throughout the facility. This spacing gives the athletic trainer the flexibility to move equipment as the program changes. In general, place electrical outlets at least 3 ft from the floor to keep power cords off the floor, which could be dangerous in the event of an accidental spill or flood, and to allow the athletic trainer to move therapeutic modalities more easily, especially if there is limited space between treatment tables. A limited number of

ground fault interrupter (gfi) A highly sensitive device designed to discontinue the flow of electricity in an electrical circuit during a power surge.

■ **Figure 5.4** Effects of 60-cycle electric current on human tissue.

Reprinted from *Journal of Athletic Training* 1981.

0–8 milliamps = Safe

8–100 milliamps = Painful

100–200 milliamps = Fibrillation

≥ 200 milliamps = Muscle contraction and tissue burns

modality outlets should be serviced by a single circuit so the probability of overload is reduced. The number will depend on the type and number of appliances that will be used simultaneously.

Many sports medicine centers, especially those located in hospitals, have designed treatment stations with pull cords that patients can use to shut off electrical power. This is especially useful when patients' electrical stimulation treatments become painful. Rather than wait for the athletic trainer to cross the room to adjust the dosage, the patient can simply pull the cord and stop the flow of electricity to the modality. Athletic trainers can also choose to place remote power switches for hydrotherapy units in their offices to prevent accidental shock. An extension of this concept would be to have a master switch in the athletic trainer's office for every outlet to which a therapeutic modality could be connected for rapid shut-off in the case of an emergency.

PLUMBING SYSTEMS

Placement of water outlets and drains is a very important consideration in the design of a sports medicine center. A mistake in the design of the plumbing system, which is usually contained inside walls and under floors, is likely to be among the most expensive to correct.

Like the electrical system, plumbing systems should be designed to be easily expandable. As a sports medicine program grows and changes, the need for water or drainage in different parts of the facility might change as well. Both hot and cold water outlets should be provided in every section of the sports medicine facility. Some of these outlets should drain into sinks and others should be free standing to fill hydrotherapy tubs. Floor drains should be placed at several strategic points around the facility. The floor should be sloped at least 1% toward each of these drains (Penman, 1977).

If the facility is to contain an ice machine, a separate cold water line and floor drain should be provided for it. Whenever possible, each hydrotherapy tank's built-in drain should be connected directly to a dedicated floor drain. The drain faucet of tanks that use a pump drain should be connected to a **standpipe drain** by a hose or similar device to prevent splashing. In every case, a hydrotherapy tank should have an overflow prevention drain.

A plumbing contractor will be able to offer a wide variety of fixtures. Most **plumbing fixtures** used in a sports medicine center can be relatively simple and inexpensive, but athletic trainers might find three exceptions desirable. The first is a **mixing valve**, which allows a more precise water temperature by combining hot and cold water and eliminates the need for separate controls. Mixing valves often have built-in thermometers and are especially useful for filling hydrotherapy tubs. Another plumbing enhancement athletic trainers might choose is a **foot-pedal activator** for hand-washing stations. These devices are especially useful for athletic trainers who use massage and other activities that cover the hands with lotions, ointments, or similar products. Finally, the athletic trainer might choose to connect hydrotherapy tanks directly to the water source. The advantage of having a dedicated source of hydrotherapy water is that accidental spills are much easier to prevent. On the other hand, using hoses to fill hydrotherapy tanks provides greater flexibility for each water outlet.

It is not uncommon to pay a great deal of attention to designing the plumbing systems and to completely overlook accessories associated with plumbing. For instance, it is often very useful to build in liquid soap dispensers next to hand-washing stations. Paper cup dispensers are desirable. The planning team could choose paper towel dispensers and wastepaper containers that are recessed into the wall—they're usually more expensive, but they save space and are more aesthetically pleas-

standpipe drain
A type of drain that is raised above floor level.

plumbing fixtures
The external hardware used to control the flow and temperature of water.

mixing valve
A type of plumbing fixture designed to blend hot and cold water, eliminating the need for separate hot-and cold-water controls.

foot-pedal activator
A water-flow device, controlled by a foot pedal, used with hand-washing stations.

ing. Finally, a drinking fountain will require a dedicated water line and drain and an electrical outlet so the water can be chilled.

VENTILATION SYSTEMS

Very little has been written about the ventilation of sports medicine facilities. But if a sports medicine center is improperly ventilated, working conditions can become extremely uncomfortable. The two most important ventilation concerns are temperature and humidity control. Penman and Penman (1982) recommend a maximum of 0.75 ft/sec draft factor with between 8 and 10 changes of air per hour during peak loads. They recommend a humidity level between 40 and 50%.

thermostat A device that controls heating and cooling equipment.

A sports medicine center should have its own **thermostat.** A common mistake in designing ventilation systems is to use a common temperature control for the sports medicine center and adjacent areas, such as locker rooms and shower areas. The result is that the sports medicine center is almost always too warm to work comfortably in. If the sports medicine center has several different rooms, it is probably desirable to have separate thermostats for each of them.

The other major ventilation concern is humidity. Excessive humidity is not only a comfort problem, but also a hygiene problem. Viruses, fungi, and bacteria survive more easily on moist surfaces than dry. Areas where water is used extensively, such as the hydrotherapy section, should be equipped with exhaust fans that are strong enough to keep humidity to reasonable levels.

Whether or not to provide air-conditioning is an important decision, because air- conditioning is very expensive to install and use. In many areas of the United States, however, the temperature and humidity are so extreme when the sports medicine center is used most heavily that air-conditioning is an essential feature. Because air conditioning cools the air by removing moisture, it is an important feature for both comfort and hygiene.

LIGHTING

Illumination is another important, but often overlooked, feature in sports medicine center design. How bright should the sports medicine center be? Arnheim and Prentice (1997) recommend that sports medicine centers be illuminated at 30 footcandles at a height of 4 ft above the floor. Other authors have suggested that a sports medicine facility requires illumination of 50 footcandles 4 ft above the floor (*Planning facilities*, 1979). Common sense dictates that different sections of the sports medicine center have different illumination requirements. Areas devoted to taping, bandaging, and wound care require more lighting than storage or hydrotherapy areas. The areas designated for physician examination and treatment of injured athletes and other physically active patients probably require the most intense illumination. Floor lamps can supplement lighting in these areas to provide extra illumination for procedures such as wound debridement and suturing.

natural lighting Outside light used to illuminate indoor spaces, usually through windows or skylights.

In addition to artificial lighting, a sports medicine center can be brightened significantly through the use of **natural lighting** from either skylights or windows and light colors on reflective surfaces like ceilings, walls, and floors. Windows have historically been eliminated from school sports medicine centers due to concerns about student-athletes' privacy. The sports medicine center, however, is not a locker room. All patients should be dressed appropriately when entering the facility, and they should be draped appropriately when receiving treatment.

SPECIALIZED FUNCTION AREAS

Eight specialized function areas are common to most sports medicine facilities: office, taping and bandaging, hydrotherapy, general treatment, rehabilitation, storage, lavatory and changing area, and private examination (see figure 5.5). Many factors determine how much space to devote to each of these functions, including the types and numbers of sports to be served, the number of athletes and other physically active patients to be served, the qualifications and expertise of the sports medicine staff, the operational budget, and the type of client to be served. See figures 5.6–5.9 for examples of how special function areas can be arranged for different types and sizes of programs.

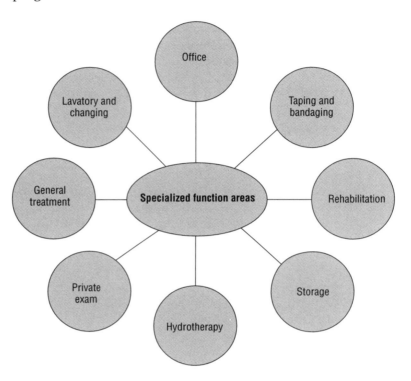

▌Figure 5.5
Specialized function areas of the sports medicine center.

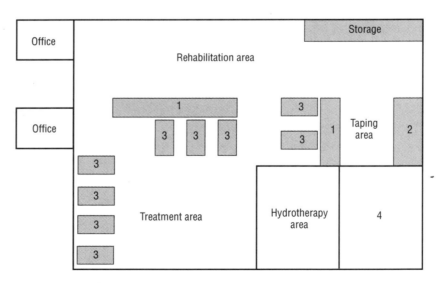

Key

1   Counter
2   Taping bench
3   Treatment tables
4   Therapy pool

▌Figure 5.6
Floor plan for a small college sports medicine facility.

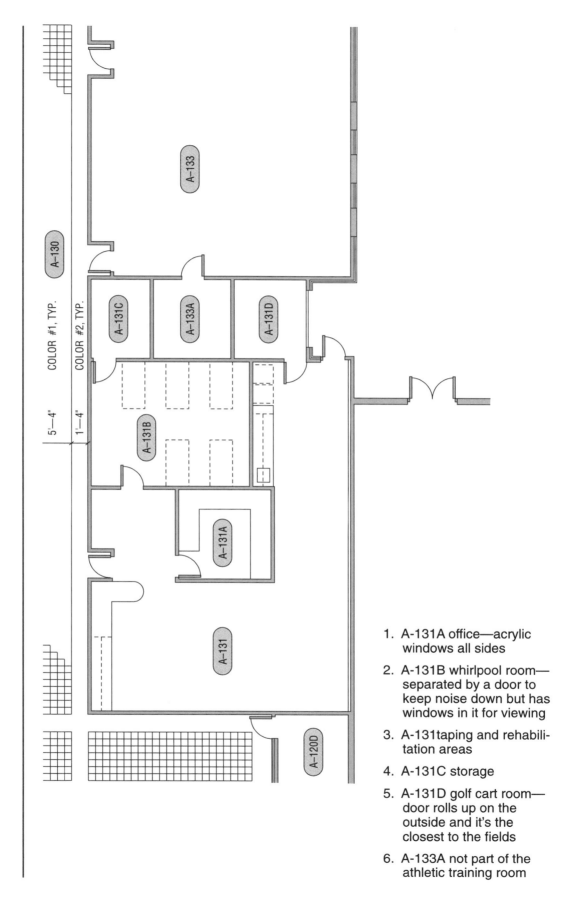

COLOR #1, TYP.

COLOR #2, TYP.

5—4"

1—4"

A-133

A-130

A-131C

A-133A

A-131D

A-131B

A-131A

A-131

A-120D

1. A-131A office—acrylic windows all sides

2. A-131B whirlpool room— separated by a door to keep noise down but has windows in it for viewing

3. A-131taping and rehabilitation areas

4. A-131C storage

5. A-131D golf cart room— door rolls up on the outside and it's the closest to the fields

6. A-133A not part of the athletic training room

▌Figure 5.7
Floor plan for a high school sports medicine facility.

From Ann Arbor Pioneer High School.

E.J. Nutter Training Center
—Athletic Training Room—

Key

A. Orthopedic office
B. General medicine office
C. Assistant athletic trainer's office
D. Head athletic trainer's office
E. Graduate assistant's office
F. Staff assistant's office
G. Taping area
H. Treatment area *= modalities
I. Storage room
J. Hydrotherapy room
   1. Hot whirlpool
   2. Cold whirlpool–2
   3. PGS machine and Paraffin bath

K. Student athletic trainer's office
L. Supply and copy room
M. Rehabilitation room
   1. VMS machine
   2. Rehabilitation device storage
   3. Versaclimber
   4. Leg extension machine
   5. Leg curl machine
   6. Leg press machine
   7. Hip machine
   8. Orthotron
   9. Nordic skier
   10. CYBEX isokinetic testing
   11. Exercise bike
   12. Liferower
   13. Impulse inertia machine
   14. Upper body ergometer
   15. Lifecycle

▌Figure 5.8
Floor plan for a large university sports medicine facility.

Reprinted with permission from the University of Kentucky.

Office

In most situations, the athletic trainer's office is located within the sports medicine facility. The athletic trainer's office should serve several purposes. First, it should be the central repository for all program records, including patients' medical files (unless kept in an adjacent health service records room as previously discussed), budget information, correspondence, insurance information, product information, and educational materials for students and clients. The athletic trainer's office can also be used for private examinations (although this presents several problems—a separate private examination area is ideal) and counseling if space is limited or unavailable. Finally, the office serves as an administrative work area for the athletic trainer. Adequate office space should be allowed to accommodate all staff athletic trainers. A common conference area within the office is a useful place for meetings or for students to do their work.

Several design features are important for the athletic trainer's office. First, the athletic trainer should have a clear view of the entire sports medicine facility from the office—windows should allow supervision of activities at all times. If the office must also be used as a private examination and consultation room, it must be

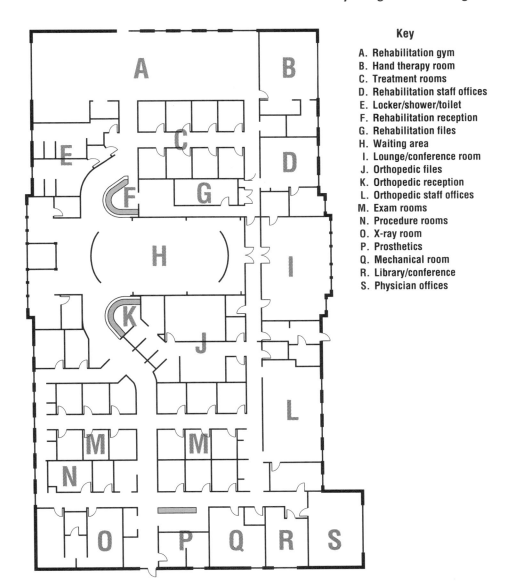

Key

A. Rehabilitation gym
B. Hand therapy room
C. Treatment rooms
D. Rehabilitation staff offices
E. Locker/shower/toilet
F. Rehabilitation reception
G. Rehabilitation files
H. Waiting area
 I. Lounge/conference room
J. Orthopedic files
K. Orthopedic reception
L. Orthopedic staff offices
M. Exam rooms
N. Procedure rooms
O. X-ray room
P. Prosthetics
Q. Mechanical room
R. Library/conference
S. Physician offices

❚ Figure 5.9 Floor plan for a combination orthopedic office and sports physical therapy clinic.

Adapted with permission from Horizon View Development, L.L.C.

data port
A dedicated phone line used to connect computers in different locations.

equipped with an exam table and blinds for the windows. Obviously, the office should contain a desk, filing cabinets, bookshelves, and a telephone with a line that is accessible without having to go through a building switchboard operator, who might not be on duty after normal business hours. Another useful feature is an extra telephone line for data transfers from a computer. In institutions with networked computer operations, a **data port** should be included as well. The office should also have enough comfortable seating to accommodate several people at one time for those occasions when the athletic trainer must consult with patients, parents, coaches, physicians, and others in groups.

Taping and Bandaging

In school-based sports medicine centers, the taping and bandaging section is often one of the busiest, especially just before practices and games. For this reason, athletic trainers designing school sports medicine centers should carefully consider the location and space devoted to this function. Private and hospital-based sports medicine clinics generally perform much less taping and bandaging in their facilities, so the area they devote to it is usually minimal.

Several design elements are important for a functional taping and bandaging area. First, it must include an adequate number of taping stations. Taping stations can be individual tables or large platforms designed to accommodate several people at one time (Cady, 1979). Whichever style is chosen, the taping table should be a minimum of 36 in. high, although some athletic trainers will be better served by taping tables that are taller.

Another important design element of the taping and bandaging area is adequate counter space. The counter should have an easily cleaned surface like Formica, be large enough to allow easy access for all athletic trainers working in the area, and offer electrical outlets every 4 ft. Although the traditional placement of the counter is along a wall, an attractive alternative is an island counter in the middle of the taping and bandaging area—the island provides taping stations on both sides, allowing easy access for twice as many athletic trainers. The taping and bandaging area should include cupboards and drawers with locks for secure short-term storage of supplies needed routinely. One way to save space in the taping and bandaging section is to combine taping stations with cupboards (Ribaric, 1980).

Finally, the type of floor covering to use in the taping and bandaging area can be a difficult problem. Both adhesive sprays and petroleum-based ointments can permanently stain carpeting and vinyl tile. For this reason, it might be wise to contract with a company that provides carpet runners for doorways and entrances. When the runners become soiled, the company will replace them with clean ones.

Hydrotherapy

The hydrotherapy section of the sports medicine center is the one specialized function area that should be physically separated because of water spills and the noisy turbines used to power whirlpool baths. The ideal design would include a glass enclosure around the area, containing the noise, heat, humidity, and accidental spilling or flooding while allowing the athletic trainer to monitor activities there from another section of the facility.

In addition to the sloped floor and expandable plumbing mentioned earlier, athletic trainers should consider other important features when planning the hydrotherapy area. Adequate space should be allotted for all the center's equipment that uses water, including hydrotherapy tanks, steam pack units, ice machines, freezers, and paraffin baths. In school sports medicine centers, water coolers and portable ice chests are usually stored here as well. Although very expensive to construct, operate, and maintain, multistation submersed whirlpools and two-lane training pools can be included in hydrotherapy areas. If so, plans must also include filtration units and water heaters. The floor of the hydrotherapy area should be covered with ceramic tile similar to what would be found in a shower room or toilet area. The walls can be constructed from cinder block if they are painted with a high-gloss epoxy paint that can be easily cleaned.

General Treatment

The general treatment area usually contains a number of treatment tables and any electrotherapeutic equipment, requiring one of the largest space commitments. After determining how many treatment tables will be required (figuring 20 patients per table per day), you can determine a square footage estimate for this area (see the formula provided on p. 137).

Allow approximately 30 in. between tables for placing three-shelved carts with therapeutic modalities. Place an electrical outlet between each treatment table. Provide a fluorescent light immediately above each table, each with its own light switch. Make sure at least some of the treatment tables have sliding drapes for privacy during treatment. Some treatment tables should also be adjustable to elevate swollen extremities. Treatment tables can double as storage cabinets if you fit them with cupboards, drawers, or shelves.

Materials for walls and floor coverings for this area should be light colored and easy to clean. Vinyl tile works well for this purpose, but it is slippery when wet. Carpet is difficult to clean, but it provides a warmer, quieter atmosphere.

Rehabilitation

In most athletic training settings, the rehabilitation area is another section that requires a great deal of space—it might take up the majority of the space in private and hospital sports medicine clinics. A few commonly used pieces of equipment to rehabilitate injured physically active patients—isokinetic equipment, treatment and exercise tables, treadmills, upper- and lower-extremity ergometers, stair climbers, and isotonic weight machines—can easily fill a large area. In addition to the equipment, adequate "dead space" must be provided between exercise stations for safety purposes. The largest part of the rehabilitation area might consist of nothing but carpeted floor space. This allows for a wide variety of functional and closed kinetic chain rehabilitation.

The location of the rehabilitation section is somewhat controversial. Most athletic trainers agree that it should not occupy the same space as the treatment or taping functions. Many athletic trainers have moved the rehabilitation function to a general-purpose weight-training facility. Although this has some advantages, exposing unsupervised patients to expensive and potentially harmful devices, such as a Cybex or Biodex, is probably unwise. The best arrangement gives the rehabilitation area its own room within the confines of the sports medicine center, especially if the institution's weight-training facility is nearby in the same building. This scheme allows for careful, supervised rehabilitation of injured physically active patients while still maintaining a quiet atmosphere in the general treatment area. When these patients are ready to advance to heavier weights and general-purpose strengthening devices, they can go to the weight room.

As in the athletic trainer's office, the best alternative for floor coverings in the rehabilitation center is probably carpeting. If dumbbells or other free weights are used, a carpeted floor will absorb the shock and noise of dropped equipment more effectively. If the rehabilitation room is located anywhere other than the ground floor, the architect might need to reinforce the floor to support heavy equipment.

Walls should be constructed of a material that allows insertion of hooks and screws, because many rehabilitation tools can be stored by hanging them on the wall. A full-length mirror is also useful to give patients visual feedback when performing rehabilitation exercises.

Storage

The storage section of the sports medicine center is commonly overlooked, perhaps because, calculated on a service-delivery-per-square-foot basis, storage rooms are expensive to construct. Given the cost, storage rooms should have several important features. First, the storage room should be located within the sports medicine center itself if at all possible. In addition, the closer the storage room is to the taping and bandaging section, the more convenient it will be for the athletic trainer to restock depleted expendable supplies. The storage room must be cool and dry at all times. Many expendable supplies commonly used in sports medicine, especially adhesive tape, deteriorate in warm, humid environments. Obviously, the storage room should be outfitted with plenty of shelves and cupboards. Finally, access to the storage room should be strictly controlled in order to prevent unauthorized removal of supplies.

Lavatory and Changing Area

Although most older athletic training facilities lack a lavatory and changing area, this highly desirable design feature is commonly included in newer facilities. This area can be designed to service both the athletic training staff and the patients who use the sports medicine facility. It should include a handicapped-accessible toilet and sink, along with a shower and lockers. A shelf for storing towels and a bin for disposing of soiled laundry should be included.

Private Examination

Many occasions in sports medicine call for private examination of an injured client to preserve modesty or to provide a calmer environment for the exam. Although the private examination area of the sports medicine center does not need to be large, it should provide a comfortable environment for the client and the athletic trainer or physician. Private examination rooms should include an examination table, a mobile lamp, a sink for washing hands, and a counter and cupboards to hold commonly needed supplies. Any supplies or equipment frequently used by the team physician should be readily available in the private examination room, as should appropriate gowns and drapes for clients. As already mentioned, the private examination room can be combined with the office if necessary.

APPLICATIONS TO ATHLETIC TRAINING: THEORY INTO PRACTICE

Use the following two case studies to help apply the concepts in this chapter to real-life situations. The questions at the end of the studies have many possible correct solutions. The case studies can be used in class discussion or for homework or test questions.

Case Study 1

Deanna Walsh is the athletic trainer for a large Wisconsin high school that offers 20 sports for 750 student-athletes. The voters of the school district recently approved a bond issue to build a new, $30 million high school. Deanna was asked by the planning committee to meet with the architect to discuss her ideas for the new athletic training room. Prior to the meeting, Deanna carefully considered the features she wanted to see incorporated into the new facility. She drew a sketch of the layout she desired, and she made a list of all the design features she wanted, including

- total size of 2500 sq ft;
- separate but connected rooms for taping, treatment, rehabilitation, office, storage, and private examination;
- a "hanging" ceiling with acoustical tiles to reduce noise;
- one treatment and taping table for every 10 athletes she would have to service during peak service hours;
- floor coverings of vinyl tile for the taping, treatment, and storage areas; ceramic tile for the hydrotherapy area; and carpeting for the office and private examination room; and
- air-conditioning, with separate thermostats for each of the six rooms.

After considering Deanna's suggestions and attempting to incorporate them into the overall design of the athletic and physical education portion of the building, the architect informed her that the new sports medicine center was too expensive as proposed and its cost would have to be reduced by one-third.

Questions for Analysis

1. Did Deanna employ the proper planning process when developing her ideas for the new athletic training room? What should she have done differently? How could she build a stronger case for her ideas?

2. What additional features should be included in Deanna's list? How can these features be justified?

3. Which features should Deanna modify or eliminate in order to meet the architect's requirement?

4. Place yourself in Deanna's position and produce your own schematic drawing of the athletic training room you would propose for the new high school. Justify each of the features you would include.

Case Study 2

Russ Emmons, AT, C/PT, operates a successful seven-year-old physical therapy and sports medicine practice. His caseload had nearly doubled when three new orthopedic surgeons moved into town a couple of years ago. When the local high school proposed a contractual relationship in which Russ would provide athletic training services for a fee plus referrals, he decided the time had come to expand out of his rented, cramped facility into his own building. Russ consulted a friend who had recently built an auto parts store for advice about hiring an architect. "I know just the architect you want," his friend told him. "He did a great job for me and I'm sure you'll like him." Russ decided to take his friend's advice, and he made an appointment to see the architect.

When they finally met a couple of weeks later, Russ was pleased with his friend's advice. The architect listened carefully to Russ' ideas and offered many helpful suggestions Russ had not considered. Toward the end of the meeting Russ asked the architect how he should go about locating a contractor to build the new clinic. "You wouldn't necessarily have to find anyone," the architect replied. "My firm could coordinate the construction internally. You'd only have to deal with one person and we could probably speed the whole construction process up quite a bit." Russ decided he liked the idea and several weeks later, after reviewing the project with his attorney and a loan officer from the bank, he signed a design/build contract with the architect's firm.

Questions For Analysis

1. What advantages will Russ have in owning his building? What disadvantages?

2. Did Russ make any mistakes in hiring an architect? What could he have done to avoid those mistakes?

3. Russ chose to use the design/build model for developing his new building. Was this a wise decision? What kinds of problems is he likely to encounter? What advantages will he realize?

4. What factors should Russ consider in the location of his new practice?

SUMMARY

1. *Understand and defend the importance of the design phase in planning and constructing new sports medicine facilities.*

   The design and construction of new sports medicine facilities is an infrequent but expensive and important task of the athletic trainer. The design stage of such projects is when athletic trainers can exert the greatest influence over the final product. Mistakes during the design phase will increase the facility's cost or decrease its function.

2. *Understand the facility design and construction process in sports medicine settings.*

   Most athletic trainers will work with planning committees consisting of program specialists and high-level administrators to design a sports medicine center. The design process involves 10 steps: assessing needs, approving the project, selecting a construction model, selecting an architect, developing schematic drawings, securing funding, bidding the construction, analyzing bids and reacting to them, commencing construction, and monitoring construction.

3. *Understand the common design elements found in a well-planned sports medicine facility.*

   Eight factors must be considered in the design of a sports medicine center: size, location, ergonomics, electrical systems, plumbing systems, ventilation systems, lighting, and specialized function areas.

4. *Describe the sports medicine facility in terms of its specialized function areas.*

   The specialized function areas of most sports medicine facilities include an office; taping and bandaging, rehabilitation, general treatment, hydrotherapy, storage, lavatory and changing areas; and a room for private examination of patients.

CHAPTER SIX

Helping Athletic Trainers Remember: Information Management

OBJECTIVES

After reading this chapter, you should be able to do the following:

1. Understand the importance of documentation as part of a complete information management system in sports medicine.

2. Understand and describe the different methods of athletic injury and treatment documentation.

3. Understand and describe the different types of information to be managed in a typical sports medicine program.

4. Understand how to use a computer in the sports medicine information management process.

Karen Thompson is the certified athletic trainer at Central City High School in addition to having a three-fifths appointment as a physical education and biology teacher. Two months ago she requested a computer for the school's athletic training room as part of a large grant proposal by the school district entitled "Computers Across the Curriculum." She hoped a computer would help her with record keeping. Because she is the only athletic trainer at the school and has to spend most of her time taking care of injured student-athletes, she usually has to take paperwork home with her in the evening to keep up.

One day in September, after teaching her classes, Karen discovered several large boxes on a treatment table in the athletic training room. Her computer had arrived! Because student-athletes were already starting to line up for taping and treatment, Karen moved the boxes to the corner of the room that doubled as her office. "Now that I finally have the equipment," she told herself, "I can start to think about how I can use it to improve our record-keeping system."

A week later the boxes were still there. When Karen called the school district's business manager to inquire about setup and training he informed her that only the equipment was covered by the grant. He suggested she consult with some of her colleagues if she had questions or problems. Karen had never worked with a computer before, so she was sure she was going to have more than a few of each.

The newest computer can only compound, at speed, the oldest problem in the relations between human beings, and in the end the communicator will be confronted with the old problem of what to say and how to say it.

Edward R. Murrow

Like many athletic trainers, Karen Thompson perceives her primary mission as providing high-quality health care to injured student-athletes. Her frustration is not due to having to meticulously document the care she administers, but rather to what she believes to be an excessive shift away from patient care to documentation for its own sake. Her view of the computer as a solution to her information management problems, whether valid or not, is common.

This chapter provides athletic trainers with the basics about information management in the athletic health care setting. We are working in an information society. Over the last century our culture has moved from its agricultural base, through a period of industrial revolution, into the information age. In the United States, approximately half of all workers are employed in jobs that involve accumulating and transferring information (Synnott & Gruber, 1981). Athletic trainers will increasingly be expected to be effective managers of information.

As health care professionals, we do not have the luxury of deciding whether or not we will manage information. The question is not "Will I choose to manage information and communicate effectively?" but rather, "What skills and tools do I need to manage information and communicate effectively?" For many reasons, athletic trainers are expected to document every patient care activity and the response to it. Athletic trainers must gather and disseminate the information necessary to accomplish a number of goals, including improvement of patient care, professional development, and improvement in education and counseling. Finally, athletic trainers are increasingly expected to be competent leaders for the sports medicine programs in their institutions. Athletic trainers who lack the information management skills to assume these leadership positions will quickly become frustrated. Their jobs, like Karen Thompson's, are likely to be characterized more by problems than by creative solutions.

WHY DOCUMENT?

Effective documentation of athletic training interventions serves at least eight purposes: legal protection, memory aid, legal requirements, professional standards, improved communication, insurance requirements, discharge decisions, and improved care.

Although documentation is only one of the information management tasks that athletic trainers must accomplish, it is common to all employment settings. Why is this skill so important? Why should busy athletic trainers concern themselves as much as they do with this task? There are many reasons.

LEGAL PROTECTION

Medical documentation helps protect the legal rights of both the physically active patient and the athletic trainer by providing a written record of the care provided by the athletic trainer. Medical records are often the only defense athletic trainers have in legal actions taken by aggrieved patients. The old adage "If it isn't written down, it didn't happen" is an increasingly appropriate guiding principle for all athletic trainers (Hawkins, 1989).

MEMORY AID

Medical documentation acts as a memory aid for athletic trainers and other professionals involved in the care of injured athletes and other physically active patients. Human memory is a poor substitute for accurate recording of medical facts, especially because a patient's medical record might not need to be referred to for months or even years.

LEGAL REQUIREMENTS

Medical documentation is, in many cases, required by law. For example, athletic trainers in professional sports are required to document player injuries for the Occupational Safety and Health Administration (OSHA). Athletic trainers in several different practice settings might be required to provide medical documentation for legally mandated workers' compensation insurance.

PROFESSIONAL STANDARDS

standards of practice
Widely accepted principles that are intended to guide the professional activities of a health care practitioner.

Medical documentation is required to meet professional **standards of practice.** The National Athletic Trainers' Association (1987) requires documentation of physician referral, initial evaluation and assessment, treatments, and dates of follow-up care for all athletes cared for in a *service program* typical of most educational settings. The requirements for athletic trainers working in *direct service programs*, typically in sports medicine clinics, are more rigorous. In addition to meeting the service program standards, an athletic trainer in this setting must provide a program plan with estimated length, methods, results, revisions, and a discontinuation or discharge assessment and summary. Other professional organizations have different documentation standards. For example, the Joint Commission on Accreditation of Healthcare Organizations (JCAHO) publishes minimum standards for health care documentation that apply to athletic trainers who work in hospitals and similar health care institutions (Marrelli, 1992).

IMPROVED COMMUNICATION

Medical documentation improves the quality of communication among the various professionals involved with the physically active patient's case (Kettenbach, 1995). Often, the only communication an athletic trainer has with the team or family physician is in writing. If the quality of the documentation is poor, either in content or writing style, misunderstandings can result between athletic trainer and physician.

INSURANCE REQUIREMENTS

Reimbursement decisions by third-party payers, such as insurance companies and health maintenance organizations, are based on medical documentation. This rationale is especially relevant for private or hospital-based sports medicine clinics, but it can also be important in professional, high school, and college sports medicine programs.

DISCHARGE DECISIONS

Medical documentation should be part of the basis for deciding when to discharge a patient from an athletic trainer's care (Kettenbach, 1995). The medical record should act as a map to guide a reader unfamiliar with the case through the entire injury, treatment, and rehabilitation process. The reader, whether a physician, athletic trainer, or physical therapist, should be able to determine by reading the record whether or not the patient is ready to be discharged.

IMPROVED CARE

When properly organized, medical documentation helps direct the athletic trainer to deliver better care. Well-written and well-organized medical documentation should be used as a tool for problem solving in difficult cases.

Medical documentation forms the raw material for program quality assessment. An athletic trainer should set both short- and long-term goals for the care of every injured patient. If the medical record shows care inconsistent with these goals, athletic trainers should be concerned that injured athletes and other physically active patients are being discharged without receiving all the care they need to function competitively.

TWO KINDS OF INFORMATION

Athletic trainers must manage two kinds of information: medical records and program administration records. Each is produced, maintained, and divulged in different ways.

medical record *Cumulative documentation of a person's medical history and health care interventions.*

Athletic trainers must differentiate between medical records and program administration records. The two types of records are separate entities, and with a few exceptions there should be little overlap between them.

MEDICAL RECORDS

A patient's medical record is a written outline of his or her health history during the time the patient was under an athletic trainer's care. **Medical records** are patient specific, and only data that is directly related to the patient's health should be included. Information not related to health, such as news clippings or academic information, has no place in the medical record and should be stored elsewhere. Marrelli (1992, 11–12) recommends the following guidelines:

- Write legibly or print neatly. The record must be readable.
- Use permanent ink (appropriate ink color depends on hospital policy).
- For every entry, identify the time and date, sign it, and provide your title.
- Describe the care provided and the patient's response.
- Describe findings objectively (i.e., in terms of behaviors).
- Write entries in consecutive and chronological order with no skipped lines or gaps.
- Write entries as soon as possible after care is provided.
- Be factual and specific.
- Use patient (or family or caregiver) quotes.

- Document patient complaints or needs and their resolution.
- Write out what you are saying, avoiding potentially confusing abbreviations.
- Chart only the care you provided.
- Promptly document a change in the patient's condition and the actions taken based on that change.
- Write the patient's, family's, or caregiver's response to teaching.

Finally, Schneller and Godwin (1983) recommend that you not erase errors. Instead, draw a line through the error, enter the proper information next to the error, and date and initial the correction.

Where and how should medical records be stored? The answer, of course, depends on the environment in which the sports medicine program operates. Two principles should be considered. First, medical records must be easily accessible by the athletic trainer at the time when they are needed the most—when the injured athlete or physically active patient is present in the sports medicine facility. The second principle is that records storage should be centralized to the greatest extent possible so that all those with a need to access the records are able to do so. These two principles can be difficult to reconcile in certain environments. For example, a university sports medicine program might operate several facilities on a campus covering a large geographic area. Similarly, a hospital-owned satellite sports medicine clinic might be part of a larger rehabilitation services department but might be physically located many miles from the hospital. How can a university athletic trainer working in an arena have immediate access to a basketball player's medical record when the files are maintained in the central athletic training room in the stadium? How can an athletic trainer in a sports medicine clinic access his patients' records when they are maintained in the central records depository of the hospital five miles across town?

Solutions to these dilemmas exist. One option for centralized records maintenance in decentralized sports medicine settings is the use of carbonless forms. With this system, one copy of every part of the patient's record is maintained in the facility where that patient's needs are primarily served. Another copy is included in an identical file in the central records storage facility. The advantage to this system is that it is relatively easy to maintain. The disadvantage is that each entry into the patient's record must be filed at least twice, thus increasing clerical time and costs.

Another option for centralization of medical records in decentralized settings is the use of electronic record keeping (Ray, 1997). Files are maintained in a computer database that can be accessed by anyone authorized to do so from computers that are linked to the central computer network. Entries into the record are made in one of three ways. Some entries are dictated directly into the system through telephone links or via voice recognition software from one of the computers linked to the records network. Other entries can be made into existing electronic forms built into the computer database. Finally, records that that do not lend themselves to either of these methods, such as communications from physicians, can be scanned into the medical record. The advantage of this system is that records can be easily accessed from a variety of locations. There are several disadvantages, however. This system is expensive to operate and maintain. Computer technology is evolving at such a rapid pace that systems built on that technology become obsolete in a short time. A second disadvantage is that computerized medical records require scrupulous attention to security measures. The confidentiality of this information is only as safe as the systems designed to prevent unauthorized access. Finally, computerized record keeping has the potential to decrease the quality of athletic trainer–patient interaction. The athletic trainer with a file folder in her hands can easily review a patient's history while asking questions regarding his present complaint. This is obviously not as easy to do when the medical information is stored on a computer in another part of the room or in the athletic trainer's office. Examples of the different types of information contained in the medical record follow.

Physical Examination Forms

The physical examination results should come first in the medical record. Not only does the physical exam normally occur first chronologically, the results can be a quick reference for athletic trainers or physicians. Some states mandate the use of specific physical examination forms for high school student-athletes. In other states and settings athletic trainers can choose from a wide variety of forms. The form chosen should ask for the following information (see figure 6.1):

- Personal data (name, address, date of birth, etc.)
- Health history
- Vital signs
- Physician's review of systems
- Special procedures (blood and urine analyses, X rays, echocardiograms, etc.)
- Functional tests (joint strength, aerobic capacity, etc.)

Injury Evaluation and Treatment Forms

Injury evaluation and treatment records should provide a concise record of the athlete's or physically active patient's progress from time of injury until time of discharge. These forms often constitute the bulk of the medical record. Although many athletic trainers maintain separate records of injury evaluations and treatments, each treatment should be easily linked to a documented injury. Athletic trainers can choose from five different methods for documenting injury evaluation and treatment data: problem-oriented medical records, focus charting, charting by exception, computerized documentation, and narrative charting.

Problem-Oriented Medical Record (POMR)

The **problem-oriented medical record (POMR)** is a system of medical record keeping that organizes information around the physically active patient's specific complaints (Berni & Readey, 1978). A cover sheet in the POMR summarizes the patient's past medical, social, and family history, as well as any personal habits that might affect the patient's health. A list of the patient's problems, along with a brief description of the plans implemented to ameliorate those problems, is also listed on the POMR cover sheet (see figure 6.2).

Another important component of the POMR is the **SOAP note** (see figure 6.3 on p. 167). Each SOAP note should be referenced on the POMR cover sheet. *SOAP* is an acronym for the following documentation parameters:

problem-oriented medical record (POMR)   A system of medical record keeping that organizes information around a patient's specific complaints.

SOAP note   Medical appraisal organized by subjective and objective evaluation, assessment of the patient's problem, and development of a plan for treatment.

S *Subjective evaluation of the patient's problem.* The subjective portion relates to how the patient conveys symptoms. It would include recording the patient's statement that "My right knee popped and gave out."

O *Objective evaluation of the patient's problem.* The objective portion of the evaluation includes physical data actually observed by the athletic trainer during evaluation. It would relate information such as the presence of intra-articular effusion, 2+ Lachmann sign, and AROM −15° in extension.

A *Assessment of the patient's problem.* Assessment is the athletic trainer's judgment of the nature of the problem based on the subjective and objective evidence. Using the same knee-injury case, a reasonable assessment of the problem would be internal derangement of the right knee with probable anterior cruciate ligament disruption.

P *Plan of action the athletic trainer will implement to resolve the problem.* Statements of both short- and long-term goals for the athlete or physically active patient should be included for quality assurance.

HOPE COLLEGE HEALTH CLINIC

ATHLETIC PHYSICAL EXAMINATION SUMMARY

1. Name _____ (M or F) _____ Age _____ Date _____

2. S.S.# _____ Year in school   Fr   So   Jr   Sr

    Sport _____

MEDICAL HISTORY SURVEY

3. Do you have now or have you had in the past, problems with:	YES	NO
a. Headaches—needing treatment		
b. Heart		
c. Breathing, e.g., asthma		
d. Abdominal pain		
e. Dizzy spells		
f. Black outs		
g. Eyes (except glasses)		
h. Hearing or ears		
i. Arthritis		
j. Joint pain or swelling		
k. Knees—injury, giving out, swelling		
l. Spine—back or neck		
m. Broken bones		
n. Kidneys		
o. Bladder		
p. Diabetes		
q. High blood pressure		
r. Cancer		
s. Operations or surgery		
t. Varicose veins		
u. Skin disorders		
v. Other major injuries		
w. Drug allergies		
x. Eating disorder		

4. If you answered yes to any of #3—give details below—identify by letter.

5. Have you ever been knocked unconscious? If yes, explain: Yes _____ No _____

6. Have you ever had a cervical spine injury? If yes, explain: Yes _____ No _____

7. Do you have any permanent handicap or disability? If yes, explain: Yes _____ No _____

8. Are you under a physician's care at the present time? If yes, explain: Yes _____ No _____

9. Are you taking any medications or drugs at the present time? If yes, explain: Yes _____ No _____

10. Year of last Tetanus.   _____

11. Women—Do you have a monthly menstrual period? Date of last period. _____ If no, explain: Yes _____ No _____

12. Do you have an intense fear of gaining weight?   Yes _____ No _____

(FOR EXAMINING PHYSICIAN ONLY)

13. Eyes:

   Rt. Eye _____ Lt. Eye _____

14. General information:

   Ht. _____ Wt. _____ B/P _____ Pulse _____

Examination	Normal	Abnormal
15. Head		
16. Eyes		
17. Nose & Throat		
18. Ears		
19. Neck		
20. Lungs		
21. Heart		
22. Abdomen		
23. Hernia		
24. G-U		
25. Extremity		
26. Shoulders		
27. Knees		
28. Other		
29. Nervous		
30. Knee Laxity		

PHYSICIAN'S STATEMENT

32. Approved for sports   Yes _____ No _____

33. Approved for further study
   Explain:

34. Approved with limitations
   Explain:

35. Disapproved comments:

36. Date _____

   Signature _____

31. Rt. _____ MCL _____ LCL _____ ACL _____ PCL _____

   Lt. _____ MCL _____ LCL _____ ACL _____ PCL _____

White copy to Health Center, yellow copy to P.E. Dept.

■ Figure 6.1 Sample of a physical examination form.

Reprinted by permission of the Hope College Health Clinic Holland, MI.

■ Figure 6.2 Cover page for problem-oriented medical record.

Problem-Oriented Medical Record Cover Sheet
Database

Past Medical Hx.

Family Hx.

Social Hx.

Habits
Tobacco:
Alcohol:
Drugs:
Seat belts:
Exercise:
Nutrition:

Problems   Dates

1.
2.
3.
4.

Plans   Dates

1.
2.
3.
4.

Follow-Up: See SOAP notes in record

For more information on this topic see chapter 2, Principles of Assessment Procedures, in the Athletic Training Education Series text *Assessment of Athletic Injuries* and chapter 4, Evaluation and Assessment Concepts, in the Athletic Training Education Series text *Therapeutic Exercise for Athletic Injuries*.

Focus Charting

focus charting
A medical record that registers a patient's complaint data, the health care practitioner actions, and the patient's response.

Focus charting is a less cumbersome alternative to the POMR medical record-keeping method (Iyer, 1991). Typical focus charting forms list pertinent *data* about the injury in the first column, describe the *action* the athletic trainer will take in response in the second column, and present the *response* to the athletic trainer's action plan in the third column (see figure 6.4). As in all other forms of medical charting, each entry should be signed and dated, and time notations should be entered if appropriate.

Charting by Exception

charting by exception *A type of medical record that notes only those patient responses that vary from predefined norms.*

Charting by exception, as its name implies, is a method in which only patient responses that vary from predefined norms are noted on the record (Murphy & Burke, 1990). This method makes record keeping more efficient and less time consuming. Although charting by exception is obviously inappropriate for recording initial

Individual Injury Evaluation and Treatment Record

Name: *Jones, Mike*　　　　Sport: *Basketball*　　　　Body Part: *R-Ankle*

Date Injury Occurred: *2/5/01*　　　　Date Injury Reported: *2/6/01*

Primary Complaint: *R-ankle pain*　　　　Secondary Complaint: *None*

Subjective data: *Pt. inverted R-ankle while playing basketball. Reports "a loud snap." No previous hx. of ankle injury. Otherwise normal medical hx. Pain w/walking is 5/10. Pain at rest is 3/10. Pain to palpation over the ant. talofibular ligament. No other bony or soft tissue tenderness noted.*

Objective data: *Moderate swelling over lateral malleolus. No discoloration, or deformity. Ankle is warm to touch. Lacks 5 deg dorsiflexion and 10 deg plantar flexion in both AROM and PROM compared to L-ankle. Strength is 4+/5 for DF, PF, Inv. & Ev. compared to 5/5 for L-ankle. Anterior drawer test is remarkably positive w/mushy end point. Talar tilt test equivocal due to swelling. Neg. Klieger's test. Pt. walks w/a noticeable limp and cannot bear wt. on the R-foot w/out assistance.*

Assessment: *Probable 3 deg ATF sprain.*

Plan: *Will refer to Dr. Jones. Appt. arranged for 3:00 pm today. Applied RICE for 20 minutes. Issued compression sleeve and ankle brace. Fitted crutches and provided instruction in crutch walking. Educated pt. on RICE techniques for home program. Provided pt. w/ankle home care brochure. Pt. indicated he understood instructions.*

Evaluator's Signature:　*David Black*

Date	Treatments and Progress
2/6/01	*RICE* × *20 min. Instructions for home care program. Crutches w/instructions. Compression sleeve and ankle brace. Pt. tolerated tx. well. Pain at rest 2/10. Swelling reduced. DB*

▌Figure 6.3　Sample evaluation and treatment form using SOAP note format.

Sports Medicine Focus Chart			
Name: *Jones, Mike*		Sport: *Basketball*	
Date	Data	Action	Response
2/6/01	*Probable 3° R. ATF sprain*	*RICE × 20 min. Compression sleeve, ankle brace, crutches issued.*	*Pain decreased to 2/10. Patient understood home care instructions.*
2/7/01	*3° R. ATF sprain*	*Cold whirlpool with AROM × 20 min. Form walking × 10 min. JOBST compression pump × 30 min.*	*Decreased limp with walking. Increased DF ROM to 5°.*
2/8/01	*3° R. ATF sprain*	*Cold whirlpool with AROM × 20 min. BAPS in PE in seated position. JOBST compression pump × 30 min.*	*Discarded crutches. Swelling reduced to minimal level. PF/DF ROM equal to L. ankle.*

■ Figure 6.4 Sample focus chart for use in recording injuries (data), treatments (action), and progress (response).

injury evaluation, it has many potential uses for recording treatments and rehabilitation. This method, however, requires maintaining tightly controlled and frequently monitored treatment protocols.

Computerized Documentation

The use of computers for keeping sports medicine records was described as early as 1982 (Abdenour, 1982), and the products available to athletic trainers have been increasing in number and utility ever since. As the quality of microcomputers has increased and their price decreased, athletic trainers have gradually shifted from using large, centralized mainframe computers toward using stand-alone and networked personal computers.

Athletic trainers see computerized record keeping as a way to decrease time spent documenting athletic injuries and treatments, thereby increasing time available for hands-on care of injured athletes and other physically active patients. But the switch to a computerized system of medical record-keeping will probably result in an initial *increase* in time spent on record keeping. It will take time to train athletic trainers to use the computer. In addition, record keeping and procedural changes will probably have to be made in order to adapt to the new technology.

As was mentioned earlier, another potential problem is maintaining the confidentiality of computerized records. It is more difficult to safeguard digitally stored data than data on paper in locked file cabinets. The use of passwords can sometimes slow unauthorized retrieval of medical records but it is very difficult to effectively thwart a motivated computer hacker. Finally, depending on the limitations of the computer software, computerized record keeping can limit the athletic trainer's flexibility in describing the case as fully as desired.

Nevertheless, athletic trainers should welcome the computer as a tool for effective and efficient medical record keeping in sports medicine. Computers allow athletic trainers to retrieve only those parts of the medical record desired for a specific purpose—we no longer need to physically search through a hundred-page medical record for a single entry. Nonprofessionals or students can perform some of the data entry, freeing the athletic trainer to spend more time with injured athletes and other physically active patients. Athletic trainers can pull information from many individual medical records for writing reports. This feature allows them to prepare year-end injury and treatment summaries that used to take weeks in much less time.

Narrative Charting

Narrative charting involves a more lengthy prose entry into the medical record. This is the most traditional method of medical record keeping. Athletic trainers make entries in paragraph form preceded by the date and time of the entry, relying very little on abbreviations or medical shorthand (see figure 6.5). **Dictation** is useful in narrative record keeping. Although clerical transcription can be expensive, dictation can significantly reduce the amount of time required to document injuries, treatments, and progress notes. Voice recognition software is now available that allows health care professionals to dictate directly to an electronic file in their computers through a microphone, thus avoiding the expense of using a transcriptionist.

narrative charting A method of recording the details of a patient's assessments and treatments using a detailed, prose-based format.

dictation The act of verbally recording, on a cassette tape or directly into a computer, the details of a health care assessment or treatment for later transcription and filing.

■ **Figure 6.5**
Example of the narrative charting method of injury documentation.

Smith, Jon

April 7, 2001

Jon is a sprinter on the school's track team. He came in today to be evaluated for pain that he has been experiencing in his anterior shins for the past three weeks. He has been icing his shins prior to and after every track practice in order to relieve the pain, but the problem has progressed to the point where it is very uncomfortable to run. He also experiences some pain when he walks. He has some pain while lying in bed at night. The pain is a dull ache unless the anterior shin is touched, when it becomes a sharp pain.

Visual examination is unspectacular. No swelling, discoloration, or deformity is noted. Palpation reveals point-specific tenderness over the anterior surface of the distal one-third of both tibias. A mild elevation in local temperature is palpable. No crepitus is noted. The gastroc and soleus are both tight bilaterally, allowing only 6° of passive dorsiflexion.

It is my impression that Jon may be suffering from bilateral tibial stress fractures. Jon is a member of an HMO and his physician while he is in college is Dr. Van Notten. I called Dr. Van Notten this morning to discuss Jon's case and was instructed to obtain a bone scan of Jon's tibias bilaterally. Jon is scheduled for the bone scan at Holland Community Hospital tomorrow morning at 9:30. He will be kept out of practice until Dr. Van Notten reviews the bone scan. He was placed on crutches and instructed to apply ice to his shins for 20 minutes every 2 hours while awake. He was told to return to the athletic training room tomorrow after his bone scan.

Signed: *Lydia Sanchez, A.T., C.*

Contact Dragon Dictate at **http://www.dragontalk.com/**.

Dictation, like writing, is a skill that takes practice to perfect. The following suggestions will help improve the effectiveness of dictation:

- Organize the data to be dictated by taking notes in medical shorthand while interviewing the patient. Use these notes to dictate a more comprehensive entry into the medical record.
- Speak clearly and slowly into the dictation machine. If possible, avoid dictating in a noisy room.
- Spell all proper names and medical terms that are used infrequently. This is especially important if the transcriber is inexperienced in medical transcription. Consider providing a medical dictionary to the transcriber.
- Review and initial all dictated narrations prior to filing them in the medical record.
- If you are planning to use voice recognition software, be sure to purchase a package designed for medical environments. Allow plenty of time (up to several hours) for the software to imprint your voice patterns and thereby reduce the number of errors.

Reports of Special Procedures

Reports of all special procedures should be included in the medical record. Although special-procedure reports should be entered into the medical record chronologically, each should be annotated to refer the reader back to an initial injury or illness assessment report. Special procedures include but are not limited to the following:

- Isokinetic strength tests
- Blood tests
- Urinalysis
- X rays or other imaging procedures
- Surgical reports
- Cardiac assessments (echocardiogram, graded exercise tests, thallium uptake scans, etc.)

Communication From Other Professionals

An athletic trainer commonly receives written documentation of a patient's medical status from physicians, physical therapists, and other health care professionals involved with the case. One type of documentation is the referral form (Gabriel, 1981) sent with an injured athlete when he or she is sent to the physician's office or the emergency room (see figure 6.6). The injured athlete referral form provides legally defensible proof that the athletic trainer consulted with a physician as required by the standards of professional practice and, in many states, by law. In addition, it improves communication between the athletic trainer and the physician by taking the burden of having to relay information off the injured athlete.

The referral form should include the athlete's name, sport, injury date, and appointment date and time. It should allow space for the athletic trainer to document the initial evaluation findings. The form should provide space for the physician to write a diagnosis and orders for treatment or rehabilitation. The athletic trainer's and the physician's notes should be dated and signed. Finally, the form should include a section—to be signed by the athlete—authorizing the physician to share the

HOPE COLLEGE SPORTS MEDICINE MEDICAL REFERRAL

Name _____   Sport _____

Date _____ Time _____   Physician _____

Athletic Trainer's Impression _____

_____

_____

_____

Physician Diagnosis & Recommendation _____

_____

_____

_____

Recommended Activity Level (Check All That Apply):

Bed Rest _____   Attend Classes Only _____   Practice as Able _____

No Practice or Competition _____   No Restrictions _____

Limited Physical Activity as Noted Above _____

Follow-Up Appointment: _____   _____
                                    Date   Time

_____
Physician Signature

PLEASE INSTRUCT THE STUDENT TO RETURN THIS FORM
TO THE ATHLETIC TRAINING ROOM

I hereby authorize _____ to release all records related to the injury/illness specified above to Richard Ray, Meg Abfall, Dr. Patrick Hulst, Dr. John Schloff, the Hope College Health Clinic, or any other representative of the Hope College medical staff. I further authorize the above-named health care provider to discuss my case with any representative of the Hope College medical staff. I waive any and all claims against the above-named health care provider, Hope College, and any of its employees or contractors in connection with the communication and disclosure of such information.

_____
Student Signature

_____   _____
Date   Witness

∎ Figure 6.6 Sample medical referral form.

Reprinted by permission of the Hope College Health Clinic.

athlete's medical information with the athletic trainer or other members of the sports medicine team. Athletic trainers can ensure that referral forms are returned in three ways. The most obvious is to ask the injured athlete to bring the form back at the next appointment. Athletic trainers can ask the physician to mail the form back, but this method delays direct feedback from the physician. Finally, the athletic trainer could ask the physician to fax a response, which provides the information quickly and avoids the possibility of the athlete's losing or forgetting the form.

A second method for communicating with other health care professionals is via the common professional courtesy of sending letters or copies of office notes to referring health care colleagues. Athletic trainers should enter these notes, often a useful source of information and documentation of the injured athlete's status, into the medical record. Athletic trainers should request a letter from all physicians and other health care professionals to whom they frequently refer injured athletes.

Emergency Information

Athletic trainers in high schools and colleges are frequently required to contact an injured student-athlete's parents or guardians, an urgent responsibility if the athlete has a serious accident or illness. To do so, the athletic trainer usually uses the emergency information form in the medical record (see figure 6.7). This form should include athlete information, such as name, address, phone number(s), date of birth, and Social Security or student identification numbers. It should also include parents' names, addresses, and telephone numbers (home and business). Some athletic trainers have suggested that the form contain the athlete's insurance information as well (Miles, 1987). This form should be readily accessible in the medical record, per-

---

Emergency Information

Name: _____   Sport: _____

Date of birth: _____   Address: _____

Social Security or ID number: _____   Phone: _____

Parents' names: _____

    Address: _____   Phone: (H) _____ (W) _____

Person to contact in an emergency: _____

    Relationship: _____   Phone: _____

Name of insurance company: _____

Policy numbers: _____

Is this insurance company a health maintenance organization (HMO)?   Yes _____ No _____

If so, list the HMO telephone number: _____

∎ **Figure 6.7** Sample emergency information form.

Adapted from *Journal of Athletic Training* 1987.

haps affixed to the inside cover of the athlete's folder. Emergency information forms could also be organized according to sport and placed in three-ring binders that teams can take with them wherever they go.

For more information on this topic see the section on emergency planning and procedures in chapter 8 of the Athletic Training Education Series text *Introduction to Athletic Training.*

Permission for Medical Treatment Forms

A widely recognized legal principle is that persons (or their parents in the case of minors) must consent to medical treatment. Any consent forms should be maintained in the medical record (see figure 6.8). Although the use of such forms has been standard operating procedure in most hospital sports medicine programs, their use in school-based settings has been limited. Consent forms are especially important in the high school setting because most of these injured student-athletes are still minors.

exculpatory clause
A signed release from a patient or parents that waives all future legal claims against an athletic trainer or the employing institution.

Along with permission forms, signed releases from patients or their parents that waive all future legal claims against the athletic trainer or the employing institution are commonly used. These **exculpatory clauses,** with very few exceptions, are legally unsupportable (Herbert, 1987). The primary legal argument against them is that such clauses are contrary to public policy and are therefore legally invalid. Because the public has a vested interest in quality health care, the courts have been hesitant to allow negligent practitioners to hide behind prospective waivers. In addition, in many states, parents cannot "sign away" the rights of their children. Any athletic trainer planning to use a prospective waiver with exculpatory language should first have it thoroughly evaluated by an attorney and liability insurance carrier.

Permission to Provide Medical Treatment Agreement

I HEREBY give my permission for my son/daughter, _____ , to undergo medical treatment for any injury or illness he/she may sustain or acquire while engaged in interscholastic athletics at Eagletown High School. I understand that the medical personnel of Eagletown High School, including athletic trainers, nurses, and team physicians will perform only those procedures that are within their training, credentialing, and scope of professional practice to prevent, care for, and rehabilitate athletic injuries. In the event that more serious medical procedures are required, such as surgery or other invasive procedures, I understand that attempts will be made to contact me for my consent. I understand that if my child suffers a potentially life-threatening injury or illness, and in the event I am unable to be contacted within a reasonable period of time, that I authorize any duly licensed medical practitioner to perform such procedures as may be medically necessary to alleviate the problem.

I have had the opportunity to ask questions regarding this release and all of my questions have been answered to my satisfaction. Having understood the above agreement, I freely sign this Permission to Provide Medical Treatment Agreement.

_____   _____
            Date   Signature of Parent or Legal Guardian

❚ **Figure 6.8** Sample agreement form for the parents or guardians of minors to grant permission to provide medical treatment.

Release of Medical Information

Another commonly understood legal principle is that health care providers may not release a person's medical records without consent. This principle has been written into the federal legal code in the form of the Family Educational Rights and Privacy Act (FERPA) of 1974 (sometimes referred to as the *Buckley Amendment*). **FERPA** requires educational institutions to receive formal written consent from students (or, in the case of minors, their parents or guardians) before "educational records" can be disclosed to a third party. The law also requires educational institutions to make available to the student all records relating to their enrollment unless the student specifically waives the right on a case-by-case basis. Several exceptions to the rule do exist. For example, employees of educational institutions may legally disclose information regarding students, without their consent, to safeguard their health in an emergency situation. Health records created or maintained by a physician, psychiatrist, psychologist, or other recognized professional or paraprofessional are also not considered "educational records" under FERPA and are therefore not covered by the law (School Records, 1996). Student-athletes do not have a legal right under FERPA to access the content of their health records. Nonetheless, good practice in health care includes receiving informed consent from patients before information regarding their health is shared with a third party.

Many parties will want access to the athlete's medical records, including coaches, the press, insurance companies, and professional sports organizations. Before providing information, the athletic trainer should make certain the athlete has formally agreed to the release by signing a waiver. If the athlete is a minor a parent or legal guardian must also sign the waiver. The athletic trainer must be certain to release only the information authorized by the athlete. Each time an athlete's medical information is released, the medical release form should show the content, purpose, and receiver of the information (see figure 6.9).

Insurance Information

Financial documents, such as patient invoices and insurance claim forms, are not medical records. They have different purposes and uses and are protected by the laws governing confidentiality in different ways. Insurance information contained in the medical record should be limited to the following (Glondys, 1988):

- Expected payer(s)
- Insured's name
- Patient's relationship to insured
- Employment data and insurance numbers

Correspondence with insurance companies and other third-party payers should be maintained separately from the medical record. Letters and copies of insurance forms often contain information directly related to the description of the injury circumstances. Copies of medical records used to document claims should not be maintained in the insurance folder; to protect confidentiality, a note referring to the supporting portion of the medical record should be used. This method protects the confidentiality of the medical record by ensuring that unauthorized individuals do not gain access through the insurance claims process.

PROGRAM ADMINISTRATION RECORDS

Much of the information athletic trainers are required to manage is administrative. Whereas medical records are specific to only one athlete or physically active patient, **program administration records** are more general in nature and usually organized

FERPA *The Family Educational Rights and Privacy Act (sometimes referred to as the* Buckley Amendment) *A 1974 federal law requiring student authorization to release educational records to a third party and ensuring access for students to their records.*

program administration records Documentation of the activities of a program.

Release of Medical Information Authorization

I, _____, DO/DO NOT give consent for the team physician, athletic trainer, or other medical personnel employed by _____ College to release such information regarding my medical history, record of injury or surgery, record of serious illness, and rehabilitation results as may be requested by either the representatives of any professional or amateur athletic organization seeking such information.

I understand that the representatives of a professional or amateur athletic organization have made representations to the team physician, athletic trainer, or other medical personnel employed by _____ College that the purpose of this request for my medical information is to assist the organization being represented in making a determination as to offering me employment.

I understand that a record will be kept of all individuals requesting information and the date of the request. This information is normally confidential and except as provided in this Release will not be otherwise released by the custodian of the information. This Release remains valid until revoked by me in writing.

I have had an opportunity to ask questions regarding this Release and the process by which my medical information may be released. All of my questions have been answered to my satisfaction. Having read and understood the above, I freely sign this Release of Medical Information Authorization.

_____   _____
Date   Signature of Student-Athlete

_____   _____
Date   Signature of Parent or Legal Guardian (for minors)

_____   _____
Date   Signature of Witness

Medical Information Release Log

Date of Release	Released to	Form of Release	Content of Release	Released by
1.				
2.				
3.				
4.				

▌**Figure 6.9**   Sample authorization form and log for release of medical information.

around subfunctions of the sports medicine program. The absolute standards for confidentiality that apply to medical records are usually, but not always, significantly relaxed for many types of program administration records. Whenever program administration records deal with specific individuals, however, confidentiality should be maintained. Examples of various types of program administration records follow.

Reports to Coaches

A common practice of most athletic trainers who work in professional, high school, and college settings is to provide coaches with daily written reports of the health status of their athletes (see figure 6.10). Daily reports can help improve communication between the athletic trainer and the coach. Coaches appreciate timely information about the health status of their athletes, because it allows them to plan more effectively. Another important benefit of the daily report to coaches is that athletic trainers can easily document recommendations for participation status. For example, assume that the athletic trainer recommends in the daily report that an athlete be limited to noncontact football drills because of a resolving neck injury. If the coach allows the athlete to participate in a full-contact scrimmage and the athlete is reinjured, the athletic trainer can at least document that he recommended a reduced activity level for the injured athlete.

Should athletic trainers be concerned about violating their ethical duty to hold athletes' medical information and health status in confidence—even from their coaches? This is a very thorny issue for a variety of reasons. First, although athletic trainers have an ethical responsibility to obtain authorization from the athlete before disclosing information to a coach, common practice in school, collegiate, and professional sports for many years has been for athletic trainers to report on the health status of athletes to their coaches (for all the reasons enumerated in the previous paragraph) even in the absence of explicit authorization. Many injury situations occur in such a manner that the coach is a witness to the injury or is the agent of referral to the athletic trainer. In situations like these, the coach is already an informed party. Even in cases where the coach doesn't know about an injury, most athletes just assume that the athletic trainer will speak to the coach about the situation. Conversely, most athletic trainers have had cases whereby athletes have specifically requested that their coaches not be informed about an injury or illness—for a wide

---

Daily Coach's Report

Sport: Football   Date: October 14, 2001

Name	Injury	Date Injured	Date Reported	Comments
Smith, Tim	L-wrist/old fx. pain	10-12-01	10-12-01	seen by Dr. West
Funk, Roger	L-shldr. sublx.	10-12-01	10-12-01	seen by Dr. West, rest
DeHaan, Dirk	R-AC contusion	10-12-01	10-13-01	treatment, seen by Dr. West
Russell, Bob	R-ankle sprain	10-12-01	10-13-01	treatment, rest
Fernandez, Scott	neck strain	10-12-01	10-13-01	seen by Dr. West, treatment, play as able
Jones, Rick	L-arm contusion	10-10-01	10-11-01	seen by Dr. West, rest

No participation	Play as able	Removed from list
Funk, Roger	Smith, Tim	Nick, Art
DeHaan, Dirk	Fernandez, Scott	Rios, Manny
Russell, Bob		
Jones, Rick		

Figure 6.10   Example of a computer-generated daily coach's report.

variety of reasons. The question is complicated even further when athletic trainers, as agents of management of professional athletic organizations, are required by the terms of their contracts to disclose the health status of all athletes to a coach or general manager.

Thompson and Sherman (1993) recommend that formal agreements should exist that specify the extent to which information will be shared with team personnel. In the absence of such agreements, all information should be held in confidence. In addition, I recommend the following guidelines for dealing with this issue:

- Inform all athletes in writing that health information that affects their ability to participate fully in team activities or where their safety might be compromised will be shared with the coach, except when an athlete makes a specific request to withhold the information. Obtain athletes' written consent for this at the beginning of each season.

- Remind athletes during their initial assessment that as part of their treatment plan you will be discussing their status with their coaches.

- Counsel athletes who are reluctant to allow you to discuss their cases with a coach as to the advantages and disadvantages of withholding the information.

- If athletes request that you hold information in confidence before you have had an opportunity to evaluate the information ("I want to tell you something but you have to promise me you won't tell the coach"), inform them that you can't make such a promise and that you'll have to hear what they have to tell you first. If they won't tell you without such an assurance, offer to refer them to another health care provider not associated with the team or institution.

- Disclose to coaches only the information they need to either plan team activities or structure a safe participation environment for the athletes in question. For example, assume an athlete has a sexually transmitted disease and must see the physician at 4:30, thus having to miss practice. I recommend you tell the coach only that the athlete is ill and will miss one day of practice.

- Document in the medical record the extent of disclosure made to a coach. In cases where the athlete will not authorize disclosure, document this as well.

Budget Information

Athletic trainers with financial authority must maintain accurate records of all financial transactions. In school, college, and professional settings, financial reports usually include monthly budget statements (produced in-house or sent from the institutional business office), purchase orders, and invoices. Documents that support budgetary decisions and **requests for proposals (RFPs)** should also be maintained in the program administration record system.

Nonmedical Correspondence

Nonmedical correspondence comprises letters and memoranda not associated with a specific patient's health status. Unlike medical correspondence, which must be meticulously recorded and preserved, much of the routine nonmedical correspondence can be discarded after action is taken. Nonmedical correspondence that must be retained should be filed under the appropriate subject heading and not in a separate folder labeled "correspondence."

Equipment and Supply Information

Equipment and supply inventories and catalogs from medical supply vendors are another kind of program administration record. Institutions often require

requests for proposals (RFPs)
Notices from internal and external funding sources announcing the details of grant programs.

nonmedical correspondence
Letters and memoranda not associated with a specific patient's health status.

administrative units to keep an inventory of nonexpendable capital equipment on file. This inventory usually includes the type of equipment, the amount or number of units, and the serial numbers. Some institutions assign their own identification numbers for nonexpendable equipment, which should also be included as part of this record. Athletic trainers in all settings are frequently called upon to purchase or recommend the purchase of sports medicine products. A well-organized file of appropriate catalogs can be useful. Warranties and equipment maintenance records should also be filed in the program administration records.

Personnel Information

Information on sports medicine staff members' employment constitutes an important part of the program administration record-keeping system. Like an individual's medical record, the personnel record is confidential and should be accessed only by those with a documented need for the information. Personnel information should be kept in a secure place, preferably a locked filing cabinet. Records on student athletic trainer performance should be treated similarly. Examples of the kinds of records normally associated with the personnel function include

- performance evaluation records;
- salary and promotion records;
- employment application information, including application forms, resumes, and letters of recommendation; and
- employment contracts.

Reporting Information

Athletic trainers are often held responsible for documenting the activities of a sports medicine program either for institutional or for outside accreditation purposes. The information required to compile such reports constitutes another aspect of the program administration record-keeping system. Documentation of patient caseloads and summaries of any special program accomplishments are often compiled in an annual report. Accreditation agencies require access to different kinds of information, depending on their purpose. Hospital accreditation agencies generally request summary statistics on patient outcomes and evidence of compliance with professional standards of practice. Agencies that accredit educational programs, such as the Commission on Accreditation of Allied Health Education Programs (CAAHEP), require data related to student outcomes such as graduation, certification, and employment rates.

OSHA bloodborne pathogen standard Federal government rules that require employers to protect employees against the accidental transmission of bloodborne pathogens, especially HIV and hepatitis B.

Another kind of reporting information is required by law to show compliance with the **OSHA bloodborne pathogen standard.** Part 1910 of Title 29 of the Code of Federal Regulations requires that employers develop programs that protect employees, including athletic trainers, from occupational exposure to bloodborne pathogens (Occupational Safety and Health Administration, 1991). These rules have significant record-keeping requirements. Records kept to comply with the OSHA rules must be retained for three years. Documents that must be entered into the employee's medical record, however, must be maintained for the duration of the employee's employment *plus* 30 years.

Training materials and forms related to compliance with the OSHA Bloodborne Pathogens Standard are available from several vendors, including Pathfinder Associates Inc., P.O. Box 5240, N. Muskegon, MI 49445-0240. Phone: 616-744-8462 Web site: **http://www.webcom.com/~pathfndr/**

Patient and Student Education Information

All athletic trainers should maintain an up-to-date database of article reprints, handouts, and other educational materials that they can provide to both patients and student athletic trainers. The maintenance of such a database as another type of program administration information is important, because the body of knowledge in athletic training and sports medicine is changing so rapidly.

FILING SPORTS MEDICINE RECORDS

The records related to a sports medicine program should be filed according to a master outline in either a primary, secondary, or tertiary position.

master outline
A guide to the major sections of a filing system.

Although it might seem rather basic, an appropriate and effective system for filing sports medicine records is important. Like Karen Thompson in the opening case, most athletic trainers are too busy to spend time searching for important documents in poorly organized files. Although different sports medicine settings will require different filing systems, the following recommendations should prove useful in most cases (Needy, 1974):

- Develop a **master outline** of files contained in the system organized under major subject headings (see figure 6.11).

- Maintain confidential files, such as medical records and personnel folders, in their own locked cabinets.

- Organize files according to major, primary, secondary, and if needed, tertiary classifications. A budget file classified in this manner would look like this:

> Major classification .... Budget
> Primary 1999
> Secondary .... Expendable supplies
> Tertiary .... Invoices

- Use file labels of different shapes or colors to differentiate between the various filing classifications.

- Do not overfill file folders. Once a folder has reached its capacity, usually 3/4 in., begin a second folder.

- Organize material within a folder chronologically or alphabetically.

- Develop separate filing systems for temporary and permanent files.

- File records promptly.

- Go through all files yearly. Discard unneeded records and update the master outline.

THE COMPUTER AS AN INFORMATION MANAGEMENT TOOL

The computer has revolutionized the way that athletic trainers manage information. Before expending institutional funds in this area, athletic trainers should weigh their options in three areas: hardware, software, and network applications for managing information.

As already mentioned, the computer has developed into a powerful tool for information management in sports medicine. Ribaric (1982) predicted nearly 20 years ago that the use of computers would become commonplace in sports medicine and he was correct. Although computers can, in most circumstances, help improve athletic trainer productivity, athletic trainers sometimes resist the change to a computerized information management system. Resistance can be overcome if the technology and specific computer applications are gradually introduced (Ray & Shire, 1986).

One of the most important questions that athletic trainers considering a change to a computerized system must answer is what specific problems the computer can provide a solution for (Priest, 1989). Mere attraction to the technology is a poor but common reason for computerizing. One of Karen Thompson's problems in the

Master Outline—Personnel

Personnel
  Applications for employment
    Current job openings and applications
  Absence from work
    Absence reports
    Absenteeism and lateness
  Bonding of employees
  Employee benefits
    Group life insurance
    Group medical and hospitalization
    Incentive awards
    Retirement program
    Severance pay
    Social Security
    Unemployment compensation
    Workers' compensation
  Employee conduct rules
    Disciplinary measures for violation of rules
  Employee relations
    Collective bargaining
    Communications
    Employee parking
    Grievance procedures
  Hiring procedures and policies
    Qualifications
    Residence requirements
    Selection procedures and recruitment
      Advertising
      College contacts
      Employment agencies
      Job interviews
      Job announcements
      References required
  Health and medical program
    OSHA bloodborne pathogen standard
    Compliance
    Working conditions
  Individual personnel folders (confidential)
  Leave
    Compensatory
    Death in family
    Holiday
    Jury duty
    Leave of absence
    Maternity
    Military
    Paternal
    Sick
    Sabbatical
    Vacation
    Voting

Payroll records
Personnel record-keeping policies
  Personnel forms
Publications
  Bulletins
  Newsletters
  Training manuals
  Requests
  Staff publications
Safety and accident program
  Accident analysis
  Accident reports
  Elimination of hazards
    Safety inspection records
  First aid policies and procedures
  Legal liability
  Safety equipment
  Safety—in-service training
  Rules
Termination of employment
  Death
  Discharge
  Layoff
  Retirement
    Early retirement program
  Resignation
  Termination interview
  Turnover analysis
Training
  Employee induction program
  Employee training records
  Time off for study program
  Tuition refund program
  Workshops and conferences
Wage and salary program
  Job analysis
  Job descriptions
  Job specifications
  Job evaluations
  Job classifications
  Organizational charts
  Pay policies
  Promotions
  Wage and salary structure
    Wage criteria
    Wage surveys
    Rate range structure

■ Figure 6.11 Example of a master outline for the personnel section of a sports medicine filing system.

Adapted from Needy 1974.

computer resources needs assessment analysis A type of needs assessment focused on the information management function and its automation.

cost-benefit analysis A type of program evaluation that estimates both the amount of resources and the potential advantages associated with a program.

opening scenario was that she had not clearly identified her record-keeping problems and their possible solutions. Like many other athletic trainers, she simply assumed that the computer would resolve her problems. Only after receiving the equipment did she begin to think about its use in a more rational and organized way. A **computer resources needs assessment analysis** is the first step the athletic trainer should take in deciding whether or not to automate the record-keeping system (see figure 6.12).

Unless an athletic trainer has extensive training in computer systems and applications, she should seek the advice of professionals prior to attempting to choose a system. Most colleges and universities employ computer specialists for this purpose. Many hospitals contract with computer consultants who can assist the hospital-based athletic trainer. Many high school athletic trainers can receive the computer advice they need by contacting the instructors who teach computer science in the school district. A computer consultant should be able to advise an athletic trainer on performing a **cost-benefit analysis**, in addition to recommending specific hardware and software.

An athletic trainer faces several important considerations in developing a computerized information management system, including hardware, software, and communication options. Priest (1989) recommends addressing the following issues:

- How will the hardware be protected, both from theft and unauthorized use?
- How will the software be protected, both from theft and unauthorized duplication?

Computer Resources Needs Assessment Questionnaire

Instructions:

All members of the sports medicine staff should complete this questionnaire in order to obtain the perspectives of as many potential users as possible. Responses from all questionnaires should be transferred to a master list. The master list will help guide the discussion between the athletic trainer and the computer resources consultant.

List the primary information needs of the sports medicine program. Some of this information may be incoming and some will be outgoing. Include both types. For each of these information needs, answer the following question:

1. From what source does the information come? (Examples include injury logs, treatment logs, telephone conversations, etc.)

Answer the following questions for each type of information that pertains to the sports medicine program:

1. Who uses the information? Who has access? How is the information used?
2. Is there anyone else who could use the information if it were provided to them? How would they use it?
3. How is the information generated? Who prepares it? Where is it sent after preparation?
4. How is information presently organized? Is an alphabetical or numerical filing system used?
5. How often is the information accessed, changed, or used?
6. Is all the information generated used in some way, or is some of it simply stored?
7. How is the accuracy of the information verified? How critical is the accuracy of the information?
8. Is the information used in reports? If so, how? How often are the reports generated?
9. How could the information be managed more effectively? If you think a computer would help, why do you think so? Are you aware of any hardware or software applications that would address this need?

❚ Figure 6.12 Computer resources needs assessment questionnaire.

- Who will be responsible for performing regular backups in order to ensure data retention? How often will backups be performed?
- How will access to computer files be regulated, especially if there will be multiple users?
- Who will update the database and how will the accuracy of the entries be verified?
- Who will maintain computer file organization?
- How will disk capacity be monitored? Who will be responsible for making sure that fixed disk space is not exhausted?
- Will the computer be networked to other computers? Is the software compatible with the network?
- Who will provide technical support and training?

HARDWARE CONSIDERATIONS

*computer hardware
The equipment
required to input,
process, and output
data.*

Computer hardware refers to the equipment required to input, process, and output data. The following items are commonly included in the array of computer hardware options (Christensen & Rupp, 1986):

- *Central processing unit (CPU):* the circuits and controls that actually process the digital data.
- *Monitor:* the cathode ray tube used for video display.
- *Printer:* the device that produces a paper copy of the computer output. Like all hardware, a large assortment of printer types is available in a wide price range.
- *Disk drives:* devices that store digital data on a magnetic platter. Hard disks are contained in the same housing as the CPU and store more data than floppy disks, which are removable.
- *Mouse:* a handheld device that allows the user to move the cursor around the monitor and select certain software options.
- *Keyboard:* the typewriter-like device used to enter data into the computer.
- *Modem:* a communications device that, when coupled with a telephone line, can be used to transfer data from one computer to another. Most modems can also send or receive documents by fax.
- *CD-ROM:* a device that uses a laser to read data digitally encoded on a compact disc. Each compact disc can hold hundreds of times as much data as a floppy disk. Most CD-ROM drives can be read only by the computer, but writable drives are now appearing on the market.
- *Network card:* a circuit board that, when installed into the computer and coupled with the appropriate network connections, allows it to communicate and share files with other computers on the same network.
- *Scanner:* a device that digitally copies and electronically stores images or text.

Kinds of Computers

*mainframe   A type
of large, powerful
computer designed for
multiple users in a
centralized institu-
tional setting.*

There are several types of computers that athletic trainers can put to use in helping them manage information. In most sports medicine settings, a personal computer will certainly be the most cost-efficient computing alternative.

A **mainframe** computer is a large, multiuser CPU capable of substantial and rapid data transformations. A mainframe is typically housed in a university's computer center or in the data management department of a hospital. Mainframe computers are usually accessed via remote **terminals** that are either directly connected (hardwired) or connected by modem and telephone line.

A **microcomputer**, also known as a **personal computer (PC)**, is a much smaller CPU designed to sit on a user's desk. It has less memory, data transformation, and storage capacity than a mainframe. PCs are usually intended to be used by one, or at most, a few users. Several PCs can be linked together to share software and communicate through a **local area network (LAN)** (Cheong & Hirschheim, 1983). In most settings, PCs connected by LANs are making the mainframe obsolete, because LANs allow users the connectivity and shared software applications without the expense of a mainframe. PCs can also act as terminals for mainframe computers if they are equipped with the appropriate communications hardware and software.

Two different kinds of PCs constitute the vast majority of the personal computer market. The first is the Macintosh produced by Apple, Inc. The other runs on the Windows® operating system manufactured by Microsoft. These are commonly known as **clones** because they were originally designed based on a standard developed by IBM and have since been produced by many other companies.

PCs come in many shapes and sizes. One increasingly popular PC is the **laptop computer**, sometimes called a **notebook**. Although designed to use the same software and perform all the functions of the normal PC, laptops are portable and are often small enough to fit into a briefcase. Although more expensive than traditional PCs, the laptop offers a great deal of computing flexibility in sports medicine settings, because it can be transported easily to remote sites like playing fields and arenas. PCs are also available in handheld "palmtop" versions.

Although PCs are attractive hardware options for many sports medicine settings, they do have their limitations. Likewise, the mainframe computer has strengths and weaknesses. The relative advantages and disadvantages of these two hardware options include the following:

- PCs can be used by only one person at a time. A mainframe can accommodate many users simultaneously.

- PC users must know how to use peripheral devices, such as disk drives and printers. The terminal is usually the only device mainframe users must manipulate.

- Mainframes have much greater data storage and computational abilities. PCs continue to be improved, however, and their data transformation and storage resources are adequate for most sports medicine needs.

- Several operations can be performed simultaneously on most mainframes, whereas some older PCs are limited to single tasks, which prevents use of the computer during long print jobs or computational processes. Most newer PCs are designed to overcome this limitation, however.

- PCs offer greater control over the computer resource because problems can be handled locally.

- There is a much greater amount and variety of software available for the PC, including software developed specifically for athletic trainers. Most of the software is also much less expensive.

- PCs are much less expensive than mainframes. Most athletic trainers could purchase the necessary PC hardware, including peripheral devices, for under $2,000. Mainframes are many orders of magnitude more expensive.

- In many universities and hospitals, the library card catalogs are maintained on a mainframe computer. If athletic trainers have access to the mainframe, they can often search for books and journals without leaving the sports medicine center.

Important Hardware Questions

The following questions should be asked and answered prior to purchasing computer hardware:

- Will the desired software applications run on the hardware?

- What level and quality of technical support and service will accompany the hardware?

- Is the computer manufacturer well established? Will service be available in five years?

- Will the manufacturer or dealer provide training? What will it cost?

- Will the computer communicate with other machines? Can it be networked to different printers?

- Can the computer's capabilities be expanded? Can more **random access memory (RAM)**, disk space, or peripheral devices be added?

- Does the cost quotation include all the necessary equipment, including CPU, hard disk drive, monitor, keyboard, printer, cables, mouse, and modem? Are other peripheral devices or software included in the purchase price?

- Does the computer offer the fastest processing speed and largest hard drive capacity you can afford to purchase?

SOFTWARE CONSIDERATIONS

Computer software, also known as a *program*, is a set of instructions that tells the computer hardware what tasks to perform and how to perform them. A kind of software that must be installed on every computer is known as the **operating system.** Most operating systems are designed to be used with particular types of computers. For example, most IBM and compatible PCs use the Windows® operating system. Apple and Macintosh computers use a completely different operating system. Another kind of computer software that athletic trainers will have to purchase is **application software.** These programs are designed to carry out specific functions, such as word processing; data storage, manipulation, and retrieval; statistical analysis; graphics production; and communications. Many of the programs needed to carry out the information management function of a sports medicine program can be relatively expensive. There are thousands of very useful programs, however, known as **shareware** programs, that can be obtained at a reasonable cost. They are available from a variety of software distributors, usually for the cost of a floppy disk plus postage. If users like the programs, they are often asked to "register" by sending a modest fee to the software developer (Nehmer, 1997).

Before purchasing application software, athletic trainers should consider the following questions:

- Will the software help you accomplish the tasks that are required? Which tasks can't be accomplished? How important are they?

- Has the software functioned well in settings similar to yours? Talk to other athletic trainers about their experiences with specific programs.

- How user friendly is the software? How much training will be required? Who will provide the training?

random access memory (RAM)
A type of computer memory in which specific information can be accessed in any order. Generally, the more powerful application software programs require greater amounts of RAM.

computer software
Also known as a computer program. A set of instructions that controls the operations of the computer hardware.

operating system
The computer software, necessary to operate the machine, that integrates and controls the functions of the hardware and application software.

application software A computer program designed to perform a specific function such as word processing, statistical analysis, or graphics production.

shareware Application software available at greatly reduced cost, usually on a trial basis.

- Do the requirements of the software match the hardware you have? Do you have enough memory and hard-drive capacity to run the software?
- Is the software compatible with your computer's operating system?
- How expensive is the software? Are less-expensive alternatives available?
- Does the software come with written documentation? What is the quality of the written documentation?
- Does your institution provide technical support for this software?
- Is the software available on a trial basis?

Word Processing Software

Word processing is one of the most basic information management functions. Athletic trainers have a wide choice of computer programs for this function. Word processing software is used for a variety of purposes, including

- writing letters and memoranda,
- compiling reports,
- integrating text with graphics,
- merging lists for large mailings,
- manipulating text without having to retype,
- producing forms,
- checking spelling,
- searching text,
- managing computer files,
- performing simple calculations, and
- maintaining simple databases.

macro   An internal program available with some application software that allows a user to reduce a complex series of keystrokes to one command.

Many word processing programs can run **macros,** internal programs that make it possible to program a complex series of keystrokes with the touch of a key or two. One application of macro use in athletic training is the automatic generation of coaches' injury reports with just a few keystrokes (Ray, 1995).

Database Software

database software Application software that allows a user to input, store, manipulate, and retrieve a specific information set. Sometimes referred to as a database management system (DBMS).

Database software allows an athletic trainer to input, store, manipulate, and retrieve a specific information set (Christensen & Rupp, 1986). In athletic training, database software has been used primarily to store and retrieve information about athletic injuries and treatments. This segment of the software industry has been the most responsive to the needs of athletic trainers. Several database software programs developed specifically for athletic trainers are available, including *T-Wiz, SportsWare,* and *Sports Injury Monitoring System.*

T-Wiz is available from Human Kinetics Publishers (http://www.hkusa.com/). SportsWare is available from Computer Sports Medicine, Inc. (http://www.csmisolutions.com/). Sports Injury Monitoring System is available from Med Sports Systems (http://www.med-sports-systems.com/).

In addition to the specialized athletic injury database management programs already mentioned, generic DBMS programs are available for every type of computer (Leroy, 1990). Some programs are quite expensive and powerful and require knowledge of database management systems (DBMS) programming. Other programs, such as Microsoft® Access, come bundled with software "suites" and are much easier to use. These programs offer athletic trainers the ability to define the kind of data they want to store and to sort the data and generate reports based only on the information desired. Many low-cost DBMS programs allow importing and exporting data to and from word processing and spreadsheet programs. This useful feature allows an athletic trainer to generate reports with graphic representations of various kinds of data. Although the commercially available sports medicine DBMS applications are the best option for most athletic trainers, athletic trainers with very limited funds might wish to experiment with a low-cost generic DBMS first.

Spreadsheet Software

spreadsheet program *A type of application software that manipulates numerical data contained in cells formed by the intersection of rows and columns.*

A **spreadsheet program** manipulates the data stored in cells made up of columns and rows in a table on the computer screen (Illingworth, 1997). Cells can contain numbers, text, or formulas. Spreadsheets are most commonly used when mathematical calculations are required. When the numerical values in a cell are changed, formulas automatically recalculate the values contained in other affected cells. The program's text capabilities describe the numerical data by providing titles and headings. Most of the best spreadsheets also have graphics capabilities that allow the athletic trainer to depict numerical data as pie charts, bar charts, and other kinds of diagrams. Applied to sports medicine, spreadsheets are most useful for budget, inventory, purchasing, statistical analysis, and payroll functions.

Other Software

Athletic trainers often find it useful to employ computer software to perform complex statistical analyses, create graphic images for slides and overhead projections, organize their personal calendars, and send data to other computers. Even drug testing has entered the computerized age; see the very informative NCAA Web site **http://www.ncaa.org/sports_sciences/**.

ELECTRONIC MAIL, THE INTERNET, AND THE WORLD WIDE WEB

electronic mail *A system that allows users to communicate via computer.*

Athletic trainers are increasingly using **electronic mail,** also known as *e-mail*, to share information with people via their computers. To do so they need a PC (or a terminal if using a mainframe computer), modem, telephone line, and the appropriate terminal emulation and communications software (which is often included in the purchase price of the modem).

bulletin board *An electronic, online, interactive electronic database system, usually organized by topic or interest group.*

Athletic trainers can use bulletin boards, networking, list servers, and the World Wide Web to access and share information regarding their profession. In this context, a **bulletin board** is an online, interactive electronic database system (Dewey, 1987). It allows a computer to call up another computer to access information. Bulletin boards are usually devoted to specific topics. For example, NATA operates an employment bulletin board at its national headquarters. Users can leave messages, read messages, and transfer files to and from the bulletin board. Some bulletin boards are free (except for the long-distance telephone charge), whereas others require a membership fee or "connect time" fees. Dewey (1994) estimates that there are over 20 000 bulletin boards operating in the United States. Athletic trainers who work with large staffs in several different locations should consider the advantages of using a bulletin board to improve communication among staff members.

network   A group of computers connected by either direct hardwire coupling or dedicated telephone lines for the purpose of communicating with each other.

A **network** is a group of computers, usually three or more, connected either by direct hardwire coupling or a dedicated telephone line, that can communicate with each other. Computer networks can be relatively simple, such as a local area network connecting computers in a single sports medicine center, or very large and complex. For example, there are over 100 networks, including the largest and best known—the Internet—that connect educational and research institutions. Athletic trainers employed in these institutions, typically colleges and universities, send electronic mail and files to each other by using the networks (Frey & Adams, 1990).

Another way an athletic trainer can gather and disseminate information over a large area is by using a network to access a list server. A **list server** is a remote computer that compiles a list of user electronic mail addresses. When new items are added to the database, the server will send the new item as an e-mail message to all the users on the list. Like bulletin boards, discussion lists are usually topic specific (see table 6.1). Although there are hundreds of topics—and nearly 80 000 lists—for discussion list users to choose from, be careful about choosing too many, because you could generate an overwhelming amount of e-mail. Discussion lists and addresses change constantly, so be sure to stay abreast of what is currently available.

list server A remote computer that compiles a directory of users' computer addresses and distributes messages contributed by the members of a particular discussion list.

A great way to find discussion lists of interest to you is by accessing CataList, the official catalog of LISTSERV lists, at **http://www.lsoft.com/lists/listref.html**.

Table 6.1   Examples of Discussion Lists Available Through List Servers

Network address	Discussion topic or group
RSA-PS-L@BROWNVM.BROWN.EDU	Research Society on Alcoholism Psychosocial Research Group
SP-ALCOHOLISM-LIST@LISTSERV.ACSU.BUFFALO.EDU	Alcoholism Information
ATHTRN-L@LISTSERV.INDIANA.EDU	Discussion list for athletic trainers
BIOMCH-L@NIC.SURFNET.NL	Biomechanics and Movement Science
BIOMED-L@LISTSERV.NODAK.EDU	Biomedical Ethics
CNM-L@PEACH.EASE.LSOFT.COM	Clinical Nutrition Management Dietetic Practice Group
FIT-L@ETSUADMN.BITNET	Exercise/Diet/Wellness
LTCARE-L@LIST.NIH.GOV	Research on Disability and Long-Term Care
BRAIN-EDU@HOME.EASE.LSOFT.COM	Education and Brain injury
INJURY-L@WVNVM.WVNET.EDU	Injury Surveillance, Control, and Intervention
DRUG-RECOGNITION-L@LISTSERV.TAMU.EDU	Drug Recognition
REGAYN@LSV.UKY.EDU	Drug Abuse Prevention
ACERT@MAELSTROM.STJOHNS.EDU	ACERT Emergency Responder
EM-NSG-L@ITSSRV1.UCSF.EDU	Emergency Nursing
EMED-L@ITSSRV1.UCSF.EDU	Emergency Medicine
EMERG-L@VM.MARIST.EDU	Emergency Services
PED-EM-L@BROWNVM.BROWN.EDU	Pediatric Emergency Medicine
FAMILY-L@LSV.UKY.EDU	Family Medicine
FINAN-HC@WUVMD.WUSTL.EDU	Health Care Finance
FOODTALK@CRCVMS.UNL.EDU	Food, Nutrition, and Food Safety
AAHB-L@SIU.EDU	American Academy of Health Behavior

(continued)

Table 6.1 *(continued)*	
Network address	**Discussion topic or group**
AGS@HEALTH.NYAM.ORG	American Geriatrics Society
BUSHEA-L@SIU.EDU	Health-Related Information for Business and Industry
CAPHIS@SHRSYS.HSLC.ORG	Consumer and Patient Health Information Service
CHERA-L@POST.QUEENSU.CA	Canadian Health Economics Research Association
CLICK4HP@YORKU.CA	Health Promotion
COMMUNITY-HEALTH-L@MAIL.MSH.ORG	Community Health
GLOBALRN@ITSSRV1.UCSF.EDU	Nursing and Other Health Professions
HEALTH-PROMOTION@INFO.MIP.KI.SE	Health Promotion and Disease Prevention
HEALTHPOL@HOME.EASE.LSOFT.COM	Health Care Policy
HLT-NET@NIC.SURFNET.NL	Initiatives in Innovation in Health Professions
HLTHPROF@MSU.EDU	Health Professions Advising
HOMEHLTH@LIST.IEX.NET	Home Health Care
MOTORDEV@UMDD.BITNET	Human Motor Skill Development
PATIENTSAFETY-L@NPSF.ORG	Patient Safety
SAFETY@LIST.UVM.EDU	Safety
SPORTPSY@VM.TEMPLE.EDU	Exercise and Sports Psychology
WISHPERD@SJSUVM1.SJSU.EDU	Women in Sport, Health, Physical Education, Recreation and Dance

browser A computer program that allows the user to search the World Wide Web for information on a given topic and display the information in text and graphic formats.

No discussion of information resources would be complete without at least some mention of the World Wide Web (the Web). The Web is an electronic information environment whereby computers search for information on a specific topic that resides on other computers—all over the globe. The information is organized into Web sites that are made up of individual Web "pages." The content of a page—both text and graphics—is displayed on your computer screen by a **browser** program.

Athletic trainers can use the Web for a variety of information gathering purposes. Some professional journals publish either their table of contents, or in some cases, entire articles on their Web sites. Vendors that service the athletic training profession advertise their products on the Web. Governmental, regulatory, and accreditation agencies that affect athletic training programs post important information on the Web (see appendix B). Many colleges and universities that offer athletic training education programs have Web sites that describe their programs, faculty, facilities, and students. A wide variety of Web sites offer useful medical information for athletic trainers and other health care professionals. In fact, the Web is fast becoming the primary information source for many athletic trainers. Like electronic discussion lists, Web sites and their addresses are in a constant state of change. An address that is current today might be changed next week, so be sure to stay abreast of the addresses for the sites you use the most.

APPLICATIONS TO ATHLETIC TRAINING: THEORY INTO PRACTICE

Apply the concepts discussed in this chapter to the following two case studies to help you prepare for such situations you might face in actual practice. The questions at the end of the studies have many possible solutions. The case studies can be used for homework, test questions, or in class discussion.

Case Study 1

When Charles Olson, the athletic trainer at Eagletown High School, met with his student athletic trainer staff at the beginning of each school year, he always covered documentation procedures for injuries and treatments. The following procedures were to be used by all student athletic trainers:

- Injury evaluation forms were to be completed only by the head athletic trainer. Student athletic trainers were expected to file the forms in individual medical files every Monday, Wednesday, and Friday.

- All treatments were to be recorded by student athletic trainers on the daily treatment log as soon as the treatment was administered. On Monday, Wednesday, and Friday afternoons, all treatments from the daily treatment log were to be copied onto the bottom half of the injury evaluation report by the student athletic trainers. Once a page of the log had been transferred, it was thrown away.

One day Charles was surprised to find a subpoena in his mail for all medical records related to a former student-athlete who had graduated five years earlier. At first, Charles could not find the student's file. Finally, after several hours of digging through boxes in a storage closet in the gymnasium, he found the file. When he looked up the injury evaluation form for the case in question, he was shocked to see that the treatment records were sloppy, often not dated, and usually illegible because they had been written with a fountain pen that had left blotches of smeared ink on the page. Although Charles complied with the subpoena and submitted all the requested records, he was left with an uneasy feeling about the quality of those records.

Questions for Analysis

1. What are the advantages of the injury and treatment recording system used at Eagletown High School? What are the disadvantages?

2. What kinds of problems is the Eagletown High School system likely to foster? How could those problems be overcome? What kinds of resources would be required to implement these solutions? How much would it cost?

3. What are the legal implications for this record-keeping system? Which legal issues should be addressed when considering changes in the system?

Case Study 2

Randy Waters is an athletic trainer for a double-A minor league professional baseball team. In addition to his duties as athletic trainer, Randy is also equipment manager and traveling secretary for the team. Because of his many duties, Randy is a very busy person without a lot of time for record keeping. He usually discusses the health of individual players with the team's manager over coffee and rolls each morning. Randy informs the manager of any new injuries and the manager can ask any questions he has.

One day in August, as the playoffs were rapidly approaching, Randy was unable to have coffee with the manager and the other coaches because he had to make arrangements for an upcoming trip. During the game that night, the team's star pitcher's knee suddenly buckled after a pitch and he fell to the ground. He had to be removed from the game and was evaluated by the team physician in the locker room. After the game, the physician told the manager the knee would be fine in a couple of days, but in the future it would be wise to rest players for a day or two following an accident like the one the pitcher had suffered. "What accident?" asked the manager with a puzzled look on his face. The physician related that during his exam the player told him he had twisted his knee in the parking lot the previous evening. He had gone to the athletic trainer and gotten some ice for it and in the morning it felt better. The manager immediately went to Randy and demanded to know why he hadn't been informed.

Questions for Analysis

1. Why is the manager so upset with Randy? Is his anger justified?

2. What steps could Randy have taken to avoid this situation? How should Randy modify his information management system to avoid problems like this in the future?

3. What legal risks does Randy's system pose, both for the club and for himself?

4. If Randy decided to use a computer to help him with his information management needs, what kinds of hardware and software might serve him best?

SUMMARY

1. *Understand the importance of documentation as part of a complete information management system in sports medicine.*

   To succeed as professionals in an information society, athletic trainers must manage and communicate information effectively. Documentation is a central task in the athletic trainer's information management role. Medical documentation helps ensure legal rights, acts as a memory aid, satisfies laws and professional standards, and provides data on which to make informed decisions.

2. *Understand and describe the different methods of athletic injury and treatment documentation.*

   There are five methods for documenting injury evaluation and treatment data, including problem-oriented medical records, focus charting, charting by exception, computerized documentation, and narrative charting.

3. *Understand and describe the different types of information to be managed in a typical sports medicine program.*

   Information in sports medicine is usually made up of medical records and program administration records. Medical records are confidential and should contain injury and treatment reports, physical examination data, reports of special procedures, communications from other health care professionals, emergency information, permission to treat and medical waiver forms, release of medical information forms, and certain kinds of insurance records. Program administration records include reports to coaches, budget information, nonmedical correspondence, equipment and supply information, personnel information, patient and student education information, and information required for writing self-studies and other kinds of evaluative reports.

4. *Understand how to use a computer in the sports medicine information management process.*

Computers can be useful tools in assisting an athletic trainer in managing information if used thoughtfully and wisely. Athletic trainers should consider cost, types of problems to be solved, amount of available support, and the number of people who will have to use the computer system, when purchasing hardware and software. Many kinds of software are available to help an athletic trainer manage information, including word processing, database, and spreadsheet. Several DBMS systems written specifically for athletic trainers are available, although a generic program might serve well. Athletic trainers can share information with other professionals by using the computer as a communication device. Bulletin boards, networks, electronic mail, list servers, and the World Wide Web are a few of the methods available to help athletic trainers use computers to expand their information base.

CHAPTER SEVEN

Athletic Trainers Paying the Bills: Athletic Injury Insurance

OBJECTIVES

After reading this chapter, you should be able to do the following:

1. Understand the difference between medical, health, and accident insurance.

2. Understand the advantages and disadvantages of self-insurance, primary coverage, and secondary coverage.

3. Define the types of injuries covered by most athletic accident policies.

4. Understand the basic legal responsibilities associated with third-party reimbursement.

5. Understand the role of procedural coding in the third-party reimbursement system.

6. Organize a claims-processing system for a sports medicine program in an educational setting.

7. Understand the steps required to file a claim for reimbursement from a third-party payer.

8. Evaluate and purchase an athletic accident insurance policy for an educational institution.

Sven Olaf, a recent transfer student and star of the New Amsterdam High School soccer team, was racing down the sidelines during a game against the crosstown rivals when he collapsed in pain. The school's certified athletic trainer, Jennifer Smith, ran onto the field and discovered that Sven was suffering from severe spasm of the paraspinous musculature. The cause of the spasm was unknown, and the lower-extremity neurological examination was normal. Because Sven was in such pain, Jennifer decided to have him transported to the local hospital by ambulance. While waiting for the ambulance to arrive, Sven's parents and the team's coach gathered around to provide support and reassurance. As Sven was being placed onto the spine board, the coach took Sven's father, who was unemployed, aside and told him, "Don't worry about the bills. The school has insurance for this kind of thing and I'm sure we'll be able to take care of it because it was an athletic injury." Two days later, Sven was discharged from the hospital after incurring a bill of over $2,000.

Because Sven had no personal medical insurance, Jennifer submitted the entire bill to the school's athletic accident insurance company. Three weeks later, Jennifer received a letter from the company denying the claim because the injury was substantially linked to a preexisting condition. Although Sven had never told Jennifer, he had suffered a similar injury two years earlier while a student at another school. The emergency room physician obtained this information during the examination and provided it to the insurance company in the medical records needed to process the claim. Because preexisting conditions were excluded in the athletic accident policy, the company denied the claim.

When Jennifer contacted Sven's parents and informed them the claim had been denied, Mr. Olaf angrily told her he had been assured the school would pay the bills. "The coach promised me!" he shouted over the phone. Jennifer told Mr. Olaf she would consult with the school administration and call him back. When Jennifer informed the athletic director of the problem, he immediately called a meeting with the coach, the school principal, and Jennifer to determine where they would find $2,000 to pay the bill that the coach, as an agent of the school, had promised they would pay.

 What can't be cured must be insured.

Oliver Herford

Athletic trainers with any experience should be able to sympathize with Jennifer Smith's situation. Athletic administrators have long felt a moral responsibility to prevent the cost associated with athletic injury from barring access to school sports programs. The soccer coach's promise to Sven's father was simply an expression of that sense of responsibility. His promise probably would have been easy to keep in the 1970s, when the majority of student-athletes' parents had their own comprehensive medical insurance. Unfortunately, this is no longer true. Stein (1996) reports that in 1979, 85% of the population was covered by some form of private health insurance. By 1996, however, this figure had dropped to approximately 70% (see figure 7.1). The percentage of the population that has access to health insurance through the employer of a family member has dropped to 61% (Bennefield, 1997). Access to private medical insurance is declining, and the terms of medical insurance policies are becoming increasingly restrictive. For example, between 1982 and 1984 alone, the number of companies that required deductibles for hospitalization doubled from 30% to 60%, while the number of employers that required employees to make a contribution to the cost of their insurance premiums also increased (Fein, 1986). Nearly all health care insurance plans now require such contributions.

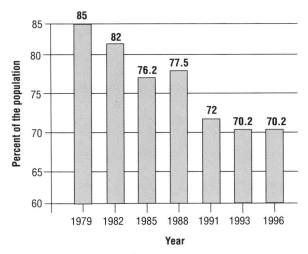

Percent of the population

85 — 85
82
80 — 76.2   77.5
75 —
72
70 — 70.2   70.2
65 —
60 —
1979 1982 1985 1988 1991 1993 1996
Year

∎ Figure 7.1 Percentage of the U.S. population with private health insurance.

Data from Health Insurance Association of America 1998 and U.S. Census reports 1996.

The cost of health care became an important political issue during the early and mid-1990s. Several proposals went before Congress and were intended to significantly modify the health care reimbursement system. These proposals ranged from minor reforms of the private health insurance system to schemes that would create a national health care system similar to the Canadian model. Although no significant federally mandated changes in the health insurance system occurred, this national discussion on health care was useful, because it pushed the marketplace to develop new, more efficient health care delivery systems that have helped hold down the rate of cost increase of medical goods and services.

In the meantime, schools and colleges face greater financial risks from medical costs than at any time in the past. This chapter, therefore, will provide athletic trainers with the information they need to manage insurance systems and more effectively safeguard the resources of the institutions they represent while living up to the moral responsibility to remove financial barriers to our nation's playing fields. In addition, this chapter will examine the third-party reimbursement process to help athletic trainers working in hospitals and clinics get paid for what they do.

INSURANCE SYSTEMS

There are many different kinds of insurance, including medical, health, athletic accident, catastrophic, and disability. Athletic accident insurance comes in one of three forms: primary coverage, secondary coverage, and self-insurance.

*medical insurance
A contract between a policyholder and an insurance company to reimburse a percentage of the cost of the policyholder's medical bills.*

policy   A contract between an insurance company and an individual or organization.

*health insurance
A type of policy designed to reimburse the cost of preventative as well as corrective medical care.*

Medical insurance is a contract between the holder of a **policy** and an insurance company to reimburse a percentage of the cost of the policyholder's medical bills, usually after a deductible has been paid by the policyholder (Rowell, 1989). **Health insurance,** on the other hand, is generally more comprehensive, because it often includes provisions for maintaining good health rather than simply paying for illnesses and injuries.

Both of these insurance classifications should be distinguished from the type of policy most educational institutions purchase for their student-athletes: **athletic accident insurance,** which is usually intended to supplement a student's family insurance plan and reimburses the cost of athletic accidents only (Chambers, Ross, & Kozubowski, 1986). The insurance industry defines *accident* differently from the concept of *injury* as understood by most athletic trainers, coaches, parents, athletes, and other physically active patients. To an insurance company, accidents usually include acute, traumatic injuries, independent of any other cause or preexisting condition, that occur during practices and games. Specific **exclusions** in most accident insurance plans include injuries caused by overuse (tendinitis, bursitis, stress fractures, etc.); illnesses; and degenerative conditions. Some athletic accident insurance companies offer **riders** to cover the costs of chronic conditions, but riders generally increase the **premium** significantly.

A fourth type of coverage is **catastrophic insurance,** which usually takes effect after the first $50,000 in medical bills has been reached and provides lifetime medical, rehabilitation, and disability coverage for athletes who have suffered long-term or permanent handicaps as a result of athletic injuries. Member institutions of the National Collegiate Athletic Association (NCAA) have received catastrophic insurance at no cost since 1991. Catastrophic insurance is also available to non-NCAA institutions and high schools through their national governing organizations.

For a complete description of NCAA-sponsored insurance programs, visit the NCAA Web site at **http://www.ncaa.org/insurance/**.

athletic accident insurance A type of insurance policy intended to reimburse medical vendors for the expenses associated with acute athletic accidents.

exclusions Situations or circumstances specifically not covered by an insurance policy.

rider Additions to a standard insurance policy that provide coverage for conditions that are normally not covered.

premium The invoiced cost of an insurance policy.

catastrophic insurance A type of accident insurance designed to provide lifelong medical, rehabilitation, and disability benefits for the victims of devastating injury.

disability insurance Insurance designed to protect an athlete against future loss of earnings due to a disabling injury or sickness.

experimental treatments Therapies not proven to be effective.

usual, customary, and reasonable fee (UCR) The charge consistent with what other medical vendors would assess.

90th-percentile fee The fee below which 90% of all other medical vendors in a particular geographic area charge for a specific service.

Disability insurance is also available through many companies; it is designed to protect athletes against future loss of earnings due to a disabling injury or sickness that occurred while they were engaged in sports activities. The NCAA sponsors a disability insurance program for exceptional student-athletes in football, men's basketball, baseball, and ice hockey. The NCAA also sponsors a special assistance fund program that may be used to pay for some medical and dental expenses for Division I student-athletes.

Finally, some insurance companies provide coverage for specific kinds of health-related problems. Dental insurance and vision insurance are two examples. These policies can be purchased separately, or they can be added to broader health care plans as riders.

EXPERIMENTAL THERAPY

Regardless of whether or not an athlete or other physically active patient is covered by medical, health, accident, or catastrophic insurance, **experimental treatments** and procedures are usually excluded under the terms of most policies (Newcomer, 1990). A variety of medical and surgical techniques now common in sports medicine began as experimental therapies. Physicians, athletic trainers, and physical therapists frequently experiment with new methods to help patients return to physical activity earlier and more safely. Unfortunately, the insurance industry often determines that a therapeutic method has made the transition from experimental to conventional several years after the medical profession does. Insurance companies define *experimental* in different ways, the best way being to simply list what they consider experimental procedures in the policy. Another method companies sometimes employ is to list the criteria by which they will determine if a procedure is experimental. This method is less exact and more difficult to defend in the courts. The final, and most common, method insurance companies use is to decide which methods are experimental on a case-by-case basis. The case-by-case decision method can be frustrating for patients and health care providers because they don't know what will be paid for and what will not.

USUAL, CUSTOMARY, AND REASONABLE FEES

Another insurance concept athletic trainers should understand is **usual, customary, and reasonable (UCR)** reimbursement for medical services. The UCR concept is a flexible-fee system originally developed by the federal government to reimburse health care providers through the Medicare system that is now used by most insurance companies. The amount of money that insurance companies will pay to health care providers for a particular service under the UCR system is determined by a combination of the following factors:

- The usual fee charged by each health care provider for the particular service
- The customary fee for the geographic area (either the average fee or the **90th-percentile fee,** whichever is lowest)
- The reasonable fee (the lower of either the usual or customary fee)

To reduce the likelihood of having a claim denied, an athletic trainer should make sure that physicians and other health care providers the patient will be referred to will perform only nonexperimental procedures and that they will accept the UCR fee as payment in full for services rendered. If the planned procedure could potentially be considered experimental, the athletic trainer should consult a representative of the insurance company before beginning it.

Even the most circumspect athletic trainer will have claims denied from time to time for reasons that might or might not seem fair. Lawsuits to recover the costs of denied claims should be the last possible option. The following suggestions might help resolve claims denied because of experimental treatment or UCR clauses:

- Find out the exact reasons the claim was denied. Insurance companies are required by law to provide this information.
- Obtain a statement from the physician or other health care provider explaining why the treatment was implemented and justifying the fee.
- If a patient is covered through a parent's employer's self-insurance fund, correspond with the employer directly. The employer, not the insurance administrator, has final legal authority to reverse the denial.
- Provide evidence from clinical studies to support your claim that the treatment should not be considered experimental.
- Try to convince the physician or other health care provider to waive the portion of the fee above the UCR amount.
- Contact the state insurance commissioner and request assistance in challenging the denial.

TYPES OF ATHLETIC INSURANCE

Educational institutions can choose from three options when designing a medical insurance system for their student-athletes: self-insurance, primary coverage, and secondary coverage (Hart & Cole, 1992). As with any management option, each system has advantages and disadvantages, including cost.

Self-Insurance

Institutions that choose to self-insure are speculating that the amount of money they pay out for medical expenses will be less than the amount they would pay for insurance premiums. The institution typically purchases no medical or accident insurance except for catastrophic coverage and pays medical bills incurred by student-athletes. Many national governing organizations such as the NCAA have rules that prevent educational institutions from paying for medical expenses not directly related to participation in intercollegiate or interscholastic athletics. Institutions that self-insure must be particularly careful to create and monitor procedures used to ensure compliance with these rules.

Self-insuring offers several advantages. Saving money is possible, because the institution retains the potential profit earned by an insurance company. Processing claims is also simplified, because there are no insurance claim forms to complete. Institutions have the flexibility to pay for procedures that might be excluded under a normal insurance policy.

Advantages and Disadvantages of Self-Insurance

Advantages	Disadvantages
• Potential savings	• High risk for large claims
• Simplified claims process	• Risk of bankrupting fund
• Greater flexibility	• Institutional dollars tied up

Although cost is an advantage with self-insurance, it can be a significant disadvantage as well. A large claim can deplete an institution's insurance fund, making it difficult or impossible to pay other, less costly claims. This is one reason why self-insurance is typically employed by large, financially healthy university athletic programs. One method for safeguarding against the possibility of a large claim is to set aside leftover insurance funds in an endowment account that will eventually provide a cushion against large claims. The disadvantage of this method is that it ties up a substantial amount of the institution's money, which could be used for more productive purposes. Institutions that self-insure can decrease their annual expenses by using a student-athlete's personal insurance as the primary source of coverage wherever possible. In this case, the institution becomes a secondary payer. See the following sections for discussions of primary and secondary coverage.

Primary Coverage

primary coverage
A type of health, medical, or accident insurance that begins to pay for covered expenses immediately after a deductible has been paid.

Primary coverage is medical or accident insurance that begins to pay for covered medical expenses as soon as the institution pays the deductible. The athlete's (or the athlete's parents') personal medical insurance is not a source for payment of medical bills arising out of athletic participation. Institutions adopt primary insurance plans for a variety of reasons. Some feel a moral obligation to pay for all athletic medical expenses without involving families or their insurance companies. Others have a student population that is substantially uninsured anyway, so it is logical to choose primary coverage. Finally, primary coverage simplifies and accelerates claims processing, because the family does not need to be involved.

> **Reasons for Purchasing Primary Insurance Coverage**
> - Sense of responsibility for paying all medical expenses
> - Large percentage of uninsured student-athletes
> - Simplified and accelerated claims processing

The disadvantage of primary coverage is the expense. Because the insurance company takes on all the risk for an institution's student-athletes, as opposed to sharing the risk with personal medical insurance, it must charge a substantially higher premium for the coverage. Hart and Cole (1992) point out that the number of schools that purchased primary coverage for their athletic medicine programs dropped from 30% in 1982 to about 5% in 1992. The percentage of educational institutions that purchased primary coverage in 1998 was less than 1% (Lyndon Cronen, conversation with author, July 1999).

Secondary Coverage

secondary coverage
A type of health, medical, or accident insurance that begins to pay for covered expenses only after all other sources of insurance coverage have been exhausted. Also known as excess insurance.

Secondary coverage, also known as *excess insurance,* is a policy that pays for covered medical expenses only after all other insurance policies, including the athlete's personal medical insurance, have reached their limit. This is the type of insurance plan selected by most institutions (Lehr, 1992). The most obvious benefit of this approach is that institutions can lower their costs by spreading the risk associated with athletic injuries to other potential payers. Because the risk is shared with personal insurance companies, the costs associated with secondary coverage can be as much as 60% lower than those associated with primary coverage. Another, less-tangible benefit to this approach is that, if used properly, it can help develop a sense of shared responsibility for safety in an athletic program. Most parents want to provide a safe environment for their children. Presumably, their interest is heightened when they have a financial interest as well. An additional advantage of the secondary approach is that it encourages athletic administrators to find ways to reduce and control medical costs. See the following section for an expanded discussion.

Advantages and Disadvantages of Secondary Insurance Coverage

Advantages	Disadvantages
• Less costly	• Longer claims process
• Shared responsibility	• Requires more communication
• Promotes cost controls	• Labor-intensive claims process

The disadvantages of secondary coverage relate to claims processing. Because personal insurance is used as a primary layer of coverage, an institution must spend substantial time and energy communicating with parents and their insurance carriers to move claims along. This can delay settling insurance claims, which can frustrate medical vendors the institution wants to keep happy. Another potential problem is that the secondary system requires more communication and understanding about the shared responsibility for paying medical costs. In the opening case, misunderstandings about how the school's policy worked were a major part of the problem. The school was eventually placed in a position in which administrators felt pressured to pay for Sven's medical treatment, even though the injury occurred before Sven arrived at the school.

REDUCING INSURANCE COSTS

Premiums for medical or accident insurance are closely linked to an institution's past claims history, enhancing the incentives for institutions to institute risk-management programs and decrease medical costs. Insurance companies track the cost of claims made by an institution and compare these costs to the premium the institution pays. Because all insurance companies must make a profit to stay in business, they will adjust the premium to help ensure that it will cover the likely cost of the claims, the administration of those claims, and the desired profit margin. Some insurance companies adjust premiums every year in an effort to balance this equation. Others make adjustments less frequently so that over the long term, say five years, their financial goals are met.

In any case, athletic trainers and other members of the sports medicine team can help their institutions keep insurance premiums to a minimum by instituting the following measures. Keep in mind that individual institutional philosophies will govern which, if any, of the following suggestions are adopted.

• Spread the risk among all concerned parties. The best way to do this is to purchase secondary coverage so that the personal insurance of athletes or their parents becomes the primary source of payment for athletic injuries.

• Adopt and communicate policies that limit the institution's financial obligations to those injuries that are covered by the school's insurance policy. For example, some athletic accident policies exclude certain kinds of injuries (e.g., stress fractures). The institution can limit its financial risk if it also refuses to pay for these kinds of injuries. To do otherwise results in institutional expenditures far in excess of the annual insurance premium.

• Insist that athletes purchase their own personal insurance. Remember, even if the institution has secondary coverage, it will end up paying from the first dollar of the claim for injured athletes without their own personal insurance. Some institutions will not allow students to participate in athletic programs without their own personal insurance. Other institutions provide their students with the opportunity to purchase university-sponsored health insurance; unfortunately, most of these policies have relatively low coverage caps and will not pay for injuries associated with intercollegiate athletics.

• Pass the cost—or some fraction of the cost—of the athletic accident insurance along to the athletes by requiring them to pay a modest sum for the insurance.

• Limit the institution's financial obligation for costs associated with athletic injuries to those medical services that have been pre-approved by an institutional representative—usually the athletic trainer or team physician. In effect, you will be creating your own HMO, because all injured athletes will be required to pass through a gatekeeper in order to have the cost of their injuries covered by the school or its insurance company. Injured athletes could still receive medical care from the provider of their choice, but they would have to pay for it if they did not use the services of the athletic trainer, team physician, or some other approved provider (Ray, 1996).

• Encourage medical providers to treat athletes from your institution on an "insurance only" basis. If the physician is willing to accept whatever the athlete's personal insurance will pay as payment in full, little or no cost will be passed on to the institution or its insurance company.

• Require injured athletes covered by managed care plans to use medical providers approved by the plan. Many managed care plans, especially HMOs, will not pay for medical services provided by out-of-plan physicians. These costs are almost always passed on to the institution.

• Conduct annual risk-assessment audits designed to help reduce the incidence of athletic injuries.

THIRD-PARTY REIMBURSEMENT

Athletic trainers who work in hospitals and clinics might earn a portion of their incomes through third-party reimbursement. Reimbursement through this system requires knowledge of diagnostic and procedural coding and strict adherence to certain legal requirements on the part of the athletic trainer.

third-party reimbursement
The process by which medical vendors are reimbursed by insurance companies for services provided to policyholders.

third party   *A medical vendor with no binding interest in a particular insurance contract.*

Third-party reimbursement is the process by which health care practitioners are reimbursed by a policyholder's insurance company for services they perform. A **third party** is defined as a person, in this case a medical vendor, who has no binding interest in a particular contract (the insurance policy). Third-party reimbursement is used as the primary mechanism to pay for medical services in the United States. Hospitals and private-practice health professionals rely very heavily on third-party reimbursement to generate the income that keeps their practices in business.

Athletic trainers have historically had a difficult time obtaining third-party reimbursement for their services. In many cases, the lack of state credentialing for athletic trainers created a barrier to third-party reimbursement. Even in those states that credential athletic trainers, however, reimbursement for athletic training services has been difficult to obtain. Insurance companies, concerned about financial issues, have been slow to cover athletic trainers' services, even though the percentage of the population demanding those services is increasing. Access to payment for athletic training services through insurance companies is becoming more available now that more states credential athletic trainers. In addition, outcome studies conducted by the NATA have demonstrated that athletic training services are cost efficient and effective in the treatment of injuries in physically active populations. As more state athletic trainers' organizations lobby their insurance commissioners and legislators for access to third-party billing (with the help of the NATA), an increase in the number of athletic trainers being paid for their services in this manner is likely.

Even though athletic trainers have historically lacked direct access to third-party reimbursement, they are often responsible for generating significant amounts of reimbursable dollars for the clinics and hospitals that employ them; therefore, they must understand this aspect of insurance. Many athletic trainers employed in sports medicine clinics perform tasks nearly identical to those performed by the physical therapists who countersign the athletic trainers' notes, thereby creating the basis for insurance reimbursement. Athletic trainers working in high school outreach programs are often responsible for bringing in referrals to the clinics that employ them. Many of these patients will pay for the services they receive by submitting a claim to their medical insurance carriers.

Some athletic trainers in university sports medicine programs have employed physical therapists, and this allows their programs to seek third-party reimbursement from their student-athletes' personal insurance companies. This practice is controversial, however, and has been criticized by some leaders in the profession, because it creates the feeling that athletic trainers might prioritize their treatment of student-athletes based on insurance coverage. (Godek, 1992).

TYPES OF THIRD-PARTY PAYERS

fee-for-service plan Also known as an indemnity plan. A type of traditional medical insurance whereby patients are free to seek medical services from any provider. The plan covers a portion of the cost of covered procedures, and the patient is responsible for the balance.

There are several models of third-party payment. Many health plans offer several models to their enrollees. Some companies even develop hybrid plans that mix the characteristics of the following models:

• Private medical insurance companies provide group and individual coverage for employees and their dependents. The medical insurance provided by these companies is typically the traditional **fee-for-service plan**. This insurance model is also known as an *indemnity plan* (DeCarlo, 1997). Patients are free to go to the medical provider of their choice. The plan reimburses a portion of the cost of covered services, and the patient is responsible for the copayment or deductible. Fee-for-service plans are rapidly being replaced by the managed care models described next.

For an excellent summary of the different health care insurance options available to consumers, see the Health Insurance Association of America's Web site at **http://www.hiaa.org/consumerinfo/ guidehi.html.**

health maintenance organization (HMO) A type of health insurance plan that requires policyholders to use only those medical vendors approved by the company. All medical services are coordinated by a primary care physician, who acts as a gatekeeper to specialty services.

capitation   A system whereby medical vendors are paid a fixed amount per patient.

• **Health maintenance organizations (HMOs)** provide participating health care practitioners with a fixed fee for services rendered to members. Fees are usually, but not always, determined using a **capitation** (per-person) system. HMOs that do not use a capitation system usually reimburse providers based on a fixed-fee schedule. Physically active patients insured by an HMO must use a primary care provider that participates in the HMO. A modest copayment is usually charged. Some HMOs provide services at medical facilities, while others provide care through a network of individual medical practitioners (**individual practice associations, or IPAs**).

• **Preferred provider organizations (PPOs)** operate similarly to HMOs, but usually allow greater choice of health care providers and pay medical vendors on a fee-for-service, rather than a capitated, basis. PPOs allow policyholders to choose any health care provider they wish, but they provide financial incentives for policyholders who use providers identified by the PPO. When physically active patients choose to see a medical provider who does not belong to the PPO, they can expect to pay for a greater percentage of the cost of the services. One variant of the PPO is the **exclusive provider organization (EPO)**, in which enrolled participants can receive benefits only from contracting medical providers (May, Schraeder, & Britt, 1996; O'Leary, 1994).

• A **point-of-service (POS)** plan is similar to a PPO. The primary difference between the two is that POS plans assign primary care physicians, who act as gatekeepers by coordinating patient care. Most PPO plans do not.

*individual practice association (IPA)
A managed care model whereby an HMO provides health care services through a network of individual medical practitioners. Care is provided in a physician's office as opposed to a large, multifunctional medical center.*

*preferred provider organization (PPO)
A type of health insurance plan that provides financial incentives to encourage policyholders to use those medical vendors approved by the company.*

*exclusive provider organization (EPO)
A type of PPO whereby medical services are reimbursed only if the patient uses contracted providers.*

point-of-service plan (POS) Managed care plans that are similar to PPOs, except that primary care physicians are assigned to patients to coordinate their care.

fraud Criminal misrepresentation for the purpose of financial gain.

*International Classification of Diseases (ICD-9-CM)
A coding system applied to illnesses, injuries, and other medical conditions for the purpose of standardizing the language associated with third-party reimbursement.*

*Current Procedural Terminology (CPT)
A coding system applied to medical procedures for the purpose of standardizing the language associated with third-party reimbursement.*

- Government-sponsored programs provide coverage for the elderly (Medicare), the needy (Medicaid), and members of the armed forces and their dependents (CHAMPUS).

LEGAL REQUIREMENTS

Among the many legal considerations in third-party reimbursement, one of the most important is the requirement that health care practitioners obtain a signed authorization from a patient for release of medical records. Unless the patient authorizes such a release, the medical vendor is bound by the patient-practitioner relationship to keep information confidential. Third-party payers, however, will not process claims unless they have access to the information to substantiate them.

Another legal issue related to confidentiality of the medical record involves answering an insurance company's questions about a patient's case over the telephone. Athletic trainers should always verify the identity of the caller and be sure the patient has signed an authorization for release of medical records before answering questions over the phone. Rowell (1989) suggests the following steps:

- Once the patient's claim form is in hand, ask the caller to read a portion of the information to verify that the caller has the original.
- If the caller is requesting a detailed explanation, ask that the questions be submitted in writing on company letterhead.
- Ask the caller for the insurance company's telephone number. Call the person back through the company switchboard to verify identity.
- Never answer questions from attorneys until the authorization for release of information is in hand, even if the attorney claims to have it. The best practice is to correspond by mail with attorneys regarding insurance reimbursement cases.

Fraud is another legal pitfall athletic trainers must avoid in the third-party reimbursement process. Fraud is a significant problem in the insurance industry. The federal government's General Accounting Office estimates that health care insurance fraud accounts for 10% of all health care expenditures—nearly $100 billion per year (Health Insurance Association of America, 1997). An athletic trainer must never change the date of an injury, treatment, or assessment, or fail to record payments from an insurance company on a patient's bill. Other fraudulent acts committed by unscrupulous health care providers include claiming reimbursement for treatments that were not provided and increasing the charges for treatments for patients with insurance. The penalties for medical fraud are substantial and can include fines of $2,000 per occurrence plus twice the amount of the false claim.

DIAGNOSTIC AND PROCEDURAL CODING

Reimbursement for sports medicine services is based on the coding system used when submitting claims to third-party payers. There are two kinds of codes that must be submitted—diagnostic and procedural.

Diagnostic coding is required for all forms of third-party billing. The **International Classification of Diseases (ICD-9-CM)** is a book that specifies the code that should be applied to every injury or condition that athletic trainers or other health professionals treat. It defines each condition as a five-digit code that must be entered on all claim forms. Table 7.1 serves as an example of the diagnostic code for acute sprains and strains of the ankle and foot.

The **Current Procedural Terminology (CPT)** is a list of codes published by the American Medical Association that represents the vast majority of medical proce-

Table 7.1   ICD-9-CM Codes for the Foot and Ankle

Code	Subcode 1	Subcode 2	Condition
845			Sprains and Strains of the Foot and Ankle
	845.0		Ankle
		845.00	Unspecified site
		845.01	Deltoid (ligament), ankle
		845.02	Calcaneofibular (ligament)
		845.03	Tibiofibular (ligament), distal
		845.09	Other
	845.1		Foot
		845.10	Unspecified site
		845.11	Tarsometatarsal (joint) (ligament)
		845.12	Metatarsalphalangeal (joint)
		845.13	Interphalangeal (joint), toe
		845.19	Other

dures. The person completing a claim form for sports medicine services selects the most appropriate code for each of the services rendered. Some examples of common CPT codes employed in sports medicine settings include those in table 7.2.

The Current Procedural Terminology is available by contacting Book and Pamphlet Fulfillment, OP-341/8, American Medical Association, P.O. Box 10946, Chicago, IL 60610-0946.

The importance of carefully checking the accuracy of the diagnostic and procedural codes listed on the claim form cannot be overstated. Using improper codes will significantly increase the time it takes the insurance company to process the claim and might result in denial of the claim.

CLAIMS PROCESSING

Claims processing is the act of formally communicating with an insurance company or other third-party payer for the purpose of seeking payment for services rendered to an injured patient. The process is different for athletic trainers working in educational settings than it is for those working in sports medicine clinics.

Filing claims quickly and properly is one of an athletic trainer's most important insurance functions. The claims process is distinctly different for athletic trainers in educational settings and athletic trainers in private or hospital-based sports medicine clinics. Athletic trainers in educational settings file all (or nearly all) claims with a single insurance company to pay other medical vendors for services rendered to the institution's student-athletes, whereas athletic trainers in sports medicine clinics file claims with a wide range of insurance companies for reimbursement for services they provide. University athletic trainers who employ physical therapists so student-athletes' insurance companies can be billed also fall into the second category. The two settings will be discussed separately, because the claims process is different in each.

CLAIMS PROCESSING IN EDUCATIONAL SETTINGS

An athletic trainer can take preliminary steps to make claims processing easier. One of the most important is to gather insurance information for every student-athlete in

Table 7.2   CPT Codes for Common Physical Medicine Procedures

Category	Code	Procedure
Modality, contact attendance, one or more areas, each 15 minutes (requires direct patient contact)		
	97034	Contrast baths
	97032	Electrical stimulation (manual)
	97033	Iontophoresis
	97035	Ultrasound
Modality, supervised, one or more areas (does not require direct patient contact)		
	97010	Cold pack
	97024	Diathermy
	97014	Electrical stimulation (unattended)
	97010	Hot pack
	97018	Paraffin bath
	97012	Traction, mechanical
	97016	Vasopneumatic devices
	97022	Whirlpool
Therapeutic exercise		
	97113	Aquatic
	97150	Group, each 15 minutes
	97530	Therapeutic activities to improve functional performance
	97110	Therapeutic exercise for strength, flexibility, range of motion
	97112	Neuromuscular reeducation
Orthotics and prosthetics		
	L1906	AFO, multiligamentous ankle support
	L0140	Cervical collar, semirigid, adjustable
	L3700	Elbow orthoses, elastic with stays
	L3458	Heel pad, removable

the program (Frankel, 1991). This task can often be accomplished well in advance of the season. For participants who are not identified until the beginning of the season, the preseason physical exam offers an excellent opportunity to collect the information. Personal insurance information forms should be updated annually. Another preparatory step that will save time and avoid confusion after an injury occurs is to communicate by letter with the parents of all student-athletes, informing them of the limits of the school's accident insurance policy and the steps they will need to take to process an insurance claim (see figure 7.2). If the school has a secondary policy, be sure to explain to parents that they must submit all medical bills to their insurance company before submitting the balance to the school.

When the athletic trainer receives a bill for processing, she should create an insurance file for the student-athlete. Because the status of the claim will change, it is useful to color code each file according to its status with adhesive labels. As the status of the claim changes, a different-colored label can be applied over the old one. Consider the following system:

insurance claim registry form A worksheet that aids in tracking the progress of an insurance claim through the entire process.

explanation of benefits form (EOB) A summary prepared by an insurance company, and sent to a policyholder, that documents how the insurance policy covered the charges associated with a particular claim.

- Red label—Bills and other information being collected, claim not yet submitted.
- Yellow label—Full claim submitted but not yet paid.
- Green label—Claim paid in full and case closed.

In addition to creating an individual insurance folder, the athletic trainer should enter each claim on an **insurance claim registry form** (see figure 7.3). This document provides the athletic trainer with a quick reference for determining which claims are paid and which are outstanding.

The athletic trainer should not submit any claim to the school's secondary insurance company before receiving an **explanation of benefits form (EOB)** from the athlete's personal insurance company. The EOB describes how benefits were paid

---

Dear Student-Athlete and Parents:

At the beginning of every sports season, the athletic department sends the parents of each student-athlete information regarding our insurance coverage. We hope all participants will be injury free; however, if an athlete is accidentally injured, the following information should be useful.

If a student-athlete is accidentally injured and generates medical expenses associated with the accident, all claims must be filed first with the student's or parents' personal insurance company. If a balance remains after the personal insurance company has paid its maximum, that balance will be submitted to the school's athletic accident insurance company. If covered, the school's insurance company will pay the balance of the eligible medical expenses not covered by the personal insurance company up to the maximum of the policy. This excess insurance program is being used at many of the nation's high schools and colleges.

The school's insurance policy covers only new accidents that are sustained during competition or supervised practice. Any bills related to injuries that fall into the category above should be mailed to the athletic department only after first being submitted to the personal insurance company. Preexisting injuries, off-season injuries, injuries incurred during the season that are not directly related to in-season competition or supervised practice (physical education injuries, intramural injuries, etc.), or routine medical care (eye care, dental care, care for illnesses) are NOT COVERED. Also not covered are injuries or "conditions" caused by overuse, such as tendinitis and stress fracture. *We strongly recommend that a personal health and accident insurance policy be maintained for all student-athletes.*

If you have any questions regarding the accident insurance program, please feel free to contact us at your convenience. We look forward to serving you again this year and hope that your experience will be enjoyable and accident free.

Sincerely,

Athletic Director   Head Athletic Trainer

▌ Figure 7.2 Sample letter to parents and student-athletes explaining the athletic accident insurance plan.

Sports Medicine Insurance Registry Form					
Date filed	Athlete name	Insurance company	Amount due	Amount paid	Date paid

▌ Figure 7.3   Sample insurance claim registry form.

Reprinted from Rowell 1989.

managed care   A growing concept in the insurance industry emphasizing cost control through coordination of medical services, such as with an HMO or PPO.

for the claim. The EOB is proof of which bills the insurance company paid and to whom—medical vendors or the parents—the checks were written (see figure 7.4).

HMOs, part of a larger concept in the medical insurance industry known as **managed care,** have become the predominant form of health insurance available (see figure 7.5). In fact, 55% of the U.S. population is covered by some form of managed care plan (Health Insurance Association of America, 1997). If a student's personal insurance carrier is an HMO, the student will be required to seek treatment from a physician designated as his or her **primary care provider** except in life-threatening emergencies. This requirement frequently poses problems for athletic trainers, because it means student-athletes must seek medical treatment from physicians not associated with the school's sports medicine program. Most HMOs refuse to pay for treatment performed by a nonparticipating physician or other health care provider without prior approval. When the athlete is a high school student living in the same town as his or her HMO physician, the problem is merely an inconvenience. When the athlete is a college student living hundreds of miles from home,

GOOD Insurance Company   Date:

EXPLANATION OF BENEFITS

EMPLOYEE: SSN:
GROUP: CLAIM #:
GROUP ID: DATE INCURRED:
PROCESSED BY: PATIENT:

TREATMENT DATES	CHARGE AMOUNT	PATIENT COPAY	NOT COVERED	REASON CODE	PPO DISCOUNT	ELIGIBLE CHARGES	DEDUCTIBLE AMOUNT	PCT	PAYMENT AMOUNT

TOTAL INDIVIDUAL DEDUCTIBLE MET $ TOTAL CHARGES $
TOTAL FAMILY DEDUCTIBLE MET $ LESS DEDUCTIBLE $
OUT-OF-POCKET YTD $ PATIENT RESPONSIBILITY $
                                               TOTAL PAYMENT $
                                               OTHER INSURANCE/ADJUSTMENTS $

PAYMENT DISTRIBUTION

CODE   PAYEE   AMOUNT   CHECK NUMBER

SERVICE CODE	REASON CODE

MESSAGES

IF THE PARTICIPANT BELIEVES THE CLAIM HAS BEEN IMPROPERLY DENIED, HE OR SHE HAS THE RIGHT TO HAVE IT REVIEWED. THE APPEAL MUST BE FILED IN WRITING WITHIN SIXTY (60) DAYS OF RECEIPT OF THIS WORKSHEET. ADDITIONAL INFORMATION ABOUT WHERE THE CLAIM SHOULD BE SENT IS CONTAINED IN THE EMPLOYEE BENEFIT HANDBOOK.

Figure 7.4 Sample explanation of benefits form.

primary care provider   The physician, selected by an HMO member, who acts as the first source of medical service for the patient. Most HMOs require members to seek a referral from the primary care provider before seeking care from another medical vendor.

however, the problem can become more serious. Most secondary carriers will not pay the full cost of an athletic accident if the student's HMO denies the claim because the student sought treatment from a physician outside the plan. Although some large university athletic programs might be able to absorb the costs incurred by avoiding the inconvenience of using a student-athlete's HMO-approved physician, the vast majority of school- and college-based programs lack the financial resources to become, in effect, primary coverage providers for these students.

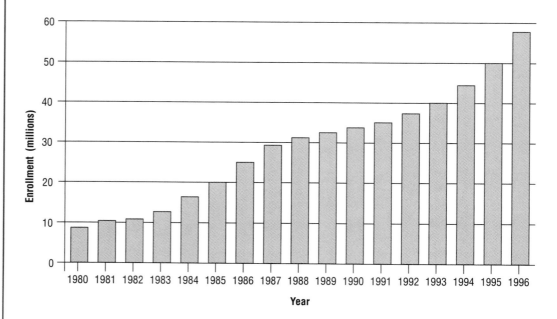

▌Figure 7.5 Enrollment in HMOs from 1980 to 1996.

Adapted, by permission, from *The Interstudy Competitive Edge* 1997.

An athletic trainer can take several steps with students who are insured through an HMO:

• Contact the HMO and request information about the procedure to be followed in the event of an athletic accident (see figure 7.6). Do this for all of the managed care plans that operate in your area so you can learn the limitations and rules for each of the policies.

• Place an "HMO ALERT" label on the athlete's medical record as a reminder to contact the HMO in the event of an injury that requires outside medical care.

• If the student is in college and lives a great distance from the HMO service area, determine if the HMO will assign a physician in the local college community as the student's primary care provider during the time the student is in school.

• Be sure to remind the parents if the school's secondary insurance policy will not honor claims rejected by their HMO for noncompliance with the HMO plan. This reminder should be part of a larger effort to educate parents and student-athletes about the institution's athletic accident insurance. There are many ways to educate parents and student-athletes, including brochures, letters, team meetings, and parent meetings. This educational effort will help prevent confusion and anger later if a claim is denied.

Insurance claim forms must be complete and accurate to be processed quickly. Athletic accident insurance claim forms have at least the following elements:

• Student's name and address (home and local when appropriate)
• Student's date of birth, sex, and year in school

HMO/PPO Authorization Form   Name of Student-Athlete _____

Name of Covered Person _____
(Parent or Guardian)

Name of Employer _____

HMO/PPO Certificate # _____

Dear (HMO/PPO name here):

_____ is a student-athlete at _____College and has indicated that he/she is covered under your plan for health and accident coverage while he/she is a student here.

_____ is participating in our intercollegiate sports program and there is a possibility that he/she may suffer an accidental injury while competing. The athletic accident coverage purchased by_____College is an excess policy that requires all medical bills be first submitted to the student's primary health plan for payment before it assumes any liability. It also requires that all student-athletes must follow any procedures required by their HMO/PPO, should they be covered by such a plan.

As the head athletic trainer, it is my responsibility to process any insurance claims that are made by our student-athletes. I am requesting your assistance in properly administering your plan for_____ _____.

If you have any printed material that would assist in this matter, please send it to me as soon as possible. If there is a phone number that should be called prior to_____ receiving any medical treatment, I request that you send it to me as well. It is most important that I be informed of all medical vendors in the immediate area of _____College that qualify under your plan to treat _____.

At various times our athletic teams will be several hundred miles from our campus and I need to know the proper procedures for handling any emergency that might take place. I also need to know whether your coverage has a particular definition of "emergency," and whether there are different procedures for treating a life-threatening emergency and a less serious problem such as a fractured leg or dislocated shoulder, that requires the immediate attention of a physician.

Thanks in advance for your help. I look forward to your early reply.

Sincerely,

Head Athletic Trainer

❚ **Figure 7.6**   Sample HMO/PPO authorization form.

Adapted with permission from First Agency, Inc., Kalamazoo, MI.

- Sport in which the student was injured
- Date, time, and place of the accident
- Description of how the accident occurred
- Nature of the injuries suffered, including specific body parts
- Names and titles of witnesses to the accident
- Parents' medical insurance information

Finally, First Agency (5071 West H Avenue, Kalamazoo, MI 49009), one of the oldest and largest athletic accident insurers, recommends that athletic trainers avoid the following claims-processing pitfalls:

- Do not wait until an injury occurs to collect the parents' insurance information from the student-athlete.

- Do not convey the impression that the institution will pay all expenses involving athletic injuries. This was one of the mistakes committed in the opening case study. One of the ways athletic departments can avoid this problem is to appoint a sole spokesperson who is responsible for managing the insurance program. All questions related to the insurance program should be directed to this person.

- Do not take primary responsibility for filing claims with the student's personal insurance company. This should be done either by the parents or the medical vendor.

- Do not prepay medical vendors from the athletic budget. Prepaying can result in duplicate payments and arouse animosity between physicians and parents.

- Do not delay filing claims with either the primary or secondary insurers. Many policies have time limits beyond which they will not pay.

- Do not assume that medical bills have been filed with the parents' insurance company. Athletic trainers should contact parents soon after an injury occurs to remind them of the process for settling claims. It is not uncommon for parents to receive a bill and assume that the institution is taking care of it, causing delays in claim processing that lead to past-due accounts.

- Do not submit incomplete claims. Make sure bills are itemized and accompanied by the parents' insurance information.

CLAIMS PROCESSING IN SPORTS MEDICINE CLINICS

The claims process in sports medicine clinics is fundamentally different from the process in educational institutions for two reasons. First, the athletic trainer or clinic administrator must integrate claims processing within the context of a larger patient billing system. Because of this, the livelihood of the sports medicine clinic depends on the ability to secure a steady flow of referrals from primary care physicians and specialists and to obtain reimbursement from third-party payers for patient bills. The second fundamental difference is that sports medicine clinics receive direct payments from third-party payers, whereas in the educational setting the money generally does not pass through the hands of an athletic trainer but is sent directly to the medical vendor. This is an important distinction, because it means that athletic trainers working in sports medicine clinics face a greater accounting burden than those working in educational institutions do.

One of the most important steps athletic trainers in sports medicine clinics can take to ensure a smooth claims process is to seek prior authorization from a patient's insurance company before providing treatment. This is a requirement for some third-party payers, such as HMOs and PPOs; reimbursement usually will not be provided without preapproval by the primary care physician. Some Blue Cross plans will reimburse for physical therapy and other sports medicine services, whereas other plans might not. The prudent clinic administrator should use the toll-free number provided by Blue Cross to determine in advance the limitations of the patient's policy.

Rowell (1989) suggests the following nine steps for filing insurance claims with third-party payers:

1. Complete the patient's charge slip, listing the patient's name, date of service, type of service, and balance due.
2. Convert all the procedures performed to CPT codes and list prices.
3. List all procedures, charges, and payments in a daily office ledger and the patient's individual ledger.
4. Complete the claim form. Most third-party payers will accept the **HCFA 1500** claim form from private-practice clinics (see figure 7.7). The **UB-92**, also known as the **HCFA 1450**, is the appropriate form for hospitals (see figure 7.8).
5. Obtain the authorized signature on the claim form. In most sports medicine clinics, the chief physical therapist must sign claims. In clinics owned by physicians, usually one of the physicians must sign.
6. Place a copy of the insurance claim form in the patient's record.
7. Enter the claim on the insurance claim registry form.
8. Mail the claim form to the insurance company.
9. Note on the patient's ledger that the claim has been submitted to the insurance company, and mail an informational copy of the ledger to the patient.

HCFA 1500   The form that private-practice clinics should use when filing a claim with an insurance company. Originally developed by the Health Care Financing Administration for Medicare claims.

UB-92   Also known as the HCFA 1450. Insurance claim form that hospitals should use.

The HCFA 1500 is available in electronic format from **http://www.hcfa.gov/medicare/edi/1500info.htm.** The UB-92, also known as the HCFA 1450, is available in electronic format from **http://www.hcfa.gov/medicare/edi/h1450.pdf**.

Medical practice software packages that help automate many of the steps for filing insurance claims are available. In addition, some insurance companies allow medical vendors to submit their claims either in the traditional manner, as just described, or in a scannable format. Preparing the scannable claim form (according to insurance company specifications) allows for quicker claims processing, because a scanner automatically enters it into the insurance company's computer system. Claims that require any written explanation, however, will usually be held for review by a processing clerk.

Another option available through some insurance companies allows medical vendors to submit claims electronically using **electronic data interchange (EDI).** A claim form is completed on the computer screen and then downloaded to the insurance company's computer with a modem and communications software. This is the quickest way to obtain reimbursement for standard claims, because the claim arrives at the insurance company, for all practical purposes, as soon as it is sent from the clinic.

electronic data interchange (EDI)   A system whereby insurance claims can be submitted electronically. Also known as paperless claims system.

PURCHASING INSURANCE SERVICES

Athletic trainers should work with an insurance agent to purchase insurance services. Although insurance can be purchased directly or by bidding, athletic trainers pursuing this option should always be sure to determine the layers and limits of the coverage, deductibles and copayments that might be required, and exclusions to the policy.

An athletic trainer might have the responsibility for evaluating and purchasing an athletic accident policy for a school sports medicine program. A variety of persons, including athletic directors, business office personnel, and risk managers, often share this function. Even if athletic trainers are not directly involved in evaluating and selecting insurance, they should not hesitate to offer their input, especially if they will be responsible for implementing the system.

Insurance is usually purchased through an **agent.** The U.S. Small Business Administration (1981) suggests that well-qualified insurance agents should be able to

- provide advice on the type and amount of insurance required,
- provide suggestions on the specific details of insurance policies, and
- provide timely service in the event of a claim.

HEALTH INSURANCE CLAIM FORM

PICA ☐☐☐ PICA ☐☐☐

1. MEDICARE ☐ (Medicare #) MEDICAID ☐ (Medicaid #) CHAMPUS ☐ (Sponsor's SSN) CHAMPVA ☐ (VA File #) GROUP HEALTH PLAN ☐ (SSN or ID) FECA BLK LUNG ☐ (SSN) OTHER ☐ (ID)

1a. INSURED'S I.D. NUMBER (FOR PROGRAM IN ITEM 1)

2. PATIENT'S NAME (Last Name, First Name, Middle Initial)

3. PATIENT'S DATE OF BIRTH   MM ꞏ DO ꞏ YY   SEX M ☐ F ☐

4. INSURED'S NAME (Last Name, First Name, Middle Initial)

5. PATIENT'S ADDRESS (No., Street)

6. PATIENT'S RELATIONSHIP TO INSURED Self ☐ Spouse ☐ Child ☐ Other ☐

7. INSURED'S ADDRESS (No., Street)

CITY   STATE

8. PATIENT'S STATUS Single ☐ Married ☐ Other ☐ Employed ☐ Full–Time Student ☐ Part–Time Student ☐

CITY   STATE

ZIP CODE   TELEPHONE INCLUDE AREA CODE ( )

ZIP CODE   TELEPHONE (INCLUDE AREA CODE) ( )

9. OTHER INSURED'S NAME (Last Name, First Name, Middle Initial)

10. IS PATIENT'S CONDITION RELATED TO:

11. INSURED'S POLICY GROUP OR FECA NUMBER

a. OTHER INSURED'S POLICY OR GROUP NUMBER

a. EMPLOYMENT? (Current or Previous) YES ☐ NO ☐

a. INSURED'S DATE OF BIRTH   MM ꞏ DO ꞏ YY   SEX M ☐ F ☐

b. OTHER INSURED'S DATE OF BIRTH   MM ꞏ DO ꞏ YY   SEX M ☐ F ☐

b. AUTO ACCIDENT?   PLACE (State)   YES ☐ NO ☐

b. EMPLOYER'S NAME OR SCHOOL NAME

c. EMPLOYER'S NAME OR SCHOOL NAME

c. OTHER ACCIDENT? YES ☐ NO ☐

c. INSURANCE PLAN NAME OR PROGRAM NAME

d. INSURANCE PLAN NAME OR PROGRAM NAME

10d. RESERVED FOR LOCAL USE

d. IS THERE ANOTHER HEALTH BENEFIT PLAN? NO ☐ YES ☐ If yes, return to and complete item 9 a—d.

READ BACK OF FORM BEFORE COMPLETING AND SIGNING THIS FORM.
12. PATIENT'S OR AUTHORIZED PERSON'S SIGNATURE I authorize the release of any medical or other information necessary to process this claim. I also request payment of government benefits either to myself or to the party who accepts assignment below.

SIGNED _____   DATE _____

13. INSURED'S OR AUTHORIZED PERSON'S SIGNATURE I authorize payment of medical benefits to the undersigned physician or supplier for services described below.

SIGNED _____

14. DATE OF CURRENT: ILLNESS (First symptom) OR INJURY (Accident) OR PREGNANCY (LMP) MM ꞏ DO ꞏ YY

15. IF PATIENT HAS HAD SAME OR SIMILAR ILLNESS, GIVE FIRST DATE   MM ꞏ DO ꞏ YY

16. DATES PATIENT UNABLE TO WORK IN CURRENT OCCUPATION FROM MM ꞏ DO ꞏ YY TO MM ꞏ DO ꞏ YY

17. NAME OF REFERRING PHYSICIAN OR OTHER SOURCE

17a. I.D. NUMBER OF REFERRING PHYSICIAN

18. HOSPITALIZATION DATES RELATED TO CURRENT SERVICES FROM MM ꞏ DO ꞏ YY TO MM ꞏ DO ꞏ YY

19. RESERVED FOR LOCAL USE

20. OUTSIDE LAB? YES ☐ NO ☐ $ CHARGES

21. DIAGNOSIS OR NATURE OF ILLNESS OR INJURY. (RELATE ITEMS 1,2,3, OR 4 TO ITEM 24E BY LINE)
1. |_____   3. |_____
2. |_____   4. |_____

22. MEDICAID RESUBMISSION CODE   ORIGINAL REF NO.

23. PRIOR AUTHORIZATION NUMBER

24. A DATE(S) OF SERVICE						B Place of Service	C Type of Service	D PROCEDURES, SERVICES, OR SUPPLIES (Explain Unusual Circumstances) CPT/HCPCS MODIFIER	E DIAGNOSIS CODE	F $ CHARGES	G Days or Units	H EPSDT Family Plan	I EMG	J COB	K RESERVED FOR LOCAL USE
FROM MM	DO	YY	TO MM	DO	YY										
1															
2															
3															
4															
5															
6															

25. FEDERAL TAX I.D. NUMBER SSN ☐ EN ☐

26. PATIENT'S ACCOUNT NO.

27. ACCEPT ASSIGNMENT? (For govt. claims, see back) YES ☐ NO ☐

28. TOTAL CHARGE $

29. AMOUNT PAID $

30. BALANCE DUE $

31. SIGNATURE OF PHYSICIAN OR SUPPLIER INCLUDING DEGREES OR CREDENTIALS (I certify that the statements on the reverse apply to this bill and are made a part thereof.)
SIGNED _____   DATE _____

32. NAME AND ADDRESS OF FACILITY WHERE SERVICES WERE RENDERED (If other than home or office)

33. PHYSICIAN'S, SUPPLIER'S, BILLING NAME, ADDRESS, ZIP CODE AND PHONE NUMBER.
PIN #   GRP#

■ Figure 7.7 HCFA 1500.

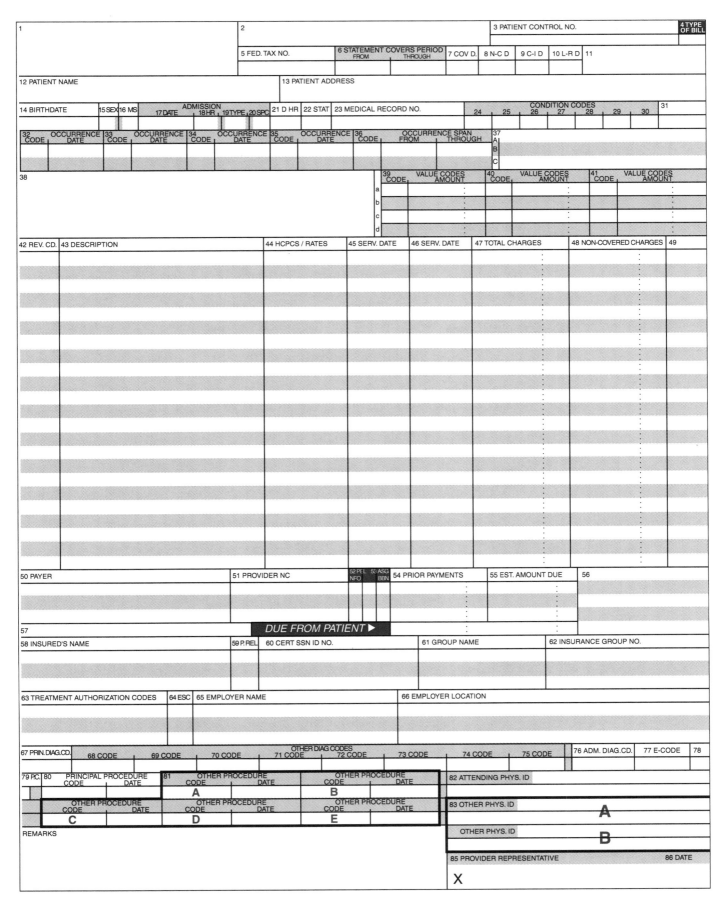

∎ Figure 7.8 UB-92 (also HCFA 1450).

insurance agent
A representative of an
insurance company or
an independent
insurance agency who
sells and services
insurance policies.

Like sports medicine supplies and equipment, athletic accident insurance can be purchased in a variety of ways. One method is to simply contact a local insurance agency and ask that a policy be written covering the elements desired by the institution. This method requires the least time and effort from the athletic trainer, but it is without question the least desirable. Investigating the wide range of insurance products and their prices is the surest method of obtaining the best protection for the lowest cost.

Another method commonly employed by educational institutions is to use a formal bidding process to purchase insurance services. The advantage to the bidding method is that it allows institutions to obtain athletic accident insurance at the lowest possible cost. There are disadvantages to this system, however. First, every insurance plan has hidden costs, the most significant of which is usually the time it takes the institution's employees to learn the system and file the claims. If an institution awards athletic accident contracts to the lowest bidder annually, employees will spend a great deal of time that could be spent on more productive work learning new insurance systems. Another disadvantage of the bidding system, especially for institutions that bid for multi-year contracts, is that the initial price of the premium might seem low, but as the institution establishes a claims history with the company, the premiums will undoubtedly rise to ensure that the company makes a profit.

An alternative to both the bidding and direct purchasing systems just described is for the athletic trainer and other institutional representatives to interview several insurance companies and carefully evaluate their products and prices. This process allows for easy clarification of questions and provides an opportunity to determine what processing claims would require.

No matter which purchasing method is used, each proposal should be evaluated with the following points in mind:

layered coverage
A method of using
different insurance
companies to under-
write different levels of
coverage in a common
policy.

- What are the monetary limits of the coverage? What are the time limits of the coverage? Does the policy offer **layered coverage?** If so, what are the limits for each layer of coverage? Is there a layer of catastrophic coverage?

- What specific exclusions to the coverage are listed? What riders are available to cover these exclusions?

- Does the policy provide primary coverage or secondary (excess) coverage? If secondary, how does it interface with personal insurance? How does it handle student-athletes whose parents are covered by HMOs or PPOs?

- What deductibles, if any, apply to the policy? Who will be responsible for paying the deductible?

copayments   The
percentage of a medical
bill not paid for by the
insurance company.

- What **copayments,** if any, are required by the policy? Who is responsible for the copayments?

- Who is covered by the policy? Are ancillary and support personnel, such as athletic trainers, coaches, student managers, and cheerleaders, covered?

- Under what circumstances are covered individuals protected? How does the policy handle out-of-season injury?

- What is the annual premium? If a multi-year contract, how and under what circumstances will the annual premium change?

- What specific steps must the institution take to file claims? How much staff time and effort will be required to do so?

APPLICATIONS TO ATHLETIC TRAINING: THEORY INTO PRACTICE

Apply the concepts discussed in this chapter to the following two case studies to prepare for situations you might face in actual practice. The questions at the end of the studies are open-ended—there are many possible correct solutions. Use the case studies for homework, exam questions, or class discussion.

Case Study 1

Barbara Cummings, A.T.,C./P.T., was beginning to have second thoughts about her decision four months earlier to sell her private sports medicine and physical therapy practice to Universal Health Care Services. She had thought that by selling the practice to Universal, a huge medical practice conglomerate operating in 47 states, she would be able to improve her bottom line while the parent company assumed the risk of adding the new, expensive equipment she so desperately needed in order to remain competitive with the local hospital's sports medicine clinic. Unfortunately, she soon discovered that Universal put so much pressure on her to increase revenue that patient care was beginning to suffer. Still, she felt she had to do something to meet Universal's expectations or she would be forced to leave the practice she had worked so long to establish.

Bob Thaxton, Universal's manager of clinic operations for 10 northern states, visited Barbara's clinic and told her she would have to institute the following billing and insurance practices immediately:

- All new patients were to be discharged immediately when their insurance limits were met.
- No patients were to be discharged until their insurance expired.
- Every patient was to be billed for a minimum of one hour of therapy to cover expenses associated with overhead at the home office.
- Patients without insurance were not to be accepted.

Although Barbara was upset with the new regulations, she felt she had no choice but to conform to the standards established by the company. The day after Bob Thaxton's visit, the new regulations were implemented.

Questions for Analysis

1. What potential legal pitfalls do the new billing and insurance regulations pose for Barbara and her staff? What ethical dilemmas, if any, are posed by these regulations?

2. How could Barbara implement the regulations without violating the law? Would her patients be well served by these actions? Why or why not?

3. What other revenue-enhancing procedures, besides those mandated by Universal, could Barbara implement? How would they serve her patients more efficiently and effectively than the procedures required by Universal?

Case Study 2

Libby Wilson, Northwest State University's head athletic trainer, was called into the athletic director's office and told that a new university policy required all service contracts to be awarded to the lowest bidder. The new rule was to take effect beginning with the next fiscal year, which was only two months away. Libby would have to put together a bidding package for the university's athletic accident insurance, the ambulance service, and the team physician's contract. The athletic director gave her one month to secure the bids. This would give him enough time, he felt, to evaluate the bids, award the contracts, and have the services in place by the time the new fiscal year began.

Although Libby was not happy about having to put these services out for bid, she went to work right away. She knew that the insurance bid would be the most complicated, so she decided to tackle this part of the project first. She put together a bidding document that requested cost quotations based on the following requirements:

- Excess coverage for 500 student-athletes in 18 sports, including football and gymnastics

- Excess coverage for all ancillary and support personnel

- Coverage limits up to $50,000 with lifetime catastrophic coverage for amounts above $50,000

Libby included a copy of the university's claims history for the previous five years (an average of 75 claims per year) and sent the bidding package to three insurance companies that specialized in athletic accident insurance. Two weeks later she received the bids. She developed table 7.3 to help the athletic director understand the bids:

Questions for Analysis

1. What advantages and disadvantages are likely to accompany the university's new policy with reference to the athletic accident insurance program?

2. If you were in Libby's position, would you have followed the same process in securing bids for insurance? Why or why not? What would you have done differently?

3. Based on the information contained in table 7.3, which company's insurance policy represents the best value? Do you need any other information to reach this conclusion?

4. The Good Insurance Company will write a policy only with a maximum of $25,000 per claim. The university's catastrophic insurance coverage does not take effect until $50,000 in medical bills have been paid. If the university decided to purchase the Good Insurance Company's policy, what options should it investigate to decrease its risk between $25,000 and $50,000?

Table 7.3   NSU Athletic Accident Insurance Bid Summary

| Company | Coverage | Premium Deductible per claim | | |
		$0	$100	$250
Professional Underwriters	$50,000	$20,000	$17,500	$15,000
Best Insurance Company	$50,000	$18,000	$16,000	$14,000
Good Insurance Company	$25,000	$12,000	$10,000	$ 8,000

SUMMARY

1. *Understand the difference between medical, health, and accident insurance.*

   As the cost of medical care continues to rise and the quality of insurance continues to fall, it is becoming increasingly important for athletic trainers to thoroughly understand insurance systems. Insurance not only protects the assets of educational institutions that sponsor athletic programs but also safeguards the income and livelihood of athletic trainers employed by sports medicine clinics. Most athletic accident policies cover only acute injuries with no connection to preexisting conditions and do not pay for illnesses or overuse conditions. Medical and health insurance policies are generally more comprehensive and are usually designed to help cover a percentage of an insured person's medical bills or to provide coverage for activities designed to maintain good health.

2. *Understand the advantages and disadvantages of self-insurance, primary coverage, and secondary coverage.*

   The three choices available to most educational institutions when purchasing insurance services are self-insurance, primary coverage, and secondary, or excess, coverage. Secondary coverage is the most common type of insurance plan, as it uses the patient's personal health insurance as a first layer of coverage. Primary insurance is very expensive; it pays all covered expenses from the first dollar. Some institutions choose to self-insure, gambling that they will not incur large claims that would drain institutional coffers.

3. *Define the types of injuries covered by most athletic accident policies.*

   Most athletic accident policies will cover only acute injuries that occur in officially sanctioned practices or games. Chronic injuries, illnesses, or degenerative conditions are usually not covered by these policies.

4. *Understand the basic legal responsibilities associated with third-party reimbursement.*

   Athletic trainers reimbursed for services through third-party insurance plans should maintain patient-practitioner confidentiality. Medical records should never be released to third-party payers unless the patient has provided written authorization. Athletic trainers commit fraud when altering the date of an injury, treatment, or assessment or when failing to record payments from an insurance company on a patient's bill. Claiming reimbursement for services not provided is also illegal and is punishable by levying substantial fines.

5. *Understand the role of procedural coding in the third-party reimbursement system.*

   CPT coding lists procedures on insurance claim forms in the form of a code. Diagnostic coding provides third-party payers with a standardized system for determining the kinds of medical conditions health care providers are treating when they seek reimbursement.

6. *Organize a claims-processing system for a sports medicine program in an educational setting.*

   Claims processing in educational settings is different than in a sports medicine clinic. In each case, patients enrolled in some managed care plans must receive authorization from primary care providers before services are rendered. Athletic trainers in educational settings should communicate the limits of the school's athletic accident insurance policy to parents. Each athlete who submits an insurance claim needs a separate file, and bills should not be submitted to the school's insurance company until the athletic trainer has received an explanation of benefits report from the athlete's personal health insurance company.

7. *Understand the steps required to file a claim for reimbursement from a third-party payer.*

   All diagnoses and procedures must be converted to coded form using the ICD-9-CM and the CPT list of codes. Claims can be submitted on the standard HCFA 1500 form for private practice settings, the UB-92 form for hospitals, on a scannable form, or electronically using a computer modem. Athletic trainers responsible for this process must keep meticulous records of all procedures, charges, and payments.

8. *Evaluate and purchase an athletic accident insurance policy for an educational institution.*

   Athletic trainers are frequently responsible for purchasing or recommending the purchase of athletic accident insurance. Price, policy exclusions, limits of coverage, deductibles, and claims processing workload should all be considered when evaluating the policies offered by various insurance companies.

CHAPTER EIGHT

Protecting Athletic Trainers: Legal Considerations in Sports Medicine

OBJECTIVES

After completing this chapter, you should be able to do the following:

1. Define and discuss the legal principles most applicable to athletic training settings.

2. Identify the types of situations most likely to hold liability concerns for athletic trainers.

3. Understand the different types of credentialing laws that affect the practice of athletic training.

4. Understand the elements required to prove negligence on the part of an athletic trainer.

5. Be aware of the various legal defenses available to athletic trainers against charges of malpractice.

6. Identify the most important elements of providing effective legal testimony.

7. Identify and put into practice methods that avoid legal liability while improving the quality of athletic training care.

As the only certified athletic trainer for a large metropolitan high school, Todd Russell has over 500 student-athletes to care for. One Thursday, as Todd was in the athletic training room packing for a Friday night football game on the other side of the state, the assistant soccer coach and one of his players carried in Enrique Vasquez, the team's back-up goalkeeper, and laid him on a treatment table. Todd examined Enrique's injured left ankle. Enrique explained that he had been involved in a collision in front of the goal, but he wasn't sure how he had injured the ankle. Most of his pain was located over the medial malleolus. Mild swelling was present. Active range of motion was painful in inversion and eversion, but not too bad in plantar and dorsiflexion. Todd told Enrique that he had probably sprained the deltoid ligament on the medial aspect of his ankle. He applied ice with an elastic bandage and elevated the injured foot. Because the team physician usually stopped in on Thursdays, Todd decided to keep Enrique in the athletic training room and have the ankle examined. Todd returned to his packing while Enrique iced the ankle.

Todd removed the ice after 30 minutes, and the team physician arrived 10 minutes later. After evaluating the problem, the physician told Enrique that Todd's assessment was probably correct, but that he wanted Enrique to be seen by his family doctor the next day to get an X ray. Todd, who was present when these instructions were given, made sure that Enrique understood what he needed to do. He gave Enrique a pair of crutches and returned to his preparation for the football game.

Because the game was to be played nearly 300 miles away, Todd was not in school on Friday. Enrique, whose parents had no medical insurance, decided not to see his family physician or get an X ray. He used the crutches only sparingly, thinking that walking on the injured ankle would decrease the stiffness he felt. When he woke up on Saturday, however, his ankle was so swollen and painful that his mother took him to the emergency room, where a displaced fracture of the tibial malleolus was diagnosed.

Enrique underwent surgery later that day to stabilize the fracture. Unfortunately, he developed an infection and was hospitalized for the next two weeks. The infection caused scarring of the articular surfaces of the joint, leaving Enrique with a permanently stiff, sore ankle.

Several months later, both Todd and the team physician were surprised to learn that they, along with the school board, were being sued by Enrique's family.

The law is sort of hocus-pocus science that smiles in yer face while it picks yer pocket.

Charles Macklin

Todd Russell faces the same pressures as many athletic trainers: too many athletes to care for and only student interns to help provide that care. Yet the expectations he faces from coaches, physicians, parents, and administrators are substantial. He is expected to be caring, thorough, tireless, and wise every day (and night and weekend) he comes to work. If he makes a mistake, it is typically overlooked. But if he were to make the wrong mistake with the wrong person, his professional standing, his personal assets, and his self-respect could be seriously jeopardized.

Athletic trainers have been aware for some time that they need a general understanding of certain legal principles to protect themselves and the institutions that employ them from the risk of lawsuit (Gieck, Lowe, & Kenna, 1984). Wise athletic trainers, however, also realize that basic knowledge of legal principles, when applied thoughtfully and consistently, helps inform and improve their professional practice. These legal standards often provide extra incentive for athletic trainers to do what they ought to be doing routinely in their professional practice, whether they will be sued or not (Danzon, 1985).

This chapter cannot, of course, provide definitive, comprehensive coverage of all the law related to the practice of athletic training. But it will present to student athletic trainers the legal issues they are likely to encounter in their professional practice. If an athletic trainer is confronted with a specific legal issue or problem, the best source of information is an attorney who is experienced in handling similar cases (Horsley & Carlova, 1983). Effective policies and procedures, formed by consultation with both attorneys and insurance companies, also help guide athletic trainers through the minefield of legal perils they face daily.

CREDENTIALING

Athletic trainers in every state are affected in some way by the laws governing medical practice (Herbert, 1990). Such laws, emanating from public interest in self-protection, help to ensure that health care providers are competent. In states without state-sponsored credentialing, athletic trainers might be able to carry out their duties by having them legally delegated by a supervising physician. But this possibility varies among states, and even in states where delegation is allowed, the circumstances under which athletic training tasks may be delegated are often unclear and open to legal interpretation (Hawkins, 1988).

Athletic trainers must become familiar with the practice acts that regulate the profession. This is important not only for practicing athletic trainers, but for students as well, because the roles and responsibilities defined in the law are likely to be different for these groups. Athletic training practice acts vary a great deal among states (see appendix B). The acts define *athlete* and *athletic trainer* differently. Some limit the scope and setting in which an athletic trainer may practice. Some allow athletic trainers to charge a fee for service, whereas others prohibit fee-for-service billing. Some limit the types of therapeutic modalities athletic trainers can use. Most have very specific educational requirements that might or might not correspond to those required for certification by the NATA Board of Certification. A majority of state laws require physician supervision. Some states also allow other health professionals, such as physical therapists, chiropractors, and dentists, to supervise an athletic trainer under certain circumstances. In those states without specific athletic training credentialing, an athletic trainer should obtain a copy of the state's **medical practice act** to determine the scope and setting of practice the law permits athletic trainers and other health care providers.

Four types of credentialing laws regulate the practice of athletic training: licensure, certification, registration, and exemption. Athletic trainers practicing in states with athletic training practice acts should review the state law to determine what type of credentialing is required—each type has different implications. In addition, the definitions and level of restrictiveness of each type of credentialing vary from state to state.

As of July 1, 1998, athletic trainers have established a legal basis for their practice in 38 states (for the most current list, contact Government Affairs, National Athletic Trainers' Association, 2952 Stemmons, Dallas, TX 75247).

*medical practice act
A state law regulating the practice of medicine, usually by specifying who may practice and under what circumstances.*

LICENSURE

Licensure is the most restrictive form of governmental credentialing. Licensure is intended to protect the public by limiting the practice of athletic training to those who have met the requirements of a licensing board established under the law. Licensure laws generally prohibit unlicensed individuals from calling themselves athletic trainers. More important, they prohibit unlicensed persons from performing the tasks reserved for athletic trainers under the law. States that license athletic trainers usually require a specific educational background that comprises both course work and experience, in addition to passing a licensing examination administered by the board. Some states that license athletic trainers accept the equivalent of the NATA Board of Certification (NATABOC) standards, but many have different requirements as well. Licensing boards are powerful legal entities, because they are

licensure *A form of state credentialing, established by statute and intended to protect the public, that regulates the practice of a trade or profession by specifying who may practice and what duties they may perform.*

usually authorized to set the rules, in accordance with the law, that govern who may practice and who may not. They also set the fee required for license applications and renewals. Because licensure is the most restrictive form of state credentialing, it is commonly viewed by athletic trainers as the most desirable of the four regulatory options.

States That License Athletic Trainers

Alabama	Iowa	North Carolina
Arkansas	Maine	North Dakota
Delaware	Massachusetts	Ohio
Florida	Mississippi	Oklahoma
Georgia	Nebraska	Rhode Island
Illinois	New Hampshire	South Dakota
Indiana	New Mexico	Texas

CERTIFICATION

certification *A form of title protection, established by state law or sponsored by professional associations, designed to ensure that practitioners possess essential knowledge and skills sufficient to protect the public.*

Certification is a less stringent form of professional regulation than licensure. A person who is certified is generally recognized to possess the basic knowledge and skills required of practitioners in the profession. Both states and professional associations can certify health care practitioners. The NATABOC, for example, is the recognized certifying agency for ensuring that athletic trainers have the basic knowledge and skills to carry out their duties as defined by the *Competencies in Athletic Training*. Athletic trainers who meet the requirements for NATABOC certification and maintain their certification are entitled to use the board's credential. Some states also certify athletic trainers. States get the authority to certify athletic trainers from a credentialing law passed by the state legislature and signed by the governor, the same process that gives them the authority for licensure. Unlike licensure, however, state certification usually protects only an athletic trainer's title, not the specific tasks he or she performs. Noncertified persons could not call themselves athletic trainers, but they could perform the duties of an athletic trainer.

States That Certify Athletic Trainers

Kentucky	Pennsylvania	Tennessee
Louisiana	South Carolina	Vermont
New York		

REGISTRATION

registration *A type of state credentialing that requires qualified members of a profession to register with the state in order to practice.*

Registration is another form of professional regulation that is less restrictive than licensure. In states that have registration laws, athletic trainers are required to register with the state before practicing. Some states allow a grace period during which athletic trainers may practice without being registered, as long as they begin their application for registration within the time frame established by the state's board. Because unregistered persons are prohibited from practicing, the registration law becomes a form of title protection for an athletic trainer. States that require registration might or might not require screening devices such as examinations, although most prescribe the educational requirements necessary to register as an athletic trainer.

States That Register Athletic Trainers		
Idaho	Minnesota	New Jersey
Kansas	Missouri	Oregon

EXEMPTION

exemption A legislative mechanism used to release members of one profession from the liability of violating another profession's practice act.

Some states have provided the legal basis for athletic trainers to practice by exempting them from complying with the practice acts of other professions, typically the physical therapy, physician assistant, medical, and masseuse practice acts. Although exemption is often viewed as the least-restrictive form of professional regulation, athletic trainers might still be required to meet a variety of standards, usually related to educational background or certification by the NATABOC, to qualify. In addition, athletic trainers are required to act according to the standards of the profession and the boundaries of their training.

States That Exempt Athletic Trainers From Other Health Professions' Practice Acts			
Arizona	Colorado	Connecticut	Hawaii

RISK MANAGEMENT

Athletic trainers can help prevent losses (physical and financial) for their employers and patients by instituting a risk-management plan. Risks can be identified through both real-world observations and controlled experiments. Preparing properly for activity, conducting safe activities, managing injuries properly, and maintaining appropriate records are all part of a risk-management plan.

risk management A process designed to prevent losses of all kinds for everyone associated with an organization, including its directors, administrators, employees, and clients.

Athletic trainers have been concerned with issues of legal liability for many years. As more athletic trainers moved into management positions or were given management responsibilities along with their clinical duties, the broader construct of risk management became more important. Although athletic trainers are still concerned with the basics of avoiding legal liability in their clinical practices, they are increasingly called upon to help their schools, professional teams, clinics, and companies manage the risks that form the foundation for this liability.

WHAT IS RISK MANAGEMENT?

At its most fundamental level, risk management is a process intended to prevent financial loss for an organization. In a broader sense, however, risk management is also intended to prevent losses of all kinds (financial, physical, property, activity, time) for everyone associated with an organization, including its directors, administrators, employees, and clients (Culp, Goemaere, & Miller, 1985). This broader application is warranted, because losses experienced at one level of an organization are almost always felt at other levels. For example, if Enrique from the opening case is successful in his lawsuit against the school district, the board of education will have fewer dollars to spend on all programs, including Todd's athletic training program. It is in everyone's best interests, then, to control the risks that led up to Enrique's injury and the subsequent difficulties he experienced.

HOW ARE RISKS IDENTIFIED?

Risk identification is rarely as easy as it seems. Some risks are obvious to anyone. If you begin to administer an ultrasound treatment to an athlete or other physically active patient and notice that the power cord is frayed and the wire is exposed, you have identified a rather obvious risk factor. You could even quantify the risk in this case, since it is safe to assume that 100% of the people who come into contact with the exposed wire will receive an injury ranging from a minor burn to a cardiac arrest –inducing electrical shock. Most risks in athletics are more difficult to identify and quantify. For example, how would you answer an athletic director who wanted to know if the rubberized gym floor was the cause of the high rate of anterior cruciate ligament (ACL) injuries among your school's female basketball players? What evidence could you provide to support your answer? Could you calculate the risk of ACL injury with any accuracy? This is obviously a difficult thing to do, since not every female basketball player at your school will suffer an ACL injury. Of those who do, not all will suffer the injury while playing in the school's gym. There are at least two ways to identify and assess risk in athletics: real-world observation and inference from controlled experiments (Graham & Rhomberg, 1996).

Real-World Observation

This is the most rudimentary form of risk assessment. It involves making inferences regarding the risk of certain activities based on clinical practice and experience. Real-world observation is usually the first step in the discovery of cause-and-effect relationships between hazardous practices and their subsequent results.

For example, athletic trainers in the 1960s who observed many cases of heat illness among athletes denied access to fluids during heavy exercise in hot weather surmised that this practice led to dehydration and all of its negative side effects. In this case, their observations led to an accurate assessment of a risk that was later validated in laboratory studies. Unfortunately, however, real-world observation can often lead to spurious conclusions. In the case of the gym floor previously mentioned, all of the women's sport coaches who used that gym were so convinced that the floor was the cause of the high incidence of ACL injuries that they lobbied the administration to tear out the rubberized floor and replace it with a wooden floor. The project cost more than $1 million. Two years later, the rate of ACL injuries was just as high on the new wooden floor as it had been on the rubberized floor. In this case, there must have been underlying causes for the ACL injuries—independent of playing surface—that were the reason for the high incidence of injury. The coaches' observations were incorrect and led to a very expensive "solution" that solved nothing.

Controlled Experiments

Another way to identify and assess risks in an athletic program is to engage in data-driven controlled studies. This method is more difficult to implement because it is time intensive, costly, and frequently impractical. Using the preceding example, the people involved would probably have gotten better information regarding the effect of playing surface on ACL injuries if they had replaced one court with wood and left another with the original rubberized surface. If they had then randomly assigned players to practice on each of the courts and tracked the incidence of ACL injury as a function of player exposures, they would have gotten a much better answer (but not a perfect one) to the question "Should we replace the rubberized floor?"

This type of controlled study—the kind used to establish the safety and efficacy of prescription drugs—is rarely practical for athletic settings. One method that is practical, however, involves using an epidemiological approach to identifying risks. Epidemiology can help athletic trainers draw inferences regarding potential risks by tracking the incidence of injuries and all their associated factors, including athlete characteristics, playing surface, weather conditions, and type of activity. Most commercially available injury-tracking database software programs allow athletic trainers to do this, and the NCAA Injury Surveillance Study also tracks this kind of information.

When the athletic trainer in the gym-floor case was asked for an opinion regarding the advisability of switching to a wooden floor, he did a 10-year analysis of knee injuries in women's basketball and volleyball using data from the school's injury-tracking database and from the NCAA Injury Surveillance Study, of which his school was a participating member. The results indicated that the rate of injury was the same for wooden and rubberized gym floors. In addition, twice as many knee injuries occurred during away contests (where the games were usually played on wood surfaces) as occurred on the rubberized floor during home games. His conclusion was that there was no basis to recommend the commitment of $1 million to switch to a wood floor. The money was spent anyway. Knee injury rates continued as before.

REDUCING RISK IN ATHLETICS

Rankin and Ingersoll (1995) recommend a four-part strategy to help control risk in athletic programs:

1. Preparation for the Activity
   - Administer preparticipation physical exams
   - Monitor fitness levels
   - Assess activity areas
   - Monitor environmental conditions
2. Conduct of the Activity
   - Maintain equipment
   - Use proper instructional techniques
   - Provide adequate work-rest intervals
3. Injury Management
   - Have a physician supervise all medical aspects of the program
   - Evaluate and treat injuries correctly and promptly
   - Supervise student athletic trainers
4. Records Management
   - Document physician orders
   - Document the treatment plan
   - Document the treatment record
   - Document the patient's progress

LEGAL PRINCIPLES

Athletic trainers can be subject to judicial claims based on a wide variety of legal theories, and those in different settings must be aware of the legal concepts specific to their setting.

malpractice Liability generating conduct associated with the adverse outcome of patient treatment (Scott, 1990, p. 6).

The common threat faced by all athletic trainers who provide sports medicine services to patients is **malpractice**. Scott (1990, p. 6) defines health care malpractice as "liability-generating conduct associated with the adverse outcome of patient treatment. Liability may be based on

- negligent patient care,
- failure to obtain informed consent,
- intentional conduct,
- breach of a contract,
- use/transfer of a defective product, or
- abnormally dangerous treatment."

TORTS

Although athletic trainers may enter patient-practitioner relationships that are implied contracts, unhappy patients are less likely to bring a legal action based on **breach of contract** than on an accusation that the athletic trainer committed a **tort** (Wadlington, Waltz, & Dworkin, 1980). A tort is a legal wrong other than breach of contract for which a remedy will be provided, usually in the form of monetary damages. Actions based on tort law are pressed by plaintiffs in civil legal proceedings, as opposed to criminal cases, which are initiated by the government. All the legal grounds for malpractice, other than breach of contract, are based on tort law. Of the three types of tort—intentional tort, negligent tort, and strict liability tort—most malpractice actions are based on negligence, which focuses on the conduct of the practitioner.

NEGLIGENCE

Athletic trainers are usually sued under a negligent tort theory (Leverenz & Helms, 1990a). **Negligence** is a type of tort in which an athletic trainer fails to act as a reasonably prudent athletic trainer would act under the circumstances (Drowatzky, 1985). Athletic trainers can demonstrate that their actions have been both reasonable and prudent by adhering to certain standards in the performance of their duties. Standards are derived from several sources, including individual, societal, institutional, and professional values (Leiske, 1985). Standards derived from individual and societal values are often implicit (e.g., patients should be treated with respect). Standards derived from institutional and professional values are typically more explicit. These standards are usually codified in policies and procedures. They can also be found in the position statements of professional associations. For example, the American College of Sports Medicine's position statement on exercise and fluid replacement creates a professional standard that athletic trainers and others involved in the health care of physically active patients should adhere to during hot, humid weather. Similarly, the American Heart Association's statement on cardiovascular preparticipation screening of competitive athletes creates a standard to which team physicians and athletic trainers should adhere when organizing and conducting preseason physical exams. Finally, the NCAA has established a comprehensive set of standards to which athletic trainers in college athletics should adhere (see the *NCAA Sports Medicine Handbook*).

Athletic trainers can be negligent through either omission or commission. **Omission** is the failure to do something that should have been done under the circumstances. **Commission** occurs when an athletic trainer performs an act that should not have been committed. To prove an athletic trainer was negligent, the aggrieved patient must be able to substantiate the following five components (Ciccolella, 1991):

- Conduct by the athletic trainer
- Existence of duty
- Breach of duty
- Causation
- Damage

Conduct

To substantiate a charge of negligence, the plaintiff must be able to prove that the athletic trainer, either by commission or omission, actually did something that links him to the case. Nonactions, such as thoughts, attitudes, or intentions, cannot render the athletic trainer negligent. Only when athletic trainers take an action (or fail to

---

breach of contract *An unexcused failure to perform the services specified in a contract, either formal or informal.*

tort *A legal wrong, other than breach of contract, for which a remedy will be provided, usually in the form of monetary damages.*

negligence *A type of tort in which an athletic trainer fails to act as a reasonably prudent athletic trainer would act under the circumstances.*

omission *A failure to act when there was a legal duty to do so.*

commission *An action that violates a legal duty.*

take an action) can they be successfully accused of negligence. In the opening case, Todd Russell's failure to contact Enrique's parents might constitute proof of the conduct portion of a negligence claim.

Duty

When does an athletic trainer owe a duty to an injured athlete or other physically active patient? Generally speaking, athletic trainers employed by educational institutions have a duty to provide athletic training services to student-athletes actively engaged in those institutions' athletic programs. Athletic trainers employed by professional sports teams have the same duty toward team members. This duty has its legal origin in the athletic trainer's contract, in which he or she agrees to provide these services in return for payment. Whether a high school or university athletic trainer owes a duty to the student who is injured in an intramural basketball game or a physical education class is less clear—it depends on the responsibilities defined by the employment contract. This is why athletic trainers should have an employment contract with a clearly written position description delineating their specific responsibilities.

Athletic trainers employed by sports medicine clinics have greater leeway in deciding whom they will accept as patients. Consequently, the injured athletes and other physically active patients they owe a duty to should, in theory, be only those patients they choose to treat in their clinics. There are enough exceptions to this general rule, however, that sports medicine clinic owners should consult with their attorneys to find out whom they might owe a duty to and under what circumstances. For example, sports medicine clinics that have a contract to provide services to an HMO might have a duty to provide services to the HMO's subscribers.

abandonment   The desertion of a patient-practitioner relationship by the health care provider without the consent of the patient.

Abandonment is another issue related to duty that affects athletic trainers. Once an athletic trainer chooses to provide services to an injured athlete or other physically active patient, whether a duty originally existed or not, the athletic trainer does not have the legal freedom to simply walk away from the case except under certain circumstances. An athletic trainer cannot forsake even patients who do not cooperate or who fail to pay their bills—unless he provides adequate warning and enough time to find alternative care.

If the physically active patient recovers and the athletic trainer and the patient agree that further treatment is no longer necessary, they can jointly terminate the relationship. If the patient has been referred, the athletic trainer has a duty to inform the referring agent, usually a physician, that treatment is being discontinued.

An athletic trainer can also discontinue services without fear of being charged with abandonment if the patient voluntarily terminates the relationship. The athletic trainer should make sure (and should be able to prove), however, that the patient understands the consequences of discontinuing the therapy. If the patient simply stops coming for treatment, the athletic trainer should be sure to document his attempts to make contact.

If the athletic trainer is away from the sports medicine center and leaves the patient's care in the hands of another practitioner, abandonment might also be charged. If the practitioner substituting for the athletic trainer commits a negligent act, the athletic trainer might be found negligent as well. Athletic trainers can avoid this problem by informing patients when they plan to be gone and making sure that patients agree to be treated by the substitute practitioner. The athletic trainer owes a duty to the patient to make sure that the substitute is competent and is capable of providing the same standard of care.

In general, the duties owed by an athletic trainer to athletes and other physically active patients are those described in the NATA's *Competencies in Athletic Training*. Specific duties identified by the courts include the duty to

- provide or obtain reasonable medical assistance for injured patients as soon as possible under the circumstances in such a way as to avoid aggravation of the injury (a probable breach of this duty occurred in the opening case). This implies having an effective emergency action plan, complete with necessary first-aid supplies and communications with ambulance services;

- maintain the confidentiality of the patient's medical records;

- provide adequate and proper supervision and instruction;

- provide safe facilities and equipment; and

- fully disclose information about the patient's medical condition to the patient in question.

Breach of Duty

standard of care
The legal duty to provide health care services consistent with what other health care practitioners of the same training, education, and credentialing would provide under the circumstances.

The next step in proving negligence against an athletic trainer requires the aggrieved athlete or other physically active patient to establish by a preponderance of the evidence that the athletic trainer actually breached a duty owed the patient. The issue here is whether the athletic trainer exercised the **standard of care** that other reasonably prudent athletic trainers would have exercised under the circumstances. The athletic trainer can consult the standards of practice of various medical and athletic professional organizations to determine a standard of care if questions arise. Note that the standard of care does not require an athletic trainer to be the *most* knowledgeable or competent athletic trainer in the profession. If this were the case, nobody could meet the standard. Instead, the standard requires athletic trainers to perform their duties as other competent athletic trainers would under similar circumstances. In determining whether athletic trainers have met the standard of care, the laws of various states require that their actions be compared to those of other athletic trainers in one of the following three settings (Scott, 1990):

- The same locality

- Similar communities

- The same or similar circumstances

For a useful guide to standards in sports medicine, see Herbert, D.L. (1992). *The sports medicine standards book.* Canton, OH: Professional Reports Corporation.

The standard of care expected of athletic trainers in fulfilling their duties to their patients can depend on whether the state has credentialed the profession. Herbert (1990) posits that in those states without statutory credentialing, the athletic trainer might be held to the standard of care of other regulated health professionals, including physicians. Indeed, in Gillespie v. Southern Utah State College, (669 P.2d. 861 [Ut. 1983]) a student athletic trainer was held to the standard of care of a physician in the treatment of a sprained ankle that later developed serious complications (Leverenz & Helms, 1990b).

Causation

actual cause
The degree to which a health care practitioner's actions are associated with the adverse outcomes of a patient's care.

Once an aggrieved athlete or other physically active patient has demonstrated that an athletic trainer breached a duty to exercise reasonable care, the patient must prove that the breach was in fact the legal cause of the injury (or made the original injury worse). The courts use two tests to determine causation. First, the plaintiff must prove **actual cause.** Actual cause is established if the patient can demonstrate that the athletic trainer's actions were a considerable determining factor in the damage claimed. The athletic trainer might be found only partially responsible for causing or aggravating the injury. Team physicians, coaches, and institutions might be named as codefendants in negligence cases, because all of them might have contributed to the injury. If more than one defendant was responsible for causing or aggravating the injury, they will be found jointly and severally liable for the negligence, which means that each defendant might end up paying a portion of the damages, consistent with his or her percentage of fault as determined by the court.

The second causation test is the requirement to demonstrate the existence of **proximate (legal) cause.** Proximate cause exists when an athletic trainer acts in a way that leads to harm or injury to another or to an event that injures another. Inherent in the notion of proximate cause is the **foreseeability** of the harm allegedly precipitated by the athletic trainer. The requirement that harm must be foreseeable is positive for athletic trainers—it doesn't penalize them for results that were improbable or unlikely. One of the problems in the opening case is that the team physician and athletic trainer did not ensure that an X ray of Enrique's injured ankle was obtained, even though they should have known that if a fracture were present it could have been aggravated by delayed or improper treatment. In short, they should have foreseen serious consequences.

proximate (legal) cause   The degree to which the harm caused by a health care practitioner was foreseeable.

foreseeability The ability to project the likely outcome of an act.

Damage

The final element in establishing negligence is to determine whether the aggrieved patient actually suffered damages. If an athletic trainer breached a duty without causing any harm, no negligence occurred. The athletic trainer who oversteps his level of training by suturing a wound, for example, cannot be found negligent unless the plaintiff can prove that she suffered harm as a result (a charge of practicing medicine without a license would probably have merit, however). Although physical damage is the most common and easily proved, the law recognizes other forms of damage as well. Emotional distress and loss of consortium (injury to the marital relationship) are just two examples (Herbert, 1990).

LEGAL DEFENSES

Athletic trainers will usually try to defend themselves against malpractice using one of five defenses: statute of limitations, sovereign immunity, assumption of risk, Good Samaritan immunity, and comparative negligence.

Athletic trainers accused of malpractice have several possible legal defenses. None of these should be viewed as ironclad protection against a lawsuit, however—each defense has exceptions that could leave the athletic trainer liable, even though the general principle might be valid. The best defense, of course, is to provide high-quality athletic training services consistent with the standard of care expected in the profession and the statutory regulations of the state. The following legal defenses might apply to claims of athletic trainer malpractice:

- The statute of limitations
- Sovereign immunity
- Assumption of risk
- Good Samaritan immunity
- Comparative negligence

STATUTE OF LIMITATIONS

statutes of limitations   Laws that fix a certain length of time beyond which legal actions cannot be initiated.

Statutes of limitations are state laws that fix a certain length of time in which an aggrieved patient may sue a health care provider. The statute of limitations applies in most states to health care providers who have been statutorily recognized by the state. States in which athletic training practice is regulated, therefore, probably extend the statutes of limitations to cover athletic trainers, but other states might not. Athletic trainers who are employed by physicians, hospitals, or physical therapists in states that don't provide credentials might also be protected, because their employers are regulated. Although the time period established by the statute of limitations is usually specified, many exceptions can lengthen the period in which an athlete or other physically active patient can bring suit.

SOVEREIGN IMMUNITY

sovereign (governmental) immunity A legal doctrine that holds that neither governments nor their agents can be held liable for negligent actions.

Sovereign (governmental) immunity is a legal doctrine that holds that neither governments nor their agents can be held liable for negligent torts (Baley & Matthews, 1984). In theory, athletic trainers employed in public schools, colleges, and universities are immune from legal liability because they are agents of governmental entities. In fact, however, many governmental units, including the federal government, have substantially lowered this traditional shield against legal liability (Herbert & Herbert, 1989). Athletic trainers employed in public institutions should not proceed as if they are immune by virtue of their positions, even though Leverenz and Helms (1990b) have identified three cases in which athletic trainers avoided liability based on a claim of governmental immunity (Garza v. Edinburg Consolidated Independent School District, 576 S.W.2d. 916 [Tx. 1979]; Lowe v. Texas Tech University, 540 S.W.2d. 297 [Tx. 1976]; and Sorey v. Kellett, 849 F.2d. 429 [5th Cir. 1988].)

ASSUMPTION OF RISK

assumption of risk A legal defense that attempts to claim that an injured plaintiff understood the risk of an activity and freely chose to undertake the activity regardless of the hazards associated with it.

One of the oldest and most common defenses that educational institutions and their employees have used against legal liability in athletic injury cases is **assumption of risk.** In this defense, the athletic trainer asserts that the injured athlete or other physically active patient was aware of the risks involved and decided to proceed anyway, thereby absolving the institution and the athletic trainer from any liability for damages. Scott (1990) points out that this defense is valid only when two conditions are met. The athlete must "fully appreciate" the type and magnitude of the risk involved in participating in the activity. The athlete must also "knowingly, voluntarily, and unequivocally" choose to participate in the activity in the face of the inherent risks. Skillful attorneys usually have little trouble defeating this defense, especially when the injured party is a minor. To protect against legal liability and improve their chances of being able to use this defense should the need arise, many schools and colleges provide educational sessions, complete with videos and printed materials, that warn student-athletes and their parents of the specific dangers inherent in their sports. Following these sessions, participants are asked to sign a statement affirming that they have been warned of the dangers associated with their sport (including permanent disability and death), that they understand these risks, that they have been offered the opportunity to ask questions regarding the risks, and that they voluntarily choose to participate regardless of the risks.

GOOD SAMARITAN IMMUNITY

Good Samaritan laws Statutes intended to shield certain health care practitioners from certain types of legal liability when they voluntarily come to the aid of injured or ill persons under specific circumstances.

A defense that can be used by athletic trainers in a very limited number of settings is immunity by virtue of a **Good Samaritan law.** Good Samaritan laws enacted in some states protect health care providers who voluntarily come to the aid of injured persons. These statutes might or might not cover athletic trainers, although about two-thirds of the states with Good Samaritan laws protect everyone who comes to the aid of an injured person, and the rest specify the classes of people who are protected under the law (Gallup, 1995). Specific Good Samaritan laws in some states protect volunteer team physicians from legal liability (Benda, 1991). If the physician receives compensation of any kind, the immunity from liability does not apply. Because athletic trainers are increasingly volunteering to serve at state games and charitable athletic events, this defense might become more popular. The injured person, of course, must consent to be treated. The statutes do not protect an athletic trainer from willful or wanton misconduct or from gross or intentional negligence.

COMPARATIVE NEGLIGENCE

comparative negligence A legal doctrine intended to determine the degree to which a plaintiff contributed to the harm caused by a defendant.

As was true in the opening case, physically active patients sometimes ignore the prescriptions of their health care providers, which leads to injury or aggravates an injury. The courts often use the doctrine of **comparative negligence** to determine if the liability for these injuries should be divided between the plaintiff and the defendant(s). Comparative negligence determines the degree of fault an athletic trainer and a patient have for causing an injury. The athletic trainer's financial liability depends on the formula used in the state in which the case is tried. In most states, patients can collect damages only if their comparative culpability is less than half the total. In some states, however, plaintiffs can be awarded financial restitution equal to the athletic trainer's percentage of fault. For instance, if Enrique's negligence accounted for 25% of the total fault for the aggravation of his injury, Todd Russell and his team physician might have to pay 75% of the damage claim.

PRODUCT LIABILITY

The explosion of lawsuits that began in the 1980s did not target only institutions and their sports medicine staffs, but also the companies that manufacture the products they use. Increased exposure to product liability lawsuits has helped drive up the costs of sports medicine supplies and athletic protective equipment. Athletic trainers can help reduce the threat of product liability lawsuits by following the practices outlined in this section.

A lengthy discussion of product liability is beyond the scope of this text. It is important, however, that athletic trainers have a basic understanding that the improper design, manufacture, or use of products can result in legal liability for both the company that made the equipment and, in some cases, for the athletic trainer that issued or used the equipment. A product can be found defective in one of four ways (Settle & Spigelmyer, 1984):

- Faulty design
- Faulty construction
- Failure to provide adequate warning
- Failure to conform to an express warranty

Injured athletes and other physically active patients can sue equipment manufacturers on the basis of any of three legal theories. First, the manufacturer can be sued for negligence. If the risk of injury from the use of its product was foreseeable and the company did not exercise due care in reducing or eliminating the risk, the company may be found negligent. A second approach involves suing a manufacturer for breach of an implied warranty. If a product is found by the court to be unfit for the purpose for which it was intended, then the plaintiff might be able to collect damages, because there is an implied warranty that equipment works in the way it is supposed to. Finally, an injured patient might be able to argue that an equipment manufacturer is strictly liable. Under this legal theory, a company can be found liable if a patient using its product is injured, regardless of the foreseeability of risk or the care the manufacturer took to prevent an injury.

Athletic trainers can help prevent lawsuits that have components of product liability by instituting the following practices:

- Read the warning labels and instruction manuals for every piece of equipment you use.
- Insist that athletes read the warning labels on all equipment they use.
- Make sure that athletes understand the information contained in the warning label. Ask them if they have any questions (this is especially important if their primary language is different from the language used on the label). Ask them

to sign a statement indicating that they have read and understand the warning label.

- Never modify, alter, or otherwise reconfigure a piece of equipment. Doing so might invalidate its express warranty and might shift a sizeable percentage of the legal liability away from the manufacturer and toward the athletic trainer.

- Inspect and maintain equipment according to the schedule recommended by the manufacturer. Keep records of all such maintenance.

PROVIDING TESTIMONY AT A DEPOSITION OR TRIAL

Although athletic trainers are sued infrequently, they might be called on to provide **testimony** in a court. An athletic trainer might give testimony either at a deposition, which is an informal series of questions posed under oath prior to a trial, or at the trial itself. He or she might be called either as a *fact* witness or as an *expert* witness.

testimony   Legally binding statements offered as evidence to the facts in a legal proceeding.

subpoena   The legal authority used to compel a person to provide testimony.

As a fact witness, the athletic trainer either had responsibility for treating an injured patient or has knowledge of the facts of the case. The athletic trainer has few choices about appearing in court under this circumstance, because the court will probably issue a subpoena ordering appearance.

An attorney might retain an athletic trainer as an expert to testify on behalf of a client. Expert witnesses are paid to provide testimony that educates the judge and jury about the standard of care that should be applied in a particular case. As an expert witness, the athletic trainer should agree with the positions she will be asked to take at trial. She should also be sure the attorney who hired her has the facts to support the case. Otherwise she will appear ignorant and foolish on the witness stand.

Whether athletic trainers are subpoenaed or appear as expert witnesses, they should observe the following guidelines to safeguard their credibility (Horsley & Carlova, 1983):

- Avoid memorizing the testimony.

- Never guess. If you're unsure of the answer to a question, admit lack of knowledge on that point.

- Testify only about issues for which you are an expert. Do not testify beyond the boundaries of your experience.

- Prepare for your testimony by carefully studying the records of the case before entering the courtroom. If you need to refer to the medical records while on the stand, understand that the records will be considered evidence that the opposing attorney will be able to access.

- Discuss your testimony with your attorney or the attorney retaining you as a witness prior to actually giving it in the courtroom.

- Use common language. Whenever you use medical language, attempt to interpret it for the judge and jury.

- Be absolutely sure that your testimony in court is consistent with any depositions you might have made prior to the beginning of the trial. Always review the deposition prior to taking the stand.

- Ask the judge if you feel the need to expand on a yes or no question posed by an attorney.

- Ask the judge if you feel that answering a question would violate the athletic trainer–patient relationship.

- Use illustrations (charts, drawings, slides, photographs, etc.) to help make your point when appropriate.

- If charged with malpractice and your malpractice insurance company has provided a lawyer you feel uncomfortable with, hire your own attorney.

- Maintain a professional, dignified demeanor at all times. Dress neatly; answer in a normal tone of voice at an even rate; and be respectful of the judge, jury, and attorneys.
- Remain composed at all times.
- Be prepared to be subjected to hostile questioning.

STRATEGIES FOR AVOIDING LEGAL LIABILITY

There are many ways athletic trainers can protect themselves against the threat of legal liability. Wise athletic trainers will take care to implement each of these strategies in their practice.

At the beginning of this chapter, I suggested that a knowledge of legal liability would help improve the quality of care offered by an athletic trainer. To place that rather sweeping statement into context, consider the following suggestions as part of a strategy to avoid the threat of legal liability (Graham, 1985).

- **Build relationships.** Develop and maintain good relations with athletes and other physically active patients, parents, coworkers, subordinates, and other health care professionals with whom you work or to whom you commonly refer patients. You should not only build trust relationships, but also promote a constant flow of two-way communication with these groups.

- **Insist on a written contract.** Have a written contract supported by a detailed position description that clearly delineates the athletic trainer's job functions. This is one of the most important defenses you can offer against a charge of negligence, because it helps establish those to whom you might owe a legal duty.

- **Obtain informed consent.** Obtain informed consent for the services you perform. In the case of minors, obtain informed consent from their parents (see figure 6.8 on p. 171). Warn athletes and parents of the dangers, including permanent disability and death, inherent in their particular sport. Repeat such warnings annually.

- **Provide physical examinations.** Be certain that every athlete undergoes a physical examination by a state-licensed medical practitioner. Make certain that the content of the physical examination is consistent with nationally recognized standards, both in terms of its content and frequency.

- **Know the profession and its standards.** Develop and maintain a database of information about injuries and illnesses that are most common to each sport you work with. This will enhance your qualifications as an expert in your field. Practice your profession unafraid, but keep in mind the standards of practice embraced by the profession.

- **Document hazards.** Make a documented attempt to reduce injuries by recommending or personally taking action to remove or modify potential hazards. Consider establishing a safety committee charged with conducting an ongoing program of risk assessment and reduction. Be aware, however, that a paper trail documenting safety hazards can also be used against you or your institution, especially if the hazards are not corrected or the corrections go undocumented.

- **Establish policies.** Adopt and scrupulously adhere to policies and procedures designed to reduce the incidence of injury and to guide the actions of sports medicine personnel when injuries do occur. Keep all emergency first-aid equipment in working order and available to those who might need to use it.

- **Document activities.** Document the details of all injuries, treatments, and rehabilitative procedures so a chronology of events can easily be determined after the fact. Maintain medical records until well after the statute of limitations for malpractice liability has expired (this will vary from state to state).

- **Maintain Cconfidentiality.** Maintain the confidentiality of the patient's medical record. When you wish to share the information with others, obtain the written permission of the patient first.

- **Provide proper instruction.** When interacting with athletes and other physically active patients, be certain that the instruction you provide allows for safe participation. If you give instructions to a patient in a rehabilitation program, for example, make sure that the patient understands how to progress and knows the warning signs associated with reinjury. If you are instructing athletes in an off-season conditioning program, make sure they can perform the exercises properly and that they use commonly accepted safety techniques; for example, spotting each other when using free weights.

- **Supervise your staff.** Insist that every staff member adhere to prescribed programmatic procedures. Make sure that supervisees understand your requests. Check to make sure that your requests are being carried out as required by the procedures specified in the program's handbook. When deviations occur, be sure to correct the supervisee's behavior.

- **Participate in continuing education.** Take part in continuing athletic training education by attending seminars and symposia and reading sports medicine literature. Alter your techniques as technology and knowledge advance. Document your continuing education activities and the changes that result.

- **Recognize your qualifications.** Practice only within the limitations of your state's law and the boundaries of your training. Be consistent with the standard of care expected of other reasonably prudent athletic trainers. Be quick to refer injured athletes and other physically active patients to physicians and be sure to follow their instructions carefully. Avoid the distribution of prescription medications and be cautious in your use of over-the-counter medications.

- **Maintain insurance coverage.** All athletic trainers, certified and student alike, should have malpractice and liability insurance to safeguard their personal assets in the event of a legal action. Even if a malpractice suit is frivolous and eventually dismissed, the costs associated with defense are usually beyond the means of most athletic trainers. In some cases, the employer's general liability policy will adequately protect you. In many cases, however, health care activities are specifically excluded from institutional liability insurance policies. In addition, the maximum benefit of institutional policies might not cover the fantastic costs associated with medical litigation. Athletic trainers who are inadequately protected through their employer's liability insurance policy should seriously consider purchasing their own policies. It is important for athletic trainers to evaluate the limits of coverage of both their employers' and their personal malpractice insurance policies. The limits of these policies often determine what kinds of activities the athletic trainer can engage in. Some policies, for example, cover job-related duties but exclude volunteer activities. Under these circumstances, an athletic trainer who provides medical services at summer sports camps would probably have to have these activities written into their job descriptions in order to be covered. Activities undertaken with malicious intent or gross negligence are frequently not covered.

The National Athletic Trainers' Association offers malpractice and liability insurance to its members through Maginnis & Associates. Contact Maginnis & Associates, 332 South Michigan Avenue, Chicago, IL 60604.

APPLICATIONS TO ATHLETIC TRAINING: THEORY INTO PRACTICE

Apply the concepts discussed in this chapter to the following two case studies to help you prepare for similar situations in actual practice. The questions at the end of the studies have many possible correct solutions. Use the case studies for homework, exam questions, or to spur class discussion.

Case Study 1

Larry Donelson was pleased when the management of the professional football team that employed him allowed him to hire an additional student athletic trainer for the preseason training camp. The preseason was always one of the most hectic times, and he was grateful for the help that students were able to provide. One of the students he had decided to hire this year, Rich Hayes, was only a sophomore. Larry usually hired only students who had completed their junior years, but Rich had come highly recommended from his supervising athletic trainer, an old friend of Larry's, so he had decided to take a chance on Rich.

James Star was a 10th-round draft choice trying to make the team that summer. James had played college football at the same university Rich was attending. Although he felt good about his performance in the first two weeks, a knee injury suffered in the first scrimmage had kept him out of practice since then. Fortunately, the knee was starting to feel better and James hoped he could return to limited practice within a couple of days.

One day the head coach surprised everybody by announcing that the team would have the next morning off. The student athletic trainers, knowing they wouldn't have to wake up at the usual 5:30 A.M., decided to visit a local pub that night. It was the only bar in the small college town where the team had its training camp, so most of the players went there as well.

Rich saw James at the pub and joined him. Three beers later, the topic of James's knee injury came up. When James told Rich he was feeling better and would probably be back in a couple of days, Rich confided that he had heard Larry Donelson, the team physician, and the head coach talking about James a couple of days ago while he was cleaning a whirlpool. When James asked what they had said, Rich told them they were simply discussing the details of James's knee injury and his prospects for full recovery. After two more beers, James had the whole story.

When James was released from the team the next week, he immediately contacted his agent, an attorney, who filed a lawsuit on his behalf alleging that the team had concealed the true nature of James's injury, which resulted in his termination and subsequent unemployment.

Questions for Analysis

1. What legal principles are involved in this case? How do they apply? Does James have a strong case? Why or why not?

2. How could this situation have been avoided? What policies and procedures should Larry Donelson institute to prevent this kind of problem?

3. Who, if anyone, is at fault in this case? If more than one person, how is a judge or jury likely to determine the percentage of each person's liability?

4. What records could Larry use to defend himself and the team?

Case Study 2

Christine Campbell, the assistant athletic trainer for Northwest State University, was off the bench like a shot when she saw the basketball team's star center fall to the floor holding her knee. After conducting an examination on the floor, Christine decided to take the player to the athletic training room for a more complete examination by the team physician. She and the student manager, who were both at least 10 inches shorter than the player, helped her hobble off the court toward the athletic training room. As they were passing the locker room, the student manager slipped on a wet spot, causing the player to put her full weight on the injured knee. She cried out in pain and told Christine that she felt a "pop."

After the team physician, a general practitioner employed by the student health service, completed his examination, he informed the player that she had torn the anterior cruciate and medial collateral ligaments in her knee and would need surgery to correct the problem. He instructed Christine to do the following things, all of which he recorded in his post-evaluation dictation for the athlete's medical record:

1. Apply an elastic wrap from the toes to midthigh.
2. Apply a knee immobilizer.
3. Fit the athlete with crutches.
4. Arrange an orthopedic consultation for the next day.
5. Give enough 600 mg ibuprofen for three days.

Later that night, a phone call from the athlete's roommate woke Christine, who found out that the athlete had become violently ill and had been rushed to the hospital by ambulance after suffering a reaction to the medication Christine had given her.

Questions for Analysis

1. What legal principles are involved in this case? What liability concerns should be addressed? What policies and procedures should be implemented to address these concerns?

2. What would you have done differently, if anything, if you had been in Christine's position?

3. Who, if anyone, is at fault in this case? If more than one person, how should a judge or jury determine the degree to which each person is liable?

SUMMARY

1. *Define and discuss the legal principles most applicable to athletic training settings.*

   Although the thought of legal action against an athletic trainer is unsettling, prudent athletic trainers will take advantage of their legal knowledge to improve the quality of the service they provide to their physically active patients. The best and most important source of legal advice, of course, is an attorney experienced in dealing with health care malpractice issues.

2. *Identify the types of situations most likely to hold liability concerns for athletic trainers.*

   Risk management is a process designed to prevent losses of all types for everyone associated with an athletic program. Risks are identified and assessed in two ways: through real-world observations and through controlled studies. The best risk-management programs use both methods. Risks can be reduced in four areas: preparation for the activity, conduct of the activity, management of injuries, and proper records management.

3. *Understand the different types of credentialing laws that affect the practice of athletic training.*

   Credentialing laws, including licensure, certification, registration, and exemption, are designed to ensure basic competencies to protect the public. All athletic trainers should become familiar with the laws in their states to determine their legal basis for practice. Athletic trainers who practice in states without credentialing laws, although they might be protected by the delegatory clause of the medical practice act, might be held to the standard of care of a physician in a malpractice case.

4. *Understand the elements required to prove negligence on the part of an athletic trainer.*

   Torts are legal wrongs, other than breach of contract, for which a court will determine a remedy, usually in the form of monetary damages. Negligence is the kind of tort most commonly charged against athletic trainers. To prove negligence, the aggrieved person must demonstrate conduct by the athletic trainer, existence of duty, breach of duty, causation (including actual and proximate cause), and damage. Athletic trainers will be held to the same standard of care as other reasonably prudent athletic trainers in the same or similar circumstances.

5. *Be aware of the various legal defenses available to athletic trainers against charges of malpractice.*

   Although several defenses against charges of malpractice exist, including statutes of limitations, sovereign immunity, assumption of risk, Good Samaritan immunity, and comparative negligence, the athletic trainer's best defense is to practice in a manner consistent with the standards of the profession.

6. *Identify the most important elements of providing effective legal testimony.*

   Should an athletic trainer be called to provide testimony, either as a fact witness or as an expert witness, he should prepare by reviewing the records of the case, consulting with the attorney, and speaking only to the facts of the case within the limits of his experience and training.

7. *Identify and put into practice methods that avoid legal liability while improving the quality of athletic training care.*

   Athletic trainers will improve their practice while simultaneously protecting themselves from liability if they will build relationships with their patients, insist on written employment contracts, obtain informed consent, screen all athletes during a physical exam, and abide by the standards of the profession. It is also important to document hazards, establish and adhere to written policies, document patient care activities, maintain confidentiality, and provide proper instruction to injured patients. Finally, athletic trainers must also supervise their staff, participate in continuing education, practice within the boundaries of their qualifications, and maintain a liability insurance policy.

CHAPTER NINE

Athletic Trainers Doing the Right Thing: Ethics in Sports Medicine

with Peter Loubert, PhD, PT, ATC

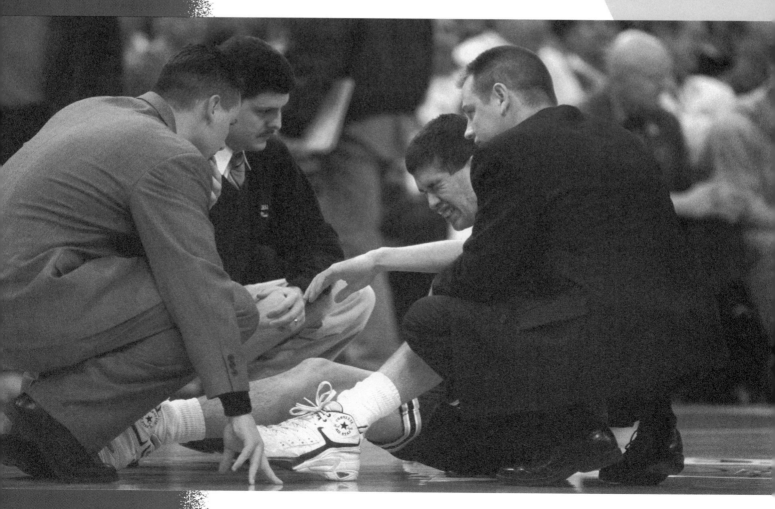

Portions of this chapter were reprinted or adapted from Ray and Wiese-Bjornstal 1999.

OBJECTIVES

After completing this chapter, you should be able to do the following:

1. Understand the definition and purpose of ethical standards and their relevance for the athletic trainer.

2. Identify the appropriate code of ethics that applies generally to the profession of athletic training, along with codes that might apply to specific settings within the profession.

3. Identify the situations and circumstances in which ethical concerns are most frequent.

4. Develop strategies for avoiding ethical problems and for dealing with them if they occur.

Tammy Johnson is the certified athletic trainer at an NCAA Division III college. As the school's first athletic trainer, Tammy was instrumental in developing and building support for a drug and alcohol program that included both educational and athlete-code-of-conduct components. Included in the athlete's code of conduct was a "zero-tolerance" clause that prohibited all athletes from consuming alcoholic beverages during their seasons. Athletes caught violating this rule would be forced to miss two games.

One night Tammy received a call at home from a student who had taken a class from her a couple of years before. The student was a waiter at a local restaurant and had observed one of the school's basketball players drinking in the restaurant's bar a couple of nights before. He had been reluctant to tell anyone about the incident, because he knew the athlete would be forced to miss the first round of the NCAA tournament later in the week if he was turned in. The student finally decided he had to do something to ease his conscience, however, so he called Tammy in the hopes she would be willing to report the violation. Tammy spent 45 minutes on the phone gathering all the details of the event, including the names of other students who had been with the basketball player. She even got the name of the waitress who had served the basketball player and his friends. She also informed the student that if he insisted on going forward with these allegations he could expect some questions from the basketball coach and the athletic director. He said that would be OK, as long as justice was served.

The next day, Tammy went to the basketball coach and informed him of the allegations. The coach, who was trying to prepare for the biggest game of the year, was upset but said he would talk to the player and try to reach resolution on the matter as soon as possible. Later that afternoon, the coach pulled Tammy aside in the hallway and told her that all of his assistants and he had confronted the player with the allegation that he had been drinking. The coach told Tammy that the athlete denied consuming any alcohol, although he did admit to being in the bar. The basketball coach told Tammy that he believed his player, and that as far as he was concerned the matter was closed. When Tammy asked the coach if he had informed the athletic director as was required in the school's drug and alcohol policy, the coach simply said he didn't think this case merited any further investigation and he didn't want to take any of the AD's time with such a trivial matter.

Fame is vapor, popularity an accident, riches take wing. . . . The only thing that endures is character.

Horace Greeley

As Tammy's case demonstrates, athletic training is a profession that places many pressures on its practitioners. Athletic trainers face pressure from coaches, whose security needs are met through winning games; from athletes and other physically active patients, who are often willing to sacrifice their health for short-term glory; and from a variety of other sources. One common by-product of this pressure is the temptation to make decisions or perform acts that, although seemingly innocent, are not in the best interests of patients or of the profession.

All athletic trainers have a responsibility to act in an ethical manner. Unfortunately, this is a responsibility that is not always easy to fulfill. Ethical decision making requires both the knowledge of ethical responsibilities and the willpower to endure the inevitable hardships that accompany ethically correct decisions. The purpose of this chapter is to introduce the topic of ethics as it applies to athletic trainers. In this chapter we will identify some of the most common situations where ethical breaches can occur, and we will consider recommendations for steps that can be taken to minimize their occurrence.

Ethical practice is not limited to the managerial roles assumed by athletic trainers; ethical dilemmas arise in other domains of the profession as well. An athletic trainer's injury management, rehabilitation, education, and counseling roles are particularly rich with potential ethical problems. However, although not all ethical problems are related to the managerial role, many are. All require some degree of decision making. Decision making is the single most common element among all managerial functions, and it is one of an athletic trainer's most important managerial skills.

DEFINING ETHICS

Ethics help define acceptable behavior among members of a group. Professions establish codes of ethics to provide behavioral guidelines for their members and to help protect the public from the actions of unethical practitoners.

ethics   The rules, standards, and principles that dictate right conduct among members of a society or profession. Ethics are based on moral values.

right conduct Behavior that is fitting, proper, or conforms to legal or moral expectations.

code of ethics   A systematized set of standards or principles that defines ethical behavior appropriate for a profession. The standards and principles are determined by moral values.

Ethics is the study of the rules, standards, and principles that dictate **right conduct** among members of a society. Such rules are based on moral values. Principles of ethics are derived from a long, rich history of philosophical debate. They are deeply embedded in our choices of how we govern and conduct ourselves as a civilized society and serve as the basis for many of our norms for social interaction. Ethics also reflect many of the tenets of a variety of religions and have been influenced by religious philosophies from around the world. All of these influences and history have led us to depend on the principles of ethics to form the moral backbone of the most important things that we do as contributors to a conscientious society. In the professions, ethics provide a perspective from which to judge the rightness or wrongness of a professional's actions; they are a reflection of the "conscience" of the profession (Appelbaum and Lawton, 1990).

WHY PROFESSIONS ESTABLISH ETHICAL STANDARDS

Professions are defined by a commitment to certain characteristics that set them apart from nonprofessional groups within our society. One of the most important of these characteristics is a commitment to high standards of ethical behavior by the members of the profession. Among the professions that provide health care services to athletes and other physically active patients, ethical standards are written in the form of a **code of ethics** by each of the respective professional organizations. The purposes of these codes are to provide a guide to appropriate conduct for members, to provide a reference by which to judge members when their conduct is brought into question, and to provide assurance and protection to the public served by members of the profession.

ETHICAL STANDARDS RELEVANT TO ATHLETIC TRAINING

Sports health care professionals should comply with the code of ethics of the national professional organization for their primary profession. Athletic trainers must adhere to several sets of professional standards. The *NATA Code of Ethics* (National Athletic Trainers' Association, 1995) is intended to guide the actions of every member of the NATA in the practice of athletic training (see appendix D). The code consists of five general principles, each with its own substatements. A breach of the principles embodied in this document would be viewed very seriously, and could result in suspension or revocation of certification. Athletic trainers who hold dual credentialing as physical therapists are expected to adhere to the American Physical Therapy Association *Code of Ethics* (American Physical Therapy Association, 1991). Similarly, athletic trainers who hold other certifications or credentials, such as nurses, occupational therapists, physicians, physician assistants, or EMTs, are bound by the codes of ethics of the organizations that represent those professions. The code of ethics documents provide guidelines for ethical conduct within the respective professions and are intended to apply to the entire range of practice patterns and settings applicable to the respective professions. Their standards are enforceable for the members of each organization but should also be considered applicable to non-members within the profession.

Five Principles of the NATA Code of Ethics

1. Members shall respect the rights, welfare, and dignity of all individuals.
2. Members shall comply with the laws and regulations governing the practice of athletic training.
3. Members shall accept responsibility for the exercise of sound judgment.
4. Members shall maintain and promote high standards in the provision of services.
5. Members shall not engage in any form of conduct that constitutes a conflict of interest or that adversely reflects on the profession.

Unfortunately, becoming informed about the NATA's code of ethics is often not enough, even for those athletic trainers without dual credentials. The various practice domains force athletic trainers to examine the ethical codes of other disciplines to make sure that they do not stray from accepted practice in those disciplines. For example, when providing counseling to student-athletes, athletic trainers should be sure to adhere to the *Code of Ethics* of the American Counseling Association (1995) or to the *Ethical Principles of Psychologists and Code of Conduct* of the American Psychological Association (1992). Athletic trainers who are also teachers might be bound by the ethical codes of professional educators' societies, such as the American Association of University Professors (1995). Finally, ethical standards exist that are specific to particular employment settings. For example, the American Hospital Association's (1992) *Ethical Conduct for Health Care Institutions* is intended to provide guidance for ethical decision making for hospital employees, including athletic trainers who work in hospital-based settings.

The American Psychological Association *Code of Conduct* is available at **http://www.apa.org/ethics/code.html**.

RELATIONSHIP BETWEEN LEGAL AND ETHICAL CONSIDERATIONS

Athletic trainers can usually act in an ethical manner by acting within the law. They can become involved in ethical dilemmas either as a primary or third party.

Ethical considerations often overlap, contradict, or otherwise interact with issues of **law**. It is convenient when a difficult ethical decision is consistent with the law; however, it is important to recognize that there are circumstances whereby an athletic trainer will find that what is ethical might not be legal, and what is legal might not be ethical. This is especially a problem in the context of a health care role when there are issues of confidentiality and protection of individual rights to privacy. The right of an athlete to privacy might well conflict with the law when the law dictates that a specific type of information be reported. The multiple roles served by athletic trainers make the issue even more difficult because of the many different types of information for which they are responsible. The most recent large-scale issue of this nature is the reporting of HIV status required by some health departments. Ideas regarding how an athletic trainer might deal with such conflicts are included later in this chapter. What is clear is that professional codes of ethics almost always dictate that it is unethical to engage in any practice activity that is illegal (Makarowski & Rickell, 1993).

laws *The rules and regulations governing the affairs of a community or society. Laws are enforced by administrative authority and an established judicial system of the community.*

THE ATHLETIC TRAINER AS A PRIMARY PARTY

An athletic trainer might face ethical issues in many different forms. The most menacing will be those in which the athletic trainer is a **primary party** to the ethical

rights Moral or
legal privileges
inherent in being a
member of a commu-
nity or society.

primary party
A person directly
involved as a
participant in an
activity.

perpetrator The
person who is respon-
sible for or has
committed an act.

*breach of
confidentiality*
Violation of a commit-
ment to privacy and
protection of informa-
tion or communica-
tions.

concern. To be a primary party means that the athletic trainer is directly involved in the situation as a person who has behaved in an ethically questionable manner or who is the victim of an unethical act committed by another person. Of primary concern in this chapter is the former situation, whereby the athletic trainer is the **perpetrator** of an unethical act.

The next few paragraphs describe four types of situations in which an athletic trainer might become entangled as a primary party in an ethical dilemma. These situations are also listed below. Although this list is not exhaustive, these are the situations that occur most often or that have the greatest potential for harm to the individuals involved. If the codes of ethics are adhered to, they will help protect both the patient and the athletic trainer.

The Most Common and/or Destructive Situations in Which an Athletic Trainer Might Become a Primary Party in an Unethical Situation

- Breach of confidentiality
- Conflict of interest
- Exploitation

Breach of Confidentiality

One of the most frequently recurring ethical situations an athletic trainer faces is **breach of confidentiality**. This is an especially difficult situation for several reasons. First, an athletic trainer often serves many roles that relate to an athlete. There is often a need for information to be shared with the team organization, with coaches, or with colleagues who are also responsible for some aspect of the athlete's care. Those needs, legitimate or not, will sometimes conflict with what is in the best interest of the athletes and with the responsibilities that the athletic trainer has for their health care. Consider Tammy's case in the opening scenario. If the basketball player who violated the school's alcohol policy had come to Tammy, admitted the violation, asked Tammy for help in treating his dependency, and asked her not to tell the coach, Tammy would have been placed in a difficult ethical position. On the one hand, she has a responsibility to maintain the confidentiality of the athletes under her care. On the other hand, she might have a contractual obligation to uphold the policies of the institution that employs her and turn the athlete in for appropriate discipline under the rules of the alcohol policy.

Confidential information obtained as part of the professional relationship that an athletic trainer has with an athlete or other physically active patient might be very personal, private, and sensitive. The athletic trainer should handle such information very carefully to avoid ethical as well as legal breaches of confidentiality. In some situations the most appropriate ethical behavior might even jeopardize an athletic trainer's job.

The second reason it might be difficult for an athletic trainer to maintain confidentiality is that there are often many people involved in the care of an athlete or other physically active patient. This is especially true where there are student and intern practitioners involved who might not be fully cognizant of concerns for confidentiality. When an athletic trainer is responsible for the supervision of students and interns, she will also be held responsible for student or intern actions. This makes the athletic trainer a primary party in a breach of confidentiality even if she was not the immediate perpetrator of the breach.

The final concern relative to confidentiality is the high profile of athletes and of the athletic industry in our society. The pressures of the press and the public's desire to know everything possible about a high-profile athlete can be significant threats to an athlete's right to privacy and to the confidentiality of information that an athletic trainer is privy to. In order to avoid breaches of confidentiality, athletic trainers should take proactive and diligent measures to protect information and communications. Several suggestions for such measures are listed below.

Measures to Protect the Confidentiality of Information and Communications

- Establish and follow responsible procedures for documentation and store records in a secure environment.
- Allow only persons with a legitimate role in providing health care to the patient access to the records.
- Release information only with written permission of the patient involved.
- Designate a specific person to handle all requests for health-related information; train all persons in the organization and remind them regularly to defer all inquiries to that person.
- Never discuss the health status of an athlete or other physically active patient in public, and never in private unless all persons present have a legitimate need and authorization to have access to the information.

reason   The basis or explanation for an action.

excuse   A reason that is considered justifiable.

There are three exceptions to the rule of confidentiality noted in the codes of ethics. No reason for a breach of confidentiality, other than those listed here, serves as an excuse for its occurrence. A professional should recognize the difference between a **reason** and an **excuse** and should only accept a reason as an excuse when it is both unavoidable and justifiable. These reasons would be considered excusable; any other reason would be inexcusable.

Exceptions to the Rule of Confidentiality

- When there is clear and imminent danger to the client.
- When there is clear and imminent danger to other persons.
- When legal requirements demand that confidential information be released.

Reprinted from Castetter 1986.

Conflict of Interest

conflict of interest   When the interests of one individual or group are discordant or in competition with those of another individual or group.

Athletic trainers are also susceptible to ethical breaches based on **conflicts of interest.** Here again, the particular threat to ethical practice is a result of the multiple roles that an athletic trainer might fill. The responsibilities that an athletic trainer has to a team organization, to the coaching staff, and to himself will often conflict with his responsibilities to an athlete or other physically active patient. The temptation to act or to advise an athlete or other patient in a manner that serves the team or protects the job or other interests of the athletic trainer might go unrecognized.

In Tammy's case the threat to confidentiality of information comes about because she has a conflict of interest. Her personal concern for her job conflicts with the best interests of the athlete to keep the information confidential. These can be particularly difficult conflicts of interest to resolve, because the coach and organization might have a legitimate need to know the information, and they might threaten to fire the athletic trainer.

A nearly universal component in most codes of ethics for health care professionals is the responsibility to place the best interests of the patient above all other concerns. This standard applies to every role assumed by an athletic trainer. Athletic trainers who receive payment to use a particular product might have a conflict of interest when treating patients with that product. An athletic trainer's role is particularly sensitive, because a high degree of trust must be developed between the athletic trainer and the patient. If the athletic trainer breaches this trust through a conflict of interest, it might be impossible to rebuild and the relationship might disintegrate. This is just one reason why athletes with sensitive counseling or psychological concerns might be better off if they are referred to a counselor not affiliated with the institution or the team. The athletic trainer's role as administrator is also subject to conflicts of interest. When decisions regarding allocation of resources, including time, money, and personnel, clash with the health care needs of the athletic patient population, a conflict of interest might be present that could lead to an ethical breach.

It is not enough to avoid conflicts of interest. Athletic trainers should be careful to avoid even the appearance of a conflict. Ethical standards are usually interpreted differently by different people. Sometimes a well-considered action will appear unethical to those who don't know why the decision was made or why the action was taken. Unfortunately, if the action appears to involve a conflict of interest, and is therefore considered unethical, the trust required to maintain a reputation of high integrity will be damaged.

Exploitation

exploitation Using another person for selfish purposes, particularly when it comes at the expense of that person and/or without their knowledge or full informed consent.

Exploitation of an athlete or other physically active patient by an athletic trainer is a particularly manipulative and self-interested form of conflict of interest. It involves the intentional use of another person or group of persons to achieve a selfish objective. When patients confide in an athletic trainer, they become particularly vulnerable to exploitation because they might reveal things about themselves that would otherwise be unknown. Under such circumstances patients are vulnerable to exploitation for money, information, sex, self-endangerment (e.g manipulating an athlete to play while injured), goods, or any number of other reasons. For an athletic trainer to perpetrate such a situation would be clearly unethical.

THE ATHLETIC TRAINER AS A THIRD PARTY

third party To be affected by, but not directly involved in, a situation. Professionals who simply have knowledge of an unethical act can be affected by it, because there is a professional responsibility to act on such knowledge.

An athletic trainer might also be involved in ethical dilemmas as a **third party.** To be a third party means that the athletic trainer is not personally involved in the dilemma but has professional responsibilities because of her knowledge of the situation. An athletic trainer has the responsibility not only to intervene in the best interest of the client but to also protect others from harm whenever there is apparent risk of harm occurring. Tammy's situation in the opening case is a good example of how an athletic trainer can become embroiled in an ethical dilemma as a third party.

One of the primary differences between being involved in a situation of ethical concern as a third party, rather than as a primary participant, is that as a third party an athletic trainer can act more appropriately to manage a solution to the situation. When an athletic trainer becomes involved in a situation as a primary participant, especially in the presence of a conflict of interest or exploitation, he must often remove himself from the situation and request that someone else intervene to help resolve it. When an athletic trainer is involved in an ethical concern as a third party the circumstance is much different. In this case the athletic trainer is often in a very good position to orchestrate a solution to the situation. The solution will often involve providing information and perspectives to the patient, or managing other people and information to resolve the ethical dilemma.

An athletic trainer can become a third party to an ethical dilemma as a result of what she learns directly from a patient or of knowledge that comes to her attention from other sources. Such knowledge can create very difficult circumstances, because there are often conflicts between the professional's responsibility to maintain confidentiality, her responsibility to protect the patient from harm, her responsibility to protect others from harm, and the many other loyalties she might have that also affect the patient.

There are five categories of knowledge that are most likely to render an athletic trainer a third party to an ethical dilemma.

Categories of Knowledge That Make an Athletic Trainer a Third Party to an Ethical Dilemma

- Knowledge of the occurrence of a breach of confidentiality, conflict of interest, or exploitation involving a patient
- Forbidden knowledge
- Knowledge of high-risk behaviors
- Knowledge of illegal activities
- Knowledge of situations wherein the welfare of the patient conflicts with the welfare of another individual or group of individuals

---

Breach of Confidentiality, Conflict of Interest, or Exploitation of a Patient

Just as when the athletic trainer is directly involved, these situations can be very harmful to patients. Knowledge of such situations makes it incumbent upon the athletic trainer to intervene on behalf of the patient. Intervention usually does not mean that the athletic trainer has responsibility for correcting the situation. It is usually sufficient to bring it to the patient's attention so that he or she can take responsibility for the situation from a fully informed perspective. In the case of patients who are **minors** or who might otherwise be unable to protect themselves in such a situation, the athletic trainer should inform the parents or **guardians,** refer the situation to the appropriate authorities (particularly when there are legal concerns), or intervene directly.

Imagine, for example, that a college women's softball player goes to her athletic trainer for advice because she is frustrated about not getting enough playing time. She states that she feels the woman playing ahead of her is getting all of the playing time, not because she is a better player but because she sleeps with the coach. The athletic trainer, as a third party having knowledge of this exploitation, would be ethically bound to intervene on behalf of both athletes.

Forbidden Knowledge

Forbidden knowledge is information about a situation that an athletic trainer is forbidden to act on. Such information might come from an athlete or other physically active patient (about themselves or others) or it might come from another person. Typically, the sharing of such information is preceded with a phrase such as "If I tell you this, you must promise not to share it with anyone" (Makarowski & Rickell, 1993).

An athletic trainer should be wary of anyone who wants to share information but refuses to allow it to be acted on. To agree to such terms might preclude the athletic trainer from taking necessary actions that would otherwise supersede the promise, including the reasons cited earlier. An athletic trainer who receives forbidden information should insist that the patient offering it trust her to act in the patient's best interests. The patient should be assured that the athletic trainer will maintain the confidentiality of the information (provided there is no threat of harm to the patient or to other persons affected by the information, and provided the athletic trainer is not legally required to release the information). If a patient is unable to agree to those terms, then he should be offered a referral to someone with whom he

minor A person under legal age for adult responsibilities and decisions.

guardian A person who has legal responsibility for the care and decisions of someone who is incompetent to act for himself or who is a minor.

forbidden knowledge Information about a situation that an athletic trainer is forbidden to act on.

can trust the information, and he should be strongly encouraged to follow through with it.

When someone other than the patient involved offers forbidden information, it is essential for an athletic trainer to clarify that she is obligated to act in the best interest of the patients under her care. It might be appropriate to offer to use the information in an anonymous fashion, if possible, but an athletic trainer must not forfeit the right to use it when necessary.

A word of caution regarding the use of knowledge is in order, particularly in the context of forbidden knowledge. To take action on knowledge that is inaccurate or untrue can be very harmful to athletic trainers, to the athletes or other physically active patients they are responsible for, or to others. The offer of forbidden knowledge by a patient or by others is a common avenue by which an athletic trainer is at risk for being **manipulated.** The athletic trainer should use any information cautiously, particularly when the accuracy of the information is in doubt. In some circumstances it might be appropriate to delay action on a piece of information until it can be verified. For example, if the student who informed on the basketball player in the opening case is known to carry a grudge against the athlete or the program, it would be wise for Tammy to try to obtain independent confirmation of his allegations before acting.

Knowledge of High-Risk Behaviors

Knowledge of **high-risk behaviors** is another area of potential ethical concern for an athletic trainer. This knowledge might come to you from your own observation, from a report from an athlete or other physically active patient under your care, or from others. This particular concern extends to situations where a patient is at risk for harm as a result of his own high-risk behaviors or the high-risk behaviors of others. It also includes situations in which the high-risk behaviors of the patient puts others at risk.

When an athletic trainer has knowledge of potentially harmful high-risk behaviors a patient is engaging in that put only the patient at risk, the ethical responsibility is not to prevent the behaviors so much as it is to be sure that the individual involved is aware of the associated risks. It might also be incumbent upon the athletic trainer to assist the person involved in finding alternatives to the high-risk behaviors. The athletic trainer's responsibilities in a case like this, therefore, are to provide the patient with information, education, and counseling so that he can make an informed choice regarding his participation in the behaviors.

When the high-risk behavior of an athlete puts others at risk, it is the responsibility of the athletic trainer to intervene, if only to be sure the other individuals are made aware of the risk so that they can protect themselves. For example, if an athletic trainer becomes aware that one of the athletes in her care is engaging in unprotected sexual activity with multiple partners, she might have an ethical duty to confront the athlete in a private setting and warn him of the consequences of such behavior.

Knowledge of Illegal Activities

Knowledge of illegal activities related to an athlete or other physically active patient can also create a difficult ethical situation. An athlete might admit to illegal activities as part of an advising session, or the information might come to the attention of the athletic trainer from an outside source, as it did in Tammy's case. That case would have been even more complicated had Tammy known, for example, that the athlete had used a false ID to obtain alcohol in the bar. In that scenario, Tammy would have an ethical responsibility to the bar and the police, in addition to her responsibility to uphold the college's policy.

manipulation
Shrewdly or deviously influencing or controlling another person or a situation. When the influence or control is for self-interested purposes, it can be exploitative.

high-risk behaviors
Behaviors that expose a person to an unnecessarily high degree of physical or psychological jeopardy.

One of the difficulties of having knowledge of illegal activities is that legal authorities might be aware of those activities and seek information from the athletic trainer. The other difficulty occurs when legal authorities are unaware of the illegal activities. Both of these circumstances demand that the athletic trainer be familiar with her legal obligations as a professional, and they also demand very careful consideration of the specific situation. Legal concerns become entangled with issues of confidentiality, responsibility to the client, privileged communication status, legal reporting requirements, and many others. Athletic trainers who have knowledge of a patient's illegal activities would be well advised to seek legal counsel in order to protect their own status and that of the patient.

Knowledge of Conflicting Interests

*self-determination
Free will to judge for oneself, to determine one's own course of action, and to manage one's own affairs.*

A central concept in ethics is that individuals have a right to self-determination (Appelbaum & Lawton, 1990). This right, however can come into conflict with the rights and welfare of other individuals or groups in society. An example would be when an athletic trainer knows that a wrestler has a contagious skin disease that is difficult to see. In this example, the right of a capable and otherwise healthy athlete to compete would conflict with the right of other athletes to be protected from the skin disease.

Knowledge of situations wherein the welfare of a patient conflicts with the welfare of another individual or group of individuals can present challenging ethical questions for the athletic trainer. Many of these types of situations are directed by social conventions or by law. However, there are also many areas that are not so clearly defined. The athletic trainer might have the opportunity to remediate some of these difficult ethical situations. Many of them can be resolved by seeking permission to take action or disclose information, or by bringing the involved parties together to develop a mutually acceptable solution to the problem. Indeed, most situations in which there is conflict between the rights and welfare of individuals can be resolved by providing an opportunity for the affected parties to become familiar with the perspectives of the other parties. Most people are reasonable and willing to compromise when they are faced with the concerns of others who might be affected by their actions.

THREE APPROACHES TO ETHICAL DECISION MAKING

There are three approaches to ethical decision making: ethical egoism, utilitarianism, and formalism. The approach you use depends on the situation at hand.

Mangus and Ingersoll (1990) describe three approaches to ethical decision making in athletic training: ethical egoism, utilitarianism, and formalism. All of these approaches are valid. Some would be best for certain situations, whereas others would only compound the ethical concern. The wise athletic trainer will weigh the benefits and drawbacks of each approach on a case-by-case basis.

ETHICAL EGOISM

The ethical egoism approach to ethical decision making involves athletic trainers' making decisions that result in the greatest benefit to themselves. Using Tammy as an example, she would be employing the ethical egoism approach if she simply dropped the issue as the coach suggested. One could argue that she did her duty by bringing the allegations to the proper authorities as specified in the school's policy. By making the decision to drop the case, Tammy is removing herself from any potential conflict that might develop were she to pursue it further. Her life gets easier. She benefits.

UTILITARIANISM

The utilitarian approach to ethical decision making involves choosing a course of action that benefits the greatest number of people. The utilitarian approach is not easily demonstrated through Tammy's case. One could argue that by dropping the case as the coach suggested, Tammy would be serving the basketball team well because it would be able to keep the star player for the upcoming tournament. One could also argue that Tammy would be serving a potentially much larger group—all of the athletes in the school's program—by more aggressively pursuing the charges against the wishes of the coach. If the player is "brought to justice" under the terms of the school's alcohol policy, a clear message will be sent to the other members of the athletic program that such behaviors will not be tolerated.

FORMALISM

The formalistic approach to ethical decision making is most likely to be followed by athletic trainers who see a clear professional duty that they believe should be implemented universally. If Tammy were a formalist, it is quite likely that she would not accept the coach's self-serving excuse for dropping the case, especially in light of the fact that the coach never informed the athletic director as required by the policy. She would probably go the athletic director herself in an effort to satisfy herself that she had fulfilled her ethical responsibility to the school, its athletic program, and ultimately, the athlete in question.

PRACTICING ETHICALLY AS AN ATHLETIC TRAINER: SPECIFIC RECOMMENDATIONS

Most athletic trainers are committed to practicing ethically but they are not interested in becoming ethicists in order to do so. Fortunately, ethical practice doesn't require becoming an ethicist, but it does require an understanding of the meaning and intent of the relevant codes of ethics, reflection on the situations and actions that occur in practice, and development of professional habits and awareness that are consistent with ethical practice.

The following recommendations are intended to serve as a functional guide to ethical practice in athletic training. The guidelines provided in this list should minimize the occurrence of ethical conflicts and facilitate the resolution of those that do occur.

- Study the relevant professional codes of ethics. Begin first with the code of ethics of the NATA, then review the codes of ethics of organizations that apply to your specific employment setting and the roles you play in that setting.

- Learn to recognize situations where ethical concerns are present or might appear to be present. This requires careful consideration of all of your personal and professional relationships, as well as how they affect the athletes or other physically active patients that you treat.

- Increase your sensitivity to situations where ethical concerns are present. Remember that ethics are relative and that the counselor needs to be aware of how a situation may appear to persons viewing the situation from their own social or cultural perspective. Sensitivity requires that you be able to appreciate a situation from the point of view of others who are affected, particularly the patients under your care. Beyond that, it is important to treat every ethical concern seriously, or you will be perceived as insensitive and uncaring—and there is no better formula for professional trouble than that.

- Consult with others whenever there are questions, especially when the answers are not clear or when they are not clearly defensible. Good consultation serves to protect the athletic trainer as well as the patient because it provides an outside, objective perspective on the situation of concern. In addition, there is often more wisdom in the careful consideration of a small group than there is within any individual.

- Refer when the concern is beyond your legal scope of practice or your competence. Everyone's best interests are served when athletic trainers make prudent use of referrals in critical, complicated, and difficult cases. In order to do this, however, athletic trainers must be acutely aware of their own limitations and must be sure to follow prescribed protocols for referral.

• Refer when you become a primary party in an ethical dilemma or when you might be perceived by a patient or outside observers to be a primary party. When an athletic trainer becomes a primary party in a situation of ethical concern, both the professional and the patient are at risk and the situation might become worse. In addition, even the perception of such a situation can be destructive. Referral to a nonconflicted health care professional is generally considered necessary and prudent in such situations.

• Document carefully and often. As in all areas of practice, careful, accurate documentation is essential.

• Follow your conscience. Good conscience requires knowledge and awareness. For the athletic trainer it requires knowledge of the moral and ethical standards applicable to the profession, and it requires awareness of the individual circumstances each patient faces. Where athletic trainers most often fail to be conscientious is not so much in knowledge as it is in awareness. To be aware, they must be reflective and considerate, which takes time and effort. As athletic trainers, we must guard against becoming too busy or too routinized to allow ourselves the time and energy to be reflective and considerate. Otherwise we risk failing to be conscientious.

• Fully disclose to a patient all your roles. More than anything else, disclosure is an ethically critical component for informed consent in an athletic trainer's relationship with an athlete or other physically active patient. Identify all the roles you assume that might involve the athlete directly or indirectly. Avoid circumstances where you are responsible for roles that have conflicting interests regarding the patient. Some examples of the types of situations that warrant disclosure include, but are not limited to, the following:

1. Athletes should be made to understand that you also have responsibility for other athletes on a team and that you might be obligated to use or act on information that affects their health or safety.

2. Athletic trainers are often employed by the same organization that an athlete plays for. This is a potential conflict of interest that the athlete needs to understand, because the practitioner might be required or have strong incentives to act in the best interest of the organization rather than of the athlete.

3. Athletic trainers often make available services, referrals, or goods in which they have a financial interest. This is a conflict of interest that should be disclosed to the athlete or other physically active patient and to which alternatives should be provided.

4. Patients should be informed that an athletic trainer also has social and legal obligations that might require him or her to divulge information that could be in conflict with the patients' own best interest. If a patient tells you about certain illegal activities, you might be required by law to report that information. Furthermore, the patient should be informed that information might be divulged when it indicates that the patient, or others, are in imminent danger.

• Consider possible courses of action carefully. When confronting an ethical dilemma, (1) identify the greatest variety of choices possible, including those that might seem extreme; (2) investigate each of the possible choices identified; and (3) judge your choices from an other-centered perspective rather than from a self-centered or egocentric perspective.

• Allow patients to make their own fully informed choices rather than imposing solutions on them. An informed perspective requires exploration of the positive and negative implications of every conceivable choice. It empowers athletes or other physically active patients to best judge which course of action is in their best interest and is a necessary prerequisite to self-determination. Allowing patients to make their own choices helps them take responsibility for their destiny.

These actions, when combined, dramatically reduce the occurrence of ethical conundrums.

APPLICATIONS TO ATHLETIC TRAINING: THEORY INTO PRACTICE

Use the following two case studies to help apply the concepts in this chapter to real-life situations. The questions at the end of the studies have many possible correct solutions. The case studies can be used in class discussion or for homework or test questions.

Case Study 1

Gerry Cramer is an athletic trainer at a large university with a very successful athletic program. One morning Gerry made a routine trip to the student health service to pick up lab reports and X rays, and while talking to a secretary, Gerry was asked if Sean O'Connor (a star basketball player) had been dating a student named Mary Johnson (a nonathlete on campus). When Gerry responded that Sean had been dating Mary a few months ago, the secretary proceeded to express how unfortunate it was that Mary had recently tested positive for HIV. Gerry was startled to hear this news, because Mary wasn't an athlete under the care of the athletic training room, nor did Gerry really even know Mary. Gerry was concerned, however, about how this might affect Sean O'Connor, who was under the care of the athletic training room.

Questions for Analysis

1. What are the major ethical issues Gerry should be concerned about following this exchange? Should Gerry pursue additional details and information from the secretary? If so, what?

2. To whom is Gerry primarily responsible in this situation? What responsibilities does Gerry have toward Sean, and what responsibilities does Gerry have toward Mary? What other persons might be involved and warrant consideration?

3. What should Gerry do with the information about Mary's HIV status? Should Gerry use the information as a basis for counseling advice to Sean? Under what conditions should Gerry use the information? What alternatives should Gerry be investigating?

4. What is the worst mistake that Gerry could make in trying to fulfill the responsibilities of an athletic trainer to an athlete in this situation? What would be the ideal resolution to this ethical situation? What alternatives fall between the two extremes? How should Gerry proceed?

5. If it is determined at some time that Sean O'Connor is HIV positive, how should this be handled in the athletic training room? Who needs to know? What permission is necessary for the information to be relayed? Who is responsible for the safety of other athletes, for coaches, for the athletic training staff, and for officials with regard to their risk of exposure?

6. What risks does Gerry face as a result of having this information? What steps should Gerry take to avoid becoming another victim in this ethical dilemma?

Case Study 2

Shawna Jackson, an athletic training student at Big Hills University, was assigned to work with the cross country team this fall. As was their custom, the team always spent the first week of the season at a mountain lodge to help facilitate both intense training and a sense of team unity. The first day at the lodge, a runner approached Shawna complaining of pain in his left great toe. Shawna examined the toe and noted that it was red, warm, and tender around the margin of the nail. "You're probably just developing a small blister from all the running you've been doing," Shawna informed the athlete. "Let's try padding and lubrication and see if that makes it feel better." Shawna applied a felt "donut" and some lubricant and the runner told her that the toe felt better. Shawna didn't see the athlete for this or any other injuries the rest of the week.

A few days after the team returned from their trip, the same runner who had seen Shawna nearly 10 days earlier limped into the training room and told Mary Ricard, the staff certified athletic trainer, that he had "pulled his left groin." When Mary asked him when this happened, the athlete shrugged his shoulders and told her that it had just started hurting a little the day before but that it was much worse today. When Mary examined the athlete, she observed several cracked calluses and blisters on his left foot. The left great toe was swollen, red, and warm. A faint red streak ran from the ankle to the posterior aspect of the knee. The left inguinal lymph nodes were swollen to golf-ball size. Mary told the runner he had a serious infection in his left leg and made an immediate appointment for the athlete to be seen by the team physician.

When Mary returned from taking the cross country runner to the hospital for IV antibiotic therapy, she checked his file and found the note that Shawna had entered describing her physical exam and treatment for the runner's "blister." Mary immediately picked up the phone and dialed Shawna's room.

Questions for Analysis

1. What are Mary's ethical responsibilities in this case? What ethical responsibilities does Shawna have? Are they the same? Are they different? Why or why not?

2. Should Mary tell the athlete that Shawna might have mishandled his toe injury? Does the athlete have a right to know this? Why or why not?

3. Which, if any, of the five principles of the NATA code of ethics applies to this case?

4. How do ethics and the law interface in this case? Where do the athletic trainers' ethical responsibilities end and the athlete's legal rights begin?

SUMMARY

1. *Understand the definition and purpose of ethical standards and their relevance for the athletic trainer.*

   Ethics is the study of the rules, standards, and principles that dictate right conduct among members of a society. Ethical standards are useful for athletic trainers because they help provide a framework for decision making that helps the athletic trainer place the needs of her patient above all other considerations. Athletic trainers who practice unethically are at risk of failing to meet the needs of their patients.

2. *Identify the appropriate code of ethics that applies generally to the profession of athletic training, along with codes that might apply to specific settings within the profession.*

   Athletic trainers are often called upon to serve in many roles while working with athletes and other physically active patients. To carry out each role well, it is essential that they be familiar with the ethical standards that are customarily applied to these roles. Athletic trainers are encouraged to review the code of ethics of the NATA as well as those of other professional groups through which they might be credentialed.

3. *Identify the situations and circumstances in which ethical concerns are most frequent.*

The most common types of ethical problems that directly involve an athletic trainer are breach of confidentiality, conflict of interest, and exploitation. Athletic trainers might also have ethical responsibilities when they have knowledge of such situations, when they are privy to forbidden knowledge, or when they have knowledge of high-risk behaviors, illegal activities, and conflicts between the welfare of different parties involved in a situation.

4. *Develop strategies for avoiding ethical problems and for dealing with them if they occur.*

Athletic trainers can reduce the occurrence of ethical dilemmas by studying the appropriate codes of ethics and learning to recognize and be sensitive to situations where ethical concerns are present. It is considered prudent practice to obtain consultation from an uninvolved professional whenever there are questions about an ethical situation and to refer patients when their problems are beyond the legal scope of practice or competence of the athletic trainer. Athletic trainers should present patients seeking their services with the conditions of the activity, including disclosure of potential conflicts between roles, and the circumstances that affect the confidentiality of information transmitted in their professional relationship. All professional activities should be documented prudently, and referral is recommended whenever a professional becomes involved as a primary party in an ethical dilemma. Whenever possible, athletes and other physically active patients should be encouraged to make their own fully informed choices regarding their care.

CHAPTER TEN

Preparticipation Physical Exams and Drug-Testing Programs

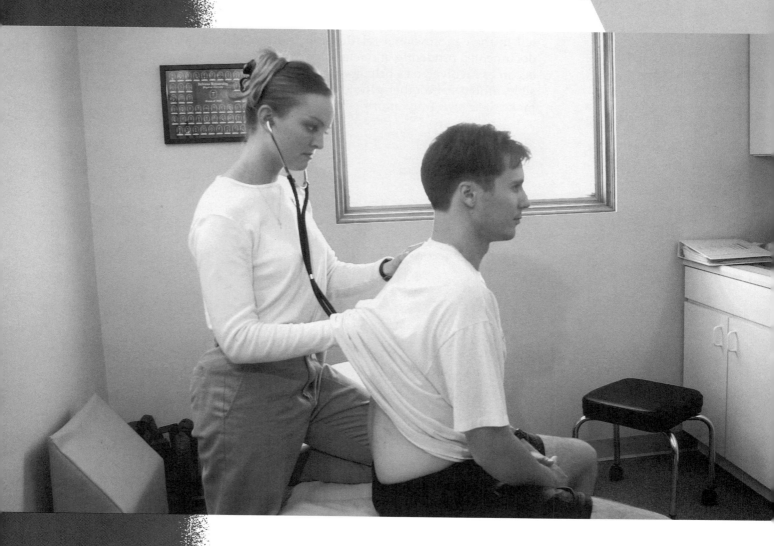

OBJECTIVES

After reading this chapter, you should be able to do the following:

1. Understand and defend the rationale for administrating preparticipation physical examinations.

2. Understand the strengths and weaknesses of the various preparticipation physical examination models.

3. Organize and implement a comprehensive preparticipation physical examination program in a variety of settings.

4. Understand and defend the rationale for administrating drug-testing programs in athletics.

5. Understand the legal ramifications of drug testing in athletic programs.

6. Organize and implement a comprehensive drug-testing program.

Randall Tate, ATC, smelled trouble when he walked into the athletic director's office to begin his first day on the job as the new athletic trainer at Eastmont Prep School. "Randy," the AD began, "we've had a few problems since you interviewed for the job last spring. I'm embarrassed to have to tell you this, but we had a big drug scandal among an influential group of our student-athletes just before graduation. I've personally always suspected that the drug problem here was bigger than most people were willing to admit, and the problems we had last year just confirmed my suspicions. I had a long meeting with the administration and the board of trustees about a month ago, and they have agreed to allow us to drug test our student-athletes beginning this fall. I know it may not seem fair to dump all this on you when you haven't been on the job for even five minutes, but you're going to be my point man on this. You are the only one with the medical expertise we need to make sure this is done right. I told the board that we would conduct our first round of testing during the fall sports physicals next month." "Are the physical examinations all arranged?" asked Randall. "I've got the date and the doctors all lined up," the AD responded. "All of the other details are up to you."

A high-grade athlete will seldom bother the trainer with his own ills. The trainer will be forced to draw him out.

Dr. Forrest "Fog" Allen

Few duties consume more of an athletic trainer's administrative time and energy than the organization and administration of preparticipation physical examinations (PPE) and drug-testing programs. Seasoned athletic trainers have experience to guide them through the many potential pitfalls involved, but new athletic trainers may require more guidance in planning for these two important activities. Although drug testing is a managerial task required of a relatively small segment of our profession, the consequences associated with poor planning in this area are significant, both for the athlete and the institution or team. PPEs, on the other hand, are an activity long associated with sports medicine and engaged in by most athletic trainers. Even athletic trainers employed in sports medicine clinics are frequently called upon to organize, conduct, or otherwise assist in the provision of PPEs to local high school athletes.

This chapter is intended to help you understand and be able to apply the principles associated with efficient organization of PPEs and drug-testing programs. Although some discussion of the medical justification for the content of the PPE and drug-testing programs is offered, the primary focus is how to plan for, organize, and otherwise manage this aspect of your professional responsibilities. A basic knowledge of the medical aspects of these two activities is assumed (see the Athletic Training Education Series text *Introduction to Athletic Training* for more on this subject).

ORGANIZING PREPARTICIPATION PHYSICAL EXAMINATIONS

The PPE is arguably the first step in injury prevention in school, college, and professional sports. Athletic trainers play an important role in helping to organize this aspect of the injury-prevention program.

WHY PPEs ARE PERFORMED

Anyone with any degree of experience in sports as a participant, coach, athletic trainer, or administrator has probably asked, "Why do we have to do these physicals every

Few administrative tasks are viewed as more fundamental to an athletic trainer's role than the planning, organization, and execution of the **preparticipation physical examination.** As the people to whom coaches, athletic directors, school administrators, and parents look for leadership in all things medical, athletic trainers are in a unique position to suggest and implement policy regarding injury prevention.

preparticipation physical examination (PPE) A medical screening procedure designed to determine an athlete's readiness for participation in a specific sport at a specific level of competition.

disqualifying conditions Injuries, illnesses, or other medical conditions that pose an undue risk to athletes, their teammates, or their competitors.

year? It just seems like a formality." This is a legitimate question. PPEs take a lot of time and energy to organize. They can be very expensive. They require a significant amount of effort on the part of many people, all of whom have other things they could be doing. Finally, they are often viewed as a necessary evil by athletes and coaches who would rather spend the time practicing. So why are PPEs so important? PPEs can be justified in at least four ways.

Injury and Illness Prevention

The most compelling reason to perform PPEs is that, properly performed and with data that is subsequently acted on, the PPE can provide information that allows an athlete to participate in sports activities with a reduced risk of injury or illness. This justification for the PPE is valid only, of course, if the medical team conducting the PPE actually uses the data generated by the exam. If seemingly minor findings are discovered during the PPE and are not followed up with appropriate treatment, then the PPE is more than a waste of time; it becomes a potential source of liability for the medical staff.

One of the functions of the PPE is to determine an athlete's readiness for participation in her chosen sport (National Collegiate Athletic Association, 1998). On rare occasions, this may involve using the information generated by the PPE to disqualify an athlete from participation. This action should be taken only when participation in that sport would foreseeably lead to an exacerbation of the athlete's medical condition or would cause harm to other participants. As the medical director of an institution's sports medicine program, the team physician should have the final authority to approve or disqualify prospective athletes for participation (Herbert, 1997). The wise team physician will consider the input of the athlete's personal physician, parents (especially in the case of a minor), and specialists involved in the case. The final authority, however, rests with the team physician (Herbert, 1996). See table 10.1 for a list of **disqualifying conditions.** The team physician has six options for determining medical qualification to participate (American Academy of Orthopaedic Surgeons, 1991):

1. **Passed.** The athlete is cleared for participation in all sports with no reservations or contraindications.

2. **Passed With Conditions.** The athlete has a medical condition that requires follow-up. The athlete may participate in some activities. The athlete may resume full activity pending satisfactory follow-up.

3. **Passed With Reservations.** The athlete may not participate in contact and/or collision sports (whichever is appropriate).

4. **Failed With Reservations.** The athlete is not cleared for his or her requested sport. Other sports may be considered. Contact and/or collision not permitted.

5. **Failed With Conditions.** The athlete must be reevaluated for participation once his or her medical condition is addressed and resolved.

6. **Failed.** The athlete may not participate in any sport at any level of exertion or competition.

Compliance With Association Rules

Most school- and college-based athletic programs are subject to the rules of the athletic associations of which they voluntarily choose to be members. At the high school level, the National Federation of State High School Athletic Associations (NFSHSAA) defers on the issue of required PPEs to the various state associations. There is great variability in the guidelines published by these organizations. Some require the

Table 10.1 Disqualifying Conditions

Condition	Contact/ collision[1]	Limited contact/ impact[2]	Noncontact Strenuous[3]	Noncontact Moderately Strenuous[4]	Noncontact Nonstrenuous[5]
Atlantoaxial instability	No	No	Yes[6]	Yes	Yes
Acute illnesses	[7]	[7]	[7]	[7]	[7]
Cardiovascular					
• Carditis	No	No	No	No	No
• Hypertension					
• Mild	Yes	Yes	Yes	Yes	Yes
• Moderate	[8]	[8]	[8]	[8]	[8]
• Severe	[8]	[8]	[8]	[8]	[8]
• Congenital heart disease	[9]	[9]	[9]	[9]	[9]
Eyes					
• Absence or loss of function of one eye	[10]	[10]	[10]	[10]	[10]
• Detached retina	[11]	[11]	[11]	[11]	[11]
Inguinal hernia	Yes	Yes	Yes	Yes	Yes
Kidney: Absence of one	No	Yes	Yes	Yes	Yes
Liver: Enlarged	No	No	Yes	Yes	Yes
Musculoskeletal disorders	[8]	[8]	[8]	[8]	[8]
Neurologic					
• History of serious head or spine trauma, repeated concussions, or craniotomy	[8]	[8]	Yes	Yes	Yes
• Convulsive disorder					
• Well controlled	No	Yes	Yes	Yes	Yes
• Poorly controlled	No	No	Yes[12]	Yes	Yes[13]
Ovary: Absence of one	Yes	Yes	Yes	Yes	Yes
Respiratory					
• Pulmonary insufficiency	[14]	[14]	[14]	[14]	[14]
• Asthma	Yes	Yes	Yes	Yes	Yes
Sickle cell trait	Yes	Yes	Yes	Yes	Yes
Skin: Boils, herpes, impetigo, scabies	[15]	[15]	Yes	Yes	Yes
Spleen: Enlarged	No	No	No	Yes	Yes
Testicle: Absence of or undescended	Yes[16]	Yes[16]	Yes	Yes	Yes

[1] Boxing, field hockey, football, ice hockey, lacrosse, martial arts, rodeo, soccer, wrestling.

[2] Baseball, basketball, bicycling, diving, high jump, pole vault, gymnastics, equestrian, skating, skiing, softball, squash, handball, volleyball.

Table 10.1

[3] Aerobic dance, crew, fencing, discus, javelin, shot put, running, swimming, tennis, track, weight lifting.

[4] Badminton, curling, table tennis.

[5] Archery, golf, riflery.

[6] Swimming: no butterfly, breast stroke, or diving starts

[7] Needs individual assessment, (e.g., contagiousness to others, risk of worsening illness).

[8] Needs individual assessment.

[9] Patients with mild forms can be allowed a full range of physical activities; patients with moderate or severe forms, or who are post-operative, should be evaluated by a cardiologist before athletic participation.

[10] Availability of American Society for Testing and Materials (ASTM)-approved eye guards may allow competitor to participate in most sports, but this must be judged on an individual basis.

[11] Consult opthamologist.

[12] No swimming or weightlifting.

[13] No archery or rifle.

[14] May be allowed to compete if oxygenation remains satisfactory during a graded exercise test.

[15] No gymnastics with mats, martial arts, wrestling, or contact sports until not contagious.

[16] Certain sports may require a protective cup.

---

completion of a standard form signed by a physician, whereas others have rules that are much more relaxed. Athletic trainers working in high school settings are cautioned to check with their state's athletic association to become familiar with the rules specific to that state.

The National Collegiate Athletic Association (NCAA, 1998) also publishes guidelines for the conduct of the PPE. Colleges belonging to this important group are instructed to provide every student-athlete with a comprehensive PPE, complete with cardiovascular screening, upon entry to the athletic program. Updated histories and blood pressure screening should be performed annually thereafter, with additional PPEs only as warranted by these histories. This guideline reflects the modified recommendations of the American Heart Association (1996).

Education and Counseling of Athletes

Because the PPE is frequently the only opportunity that many adolescent athletes have to interact with a physician, it has been suggested that the focus of the PPE be redirected toward counseling and educating young athletes on a variety of health-related issues (Goldberg et al., 1980; Koester, 1995). Koester's HEADS topics (Home life, Education, Activities, Drugs, Sex, Suicide) provide a useful guide to initiating conversations with young athletes in an effort to prevent the kinds of health problems that they are most likely to experience (see tables 10.2 and 10.3). Some institutions also use the PPE as an opportunity to educate athletes about the benefits of hepatitis B vaccination.

The ability of a health care professional to elicit high-quality information and to provide meaningful feedback regarding an adolescent's potential health risks is dependent on several factors. The typical mass screening in the gym or locker room is a poor setting for this kind of activity. The level of training and comfort of the examiner is also important. Finally, young athletes are only likely to open up to those they know and trust, so it is important to use health care professionals who are familiar with this sample of athletes for this portion of the PPE.

mass screening
A PPE method whereby many athletes are screened simultaneously, usually in a school gymnasium or locker room.

Table 10.2	HEADS Topics and Sample Questions for the Mature Adolescent
Topic	**Sample questions**
Home life	Problems with parents or siblings, living arrangements, parents' drug use?
Education	Grade level, grades, enjoy school, future plans?
Activities	What do you do for fun, extracurricular activities, who are your friends, what are weekends like?
Drugs	Do you or your friends drink alcohol, how much, how often, do you drink until you are drunk, use marijuana, cocaine, inhalants, other drugs?
Sex	Are you sexually active, use birth control, condoms, sexual preference, number of partners, do you know about risks (pregnancy, STDs, HIV)?
Suicide	Have you ever been depressed, do you feel like you are under too much pressure, thought of or attempted suicide?

Reprinted from *Journal of Athletic Training* 1995.

Table 10.3	HEADS Topics and Sample Questions for the Younger Adolescent
Topic	**Sample questions**
Home life	Problems with siblings or parents, living arrangements, adequate diet?
Education	Grade level, grades, enjoy school, future plans?
Activities	What do you do for fun, extracurricular activities, who are your friends, what are weekends like?
Depression	Ever stressed out or depressed, how do you handle it?
Safety	Seat belts, helmets, guns in the house or at a friend's house?

Reprinted from *Journal of Athletic Training* 1995.

Compliance With Standards of Practice

Although not codified in federal or state statutes, the requirement to provide a PPE that at the very least meets minimal standards is well understood and accepted in both the athletic and medical communities. Failure to provide such a PPE would be considered a gross violation of the standards of practice for anyone charged with safeguarding the health of athletes. No fewer than six explicit national standards, not counting all those promulgated by individual state associations, have been published (Herbert, 1992). See table 10.4 for a list of national standards for PPEs.

WHEN PPEs SHOULD BE CONDUCTED

The ideal time to conduct PPEs is six to eight weeks before athletes intend to begin vigorous training for their sports (Anderson & Hall, 1995). This allows adequate time for remediation of most problems the PPEs are likely to detect. An option common in many school and college settings is to conduct PPEs one season before athletes intend to participate in their sports. For example, a football player would be screened just before the summer recess. A basketball player would be screened in the early fall at the beginning of the school year. Spring sport athletes would be screened around the end of December. Although this system works well for high schools and small colleges where sports seasons are conducted exclusively during specific times of the year, larger schools that sponsor nontraditional seasons may be

Table 10.4   National Standards for Preparticipation Physical Examination

Sponsoring organization	Document name
American Academy of Pediatrics	*Recommendations for Participation in Competitive Sports*
American Medical Association	*Medical Evaluation of the Athlete: A Guide*
American College of Cardiology	*Twenty-Sixth Bethesda Conference: Recommendations for Determining Eligibility for Competition in Athletes with Cardiovascular Abnormalities*
American Heart Association	*Cardiovascular Preparticipation Screening of Competitive Athletes*
National Collegiate Athletic Association	*Sports Medicine Handbook (Guideline 1B: Medical Evaluations, Immunizations, and Records)*
American Academy of Family Physicians American Academy of Pediatrics American Medical Society for Sports Medicine American Orthopaedic Society for Sports Medicine American Osteopathic Academy of Sports Medicine	*Preparticipation Physical Evaluation*

health history update A brief questionnaire designed to determine whether an athlete suffered any injuries or developed any medical conditions since the last comprehensive PPE.

forced to screen all their athletes in either the late spring or summer since even spring sports jump into full gear as soon as school begins in the fall.

As was addressed earlier, the frequency with which PPEs should be conducted is a matter of some debate. The least rigorous standard requires a complete and comprehensive PPE when an athlete enters an athletic program, with annual **health history updates** thereafter (see figure 10.1). Most high school programs require a PPE every year, although a few states require only one PPE every three years (Kibler, 1990). Although athletic trainers are obligated to comply with the standards for their particular settings, the fact remains that the frequency of the PPE is closely related to its content. The more comprehensive and detailed the PPE, the less frequently it needs to be repeated. More cursory PPEs should probably be repeated with greater frequency. The nature of the sport is another factor that should influence the frequency with which PPEs should be repeated. Contact and collision sports with high injury rates may warrant more frequent repetition of the PPE than those sports for which injuries are less frequent and serious.

WHERE AND HOW PPEs SHOULD BE CONDUCTED

Much debate exists regarding the optimal setting for the PPE. Before attempting to decide where and how PPEs will be conducted, I suggest that athletic trainers try to answer the following questions:

1. What kind of information do we need to get from the PPEs?
2. How many people will we be able to recruit to help conduct the PPEs?
3. How many of the people we recruit will be trained medical personnel with an interest and experience in sports health care?
4. What options do we have in terms of physical facilities for the PPEs?
5. Do the facilities to which we have access have adequate provisions for privacy?

HOPE COLLEGE HEALTH CLINIC
ATHLETIC PHYSICAL UPDATE

Name ———————————————— (M or F) —— Age ———— Date ————

S.S. # ————————————————   Year in school   Fr   So   Jr   Sr

Sport ————————————————

1. List any significant illnesses, injuries, or surgery you have had since your last Hope College physical exam. (mono, pneumonia, knee or joint injury, etc.)

2. What past or present medical problems (injuries, illnesses, etc.) do you feel we should check?

3. Are you now suffering from any medical problems?

Signature ————————————————————————

White copy to Health Center, yellow copy to Athletic Dept.

Figure 10.1   Sample annual health history update form.

6. How much time do we have for conducting PPEs?
7. What expenses will be incurred?
8. Will the people conducting the PPEs be volunteers, or will they expect to be paid?
9. How many athletes will we need to service?
10. What are the characteristics of the athletes to be screened? Adults? Children? Male? Female?

Office-Based PPEs

There are many important issues to consider in determining the methods to be employed in conducting PPEs (see table 10.5). All other factors being equal—which they never are—the privacy of a physician's office is probably the ideal place. This setting allows the physician to examine and counsel the athlete with a minimum of interruption. It also allows the physician to focus on the athlete and his or her problems. Finally, physicians who conduct PPEs in their offices have the advantage of being able to more easily call on the wide range of medical equipment and services they may need to provide the comprehensive care the athlete requires. This can be very difficult to accomplish in a mass screening in a gymnasium.

If an office-based PPE is the technique of choice, the next issue is to identify the appropriate physician to conduct the examination. Should all athletes be examined in the team physician's office, or should they be screened by their personal physicians? This is another question about which a good many people disagree.

On one hand, the team physician is presumably more versed in sports health care issues and may be better able to make judgments regarding participation status and follow-up treatment for conditions discovered during the PPE. The team physician, as medical director of the school's athletic program, may also be legally responsible for judging an athlete's participation status. On the other hand, the athlete's family physician may be more familiar with the athlete's personal and family history. This level of familiarity can be important in establishing the confidence the athlete will need to both confide in and be receptive to the physician. Finally, many would argue that the technical skills required to perform an adequate PPE are commonplace enough that most primary care physicians have the required competence to provide this service.

In the final analysis, it is the nature of the patient that will determine who is best suited to conduct the PPE. Most young adolescents can be screened very effectively by their personal physicians. As children grow older and routine visits to the family

Table 10.5 Strengths and Weaknesses of Office and Station PPEs

Strengths	Weaknesses
Office-Based PPE	
1. Greater privacy	1. Greater potential for breakdown in communication to school-based health care personnel
2. Easier access to patient records	2. Greater potential for lack of familiarity with specific sport demands
3. Easier access to medical supplies and equipment	3. Less efficient
4. More conducive to athlete counseling	4. Incorporation of fitness testing more difficult
5. Athlete has more feedom to choose physician	
Station PPE	
1. Greater efficiency	1. Little to no privacy
2. Easier access to the whole sports medicine team	2. Difficult to counsel athletes
3. Easier to include fitness testing as part of the PPE	3. Can be noisy
4. Use of volunteers promotes the concept of shared responsibility for safety	4. Volunteers must be recruited and trained
	5. Facilities and transport of supplies must be arranged
	6. Athletes' records are usually not available

physician become less frequent, it may be more appropriate for the team physician to take over the administration of the PPE. Who, after all, is likely to provide athletes with the medical care they need if they become injured or ill during the course of their seasons? For most junior and some senior high school students, this person will be their family physician. For many senior high school and most college and professional athletes, it will be the team physician. Whoever is most likely to take care of the athletes during their seasons should probably conduct their PPEs. For the growing segment of the population without a family physician, the issue becomes more problematic. Similarly, the high school without a team physician faces difficulty in attempting to organize an effective PPE program.

station PPE   A group screening process whereby information for individual athletes is collected at a variety of stations staffed by a combination of medical and nonmedical personnel, usually in the context of a school environment.

Group PPEs and the Station Method

The preceding arguments in favor of office-based PPEs notwithstanding, the method that many schools employ involves a screening of many athletes at a common site using a variety of stations to collect information about their health. Although it is very difficult to obtain the degree of privacy required for one-on-one counseling between a physician and an athlete in this setting, this method has proven successful in helping detect the more serious and common conditions that are likely to impair an athlete's ability to participate in sports with a relative degree of safety.

The answers to the questions on pages 261 and 262 will determine the form the **station PPE** takes. Many nonmedical volunteers can play an important role in helping conduct an organized, efficient mass PPE. The role of the athletic trainer is to identify the number of stations, recruit an adequate number of volunteers for each station, and where appropriate, provide the training the volunteers will need to perform their duties. Parents, coaches, and student interns are capable of performing a wide variety of tasks, including checking height and weight, controlling flow through the various stations, collecting money (for those programs that charge a fee for the PPE—see Heinzman, 1991), and checking to make sure that all the required forms have been completed before the athlete leaves the examination area. For PPEs that incorporate fitness testing, coaches who are trained in the techniques are an excellent choice to operate these stations. See figure 10.2 for a schematic of a typical station approach to the PPE.

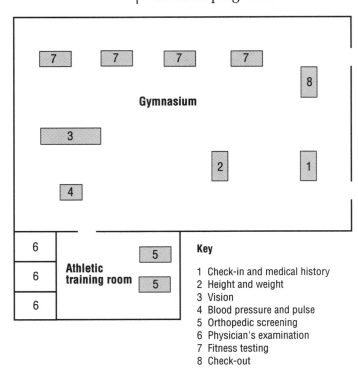

Figure 10.2   Station PPE schematic.

Key

1 Check-in and medical history
2 Height and weight
3 Vision
4 Blood pressure and pulse
5 Orthopedic screening
6 Physician's examination
7 Fitness testing
8 Check-out

WHAT SHOULD BE EVALUATED DURING THE PPE

A surprising amount of disagreement exists among professionals regarding the content of the ideal PPE. Athletic trainers should consider the following factors when designing the PPE.

Athlete Age and Level of Competition

Obvious differences exist between a 30-year-old professional football player and a 12-year-old seventh-grade basketball player. Although the elements of the PPE may be the same for both patients, the degree to which those elements are emphasized is likely to be different. The PPE for the 12-year-old, for example, should include a greater emphasis on developmental problems common to that age group. The NFL athlete will probably require a much more extensive orthopedic examination, perhaps even including MRI and other imaging studies. Both athletes need an orthopedic screening, but the screening should be tailored to the athlete and will differ greatly for each.

Sport

Although certain aspects of the PPE should be included for all athletes, the exam should be as sport-specific as possible. This is especially true in that part of the PPE designed to determine an athlete's physical fitness. For example, an isokinetic evaluation of a sprinter's hamstrings/quadriceps ratio may yield useful information that could help the athlete undertake an exercise program designed to help her prevent a hamstring strain while sprinting. To do the same test on a golfer would be interesting, but not particularly useful. Similarly, the Wingate test of anaerobic power might be useful for an ice hockey player, but not that important for a 10 000 m runner on the track team, who would benefit more from a test of his $\dot{V}O_2$max.

Follow-Up

The information collected during the PPE is valuable only if the problems discovered are acted on. Too often the PPE becomes a routine process by which a massive amount of information is collected but for which no follow-up is provided (Briner, 1993). Vision screening is useful only if athletes with problems are referred for follow-up evaluation by an optometrist or ophthalmologist. Strength and fitness screening is useful only if conditioning specialists are available to provide the athlete with feedback and advice for improvement. Questions on the medical history form designed to reveal the potential for disordered eating are useful only if they are addressed by the physician during the PPE and appropriate referrals are arranged for the athlete. As part of the team that designs the PPE, the athletic trainer ought to ask the question "What will we do if . . . ?" for each component of the exam. If the institutional or community resources are so limited that the information collected cannot be acted on, a careful interdisciplinary review of that portion of the PPE ought to be undertaken.

Predictability of Tests

Unfortunately, the majority of the screening activities normally undertaken during the PPE are relatively weak and insensitive predictors of athletic injury (DuRant et al., 1992). The orthopedic exam, especially among those athletes with no previous history of injury, is a surprisingly poor predictor of future athletic injury. Relatively sophisticated noninvasive tests for cardiac abnormalities, including two-dimensional echocardiography and 12-lead electrocardiogram, are not only prohibitively expensive to use on a routine basis, they are unlikely to detect many problem cases (American Heart Association, 1996).

The one portion of the PPE that seems to have the best predictive value is the medical history. Most athletic injuries are, in fact, reinjuries (Lysens, Steverlynck, & van den Auweele, 1984). The medical history, therefore, constitutes the most important part of the PPE for the vast majority of athletes. As part of the team charged with designing the PPE, the athletic trainer ought to ask "How likely is this test to uncover a problem?" for each element of the PPE.

Common Elements of the PPE

The preceding cautions notwithstanding, there are at least five elements that most practitioners agree should be part of the PPE.

Health History

A detailed questionnaire designed to elicit information regarding an athlete's past medical problems is arguably the most important part of the PPE. The answers provided on the questionnaire should guide the medical team in designing specific tests for each particular athlete to address his or her problems. See figure 6.1 on page 165 for an example of a **health history form**. A sense of confidentiality is an important aspect of this part of the PPE. If athletes think that the information they record on the health history form is likely to be shared too widely, they may not answer the questions truthfully and completely. Athletes need to be reassured that the information will be held in confidence and will not be shared with anyone outside the medical staff unless they specifically authorize such a release in writing.

health history form
A detailed questionnaire designed to document an athlete's previous injuries, illnesses, and other medical conditions. This form often serves as the basis for additional medical follow-up and evaluation.

Physician's Examination

A physician should examine every athlete during the course of the PPE. In fact, in most states an athlete is not considered to have undergone a PPE unless a physician has examined her and verified in writing that she is fit to participate. The major components of the physician's examination include a general review of systems, including examination of the head, eyes, ears, nose, throat, chest and abdomen, and genitalia (Kibler, 1990). Every examination should include a general cardiac screening, including standing and supine precordial auscultation, brachial blood pressure in the sitting position, palpation of the femoral artery pulses, and screening for the physical stigmata of Marfan's syndrome (American Heart Association, 1996). Some physicians (McKeag & Hough, 1993) recommend **maturational assessment** for junior and senior high school athletes, but little is known about the usefulness of this technique in actually preventing injuries (Smith, 1994).

maturational assessment A medical screening procedure based on Tanner's stages of maturational development. It is often used to classify children and adolescents for the purpose of matching them with appropriate athletic opponents.

Orthopedic Examination

Although the orthopedic examination may not be a strong predictor of injury for those athletes with no previous history of injury, it is a very important part of the PPE for those athletes who have suffered an injury. The majority of the orthopedic exam should be focused on problems the athlete identifies in the health history questionnaire using evaluation techniques specific to those body parts. McKeag and Hough (1993) recommend a quick general orthopedic examination for all athletes (see table 10.6), although the efficacy of this procedure in detecting problems that might lead to injury is unknown. The general orthopedic examination need not be performed by a physician unless required by association rules. Athletic trainers, physical therapists, and physician assistants with the proper training can assume this responsibility.

Special Tests

This portion of the PPE will vary greatly depending on the financial resources available and the philosophy of the physician. Common special tests include simple urinalysis to detect protein or sugar. Simple tests of visual acuity using a Snellen chart can also be performed at little cost. Routine X rays and cardiovascular or other assessments are not recommended unless warranted by the health history questionnaire or the physician's examination.

Physical Fitness Testing

Many athletic programs use the PPE as an opportunity to establish a baseline for the athlete's physical fitness. Although this aspect of the PPE is usually not medically necessary to clear an athlete for participation, the information obtained can be useful to athletes and staff members in providing an assessment of the athlete's conditioning status. A wide variety of physical fitness tests are available, a list of which is beyond the scope of this text.

Two important points should be made regarding this portion of the PPE. First, all physical fitness tests should be designed to provide data that are important to

Table 10.6   Musculoskeletal Physical Examination

Athletic activity (instructions)	Observations
1. Stand facing examiner.	AC joints, general habitus
2. Look: at ceiling, at floor, over both shoulders. Touch ears to shoulders.	Cervical spine motion
3. Shrug shoulders (examiner resists).	Trapezius strength
4. Abduct shoulders 90° (examiner resists at 90°).	Deltoid strength
5. Full external rotation of arms.	Shoulder motion
6. Flex and extend elbows.	Elbow motion
7. Arms at sides, elbows at 90° flexed; pronate and supinate wrists.	Elbow and wrist motion
8. Spread fingers; make fist.	Hand/finger motion and deformities
9. Tighten (contract) quadriceps; relax quadriceps.	Symmetry and knee effusion
10. "Duck walk" four steps (away from examiner).	Hip, knee, and ankle motion
11. Back to examiner.	Shoulder symmetry; scoliosis
12. Knees straight, touch toes.	Scoliosis, hip motion, hamstring tightness
13. Raise up on toes, heels.	Calf symmetry, leg strength
OR (shortened version)	
1. Nod your head *yes*; shake your head *no*.	
2. Hands behind your head; hands behind your back.	
3. Slowly bend forward and touch your toes.	
4. Stand up straight; jump on your left foot, now on your right foot.	
5. Squat like a baseball player.	
6. Walk toward me like a duck.	

Reprinted from D.B. McKeag and D.O. Hough, 1993, *Primary care sports medicine* (Dubuque, IA: Brown), 102. Reproduced with permission of The McGraw-Hill Companies.

normal physiological function for a specific sport. Second, if fitness testing is to be included as part of the PPE, it should always be the last element completed. The athlete should always be subjected to the health history, physician's exam, and orthopedic exam prior to engaging in strenuous exercise so any problems that might preclude such exercise can be identified first. Positioning the fitness tests at the end of the PPE also allows the athlete to be examined in a resting state, which is an important factor in the collection of baseline cardiovascular data.

LEGAL CONSIDERATIONS

The legal precautions for conducting PPEs are similar to other aspects of medical and allied health care practice. Athletic trainers, physicians, and other health care professionals involved in the PPE will be held to the same standards of practice for this activity as for the other aspects of their professional practice. Two areas of emphasis are particularly important, however.

Consent

As for any medical procedure, an athlete must consent to be examined during the PPE. In order for athletes to provide informed consent, they must be told what will happen to them during the PPE, they must understand what they were told, they should have the opportunity to ask questions, and they must sign a document indicating that they agree to submit to the procedure. The parents or guardians of minor children must provide informed consent on behalf of young athletes. Athletes past the age of majority can provide informed consent for themselves. See figure 10.3 for an example of an informed consent form for the PPE.

Statement of Informed Consent to a Preparticipation Physical Examination

It is the policy of Ohio Technological University that all students must undergo a preparticipation physical examination (PPE) by an OTU physician prior to the beginning of practice or competition in intercollegiate athletics. We insist that you undergo a PPE for the following reasons:

- We want to help you prevent injuries and illnesses.
- We want to make sure that you are ready for vigorous athletic participation.
- We want to establish a medical basis for your participation.
- We must comply with the NCAA requirement that all athletes be medically cleared for participation.
- We want to use the PPE to talk to you about your personal health issues.

The PPE has three parts:

- A health history questionnaire that you complete (please be honest and complete).
- Several special tests (vision, blood pressure, weight/height, etc.) performed by the athletic training or nursing staff.
- An examination by a physician.

Things you should know about your PPE:

- The information derived from the PPE is kept confidential. Only the medical staff will have access to the information unless you authorize its release to others in writing.
- You will be asked to partially undress for the physician's examination. The physician may have to touch you in private areas in order to complete the examination. If you would be more comfortable having a nurse or athletic trainer of your own gender in the room during the physician's exam, just ask and we'd be happy to do this.
- The physician may ask you a few questions that seem "personal" and not necessarily related to athletics. We want to use this opportunity to talk about your health, because illnesses and other nonathletic problems can interfere with your season as easily as an ankle sprain or a dislocated shoulder.

I,_____, have read the statement above and understand the reasons and components of the preparticipation physical examination. I freely consent to the examination. I have had an opportunity to ask questions regarding the preparticipation physical examination. All my questions have been answered.

_____
Student-athlete signature

_____
Witness signature

_____
Parent or guardian signature

_____
Date

∎ **Figure 10.3**   Sample Informed Consent Form for the PPE.

Waiver of Liability

The primary purpose of the PPE is to prevent athletes from participating when they have a medical condition that endangers their health or that of their teammates or opponents. From time to time, a team physician will decide that an athlete should not be allowed to participate in a given sport. Unfortunately, this is often not the last word. Athletes and their parents frequently challenge the decision of the team physician and demand their right to participate, no matter the risk for permanent disability or death. Frequently, these athletes will seek second, third, or even fourth opinions to justify their desire to participate. The actions of the medical staff, including the team physician and the athletic trainer, are very important in cases like these, because they can often involve litigation to resolve the matter.

One approach the medical team can take is to require athletes (and their parents in the case of minors) to sign waivers when they wish to participate against the advice of the physician. Such waivers must be individually tailored to each specific case and should include a full description of the medical condition, the findings of the PPE and other associated examinations connected to the condition, and a complete list of all the possible medical complications that could arise as a result of athletic participation, including permanent disability and death. If temporary or permanent disability is a potential outcome, the financial implications of such a disability should be described in the waiver. If the athlete is married, the spouse should be asked to sign a similar document waiving her right to sue for **loss of consortium**. The waiver should be written in simple language and all medical terms should be explained. The athlete, his parents, and his spouse should be offered the opportunity to ask questions regarding the contents of the waiver. The language of the waiver should be such that the athlete admits to having read the waiver, understanding it, and agreeing to hold the institution and its medical staff harmless for any future injuries associated with the condition in question. Although waivers have been upheld in some courts, they are often viewed as a violation of the public interest and are frequently not upheld, no matter how detailed or explicit.

loss of consortium A legal claim of damages for injuries to a spouse or for alienation of a spouse's affection.

The second approach the medical team should consider in these cases is to simply stick to their decision to deny medical clearance for participation and allow the athlete to bring suit. This forces the courts to make a decision as to the reasonableness of the physician's decision (Herbert, 1997). Any orders issued by the court should be included in the athlete's medical file as a record of the facts of the case should an injury result from participation at a later date.

ORGANIZING DRUG-TESTING PROGRAMS

Athletic trainers in professional sports and NCAA Division I and II universities are often charged with development and implementation of drug-testing programs. These programs may occur year-round. Even athletic trainers in Division III settings should become familiar with the issues of organizing drug-testing programs, because they may be asked to help administer post-championship testing.

As Randy Tate in the opening case is now aware, even some high schools have implemented drug-testing programs. Regardless of the setting, all athletic trainers have the responsibility of educating the athletes in their care regarding the rules and mechanics of drug testing.

WHY DRUG TESTING SHOULD BE PERFORMED

The reasons for drug testing are as varied as the number of people who have written about this controversial subject since it gained widespread popularity in the 1980s. Some institutions envision drug testing as a means of promoting order and discipline on an athletic team. Others see it as a way to prevent or discourage potentially illegal activity. One would hope that most are genuinely concerned about instituting drug-testing programs as a means of helping those with chemical addictions come to grips with their problems.

The NCAA (1995) has identified two overarching goals for its drug-testing program, which is generally viewed as the standard for collegiate sports in the United

States. The first goal is to promote fair and equitable competition. At least two objectives can be implied from this goal. First is the proposition that all athletes should compete on a "level playing field" where only the sum of their training and talent should determine the outcome of a contest. The second part of this goal is the idea that no athlete should feel pressure to take drugs in order to have a chance to win. Drug testing should be designed to ensure that these two objectives are met. Unfortunately, too many examples of athletes who have been caught using drugs after world-record performances exist to allow athletes to believe that a level playing field exists. The ability of athletes to keep technologically one step ahead of the drug-testing labs has greatly impaired the achievement of this goal (Thorland, 1990).

The second goal identified by the NCAA is to safeguard the health and safety of athletes by discouraging drug use through drug testing. The potentially detrimental effects of drug use are well understood and universally acknowledged. The hope is that athletes who use drugs will be caught so they may be counseled and, where appropriate, receive treatment for any problems their drug use may have engendered. Unfortunately, many, if not most, highly motivated athletes are too willing to sacrifice their health for short-term glory on the athletic field. When asked if they would take performance enhancing drugs, even if they knew they would suffer serious heart or liver disease as a result, a significant percentage of the athletes have said they would do so (NCAA, 1988). Drug testing seems like weak ammunition in a fight where such strong motivating forces are at work.

WHEN DRUG TESTING SHOULD BE PERFORMED

There are three models for the timing of drug testing that account for the majority of all drug tests performed in collegiate, professional, and Olympic sports: post-championship testing, preseason testing, and year-round testing.

Post-Championship Testing

Many college athletes are exposed to drug testing after their teams participate in an NCAA championship event. Choice of athletes to be tested at these events can be based on random selection, position of finish, playing position, or playing time. For testing that takes place at non-championship events like postseason football bowl games, athlete selection can also be based on financial aid status.

Preseason Testing

Professional athletes are frequently drug tested prior to their first season of competition. This test is usually part of the preparticipation physical examination and is considered to be a **preemployment test**. In the National Football League (NFL), all rookies are tested for anabolic steroids and drugs of abuse at the league combine.

preemployment test
Any procedure (including a drug test), conducted on a potential employee, that is used to determine the applicant's suitability for employment.

Year-Round Testing

The NCAA requires athletes in Division I and II football and Division I indoor and outdoor track and field to submit to drug testing on a year-round basis. In addition, the NFL and several Olympic sports national governing bodies require year-round testing of athletes for a variety of performance-enhancing drugs, including anabolic steroids. Many universities with large athletic programs also engage in year-round testing as a way of discouraging off-season drug use.

HOW DRUG TESTING SHOULD BE CONDUCTED

Many important decisions regarding the mechanics of a drug-testing program will affect the eventual success or failure of the program. In order to fully implement the directive from his athletic director, Randy Tate will have to consider each of the following elements:

Consent

All athletes should sign a consent form agreeing to submit to drug testing. Although the language of the consent form indicates that this activity is voluntary, the sanction imposed when an athlete chooses not to sign is usually athletic ineligibility. Figures 10.4 through 10.6 contain the forms used by NCAA Division I, II, and III universities. Universities that conduct their own drug-testing programs in addition to those required by the NCAA should also develop their own consent forms (see figure 10.7 on p. 278).

Selection of Subjects

random selection
A method for choosing subjects for drug testing based on permutations of timing, subject characteristics, or both. Implies an equal probability for any subject within a given population to be chosen for testing.

Few issues related to drug testing are more riddled with potential liability than selection of the athletes to be tested. Although most drug-testing programs associated with college, professional, and Olympic sports are purported to use **random selection,** this term can be defined in many ways. In some cases it means that the testing is random with regard to the subjects selected and in other cases it means that the timing of testing is random (Elkouri & Elkouri, 1993). Each category has several permutations, including the following:

Random Selection of Subjects by Sport

The NCAA and some universities may randomly choose a sport to test during any given testing period. Under this system, athletes might be able to avoid being tested at all during their college careers if their teams are never chosen or never participate in NCAA postseason championships.

Random Selection of Subjects by Position

Some athletes are selected for testing based on the position they play on the team. For instance, Randy Tate may choose to test only the defensive players on the football team during any given testing period, saving the offensive players until another testing period.

Random Selection of Subjects by Playing Time or Finish Position

The NCAA frequently chooses to test only within that group of athletes that actually contributed to the outcome of a particular contest by virtue of their playing time. A similar method involves selecting subjects who placed high in individual sport championships.

Random Selection of Subjects by Financial Aid Status

In some cases, especially those involving NCAA Division I sports, subjects for drug testing are drawn from the pool of those athletes on athletic scholarship. Non-scholarship athletes are often eliminated from the pool.

Random Timing—No Notice

One method frequently used in drug testing is to conduct unannounced spot-checks at random intervals. This often involves taking an athlete off the field to administer a drug test with no warning. Many experts believe this is one of the only ways to discourage cheating the system, because athletes who know when they will be tested can often mask their drug use by abstaining for as little as a few days prior to the test.

Random Timing—Some Notice

The alternative to unannounced random testing is to provide subjects with some notice that they will be tested. The further in advance an athlete knows about the test, however, the greater the chances she will be able to manipulate the results.

In order to demonstrate that subjects were actually selected for testing at random, an athletic trainer must develop a system that equalizes the probability that one athlete has as much of a chance of being tested as any other athlete. Randomization can occur in many ways. Athletes are usually assigned a number. Their number

Form 97-3a   Academic Year 1997-98

Student-Athlete Statement—Division I

For:	Student-athletes
Action:	Sign and return to your director of athletics
Due date:	Before you first compete each year
Required by:	NCAA Constitution 3.2.4.5 and Bylaws 14.1.3.1 and 30.12
Purpose:	To assist in certifying eligibility

TO STUDENT-ATHLETE

Name of your institution: _____

This form has three parts: a statement concerning eligibility, a Buckley Amendment consent and an affirmation of a valid ACT or SAT score. You must sign all three parts to participate in intercollegiate competition.

Before you sign this form, you should read the Summary of NCAA Regulations provided by your director of athletics or read the bylaws of the NCAA Division I Manual that deal with your eligibility. If you have any questions, you should discuss them with your director of athletics.

The conditions that you must meet to be eligible and the requirement that you sign this form are spelled out in the following articles and bylaws of the NCAA Division I Manual:

• Articles 10, 12, 13, 14, 15 and 16 • Bylaws 14.1.3.1, 18.4 and 31.2.3

Part I: Statement Concerning Eligibility

By signing this part of the form, you affirm that, to the best of your knowledge, you are eligible to compete in intercollegiate competition.

You affirm that you have read the Summary of NCAA Regulations or the relevant sections of the NCAA Division I Manual, and that your director of athletics (or his or her designee) gave you the opportunity to ask questions about them.

You affirm that you meet the NCAA regulations for student-athletes regarding eligibility, recruitment, financial aid, amateur status and involvement in organized gambling.

You affirm that you are aware of the NCAA drug-testing program and that you have signed the 1997-98 Drug-Testing Consent (Form 97-3d).

You affirm that you have reported to the director of athletics of your institution any violations of NCAA regulations involving you and your institution.

You affirm that you understand that if you sign this statement falsely or erroneously, you violate NCAA legislation on ethical conduct and you will further jeopardize your eligibility.

_____   _____
Name (please print)   Date of Birth

_____   _____
Signature of Student-Athlete   Home Address

_____   _____
Date

_____
Sport(s)

Figure 10.4 NCAA Division I drug-testing consent form.
Reprinted with permission from the NCAA.

Part II: Buckley Amendment Consent

By signing this part of the form, you certify that you agree to disclose your education records.

You understand that this entire form and the results of any NCAA drug test you may take are part of your education records. These records are protected by the Family Educational Rights and Privacy Act of 1974, and they may not be disclosed without your consent.

You give your consent to disclose only to authorized representatives of this institution, its athletics conference (if any) and the NCAA, the following documents:

- This form;
- Results of NCAA drug tests;
- Any transcript from your high school, this institution, or any junior college or any other four-year institutions you have attended;
- Precollege test scores, appropriately related information and correspondence (e.g., testing sites and dates, and letters of test-score certification or appeal), and, where applicable, information relating to eligibility for or conduct of nonstandard testing;
- Records concerning your financial aid; and
- Any other papers or information pertaining to your NCAA eligibility.

You agree to disclose these records only to determine your eligibility for intercollegiate athletics, your eligibility for athletically related financial aid, for purposes of inclusion in summary institutional information reported to the NCAA (and which may be publicly released by it), for NCAA longitudinal research studies and for activities related to the NCAA athletics certification program and NCAA compliance reviews.

_____   _____
Date   Signature of Student-Athlete

Part III: Incoming Freshman—Affirmation of Valid ACT or SAT Score

You affirm that, to the best of your knowledge, you have received a validated ACT and/or SAT score.

You agree that, in the event you are or have been notified by ACT or SAT of the possibility of an invalidated test score, you will immediately notify the director of athletics of your institution.

_____   _____
Name   Date

_____
Signature of Student-Athlete

What to do with this form: Sign and return it to your director of athletics before you first compete. This form is to be kept in the director of athletics' office for six years.

▌**Figure 10.4** (continued)

273

Form 97-3b

Academic Year 1997-98

Student-Athlete Statement—Division II

For: Student-athletes
Action: Sign and return to your director of athletics
Due date: Before you first compete each year
Required by: NCAA Constitution 3.2.4.5 and Bylaws 14.1.3.1 and 30.12
Purpose: To assist in certifying eligibility

TO STUDENT-ATHLETE

Name of your institution: _____

This form has three parts: a statement concerning eligibility, a Buckley Amendment consent and an affirmation of a valid ACT or SAT score. You must sign all three parts to participate in intercollegiate competition.

Before you sign this form, you should read the Summary of NCAA Regulations provided by your director of athletics or read the bylaws of the NCAA Division II Manual that deal with your eligibility. If you have any questions, you should discuss them with your director of athletics.

The conditions that you must meet to be eligible and the requirement that you sign this form are spelled out in the following articles and bylaws of the NCAA Division II Manual:

• Articles 10, 12, 13, 14, 15 and 16   • Bylaws 14.1.3.1, 18.4 and 31.2.3

Part I: Statement Concerning Eligibility

By signing this part of the form, you affirm that, to the best of your knowledge, you are eligible to compete in intercollegiate competition.

You affirm that you have read the Summary of NCAA Regulations or the relevant sections of the NCAA Division II Manual, and that your director of athletics (or his or her designee) gave you the opportunity to ask questions about them.

You affirm that you meet the NCAA regulations for student-athletes regarding eligibility, recruitment, financial aid, amateur status and involvement in organized gambling.

You affirm that you are aware of the NCAA drug-testing program and that you have signed the 1997-98 Drug-Testing Consent (Form 97-3e).

You affirm that you have reported to the director of athletics of your institution any violations of NCAA regulations involving you and your institution.

You affirm that you understand that if you sign this statement falsely or erroneously, you violate NCAA legislation on ethical conduct and you will further jeopardize your eligibility.

_____
Name (please print)

_____
Date of Birth

_____
Signature of Student-Athlete

_____
Home Address

_____
Date

_____

_____
Sport(s)

▌Figure 10.5 NCAA Division II drug-testing consent form.

Reprinted with permission from the NCAA.

Part II: Buckley Amendment Consent

By signing this part of the form, you certify that you agree to disclose your education records.

You understand that this entire form and the results of any NCAA drug test you may take are part of your education records. These records are protected by the Family Educational Rights and Privacy Act of 1974, and they may not be disclosed without your consent.

You give your consent to disclose only to authorized representatives of this institution, its athletics conference (if any) and the NCAA, the following documents:

- This form;
- Results of NCAA drug tests;
- Any transcript from your high school, this institution, or any junior college or any other four-year institutions you have attended;
- Precollege test scores, appropriately related information and correspondence (e.g., testing sites and dates, and letters of test-score certification or appeal), and, where applicable, information relating to eligibility for or conduct of nonstandard testing;
- Records concerning your financial aid; and
- Any other papers or information pertaining to your NCAA eligibility.

You agree to disclose these records only to determine your eligibility for intercollegiate athletics, your eligibility for athletically related financial aid, for purposes of inclusion in summary institutional information reported to the NCAA (and which may be publicly released by it), for NCAA longitudinal research studies and for activities related to the NCAA athletics certification program and NCAA compliance reviews.

_____   _____
Date   Signature of Student-Athlete

Part III: Incoming Freshman—Affirmation of Valid ACT or SAT Score

You affirm that, to the best of your knowledge, you have received a validated ACT and/or SAT score.

You agree that, in the event you are or have been notified by ACT or SAT of the possibility of an invalidated test score, you will immediately notify the director of athletics of your institution.

_____   _____
Name   Date

_____
Signature of Student-Athlete

What to do with this form: Sign and return it to your director of athletics before you first compete. This form is to be kept in the director of athletics' office for six years.

■ **Figure 10.5** _(continued)_

Form 97-3c   Academic Year 1997-98

Student-Athlete Statement—Division III

For:	Student-athletes
Action:	Sign and return to your director of athletics
Due date:	Before you first compete each year
Required by:	NCAA Constitution 3.2.4.5 and Bylaws 14.1.3.1 and 30.12
Purpose:	To assist in certifying eligibility

TO STUDENT-ATHLETE

Name of your institution: _____

This form has two parts: a statement concerning eligibility and a Buckley Amendment consent. You must sign both parts to participate in intercollegiate competition.

Before you sign this form, you should read the Summary of NCAA Regulations provided by your director of athletics or read the bylaws of the NCAA Division III Manual that deal with your eligibility. If you have any questions, you should discuss them with your director of athletics.

The conditions that you must meet to be eligible and the requirement that you sign this form are spelled out in the following articles and bylaws of the NCAA Division III Manual:

• Articles 10, 12, 13, 14, 15 and 16   • Bylaws 14.1.3.1, 18.4 and 31.2.3

Part I: Statement Concerning Eligibility

By signing this part of the form, you affirm that, to the best of your knowledge, you are eligible to compete in intercollegiate competition.

You affirm that you have read the Summary of NCAA Regulations or the relevant sections of the NCAA Division III Manual, and that your director of athletics (or his or her designee) gave you the opportunity to ask questions about them.

You affirm that you meet the NCAA regulations for student-athletes regarding eligibility, recruitment, financial aid, amateur status and involvement in organized gambling.

You affirm that you are aware of the NCAA drug-testing program and that you have signed the 1997-98 Drug-Testing Consent (Form 97-3f).

You affirm that you have reported to the director of athletics of your institution any violations of NCAA regulations involving you and your institution.

You affirm that you understand that if you sign this statement falsely or erroneously, you violate NCAA legislation on ethical conduct and you will further jeopardize your eligibility.

_____	_____
Name (please print)	Date of Birth
_____	_____
Signature of Student-Athlete	Home Address
_____	
Date	_____
_____	
Sport(s)	

Figure 10.6   NCAA Division III drug-testing consent form.

Reprinted with permission from the NCAA.

Part II: Buckley Amendment Consent

By signing this part of the form, you certify that you agree to disclose your education records.

You understand that this entire form and the results of any NCAA drug test you may take are part of your education records. These records are protected by the Family Educational Rights and Privacy Act of 1974, and they may not be disclosed without your consent.

You give your consent to disclose only to authorized representatives of this institution, its athletics conference (if any) and the NCAA, the following documents:

- This form;
- Results of NCAA drug tests;
- Any transcript from your high school, this institution, or any junior college or any other four-year institutions you have attended;
- Precollege test scores and appropriately related information and correspondence (e.g., testing sites and dates, and letters of test-score certification or appeal);
- Records concerning your financial aid; and
- Any other papers or information pertaining to your NCAA eligibility.

You agree to disclose these records only to determine your eligibility for intercollegiate athletics, your eligibility for athletically related financial aid, for purposes of inclusion in summary institutional information reported to the NCAA (and which may be publicly released by it), for NCAA longitudinal research studies and for activities related to NCAA compliance reviews.

_____   _____
Date   Signature of Student-Athlete

What to do with this form: Sign and return it to your director of athletics before you first compete. This form is to be kept in the director of athletics' office for six years.

▌Figure 10.6   _(continued)_

---

can be selected either by consulting a table of random numbers or by generating a list of random numbers from a computer statistics program. In any case, it is important to document which method is used in the event that the validity of the selection procedure is ever challenged.

Reasonable Suspicion

An alternative to random testing is to select subjects on the basis of **reasonable suspicion**. Reasonable suspicion, also known as _reasonable cause_ or _probable cause_, is based on specific signs of drug use in an individual. These signs are usually associated with observed behavior abnormalities that may or may not be related to the athlete's participation in sports. For example, an athlete may be asked to submit to a drug test after demonstrating rapid gains in muscle bulk and other signs of anabolic steroid use—a situation obviously related to the athlete's participation in sports. The same athlete may be asked to submit to drug testing after being involved in a traffic accident in which he was under the influence of drugs—an incident unrelated to the athlete's involvement in sports. Drug testing that involves reasonable suspicion as a selection criterion should be approached with great caution. What is reasonable to one person is often unreasonable to another, especially when sanctions may be involved. Suspicious behaviors must be carefully documented. Selection by reasonable suspicion is enhanced when more than one person observes the suspicious

reasonable suspicion
A basis for selecting subjects for drug testing based on observable signs of drug use. Also known as reasonable cause or probable cause.

INDIANA UNIVERSITY DEPARTMENT OF INTERCOLLEGIATE ATHLETICS ALCOHOL AND DRUG SCREENING PROGRAM CONSENT FORM
READ CAREFULLY BEFORE SIGNING

PRINT NAME _____

SPORT_____

1.　　AGREEMENT

I have carefully read the *Indiana University Department of Intercollegiate Athletics Alcohol and Drug Screening Program and Policies* and know the contents thereof, and I understand that by my signature, I agree to abide by the policies and I acknowledge that I have received a copy of these policies. I also understand that failure to show for a substance-screening test may be treated as a positive test result.

Student-Athlete Signature _____ Date _____

2.　　CONSENT TO URINALYSIS

For the 1998-99 year (which includes the summer 1999 vacation period), I hereby consent to have a sample of my urine collected and tested during my annual physical examination and at other such times as necessary or required, for the presence of certain drugs or substances in accordance with the provisions of the *Indiana University Department of Intercollegiate Athletics Alcohol and Drug Screening Program and Policies.*

Student-Athlete Signature _____ Date _____

Parent/Guardian Signature _____ Date _____

3.　　AUTHORIZATION FOR RELEASE OF INFORMATION

I further authorize you to release to the head coach of any intercollegiate sport in which I am a participant, my parent(s) or legal guardian(s), the athletic director and the team physician at Indiana University all the information and records, including test results, you may have relating to the screening or testing of my urine sample(s) in accordance with the provisions of the *Indiana University Department of Intercollegiate Athletics Alcohol and Drug Screening Program and Policies.* To the extent set forth in this document, I waive any privilege I may have in connection with such information.

I understand that my urine sample will be sent to the Indiana University Medical Center, Indianapolis, Indiana, for actual testing.

Student-Athlete Signature _____ Date _____

Parent/Guardian Signature _____ Date _____

4.　　RELEASE OF LIABILITY

The trustees of Indiana University, its officers, employees, and agents are hereby released from legal responsibility or liability for the release of such information and records as authorized by this form.

Student-Athlete Signature _____ Date _____

Parent/Guardian Signature _____ Date _____

■ **Figure 10.7** Institutional drug-testing consent form.

Reprinted with permission from the Indiana University Athletic Department.

behavior on more than one occasion. Behaviors or qualities that are measurable (documented increases in size and strength, number of motor vehicle accidents, drop in grade point average) are more useful in defending the reasonableness of suspicion of drug use.

Drug-Testing Methods

The most common method for drug testing in sports is urinalysis. Tests involving blood, saliva, hair, and breath analysis are also available but are used with less frequency. A method frequently employed as a first-level screening for many drugs is the **enzyme multiplied immunoassay technique (EMIT)**. This method uses light absorption to establish the level of a drug in a subject's urine. The amount of light absorption is compared to norms for a variety of drugs commonly tested for in athletic settings. Although this method is relatively inexpensive, it is associated with a high percentage of false-positive tests.

Because the EMIT tests can indicate the presence of drugs in an athlete's urine higher than what is actually present, it is critical that positive tests be confirmed by a process known as **gas chromatography–mass spectrometry (GC–MS)**. This method, although more expensive, is widely regarded as the gold standard in urinalysis (Thorland, 1990). This method is also the method of choice for determining the presence of anabolic steroids in the urine. The EMIT test is not sensitive to the presence of anabolic steroids. GC–MS works by separating the compounds found in the urine and developing "fingerprints" for each compound. These fingerprints can then be compared to those of known drugs. Although GC–MS is a very sensitive method, athletes frequently beat the system by using "designer" drugs for which no reference fingerprints are available.

Specimen Handling and Chain of Custody

Although distasteful to all involved, a urine sample that was not observed by a reliable witness while it was being collected, labeled, and packaged is of no value. Athletes should be observed while they deliver their urine samples. This obviously requires the presence of a toilet facility in the immediate vicinity of the drug-testing area. In the event the athlete is having difficulty producing a specimen, caffeine and alcohol-free beverages from sealed containers should be provided. The athlete should be allowed to observe the handling of the sample until it has been transferred to an appropriate bottle provided by the testing lab. The athlete should also be allowed to observe the bottle as it is being sealed and labeled. After the specimen has been labeled and sealed, the athlete should sign a form indicating that the specimen she provided was indeed her own, that she did not tamper with the specimen or any of the containers used to collect or store it, that she observed the transfer of the specimen to the storage bottle and the sealing thereof, and that the name on the storage bottle is hers.

Testing the Sample

Although simple immunoassay kits are available that athletic trainers can use to test urine samples in the athletic training room, this practice should be discouraged for several reasons. First, because of the potential for loss of athletic eligibility and its associated social and financial consequences, a reliable, disinterested third party should be used to test the samples. Ideally, a laboratory experienced in athletic drug testing should be contracted for every phase of the program, including subject selection, specimen collection, sample testing, and results reporting. The NCAA (1995) recommends that institutions contract only with labs that can provide information on **false-positive** and **false-negative** rates for the specific tests to be conducted .

---

enzyme multiplied immunoassay technique (EMIT) A first-line screening procedure designed to detect abuse of drugs or the presence of performance-enhancing drugs by testing an athlete's urine.

gas chromatography–mass spectrometry (GC–MS) A highly accurate method for detecting the presence of performance-enhancing and other drugs, including anabolic steroids, in an athlete's urine.

false-positive test The results of a drug test that indicate the presence of a banned compound above an acceptable level, when in fact the compound is either absent or present below acceptable levels.

false-negative test The results of a drug test that indicate either the absence of a banned compound or its presence below an acceptable level, when in fact the compound is present above acceptable levels.

The NCAA accredits laboratories for the purpose of conducting athletic drug testing. A list of NCAA accredited drug-testing laboratories is available from the NCAA, 700 W. Washington Ave., P.O. Box 6222, Indianapolis, IN 46206-6222. Phone: 317-917-6222.

Reporting the Results

The results of positive drug tests should be reported only to those people with a legitimate need to have the information. This can become a very difficult issue, because denial of athletic eligibility is often the result of a positive drug test. How should Randy Tate respond to a reporter's question about why the star quarterback is on the bench, even though he's been playing so well this year? Is he injured? What happened? Institutions that choose to implement drug-testing programs must develop ironclad procedures regarding the dissemination of this information. People with a need to know might include the athlete, the team physician, the athletic trainer, and the head coach; this list will vary from institution to institution. Personnel who are included on the list should be warned of the potential negative consequences of releasing the information. The damage to an athlete's reputation and potential loss of income make this area especially ripe for litigation.

WHAT TO TEST FOR

Which drugs should Randy Tate test for? On what basis should the list of banned drugs be developed? The two most common lists of banned drugs are those published by the NCAA and the list of drugs tested for in athletes who compete in the Olympic games. The Olympic list is longer and more restrictive than the NCAA list. In general, drugs that are banned from use include certain kinds of stimulants (amphetamine, cocaine), anabolic agents (testosterone, clenbuterol), diuretics (acetazolamide, furosemide), street drugs (heroin, marijuana), and peptide hormones and analogues (human growth hormone, erythropoietin). In addition, some drugs are prohibited in certain sports but allowed in others. Interestingly, many institutional drug-testing programs do not test for alcohol, even though this is clearly the drug with the greatest rate of abuse among high school and college-aged students.

PROCEEDING WITH CAUTION

Drug testing is a very controversial subject. It has been widely litigated—a trend that will probably continue into the future. Legal counsel is an essential element of the drug-testing program. Athletic trainers asked to design a drug-testing program must be very careful to incorporate a number of elements in order to lend validity and reliability to the procedures as well as to protect the rights of those to be tested. When Randy Tate designs his program, he should be sure to build the following 10 elements into the process (Pickett, 1986):

1. **Clearly articulate the purpose of the program.** It is particularly important that everyone associated with a drug-testing program understand its purpose. If the purpose of the program is not clearly articulated, it can easily be manipulated and turned into something that its creators never intended.

2. **Make testing as sport-specific as possible.** It is easier to defend a drug-testing program if you can demonstrate that it is designed to prevent or detect problems clearly associated with a particular sport. Testing the entire cross country team for anabolic steroids and human growth hormone five times per year would be an example of testing for a problem that is unlikely to exist.

3. **Use valid and reliable methods.** You must be able to prove that each positive result is associated with a particular athlete's sample through a carefully documented chain of custody. Positive results should always be confirmed using GC/MS.

4. **Incorporate an appeal mechanism.** If athletes have a property interest in retaining their athletic scholarship, eligibility, or position on a professional team, they must be allowed access to due process before they can be sanctioned. All athletes who test positive should be allowed to appeal the results. The more severe the sanction, the more formal the process should be.

5. **Protect the athlete's privacy.** Only those personnel with a legitimate need to know should be informed about positive drug tests. This list should be codified in written policies and procedures. Nobody else should have access to the information without the written permission of the athlete.

6. **Develop written policies and procedures.** The first step in instituting a drug-testing program is to codify the process in a written document that prescribes every step of the program. The process described in the *1995-1996 NCAA Drug Education and Testing Programs* (NCAA, 1995) booklet is a useful template for institutions who wish to implement their own programs.

7. **Obtain consent.** Athletes may not be tested for drugs against their will. In order for the athlete's consent to be valid, the document they sign should include a detailed description of the drug-testing process and the sanctions associated with positive tests.

8. **Inform potential athletes.** Athletes being recruited to participate in an institution's athletic program should be informed that a drug-testing program exists to which they may be subjected. This information should be reiterated when the student actually enrolls. Such information helps establish the evidence required to prove informed consent.

9. **Inform current athletes.** All athletes with the potential to be tested should be informed, in writing, of the purposes of the program, the procedures for selection and testing, the sanctions associated with positive tests, and the appeal procedures. They should also be informed of the risk that information regarding positive tests may be accessible to third parties (through court order or other legal means).

10. **Train and retrain personnel.** All personnel associated with the drug-testing program should be thoroughly trained in their responsibilities. In addition, this training should be repeated on a regular basis to ensure that changes in the program are communicated and that personnel are performing their duties correctly.

APPLICATIONS TO ATHLETIC TRAINING: THEORY INTO PRACTICE

Use the following two case studies to help apply the concepts in this chapter to real-life situations. The questions at the end of the studies have many possible correct solutions. The case studies can be used in class discussion or for homework or test questions.

Case Study 1

Glenda Hathaway's phone rang in her office at Northline Sports Medicine Clinic, where she was one of several certified athletic trainers. Her supervisor, James Jones, asked her if she would stop by his office later to discuss a new project he had in mind. When Glenda arrived 20 minutes later, James told her that the clinic would be offering a new service in the fall. "We want to expand our outreach services by offering to coordinate preparticipation physical examinations for the high schools we want to develop contracts with. We want you to pilot the program at Truman High in August. Here's the phone number of the athletic director at Truman. I've spoken with him already and he's really excited to have us doing this for him. Let me know how I can help."

Although Glenda was excited to get started on this project, she came away from her first meeting with Truman's athletic director a bit worried. The facilities were dark, in poor repair, and dirty. The athletic training room was a converted custodial closet. The boys' locker room was next to the gym, but the girls' locker room was down the hall in another wing of the building. Truman had a doctor—the parent of one of the student-athletes—but he only came to home football games on Friday nights. The athletic director told Glenda that he anticipated 500 students would need physical exams. The date was less than one month away.

Questions for Analysis

1. What alternatives does Glenda have for the physical facilities she needs to conduct Truman's PPEs?
2. Of all the obstacles that Glenda faces, which are the most important? Why?
3. Assuming that Glenda can pull together a team of physicians for Truman's PPEs, who will decide the final participation status of each athlete? If an athlete challenges one of Glenda's physicians on his decision to deny clearance, how should Glenda handle it?
4. Put yourself in Glenda's position and develop a plan to organize and administer PPEs to Truman High's 500 student-athletes. Be sure to include a floor plan of whatever facility you plan to use, along with staffing and supply lists. Develop all the forms you'll need to document each step of the PPE.

Case Study 2

Mark Thomas, ATC, walked into the locker room to tell Bill Williams that his number had come up. "Bill," Mark began, "I know you're just a freshman on the football team, but everybody has to get drug tested if their number is drawn. Yours just came up, so I'll need a urine sample from you. Right now." "Mr. Thomas," responded Bill, "I've only been here five days, and besides, my religion doesn't permit me to do this. I think I should talk to my parents first." "Bill," Mark said, "you don't have a choice. You signed the drug-testing consent form when you arrived last

week, so you should have known this was going to happen. I don't have all day to stand here and argue. Either fill the cup or I'll have to go to the coach." Bill reluctantly went into the bathroom where Mark watched him provide a specimen. After he was finished, Bill said to Mark, "Please don't let my folks know that I did this. They'd really be upset. They're pretty conservative." "If you don't test positive there's nothing to worry about," responded Mark. After that he turned and walked out of the locker room with Bill's specimen.

Questions for Analysis

1. Based on what you read in this case, what potential flaws exist in Mark's drug-testing program? How could these flaws be corrected?

2. Mark told Bill that he had no choice but to submit to the drug test. Is he right? Why or why not?

3. Assume that Bill's test was positive for the presence of anabolic steroids. Further assume that he was suspended for the season and that a story appeared in the newspaper reporting that Bill was being disciplined for "violating team rules." If Bill's parents called Mark wanting to know why their son was being suspended, how should Mark respond?

4. Would you challenge the results of this test and the resulting suspension if you were Bill? On what grounds?

5. Design a policies and procedures manual for a drug-testing program at an NCAA Division I university. Be sure to include a comprehensive list of procedures, including subject selection, drugs to be tested for, and sample collection and chain of custody. Develop an RFP to be sent to various laboratories who might do the testing. Develop an appeal process and a list of sanctions for positive tests.

SUMMARY

1. *Understand and defend the rationale for administrating preparticipation physical examinations.*

   The preparticipation physical examination is the first step in injury prevention and is a process that most athletic trainers are eventually involved with. In addition to helping prevent injury, the PPE allows institutions to comply with association rules, provides an opportunity for counseling and education, and helps improve compliance with standards of practice.

2. *Understand the strengths and weaknesses of the various preparticipation physical examination models.*

   There are advantages and disadvantages to conducting PPEs in either the physician's office or in a station technique in a school setting. The decision to use the family physician or the team physician also has advantages and disadvantages. Considerations for each setting include privacy, availability of equipment and supplies, and the thoroughness of the examination.

3. *Organize and implement a comprehensive preparticipation physical examination program in a variety of settings.*

   PPEs should ideally be conducted six to eight weeks prior to the beginning of the season. The NCAA requires a comprehensive PPE only upon entry into the athletic program, whereas most state high school associations require an annual PPE. The content of the PPE should be based on the athlete's age and level of competition, the sport to be played, the level of follow-up available, and the predictability of the tests to be used. Common elements of the PPE include a comprehensive health history, physician's examination, orthopedic examination, special tests, and fitness tests. Athletes (or their parents) must give written informed consent to be examined during the PPE. Athletes who wish to challenge the judgment of the medical staff regarding their participation status should be required to sign a detailed waiver of liability. Even this may not be enough to shield the medical staff from liability in the event of a serious injury or illness, however. A more prudent approach may be to allow the courts to rule on the reasonableness of the physician's participation decision.

4. *Understand and defend the rationale for administrating drug-testing programs in athletics.*

   Drug testing is intended to safeguard athletes' health while providing a level playing field for equitable competition.

5. *Understand the legal ramifications of drug testing in athletic programs.*

   Athletes should be observed as they provide the specimen, and they should be allowed to witness the handling of the specimen. Reporting of positive tests should be limited to those with a legitimate need to have the information. The NCAA list of banned drugs is not as extensive as that used for the Olympics but still contains a wide range of drugs of abuse and performance-enhancing drugs. Athletic trainers who are charged with developing drug-testing programs should always seek legal counsel and should comply with the 10 principles listed in the chapter.

6. *Organize and implement a comprehensive drug-testing program.*

   Drug tests are normally conducted after championship games, as part of the PPE, or as part of a year-round program. Athletes must consent to be tested, but lack of consent usually results in ineligibility. Random selection of subjects for testing is the norm, but can have several permutations based on timing of the test or characteristics of the athlete. Testing on the basis of reasonable suspicion requires identification of objective signs of drug use, preferably by more than one observer on more than one occasion. Urinalysis is the usual method employed in athletic drug-testing programs. Initial positive tests conducted with immunoassay techniques should be confirmed with gas chromatography and mass spectrometry. Only reputable labs that can report their false-positive and false-negative rates should be used to test the samples.

APPENDIX A
WOTS UP ANALYSIS
FOR A SPORTS MEDICINE PROGRAM

The following nine worksheets comprise a WOTS UP analysis for a sports medicine program. This worksheet package has been adapted by permission of Donald A. Campbell and Company.

WORKSHEET 1 BENEFITS AND CONCERNS RELATIVE TO STRATEGIC PLANNING

Instructions:

1. List the benefits you expect from our strategic planning as well as any concerns.
2. Note possible ways to overcome each of your concerns. Circle the best ideas.

Benefits expected:

Concerns:

Ways to overcome concerns:

WORKSHEET 2 ORGANIZING THE PLANNING PROCESS

Instructions:

Indicate how each of the following issues should be handled. Outline the steps, responsibilities, and time lines for developing the strategic plan.

1. What are we developing a strategic plan for?

   The entire sports medicine program

   Only part of the sports medicine program (which part?)

   The entire sports medicine program and each of its subprograms

   Other

2. For what period of time should we plan?

   Next 2 years   Next 4 years

   Next 3 years   Next 5 years

   Next 6 years   Other

3. What critical issues do you hope the planning will address?

4. How much time should we spend planning?

5. Should we use a consultant or other resource person in developing our plan?

   Yes

   No

   Unsure

   If so, what kind of help do we need?

6. Who should be part of the planning team? Circle all that apply.

   Athletic trainers

   Team physicians

   Athletic administrators

   Coaches

   Consultants

   Student athletic trainers

   Patients

   Others

7. How large should the planning team be?

   5–8

   9–12

   13–16

   17–20

   More than 20

8. Are there any others we should involve in the development of the plan? In the review of the plan?

9. Who should manage the overall planning effort?

10. Who should lead or chair the planning meetings?

11. By what date should we have the plan completed for approval?

12. Outline the steps you envision us using as we develop our plan.

Steps	Person(s) Responsible	Deadline

WORKSHEET 3 HISTORY AND PRESENT SITUATION

Instructions:

Review the history and present situation of the sports medicine program as they pertain to your area of responsibility. List any historical trends that will need attention as we plan for the future. Do not hesitate to comment on areas *outside* of your realm of responsibility if you so desire.

WORKSHEET 4 QUESTIONS ABOUT MISSION

1. Describe below what you understand the mission of the sports medicine program to be.

2. List any questions, ideas, or concerns you have about the present mission of the sports medicine program.

3. Do you envision any changes in the mission of the sports medicine program? If so, what do you want to accomplish? Who will be served by such a change?

WORKSHEET 5 CLIENT, CUSTOMER, AND STAKEHOLDER NEEDS

Instructions:

1. List the needs of present or potential "customers" that the sports medicine program might address. Note ideas for how the sports medicine program might meet those needs.

2. List the significant groups who have a stake in what the sports medicine program does. How can the program meet their needs?

Clients and Customers

Describe Existing or Possible New Target groups	Their Needs	Ways to Meet Those Needs

Other Stakeholders	Their Needs	Ways to meet Those Needs

WORKSHEET 6 COMPETITORS AND ALLIES

Instructions:

1. List present and potential new competitors, what the sports medicine program competes for, and our program's relative advantages and disadvantages (price, services, etc.)

2. List possible allies and how the sports medicine program might team up with each organization, person, or group.

Competitors   What We Compete For

Existing:

New:

Our Advantages   Our Disadvantages

Allies of the sports medicine program:

How can we team up with our allies?

WORKSHEET 7 OPPORTUNITIES AND THREATS

Instructions:

1. List and rank the major opportunities and threats that you believe the sports medicine program will face in the next five years that will determine its success or failure.

2. Use the information from worksheets 5 and 6 to help provide a more detailed analysis of our clients and stakeholders.

3. Be sure to consider the social, cultural, economic, political, and technological forces that may impact the sports medicine program in the next five years.

Opportunities:

Threats:

WORKSHEET 8 STRENGTHS AND WEAKNESSES

Instructions:

List the major strengths and weaknesses of the sports medicine program as it looks toward the future.

Strengths and assets:

Weaknesses and liabilities:

WORKSHEET 9 CRITICAL ISSUES FOR THE FUTURE

Instructions:

Review worksheets 3 through 8 and list critical issues or choices that the sports medicine program faces over the next five years.

Critical issues or choices:

APPENDIX B
STATE BOARDS REGULATING ATHLETIC TRAINING

The following list includes the names, addresses, and phone numbers (at the time of publication) of the state boards regulating athletic training through licensure, certification, or registration laws in the United States. The boards can provide information on regulatory requirements, fees, and forms. Although 38 states regulate athletic training, only the 35 states listed have regulatory boards. Arizona, Connecticut, and Hawaii regulate through exemption laws and do not have regulatory boards.

Alabama
Alabama Board of Athletic Trainers
415 Monroe Street
Montgomery, AL 36104
(334) 284-1929
Fax (334) 284-2663
Louise Porter, Executive Secretary

Arkansas
Arkansas Board of Physical Therapy
900 Shackleford Place, Suite 1
Little Rock, AR 72211
(501) 228-7100
Fax (501) 228-5535
Jennifer Coleman, Executive Director
Jcole10145@aol.com

Colorado
Colorado Board of Medicine
1560 Broadway, Suite 1300
Denver, CO 80202-5140
(303) 894-7690
Fax (303) 894-7692
Susan Miller, Program Administrator
Susan.miller@dora.state.co.us
http://www.dora.state.co.us/medical/

Delaware
Delaware Board of Physical Therapy
Cannon Building, Suite 203
861 Silver Lake Blvd.
Dover, DE 19904
(302) 739-4522
Fax (302) 739-2711
Susan Miccio, Administrative Assistant
Smiccio@state.de.us

Florida
Florida Department of Health
Division of Medical Quality Assurance
Northwood Centre
2020 Capitol Circle SE
Bin COA
Tallahassee, FL 32399-3258
(850) 487-9603
Fax (850) 921-5389
Theresa Skelton, Board Staff
Theresa_Skelton@doh.state.fl.us
http://www.doh.state.fl.us/mqa/

Georgia
Georgia Board of Athletic Trainers
237 Coliseum Dr.
Macon, GA 31217-3858
(912) 207-1670
Fax (912) 207-1676
Lasharn Hughes, Executive Director
Lmhughes@sos.state.ga.us
http://www.sos.state.ga.us/

Idaho
Idaho State Board of Medicine
PO Box 83720
Boise, ID 83720-0058
(208) 334-2822 or (800) 333-0073
Fax (208) 334-2801
Dee Parrott, Technical Records Specialist

Illinois
Department of Professional Regulation
Technical Assistance
096 Athletic Training
Illinois Board of Athletic Training
320 West Washington Street, 3rd Floor
Springfield, IL 62786
(217) 782-8556
Fax (217) 782-7645
http://www.state.il.us/dpr/

Indiana
Health Professions Bureau
402 West Washington Street
Room 041
Indianapolis, IN 46204
(317) 233-4435 or (888) 333-7515
Fax (317) 233-4236
Barbara Buck, Board Director
Bbuck@hpb.state.in.us
http://www.ai.org/hpb/

Iowa
Iowa Department of Public Health
Lucas State Office Building
Des Moines, IA 50319-0075
(515) 242-5938
Fax (515) 281-3121
Roxanne Sparks, Board Administrator
Rsparks@idth.state.ia.us

Kansas
Kansas State Board of Healing Arts
235 South Topeka Boulevard
Topeka, KS 66603-3068
(785) 296-7413
Fax (785) 296-0852
Larry Buening, Executive Director
http://www.ink.org/public/boha/

Kentucky
Kentucky Board of Medical Licensure
310 Whittington Parkway, Suite 1B
Louisville, KY 40222
(502) 429-8046
Fax (502) 429-9923
Sandy Brooks, Assistant Licensure Coordinator
Sandy.brooks@mail.state.ky.us
http://www.state.ky.us/agencies/kbml/

Louisiana
Louisiana State Board of Medical Examiners
630 Camp Street
New Orleans, LA 70130
Mailing Address:
PO Box 30250
New Orleans, LA 70190-0250
(504) 524-6763
Fax (504) 568-8893 or (504) 599-0503
Marian Glasper, Acting Licensure Director
Bmexmg@lsumc.edu

Maine
Maine Department of Professional
  and Financial Regulation
Office of Licensing and Regulation
State House
Station 35
Augusta, ME 04333
(207) 624-8603
Fax (207) 624-8637
Marleen McFadden, Clerk
Marleen.m.mcfadden@state.me.us
http://www.maineprofessionalreg.org/

Massachusetts
Board of Allied Health Professions
239 Causeway St., 5th Floor
Boston, MA 02114
(617) 727-3071
Fax (617) 727-2669
Kim Hamel, Administrative Assistant
http://www.state.ma.us/reg/

Minnesota
Athletic Trainers' Advisory Council
Minnesota Board of Medical Practice
University Park Plaza
2829 University Avenue SE, Suite 400
Minneapolis, MN 55414
(612) 617-2130 or (800) 657-3709
Fax (612) 617-2166
Jeanne Hoffman, Licensure Supervisor
Jeanneh@bmp.state.mn.us
http://www.bmp.state.mn.us/

Mississippi
Mississippi State Department of Health
Office of Professional Licensure
PO Box 1700, 2423 North State Street
Jackson, MS 39215-1700
(601) 987-4153
Fax (601) 987-3784
David Kweller, Health Facility Surveyor
http://www.msdh.state.ms.us/

Missouri
Missouri State Board for the Healing Arts
PO Box 4
Jefferson City, MO 65102
751-0098
Fax (573) 751-3166
Nicole Wieberg, Licensure Technician
Nwieberg@mail.state.mo.us
http://www.ecodev.state.mo.us/pr/healarts/

Nebraska
Department of Health
Bureau of Examining Boards
301 Centennial Mall South
PO Box 95007
Lincoln, NE 68509-5007
(402) 471-2115
Fax (402) 471-0383
Delores James
http://www.hhs.state.ne.us/

New Hampshire
Office of Allied Health Professions
2 Industrial Park Drive
Concord, NH 03301
(603) 271-8389
Fax (603) 271-6702
Veronique Sucey, Administrative Assistant

New Jersey
The State Board of Medical Examiners
140 East Front Street
Trenton, NJ 08608
(609) 826-7100
Fax (609) 984-3930
Mary Lou Mattola

New Mexico
Regulation & Licensing Department
Athletic Trainers' Practice Board
PO Box 25101
Santa Fe, NM 87504
(505) 476-7100
Fax (505) 476-7094
Becky Armijo, Administrator
Athletictrainerboard@state.nm.us

New York
State Committee for Athletic Trainers
Room 3023
Cultural Education Center
Albany, NY 12230
(518) 474-3842
Fax (518) 473-6995
Thomas Monahan
athl@mail.nysed.gov

North Carolina
North Carolina Board
  of Athletic Trainer Examiners
PO Box 10769
Raleigh, NC 27605
(919) 821-4980
Fax (919) 833-5743
Jim Scarborough, Administrator
Scarboro@interpath.com

North Dakota
Board of Licensure
University of Mary
Department of Athletics
7500 South University Dr.
Bismark, ND 58504
(701) 255-7500
Fax (701) 255-7687
Tim McCrory, Chair

Ohio
Executive Secretary
OT, PT, AT Board
77 South High Street, 16th Floor
Columbus, OH 43266-0317
(614) 466-3774 or (800) 871-1921
Fax (614) 644-8112 or (614) 995-0816
Carl Gabriel Williams, Executive Director
Carlwilliams14@yahoo.com
http://www.state.oh.us/pyt/

Oklahoma
State Board of Medical Licensure & Supervision
State of Oklahoma
5140 North Francis Steet, Suite C
Oklahoma City, OK 73118
(405) 848-6841
Fax (405) 848-8240
Robyn Kemp, Director of Licensing
Rkemp@osbmls.state.ok.us
http://www.osbmls.state.ok.us/

Oregon
Health Division Licensing Programs
700 Summer Street NE, Suite 320
Salem, OR 97301-1287
(503) 378-8667
Fax (503) 370-9004
Tricia Albritton, Programs Operation Manager
hdlp.mail@state.or.us
http://www.hdlp.hr.state.or.us/

Pennsylvania
State Board of Physical Therapy
PO Box 2649
Harrisburg, PA 17105-2649
(717) 783-7134
Fax (717) 787-7769
Robert Kline, Board Administrator
Physical@pados.dos.state.pa.us
http://www.dos.state.pa.us/bpoa/pt/bd.htm

Rhode Island
Rhode Island Department of Health
Professional Regulations
3 Capital Hill, Room 104
Providence, RI 02908
(401) 222-2827
Fax (401) 222-1272
Maureen Sowik, Physical Clerk

South Carolina
South Carolina Department of Health
  and Environmental Control
Division of Emergency Medical Services
2600 Bull Street
Columbia, SC 29201
737-7204
Fax (803) 737-7212
Jim Catoe, Program Administrator
Catoekc@columb54.dhec.state.sc.us

South Dakota
South Dakota Board of Medical Examiners
1323 South Minnesota Avenue
Sioux Falls, SD 57105
(605) 336-1965
Fax (605) 336-0270
Mitzi Turley, Administrative Assistant

Tennessee
Board of Medical Examiners
State Department of Health
Council on Athletic Training
1st Floor, Cordell Hull Building
425 Fifth Avenue North
Nashville, TN 37247-1010
(615) 532-3202 or (888) 310-4650
http://www.state.tn.us/health/

Texas
Texas Department of Health
Professional Licensing & Certification Division
Advisory Board of Athletic Trainers
1100 West 49th Street
Austin, TX 78756-3183
(512) 834-6615
Fax (512) 834-6677
Becky Berryhill, Technician
At@licc.tdh.state.tx.us
http://www.tdh.state.tx.us/hcqs/plc/at.htm

West Virginia
West Virginia Department of Education
Building 6, Room 309
1900 Kanawha Boulevard East
Charleston, WV 25305-0330
(304) 558-8830
Fax (304) 558-0048
John Ray, Coordinator of Health and Physical Education
Jbray@access.k12.wv.us
http://www.wvde.state.wv.us/

APPENDIX C
ORGANIZATIONAL STRUCTURE OF THE NATIONAL ATHLETIC TRAINERS' ASSOCIATION

The figure below depicts the organizational structure of the NATA, its affiliated organizations, and its committees and task forces. The committee structure changes periodically. The structure shown below was accurate as of November 1, 1999.

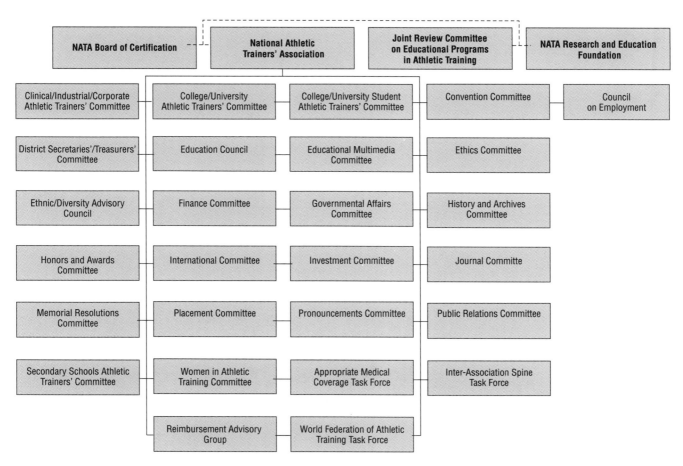

Reprinted with permission from the National Athletic Trainers' Association.

APPENDIX D
NATA CODE OF ETHICS

PREAMBLE

The Code of Ethics of the National Athletic Trainers' Association has been written to make the membership aware of the principles of ethical behavior that should be followed in the practice of athletic training. The primary goal of the Code is the assurance of high-quality health care. The Code presents aspirational standards of behavior that all members should strive to achieve.

The principles cannot be expected to cover all specific situations that may be encountered by the practicing athletic trainer, but should be considered representative of the spirit with which athletic trainers should make decisions. The principles are written generally, and the circumstances of a situation will determine the interpretation and application of a given principle and of the Code as a whole. Whenever there is a conflict between the Code and legality, the laws prevail.

The guidelines set forth in this Code are subject to continual review and revision as the athletic training profession develops and changes.

PRINCIPLE 1:

Members shall respect the rights, welfare, and dignity of all individuals.

1.1 Members shall not discriminate against any legally protected class.

1.2 Members shall be committed to providing competent care consistent with both the requirements and the limitations of their profession.

1.3 Members shall preserve the confidentiality of privileged information and shall not release such information to a third party not involved in the patient's care unless the person consents to such release or release is permitted or required by law.

PRINCIPLE 2:

Members shall comply with the laws and regulations governing the practice of athletic training.

2.1 Members shall comply with applicable local, state, and federal laws and institutional guidelines.

2.2 Members shall be familiar with and adhere to all National Athletic Trainers' Association guidelines and ethical standards.

2.3 Members are encouraged to report illegal or unethical practice pertaining to athletic training to the appropriate person or authority.

2.4 Members shall avoid substance abuse and, when necessary, seek rehabilitation for chemical dependency.

PRINCIPLE 3:

Members shall accept responsibility for the exercise of sound judgment.

3.1   Members shall not misrepresent in any manner, either directly or indirectly, their skills, training, professional credentials, identity, or services.

3.2   Members shall provide only those services for which they are qualified via education and/or experience and by pertinent legal regulatory process.

3.3   Members shall provide services, make referrals, and seek compensation only for those services that are necessary.

PRINCIPLE 4:

Members shall maintain and promote high standards in the provision of services.

4.1   Members shall recognize the need for continuing education and participate in various types of educational activities that enhance their skills and knowledge.

4.2   Members who have the responsibility for employing and evaluating the performance of other staff members shall fulfill such responsibility in a fair, considerate, and equitable manner, on the basis of clearly enunciated criteria.

4.3   Members who have the responsibility for evaluating the performance of employees, supervisees, or students, are encouraged to share evaluations with them and allow them the opportunity to respond to those evaluations.

4.4   Members shall educate those whom they supervise in the practice of athletic training with regard to the Code of Ethics and encourage their adherence to it.

4.5   Whenever possible, members are encouraged to participate and support others in the conduct and communication of research and educational activities that may contribute knowledge for improved patient care, patient or student education, and the growth of athletic training as a profession.

4.6   When members are researchers or educators, they are responsible for maintaining and promoting ethical conduct in research and educational activities.

PRINCIPLE 5:

Members shall not engage in any form of conduct that constitutes a conflict of interest or that adversely reflects on the profession.

5.1   The private conduct of the member is a personal matter to the same degree as is any other person's except when such conduct compromises the fulfillment of professional responsibilities.

5.2   Members of the National Athletic Trainers' Association and others serving on the Association's committees or acting as consultants shall not use, directly or by implication, the Association's name or logo or their affiliation with the Association in the endorsement of products or services.

5.3   Members shall not place financial gain above the welfare of the patient being treated and shall not participate in any arrangement that exploits the patient.

5.4   Members may seek remuneration for their services that is commensurate with their services and in compliance with applicable law.

Reprinted from National Athletic Trainers' Association 1995.

GLOSSARY

90th-percentile fee The fee below which 90% of all other medical vendors in a particular geographic area charge for a specific service.

abandonment The desertion of a patient-practitioner relationship by the health care provider without the consent of the patient.

accreditation Formal recognition provided to an organization or one of its programs indicating that it meets certain prescribed quality standards.

accuracy standards Performance evaluation standards intended to improve the validity and reliability of the employee appraisal process.

actual cause The degree to which a health care practitioner's actions are associated with the adverse outcomes of a patient's care.

adversaries Persons who are unsupportive of both a program and a particular plan related to the program.

agreement-trust matrix A model that identifies and types the most important people in developing support for a plan.

allies Persons who exhibit a high level of support for a plan.

allocator of resources role A type of decisional role in which the leader exercises authority to determine how organizational assets will be deployed.

application software A computer program designed to perform a specific function such as word processing, statistical analysis, or graphics production.

assumption of risk A legal defense that attempts to claim that an injured plaintiff understood the risk of an activity and freely chose to undertake the activity regardless of the hazards associated with it.

athletic accident insurance A type of insurance policy intended to reimburse medical vendors for the expenses associated with acute athletic accidents.

authority That aspect of power, granted to either groups or individuals, that legitimizes the right of the group or individual to make decisions on behalf of others.

bedfellows Persons who exhibit support for a particular plan but who have a history of untrustworthy behavior and vacillation.

bidding A process whereby vendors provide cost quotations for goods and services they wish to sell.

bidding documents The package of materials prepared by the architect and sent to contractors, including the invitation to bid, the bid form, and special bidding instructions.

breach of confidentiality Violation of a commitment to privacy and protection of information and/or communications.

breach of contract An unexcused failure to perform the services specified in a contract, either formal or informal.

browser A computer program that allows the user to search the World Wide Web for information on a given topic and display the information in text and graphic formats.

bubble diagram An abstract, graphic representation of the relationship of one function of a building to another based on the "closeness" factor established by the relationship chart.

budget A type of operational plan for the coordination of resources and expenditures.

bulletin board An electronic, online, interactive electronic database system, usually organized by topic or interest group.

business plan Used by commercial loan officers to assess the viability of a business. Includes a written description of the activities the business will engage in, a market analysis, historical and projected financial statements, and other associated information.

capital campaign A program, usually of fixed length, designed to raise funds for program creation, development, and improvement.

capitation A system whereby medical vendors are paid a fixed amount per patient.

carrier Charge-based providers contracted by the federal government charged with reviewing Medicare claims made by physician or other health care providers.

catastrophic insurance A type of accident insurance designed to provide lifelong medical, rehabilitation, and disability benefits for the victims of devastating injury.

certification A form of title protection, established by state law or sponsored by professional associations, designed to ensure that practitioners possess essential knowledge and skills sufficient to protect the public.

charting by exception A type of medical record that notes only those patient responses that vary from predefined norms.

clinical supervision The process of direct observation of an employee's work, with emphasis on measurement of specific behaviors, and the subsequent development of plans to remediate deficiencies in performance.

clones Lower-cost, generic PCs designed to be compatible with those produced by IBM.

code of ethics A systematized set of standards or principles that defines ethical behavior appropriate for a profession. The standards and principles are determined by moral values.

collegial culture A type of organizational culture characterized by consensus, teamwork, and participatory decision making.

commercial loan An amount of money, borrowed from a lending institution, for the purpose of establishing, improving, or maintaining a business.

commission An action that violates a legal duty.

Commission on Accreditation of Rehabilitation Facilities (CARF) A nonprofit agency that sets quality standards for rehabilitation services and facilities.

comparative negligence A legal doctrine intended to determine the degree to which a plaintiff contributed to the harm caused by a defendant.

computer hardware The equipment required to input, process, and output data.

computer resources needs assessment analysis A type of needs assessment focused on the information management function and its automation.

computer software Also known as a *computer program*. A set of instructions that controls the operations of the computer hardware.

conflict of interest When the interests of one individual or group are discordant or in competition with those of another individual or group.

construction documents The highly detailed technical drawings a contractor will use to determine building costs and to guide construction.

construction management A method that involves the general contractor as part of the design team from the beginning of the building process.

copayments The percentage of a medical bill not paid for by the insurance company.

cost-benefit analysis A type of program evaluation that estimates both the amount of resources and the potential advantages associated with a program.

counterpower The potential to influence the behavior of a superior.

criteria Quantifiable measures used to determine whether a particular objective has been accomplished.

current procedural terminology (CPT) A coding system applied to medical procedures for the purpose of standardizing the language associated with third-party reimbursement.

data port A dedicated phone line used to connect computers in different locations.

database software Application software that allows a user to input, store, manipulate, and retrieve a specific information set. Sometimes referred to as a *database management system* (DBMS).

decisional role That portion of a manager's work that requires her to use authority to make decisions.

definers People who use or receive the services of a program.

design/build A method that uses only one firm to both design and construct a new building.

developmental supervision A supervisory model that emphasizes collaboration between supervisors and supervisees in order to help them solve problems and develop professionally.

dictation The act of verbally recording, on a cassette tape or directly into a computer, the details of a health care assessment or treatment for later transcription and filing.

disability insurance Insurance designed to protect an athlete against future loss of earnings due to a disabling injury or sickness.

disqualifying conditions Injuries, illnesses, or other medical conditions that pose an undue risk to athletes, their teammates, or their competitors.

disseminator role A type of informational role that requires the leader to communicate with members of the group.

disturbance handler role A type of decisional role in which the leader manages conflict.

electronic data interchange (EDI) A system whereby insurance claims can be submitted electronically. Also known as *paperless claims system*.

electronic mail A system that allows users to communicate via computer.

endowment That portion of an institution's assets in cash and investments not normally used for operational purposes.

entrepreneurial role A type of decisional role in which the leader initiates and designs controlled change within an organization.

enzyme multiplied immunoassay technique (EMIT) A first-line screening procedure designed to detect abuse of drugs or the presence of performance-enhancing drugs by testing an athlete's urine.

ergonomics The scientific study of human work.

ethics The rules, standards, and principles that dictate right conduct among members of a society or profession. Ethics are based on moral values.

exclusions Situations or circumstances specifically not covered by an insurance policy.

exclusive provider organization (EPO) A type of preferred provider organization whereby medical services are reimbursed only if the patient uses contracted providers.

exculpatory clause A signed release from a patient or parents that waives all future legal claims against an athletic trainer or the employing institution.

excuse A reason that is considered justifiable.

exemption A legislative mechanism used to release members of one profession from the liability of violating another profession's practice act.

experimental treatments Therapies not proven to be effective.

explanation of benefits form (EOB) A summary prepared by an insurance company, and sent to a policyholder, that documents how the insurance policy covered the charges associated with a particular claim.

exploitation Using another person for selfish purposes, particularly when it comes at the expense of that person and/or without their knowledge or full informed consent.

express warranty An explicit statement specifying the conditions, circumstances, and terms under which a vendor will replace or repair a product if found to be faulty.

external chart audit A patient records review technique, performed by an accreditation agency or a payer, intended to ensure that patient care is appropriate and meets certain minimum standards.

external evaluators Experts not affiliated with an organization who are retained to assess the various programs within the organization.

f.o.b. point Freight-on-board point. The point at which the title for shipped goods passes from vendor to purchaser.

false-negative test The results of a drug test that indicate either the absence of a banned compound or its presence below an acceptable level, when in fact the compound is present above acceptable levels.

false-positive test The results of a drug test that indicate the presence of a banned compound above an acceptable level, when in fact the compound is either absent or present below acceptable levels.

feasibility standards Performance evaluation standards intended to help foster practicality in the employee appraisal process.

fee-for-service plan Also known as an *indemnity plan*. A type of traditional medical insurance whereby patients are free to seek medical services from any provider. The plan covers a portion of the cost of covered procedures, and the patient is responsible for the balance.

FERPA (The Family Educational Rights and Privacy Act) Sometimes referred to as the *Buckley Amendment*. A 1974 federal law requiring student authorization to release educational records to a third party and ensuring access for students to their records.

figurehead role An interpersonal role that requires the authority holder to represent the group, usually in a visible public capacity.

fixed budgeting A method in which expenditures and revenues are projected on a monthly basis, thereby providing an estimate of cash flow.

focus charting A medical record that registers a patient's complaint *data,* the health care practitioner *actions,* and the patient's *response.*

foot-pedal activator A water-flow device, controlled by a foot pedal, used with hand-washing stations.

forbidden knowledge Information about a situation that an athletic trainer is forbidden to act on.

forecast A prediction of future conditions, based on various statistics and indicators, that describes an athletic training program's past and present situations.

foreseeability The ability to project the likely outcome of an act.

formalistic culture A type of organizational culture characterized by a clear chain of command and well-defined lines of formal authority.

formative evaluation An assessment designed primarily for improvement of a program.

fraud Criminal misrepresentation for the purpose of financial gain.

Gannt chart A graphic planning and control technique that maps discrete tasks on a calendar.

gas chromatography–mass spectrometry (GC–MS) A highly accurate method for detecting the presence of performance-enhancing and other drugs, including anabolic steroids, in an athlete's urine.

general contractor The company responsible for coordinating the actual construction of a building.

goals General statements of program intent.

Good Samaritan laws Statutes intended to shield certain health care practitioners from certain types of legal liability when they voluntarily come to the aid of injured or ill persons under specific circumstances.

ground fault interrupter (gfi) A highly sensitive device designed to discontinue the flow of electricity in an electrical circuit during a power surge.

guardian A person who has legal responsibility for the care and decisions of someone who is incompetent to act for himself or who is a minor.

Hawthorne effect Also known as the placebo effect. A phenomenon whereby the subjects in an experimental study alter their behavior simply as a result of the process of being studied, even when there is no effect from the independent variable.

HCFA 1500 The form that private-practice clinics should use when filing a claim with an insurance company. Originally developed by the Health Care Financing Administration for Medicare claims.

health history form A detailed questionnaire designed to document an athlete's previous injuries, illnesses, and other medical conditions. This form often serves as the basis for additional medical follow-up and evaluation.

health history update A brief questionnaire designed to determine whether an athlete suffered any injuries or developed any medical conditions since the last comprehensive PPE.

health insurance A type of policy designed to reimburse the cost of preventative as well as corrective medical care.

health maintenance organization (HMO) A type of health insurance plan that requires policyholders to use only those medical vendors approved by the company. All medical services are coordinated by a primary care physician, who acts as a gatekeeper to specialty services.

high-risk behaviors Behaviors that expose a person to an unnecessarily high degree of physical or psychological jeopardy.

honeymoon effect The period of time, usually immediately after arriving in a new position, in which persons are more likely to be granted extra authority to make decisions.

implied warranty An unstated understanding that a vendor will "make good" if a product is faulty.

individual practice association (IPA) A managed care model whereby an HMO provides health care services through a network of individual medical practitioners. Care is provided in a physician's office as opposed to a large, multifunctional medical center.

informational role Those functions that require the manager to collect, use, and disseminate information.

inspection-production A supervisory model that emphasizes the use of formal authority and managerial prerogatives in order to improve employee efficiency and efficacy.

insurance agent A representative of an insurance company or an independent insurance agency who sells and services insurance policies.

insurance claim registry form A worksheet that aids in tracking the progress of an insurance claim through the entire process.

interference Anything, including environmental elements or characteristics of the communication medium, that distorts the message sent from the sender to the receiver.

intermediary Cost-based providers contracted by the federal government charged with reviewing Medicare claims made by hospitals.

internal chart audit A patient records review technique performed by the sports medicine staff as part of a quality-assurance program.

internal influencers Organization decision makers.

International Classification of Diseases (ICD-9-CM) A coding system applied to illnesses, injuries, and other medical conditions for the purpose of standardizing the language associated with third-party reimbursement.

interpersonal role A managerial role, emanating from the possession of formal authority, that requires the manager to interact and form relationships with others in the organization.

inventory management The process of controlling equipment and supply stocks so that services can be provided without interruption while the use of institutional resources is maximized.

job description A written description of the specific responsibilities a position holder will be accountable for in an organization.

job specification A written description of the requirements or qualifications a person should possess in order to fill a particular role in an organization.

Joint Commission on Accreditation of Healthcare Organizations (JCAHO) The oldest and largest health care standards organization in the country. JCAHO accredits ambulatory health care facilities.

laptop computer Personal computers that have been reduced in size in order to achieve portability. Smaller laptops are known as **notebooks**.

laws The rules and regulations governing the affairs of a community or society. Laws are enforced by administrative authority and an established judicial system of the community.

layered coverage A method of using different insurance companies to underwrite different levels of coverage in a common policy.

leadership A subset of power that involves influencing the behavior and attitudes of others to achieve intended outcomes.

legitimacy That aspect of power that gives the leader the right to make a request and provides the obligation of the subordinate to comply.

liaison role An interpersonal role that requires the leader to interface with others in the group, including superiors, subordinates, and coequals.

licensure A form of state credentialing, established by statute and intended to protect the public, that regulates the practice of a trade or profession by specifying who may practice and what duties they may perform.

line-item budgeting A method that allocates a fixed amount of money for each subfunction of a program.

list server A remote computer that compiles a directory of users' computer addresses and distributes messages contributed by the members of a particular discussion list.

local area network (LAN) A system that connects two or more personal computers in different places so that users can communicate and share software and data.

loss of consortium A legal claim of damages for injuries to a spouse or for alienation of a spouse's affection.

lump-sum bidding A process whereby general contractors provide cost quotations for the right to construct or renovate a building.

lump-sum budgeting A method that allocates a fixed amount of money for an entire program without specifying how the money will be spent.

macro An internal program available with some application software that allows a user to reduce a complex series of keystrokes to one command.

mainframe A type of large, powerful computer designed for multiple users in a centralized institutional setting.

malpractice Liability generating conduct associated with the adverse outcome of patient treatment (Scott, 1990).

managed care A growing concept in the insurance industry emphasizing cost control through coordination of medical services, such as with an HMO or PPO.

management The element of leadership that involves planning, decision making, and coordination of the activities of a group.

manipulation Shrewdly or deviously influencing or controlling another person or a situation. When the influence or control is for self-interested purposes it can be exploitative.

market analysis Includes a written description of the competitive advantages of a business, analysis of the competition, pricing structure, and marketing plan.

mass screening A preparticipation physical examination method whereby many athletes are screened simultaneously, usually in a school gymnasium or locker room.

master outline A guide to the major sections of a filing system.

matrix structure A type of chart that describes an organizational structure in terms of both functions and services.

maturational assessment A medical screening procedure based on Tanner's stages of maturational development. It is often used to classify children and adolescents for the purpose of matching them with appropriate athletic opponents.

medical insurance A contract between a policyholder and an insurance company to reimburse a percentage of the cost of the policyholder's medical bills.

medical practice act A state law regulating the practice of medicine, usually by specifying who may practice and under what circumstances.

medical record Cumulative documentation of a person's medical history and health care interventions.

microcomputer Also known as a **personal computer (PC)**. A type of computer designed to sit on a desk and serve the needs of one, or at most, a few users.

minor A person under legal age for adult responsibilities and decisions.

mission statement A written expression of an organization's philosophy, purposes, and characteristics.

mixing valve A type of plumbing fixture designed to blend hot and cold water, eliminating the need for separate hot- and cold-water controls.

monitor role A type of informational role that requires the leader to observe and keep abreast of changes that will affect the group and its activity.

narrative charting A method of recording the details of a patient's assessments and treatments using a detailed, prose-based format.

natural lighting Outside light used to illuminate indoor spaces, usually through windows or skylights.

need The discrepancy between the present program status and the desired future state of one or more aspects of the program.

needs assessment A systematic set of procedures undertaken to set organizational or programmatic priorities based on identified needs.

negligence A type of tort whereby an athletic trainer fails to act as a reasonably prudent athletic trainer would act under the circumstances.

negotiations The process of bargaining.

negotiator role A type of decisional role in which the leader uses authority to bargain with members of the internal or external audience.

network A group of computers connected by either direct hardwire coupling or dedicated telephone lines for the purpose of communicating with each other.

nonmedical correspondence Letters and memoranda not associated with a specific patient's health status.

objectives Specific statements of how a program intends to accomplish a particular goal.

omission A failure to act when there was a legal duty to do so.

operating system The computer software, necessary to operate the machine, that integrates and controls the functions of the hardware and application software.

operational plan A type of plan that defines organizational activities in the short term, usually no longer than two years.

opponents Persons who support a particular program but dispute the implementation of a plan related to that program.

organizational chart A graphic representation of an organization's structure, usually arranged by function, service, or in a matrix format.

organizational culture The values, beliefs, assumptions, and norms that form the infrastructure of the organizational ethos.

organizational structure A model that defines the relationships among the members of an organization.

OSHA bloodborne pathogen standard Federal government rules that require employers to protect employees against the accidental transmission of bloodborne pathogens, especially HIV and hepatitis B.

outcomes assessment An evaluation method used in health care that seeks objective evidence that a patient's functional ability was enhanced through the care provided by the athletic trainer.

performance budgeting A method that allocates funds for discrete activities.

performance evaluation The process of placing a value on the quality of an employee's work.

perpetrator The person who is responsible for and/or has committed an act.

person specification A specific delineation, based on the job specification, of the qualities, skills, and characteristics a person must have in order to fill a particular role.

personal power The potential to influence others by virtue of personal characteristics and personality attributes.

personalistic culture A type of organizational culture characterized by autonomy in decision making and problem solving.

PERT (Program Evaluation and Review Technique) A method of graphically depicting the time line for and interrelationships of the different stages of a program.

planning A type of decision-making process in which a course of action is determined in order to bring about a future state of affairs.

planning committee A group of institutional employees who work with an architect to develop the design of a building.

plumbing fixtures The external hardware used to control the flow and temperature of water.

point-of-service plan (POS) Managed care plans that are similar to PPOs, except that primary care physicians are assigned to patients to coordinate their care.

[1]**policy** A contract between an insurance company and an individual or organization.

[2]**policy** A type of plan that expresses an organization's intended behavior relative to a specific program subfunction.

pooled buying consortium A group of similar institutions that merge resources to purchase goods in large quantities for the purpose of receiving volume discounts.

position description A formal document that describes the qualifications, work content, accountability, and scope of a job.

position power The power vested in people by virtue of the roles they play in an organization.

power The potential to influence others.

practice The action that actually takes place in response to administrative problems.

preemployment test Any procedure (including a drug test), conducted on a potential employee, that is used to determine the applicant's suitability for employment.

preferred provider organization (PPO) A type of health insurance plan that provides financial incentives to encourage policyholders to use those medical vendors approved by the company.

premium The invoiced cost of an insurance policy.

preparticipation physical examination (PPE) A medical screening procedure designed to determine an athlete's readiness for participation in a specific sport at a specific level of competition.

primary care provider The physician, selected by an HMO member, who acts as the first source of medical service for the patient. Most HMOs require members to seek a referral from the primary care provider before seeking care from another medical vendor.

primary coverage A type of health, medical, or accident insurance that begins to pay for covered expenses immediately after a deductible has been paid.

primary decision makers Institutional members who have formal authority over large units or sub-units of an organization.

primary party A person directly involved as a participant in an activity.

problem-oriented medical record (POMR) A system of medical record keeping that organizes information around a patient's specific complaints.

procedure A type of operational plan that provides specific directions for members of an organization to follow.

process A collection of incremental and mutually dependent steps designed to direct the most important tasks of an organization.

program administration records Documentation of the activities of a program.

program evaluation A systematic and comprehensive assessment of the worth of a particular program.

program statement A document, prepared by the users, the architect, or both, that specifies the anticipated space requirements based on known work patterns provided by the users.

propriety standards Performance evaluation standards intended to help ensure that the process is legal and fair.

proximate (legal) cause The degree to which the harm caused by a health care practitioner was foreseeable.

purchase order A document that formalizes the terms of a purchase and transmits the intentions of the buyer to purchase goods or services from a vendor.

purchasing The process of acquiring goods and services.

random access memory (RAM) A type of computer memory in which specific information can be accessed in any order. Generally, the more powerful application software programs require greater amounts of RAM.

random selection A method for choosing subjects for drug testing based on permutations of timing, subject characteristics, or both. Implies an equal probability for any subject within a given population to be chosen for testing.

reason The basis or explanation for an action.

reasonable suspicion A basis for selecting subjects for drug testing based on observable signs of drug use. Also known as reasonable cause or probable cause.

receiving The process of accepting delivery of goods purchased from a vendor.

recruitment The process of planning for human resources needs and identifying potential candidates to meet those needs.

registration A type of state credentialing that requires qualified members of a profession to register with the state in order to practice.

relationship chart A table used to justify the placement of various rooms within a building.

reliability (in staff selection) Consistency of staff selection procedures.

request for quotation (RFQ) A document that provides vendors with the specifications for bidding on the sale of goods and services.

requests for proposals (RFPs) Notices from internal and external funding sources announcing the details of grant programs.

requisition A type of formal or informal communication, usually written, used for requesting authorization to purchase goods or services.

riders Additions to a standard insurance policy that provide coverage for conditions that are normally not covered.

right conduct Behavior that is fitting, proper, or conforms to legal or moral expectations.

rights Moral and/or legal privileges inherent in being a member of a community or society.

risk management A process designed to prevent losses of all kinds for everyone associated with an organization, including its directors, administrators, employees, and clients.

schematic drawings A graphic representation, derived from the program statement, that illustrates the relationships among the principal functions of a building.

scientific management A collection of management theories developed in the early 1900s whose emphasis is on the strict control of work in order to maximize production through increases in efficiency.

secondary coverage A type of health, medical, or accident insurance that begins to pay for covered expenses only after all other sources of insurance coverage have been exhausted. Also known as *excess insurance.*

secondary decision makers Professional staff members primarily responsible for delivering a program within an organization.

self-determination Free will to judge for oneself, to determine one's own course of action, and to manage one's own affairs.

shareware Application software available at greatly reduced cost, usually on a trial basis.

SOAP note Medical appraisal organized by subjective and objective evaluation, assessment of the patient's problem, and development of a plan for treatment.

sovereign (governmental) immunity A legal doctrine that holds that neither governments nor their agents can be held liable for negligent actions.

span of control The number of subordinates supervised by a particular individual in an organizational setting.

spending ceiling model A type of expenditure budgeting that requires justification only for those expenses that exceed those of the previous budget cycle. Also known as the *incremental model.*

spending reduction model A type of budgeting used during periods of financial retrenchment that requires reallocation of institutional funds, resulting in reduced spending levels for some programs.

spokesperson's role A type of informational role that requires the leader to communicate with organizational influencers and members of the organization's public.

spreadsheet program A type of application software that manipulates numerical data contained in cells formed by the intersection of rows and columns.

staff selection The procedures used as the basis for any employment decision, including recruitment, hiring, promotion, demotion, retention, and performance evaluation.

standard of care The legal duty to provide health care services consistent with what other health care practitioners of the same training, education, and credentialing would provide under the circumstances.

standards of practice Widely accepted principles that are intended to guide the professional activities of a health care practitioner.

standpipe drain A type of drain that is raised above floor level.

station PPE A group screening process whereby information for individual athletes is collected at a variety of stations staffed by a combination of medical and nonmedical personnel, usually in the context of a school environment.

statutes of limitations Laws that fix a certain length of time beyond which legal actions cannot be initiated.

strategic planning A type of planning that involves critical self-examination in order to bring about organizational improvement.

subcontractor A company hired by the general contractor to complete a particular portion of the building project. The subcontractor's work is usually devoted to a particular skilled trade, such as plumbing, electrical, or landscaping.

subpoena The legal authority used to compel a person to provide testimony.

summative evaluation An assessment designed primarily to describe the effectiveness or accomplishments of a program.

supervision A process whereby authority holders observe the work activities of an employee in order to improve the outcomes of the employee's work or to improve the employee's professional development.

tax-exempt bonds Bonds authorized and sold by governmental agencies to provide funding for construction projects.

terminal A combination cathode ray tube and keyboard that allows users to access a mainframe computer.

testimony Legally binding statements offered as evidence to the facts in a legal proceeding.

thermostat A device that controls heating and cooling equipment.

third party *1:* To be affected by, but not directly involved in, a situation. Professionals who simply have knowledge of an unethical act can be affected by it, because there is a professional responsibility to act on such knowledge. *2:* A medical vendor with no binding interest in a particular insurance contract.

third-party reimbursement The process by which medical vendors are reimbursed by insurance companies for services provided to policyholders.

tort A legal wrong, other than breach of contract, for which a remedy will be provided, usually in the form of monetary damages.

Total Quality Management (TQM) Also known as continuous quality improvement. A management system that emphasizes continuous improvement in the process by which work is accomplished for the purpose of creating improvements in a product. A continuous focus on the needs and desires of clients is a major focus of TQM.

traffic patterns The anticipated flow of people from one area of a building to another.

transactional leadership The simple exchange between leaders and followers of one thing for another.

transformational leadership That aspect of leadership that uses both change and conflict to elevate the standards of the social system.

UB-92 Also known as the **HCFA 1450.** Insurance claim form that hospitals should use.

unity of command A principle of scientific management that requires that the work of an employee be directed by a single superior.

usual, customary, and reasonable fee (UCR) The charge consistent with what other medical vendors would assess.

utility standards Performance evaluation standards intended to help ensure that employee appraisal is useful to workers, employers, and others who need to use the information.

validity (in staff selection) The employment of criteria that predict how well a candidate will perform in a role.

variable budgeting A method requiring that monthly expenditures be adjusted so they do not exceed revenues.

vision statement A concise statement that describes the ideal state to which an organization aspires.

WOTS UP analysis A data collection and appraisal technique designed to determine an organization's strengths, weaknesses, opportunities, and threats in order to facilitate planning.

zero-based budgeting A model that requires justification for every budget line item without reference to previous spending patterns.

zone of indifference A hypothetical boundary of legitimacy, outside of which requests or orders will be met with mere compliance or refusal.

BIBLIOGRAPHY

Abdenour, T.E. (1982). Computerized training room records. *Athletic Training,* 17(3), 191.

Acheson, K.A., & Gall, M.D. (1987). *Techniques in the clinical supervision of teachers* (2nd ed.). New York: Longman.

Ackoff, R.L. (1970). *A concept of corporate planning.* New York: Wiley Interscience.

Aldrich, J.W. (1985). Staffing concepts and principles. In W. Tracey (Ed.), *Human resources management and development handbook* (pp. 165–173). New York: AMACOM.

American Academy of Orthopaedic Surgeons. (1991). *Athletic training and sports medicine.* 2nd ed. Park Ridge, IL: Author.

American Association of University Professors (1995). *AAUP policy documents and reports: Statement on professional ethics.* Washington, DC: Author.

American Counseling Association (1995). *Code of ethics.* Alexandria, VA: Author.

American Heart Association. (1996). Cardiovascular preparticipation screening of competitive athletes. *Circulation,* 94, 850–856.

American Hospital Association (1992). *Ethical conduct for health care institutions.* Chicago: Author.

American Medical Association (1980). *Principles of medical ethics.* Chicago: Author.

American Physical Therapy Association (1991). *Code of ethics.* Alexandria, VA: Author.

American Psychological Association (1992). *Ethical principles of psychologists and code of conduct.* Washington, DC: Author.

Ammer, C., & Ammer, D.S. (1984). *Dictionary of business and economics* (2nd ed.). New York: The Free Press.

Anderson, M.K., & Hall, S.J. (1995). *Sports injury management.* Media, PA: Williams & Wilkins.

Appelbaum, D., & Lawton, S.V. (1990). *Ethics and the professions.* Englewood Cliffs, NJ: Prentice Hall.

Arnheim, D.D., & Prentice, W.E. (1997). *Principles of athletic training* (9th ed.). Dubuque, IA: Brown and Benchmark.

Baley, J.A., & Matthews, D.L. (1984). *Law and liability in athletics, physical education, and recreation.* Boston: Allyn & Bacon.

Barlow, C.W. (1982). *Negotiating skills for the purchasing agent.* New York: American Management Association Membership Publications Division.

Barnard, C.I. (1938). *The functions of the executive.* Cambridge, MA: Harvard University Press.

Bass, B.M. (1990). *Bass & Stogdill's handbook of leadership* (3rd ed.). New York: Macmillan.

Benda, C. (1991). Sideline Samaritans. *The Physician and Sportsmedicine,* 19(11), 132–142.

Bennefield, R.L. (1997). Health insurance coverage: 1996. *Current Population Reports,* P60–199, September.

Bennis, W., & Nanus, B. (1985). *Leaders.* New York: Harper & Row.

Berni, R., & Readey, H. (1978). Problem-oriented medical record implementation. St. Louis: Mosby.

Biehle, J.T. (1982). Construction costs and the "oh my gosh!" syndrome. *American School and University,* 54, C10–C14.

Blake, R.R., & Mouton, J.S. (1984). *Solving costly organizational conflicts.* San Francisco: Jossey-Bass.

Block, P. (1987). *The empowered manager: Positive political skills at work.* San Francisco: Jossey-Bass.

Briner, W.W. (1993). Getting more out of athletic examinations. *American Family Physician,* 48, 225.

Bruce, S.D. (1986). *Prewritten job descriptions.* Madison, CT: Business and Legal Reports.

Burns, J.M. (1978). *Leadership.* New York: Harper & Row.

Cady, C. (1979). A space saving taping table. *Athletic Training,* 14(4), 224.

Campbell, D. (1999, April). Researchers update data from athletic training outcomes study. *NATA News,* 26–27.

Cascio, W.F., & Bernardin, H.J. (1981). Implications of performance appraisal litigation for personnel decisions. *Personnel Psychology,* 34, 211–226.

Castetter, W.B. (1986). *The personnel function in educational administration* (4th ed.). New York: Macmillan.

Chambers, R.L., Ross, N.V., & Kozubowski, J. (1986). Insurance types and coverages: Knowledge to plan for the future (with a focus on motor skill activities and athletics). *Physical Educator,* 44(l), 233–240.

Cheong, V.E., & Hirschheim, R.A. (1983). *Local area networks.* New York: Wiley & Sons.

Christensen, W.W., & Rupp, P.R. (1986). *The nurse manager's guide to computers.* Rockville, MD: Aspen.

Ciccolella, M. (1991). Caught in court. *College Athletic Management,* 3(4), 10–13.

Cohen, A., & Cohen, E. (1979). *Designing and space planning for libraries.* New York: Bowker.

Culp, B., Goemaere, N.D., & Miller, E. (1985). Risk management: An integral part of quality assurance. In Meisenheimer, C.G. (1985). *Quality assurance: A complete guide to effective programs.* Rockville, MD: Aspen, pp. 169–192.

Dale, E. (1965). *Management: Theory and practice.* New York: McGraw-Hill.

Danzon, P.M. (1985). *Medical malpractice.* Cambridge, MA: Harvard University Press.

DeCarlo, M.S. (1997). Reimbursement for health care services. In Konin, J.G. (Ed.) *Clinical athletic training* (pp. 89–104). Thorofare, NJ: Slack.

Dejnozka, E.L. (1983). *Educational administration glossary.* Westport, CT: Greenwood Press.

Demos, G.D., & Grant, B. (1973). *An introduction to counseling: A handbook.* Los Angeles: Western Psychological Services.

Dewey, P.R. (1987). *Essential guide to bulletin board systems.* Westport, CN: Meckler.

Dewey, P.R. (Ed.) (1994). *National directory of bulletin board systems—1994.* Westport, CN: Meckler.

Dibner, D.R. (1982). *You and your architect.* Washington, DC: The American Institute of Architects.

Directory of architects. (1998). *Athletic Business,* 22(2), 289–302.

Dobbins, G.H., & Russell, J.M. (1986). The biasing effects of subordinate likableness on the leaders' responses to poor performers: A laboratory and a field study. *Personnel Psychology,* 39, 759–777.

Dorfman, P.W., Stephan, W.G., & Loveland, J. (1986). Performance appraisal behaviors: Supervisor perceptions and subordinate reactions. *Personnel Psychology,* 39, 579–597.

Dougherty, N.J., & Bonanno, D. (1985). *Management service in sport and leisure services.* Minneapolis, MN: Burgess International.

Drafke, M.W. (1994). *Working in health care: What you need to know to succeed.* Philadelphia: F.A. Davis.

Drake, J.D. (1982). *Interviewing for managers.* New York: AMACOM.

Drowatzky, J.N. (1985). Legal duties and liability in athletic training. *Athletic Training,* 20(l), 10–13.

DuRant, R.H., Pendergrast, R.A., Seymore, C., Gaillard, G., & Donner, J. (1992). Findings from the preparticipation athletic examination and athletic injuries. *American Journal of Diseases of Children,* 146, 85–91.

Elkouri, F., & Elkouri, E.A. (1993). *Resolving drug issues.* Washington, DC: Bureau of National Affairs.

Equal Employment Opportunity Commission. (1979). *Uniform guidelines on employee selection procedures.* Washington, DC: Bureau of National Affairs.

Esposto, L. (1993). Applying functional outcome assessment to Medicare documentation. In Keirns, M.A., Knudsen, L., & Webster, K.J. (1997). Outcomes assessment in athletic training. In Konin, J.G. (Ed.). *Clinical athletic training.* Thorofare, NJ: Slack. pp. 245–253.

Fahey, T.D. (1986). *Athletic training: Principles and practice.* Palo Alto, CA: Mayfield.

Falcone, P. (1997). *96 great interview questions to ask before you hire.* New York: AMACOM.

Fayol, H. (1949). *General and industrial management.* London: Pitman & Sons.

Fein, R. (1986). *Medical care, medical costs.* Cambridge, MA: Harvard University Press.

Fitz-Gibbon, C.T., & Morris, L.L. (1987). *How to design a program evaluation.* Newbury Park, CA: Sage.

Fletcher, M.E., & Ranck, S.L. (1991). Building a committee. *Athletic Business,* 15(8), 49–50.

Forseth, E.A. (1986). Consideration in planning small college athletic training facilities. *Athletic Training,* 21(1), 22–25.

Fowler, A.R., & Bushardt, S.C. (1986). T.O.P.E.S.: Developing a task oriented performance evaluation system. *Advanced Management Journal,* 51(4), 4–8.

Frankel, E. (1991). Handle with care. *College Athletic Management,* 3(3), 11–13.

French, J.R.P., & Raven, B. (1959). The bases of social power. In D. Cartwright (Ed.), *Studies in social power* (pp. 150–167). Ann Arbor, MI: Institute for Social Research.

Frey, D., & Adams, R. (1994). *!%@:: A directory of electronic mail addressing and networks.* Sebastopol, 4th ed., CA: O'Reilly & Associates.

Friedrich, C.J. (1963). *Man and his government: An empirical theory of politics.* New York: McGraw-Hill.

Fry, R. (1993). *Your first interview.* 2nd ed. Hawthorne, NJ: Career Press.

Gabriel, A.J. (1981). Medical communications: Records for the professional athletic trainer. *Athletic Training,* 16(1), 68–69.

Gallup, E.M. (1995). *Law and the team physician.* Champaign, IL: Human Kinetics.

Garofalo, M.J. (1989). How strategies can get lost in the translation. *Business Month,* 134(10), 82–83.

Gibson, C.K., Newton, D.J., & Cochran, D.S. (1990). An empirical investigation of the nature of hospital mission statements. *Health Care Management Review,* 15(3), 35–45.

Gieck, J., Lowe, J., & Kenna, K. (1984). Trainer malpractice: A sleeping giant. *Athletic Training,* 19(1), 41–46.

Gillies, D.A. (1994). *Nursing management: A systems approach.* 3rd ed. Philadelphia: Saunders.

Glondys, B.A. (1988). *Today's challenge: Content of the health record.* Chicago: American Medical Records Association.

Godek, J.J. (1992). Sports rehabilitation in the '90s: Who's who? *Journal of Sport Rehabilitation,* 1, 87–94.

Goldberg, B., Saratini, A., Witman, P., Gavin, M., & Nicholas, J. (1980). Preparticipation sports assessment—An objective evaluation. *Pediatrics,* 67, 736–745.

Good, C.V. (Ed.). (1973). *Dictionary of education.* New York: McGraw-Hill.

Gorlin, R.A. (Ed.). (1990). *Codes of professional responsibility.* 2nd ed. Washington, D.C.: The Bureau of National Affairs, Inc.

Graham, J.D., & Rhomberg, L. (1996). How risks are identified and managed. In H. Kunreuter & P. Slovic (Eds.). *The Annals of the American Academy of Political and Social Science,* vol. 545, May 1996, pp. 15–24.

Graham, L.S. (1985). Ten ways to dodge the malpractice bullet. *Athletic Training,* 20(2), 117–119.

Gulick, L., & Urwick, L. (Eds.). (1977). *Papers on the science of administration.* Fairfield, NJ: Kelley.

Haddad, S.A. (1985). Compensation and benefits. In W. Tracey (Ed.), *Human resources management and development handbook* (pp. 638–660). New York: AMACOM.

Hagerty, B.K., Chang, R.S., & Spengler, C.D. (1985). Work sampling: Analyzing nursing staff productivity. *Journal of Nursing Administration,* 15(9), 9–14.

Hart, P.M., & Cole, S.L. (1992). Subtracting insult from injury. *Athletic Business,* 16(5), 39–42.

Hawkins, J. (1988). The legal status of athletic trainers. *The Sports, Parks and Recreation Law Reporter,* 2(1), 6–9.

Hawkins, J.D. (1989). Sports medicine record keeping: The key to effective communication and documentation. *Sports Medicine Standards and Malpractice Reporter,* 1(2), 31–35.

Health Insurance Association of America (1997). *Fundamentals of health insurance.* Washington, DC: Author.

Health Insurance Association of America (1997). *Federal perspectives*, p. 4. Available: **http://www.hiaa.org/consumerinfo/fedpers2.html/**.

Heinzman, S.E. (1991). Quality physicals that generate funds for the training room. *Athletic Training, JNATA*, 26, 66–69.

Herbert, D.L. (1987). The use of prospective releases containing exculpatory language in exercise and fitness programs. *The Exercise Standards and Malpractice Reporter*, 1(6), 89–90.

Herbert, D.L. (1990). *Legal aspects of sports medicine*. Canton, OH: Professional Reports Corporation.

Herbert, D.L. (1992). *The sports medicine standards book*. Canton, OH: Professional Reports Corporation.

Herbert, D.L. (1996). Athlete's exclusion from participation does not violate Federal Rehabilitation Act. *Sports Medicine Standards and Malpractice Reporter*, 8, 40–43.

Herbert, D.L. (1997). Sports medicine physician has "final say" in exclusion of athlete from participation. *Sports Medicine Standards and Malpractice Reporter*, 9(17), 20–23.

Herbert, D.L., & Herbert, W.G. (1989). *Legal aspects of preventative and rehabilitative exercise programs*, (2nd ed.). Canton, OH: Professional Reports Corporation.

Hollander, E.P. (1978). *Leadership dynamics: A practical guide to effective relationships*. New York: Macmillan.

Horine, L. (1991). *Administration of physical education and sport programs* (2nd ed.). Dubuque, IA: Brown.

Horn, J. (1992). HCFA considers revisions of coding system. *P.T. Bulletin*, 7(28), 3, 40.

Horsley, J.E., & Carlova, J. (1983). *Testifying in court*. Oradell, NJ: Medical Economics.

Huber, V.L., Podsakoff, P.M., & Todor, W.D. (1986). An investigation of biasing factors in the attributions of subordinates and their supervisors. *Journal of Business Research*, 14, 83–97.

Illingworth, V. (1997). *Dictionary of computing* (4th ed.). New York: Oxford University Press.

Iyer, P.W. (1991). *Nursing documentation: A nursing process approach*. St. Louis: Mosby Year Book.

Jacobs, T.O. (1970). *Leadership and exchange in formal organizations*. Alexandria, VA: Human Resources Research Organization.

Joint Committee on Standards for Educational Evaluation. (1981). *Standards for evaluations of educational programs, projects, and materials*. New York: McGraw-Hill.

Joint Committee on Standards for Educational Evaluation. (1988). *The personnel evaluation standards*. Beverly Hills, CA: Sage.

Jones, R.L., & Trentin, H.G. (1971). *Budgeting: Key to planning and control* (2nd ed.). New York: American Management Association.

Kahn, R.F. (1968). A note on the concept of authority. In G. Wijeyewardene (Ed.), *Leadership and authority* (pp. 6–14). Kuala Lumpur, Malaysia: University of Malaysia Press.

Karelis, C.H. (1987). The limits of leadership. *Liberal Education*, 73(2), 20–33.

Katz, D., & Kahn, R.L. (1966). *The social psychology of organizations*. New York: Wiley & Sons.

Kauffman, R., Rojas, A. M., & Mayer, H. (1993). *Needs assessment: A user's guide*. Englewood Cliffs, NJ: Educational Technology.

Keaveny, T.J., & McGann, A.F. (1980). Performance appraisal format: Role clarity and evaluation criteria. *Research in Higher Education*, 13(3), 225–232.

Keirns, M.A., Knudsen, L., & Webster, K.J. (1997). Outcomes assessment in athletic training. In J.G. Konin (Ed.), *Clinical athletic training* (pp. 245–253). Thorofare, NJ: SLACK.

Kess, S., & Westlin, B. (1987). *Business strategies*. Chicago: Commerce Clearinghouse.

Kettenbach, G. (1995). *Writing S.O.A.P. notes*. (2nd ed.) Philadelphia: Davis.

Kibler, W.B. (1990). *The sport preparticipation fitness examination*. Champaign, IL: Human Kinetics.

King, A.A. (1987). *Power and communication*. Prospect Heights, IL: Waveland.

Koester, M.C. (1995). Refocusing the adolescent preparticipation physical evaluation toward preventive health care. *Journal of Athletic Training*, 30, 352–360.

Kolodny, H.F. (1979). Evolution to a matrix organization. *Academy of Management Review*, 4(4), 543–553.

Lasswell, H.D., & Kaplan, A. (1950). Power and society: A framework for political inquiry. *Yale Law School Studies, 2*, 133.

Lehr, C. (1992). Status of medical insurance provided to student-athletes at NCAA schools. *Journal of Legal Aspects of Sport, 2*(l), 12–22.

Leiske, A.M. (1985). Standards: The basis of a quality assurance program. In C.G. Meisenheimer (1985), *Quality assurance: A complete guide to effective programs.* Rockville, MD: Aspen, pp. 45–72.

Leroy, L. (1990). A review of record keeping sports medicine computer software. *Athletic Training, 25*(4), 321–328.

Leverenz, L.J., & Helms, L.B. (1990a). Suing athletic trainers: Part I. *Athletic Training, 25*(3), 212–216.

Leverenz, L.J., & Helms, L.B. (1990b). Suing athletic trainers: Part II. *Athletic Training, 25*(3), 219–226.

Locke, L.F., Spirduso, W.W., & Silverman, S.J. (1993). *Proposals that work: A guide for planning dissertations and grant proposals.* 3rd ed. Newbury Park, CA: Sage.

Lyer, P.W. (1991). New trends in charting. *Nursing 91, 21*(l), 48–50.

Lysens, R., Steverlynck, A., & van den Auweele, Y. (1984). The predictability of sports injuries. *Sports Medicine, 1*, 6–10.

Makarowski, L.M., & Rickell, J.B. (1993). Ethical and legal issues for sport professionals counseling injured athletes. In D. Pargman (Ed.), *Psychological bases of sport injuries* (pp. 45–65). Morgantown, WV: Fitness Information Technology, Inc.

Mangus, B.C., & Ingersoll, C.D. (1990). Approaches to ethical decision making in athletic training. *Athletic Training, JNATA, 25*, 340–343.

Margolin, J.B. (1983). *The individual's guide to grants.* New York: Plenum.

Marrelli, T.M. (1992). *Nursing documentation handbook.* St. Louis: Mosby.

May, C.A., Schraeder, C., & Britt, T. (1996). *Managed care and case management: Roles for professional nursing.* Washington, DC: American Nurses Publishing.

Mayo, H.B. (1978). *Basic finance.* Philadelphia: Saunders.

McCarthy, M.M. (1983). Discrimination in employment. In J. Beckham & P. Zirkel (Eds.), *Legal issues in public school employment* (pp. 46–47). Bloomington, IN: Phi Delta Kappan.

McKeag, D.B., & Hough, D.O. (1993). *Primary care sports medicine.* Dubuque, IA: Wm. C. Brown.

Mehrabian, A. (1981). *Silent messages.* 2nd ed. Belmont, CA: Wadsworth.

Miles, B.J. (1987). Injuries on the road: Good information reduces problems. *Athletic Training, 22*(2), 127.

Mintzberg, H. (1973). *The nature of managerial work.* New York: Harper & Row.

Morris, L.L., & Fitz-Gibbon, C.T. (1978). *How to present an evaluation report.* Newbury Park, CA: Sage.

Murphy, J., & Burke, L.J. (1990). Charting by exception. *Nursing 90, 20*(5), 65–69.

Muther, R., & Wheeler, J.D. (1973). *Simplified systematic layout planning.* Kansas City, MO: Management & Industrial Research Publications.

Myers, O.J. (1985). Myths concerning employees' performance appraisal. *Supervision, 47*(12), 14–16.

National Athletic Trainers' Association (1987). *Standards of practice for athletic trainers.* Dallas, TX: Author.

National Athletic Trainers' Association (1995). *NATA code of ethics.* Dallas, TX: Author.

National Athletic Trainers' Association, Professional Education Committee (1992). *Competencies in Athletic Training.* Dallas, TX: Author.

National Collegiate Athletic Association. (1995). *1995–1996 NCAA drug education and testing programs.* Overland Park, KS: Author.

National Collegiate Athletic Association. (1998). *1998–1999 NCAA sports medicine handbook.* Overland Park, KS: Author.

National Collegiate Athletic Association Committee on Competitive Safeguards and Medical Aspects of Sports. (1988). *Drugs and the intercollegiate athlete.* Overland Park, KS: Author.

Needy, J.R. (1974). *Filing systems.* Arlington, VA: National Recreation and Park Association.

Nehmer, K.S. (Ed.) (1997). *Guide to free computer materials.* (15th ed.) Randolph, WI: Educators Progress Service.

Newcomer, L.N. (1990). Defining experimental therapy: A third-party payer's dilemma. *The New England Journal of Medicine, 323*(24), 1702–1704.

O'Leary, M.R. (1994). *Lexicon.* Oakbrook Terrace, IL: Joint Commission on Accreditation of Healthcare Organizations.

Occupational Safety and Health Administration. (1991). Occupational exposure to bloodborne pathogens. *Federal Register, 56*(235), 64175–64182.

Organ, D.W., & Bateman, T. (1986). *Organizational behavior: An applied psychological approach.* Plano, TX: Business Publications.

Ouchi, W.G., & Dowling, J.B. (1974). Defining the span of control. *Administrative Science Quarterly, 19,* 357–365.

Owens, R.G. (1987). *Organizational behavior in education* (3rd ed.). Englewood Cliffs, NJ: Prentice Hall.

Parks, J. (1977). Athletic trainer evaluation. *Athletic Training, 12*(2), 92–93.

Pearce, J.A. (1982). The company mission as a strategic tool. *Sloan Management Review, 23*(2), 15–23.

Penman, K.A. (1977). *Planning physical education and athletic facilities in schools.* New York: Wiley & Sons.

Penman, K.A., & Adams, S.H. (1980). *Assessing athletic and physical education programs.* Boston: Allyn & Bacon.

Penman, K.A., & Penman, T.M. (1982). Training rooms aren't just for colleges. *Athletic Purchasing and Facilities, 6*(9), 34–37.

Penton/IPC Education Division. (1982). *Fundamentals of PERT.* Cleveland, OH: Author.

Pettigrew, A.M. (1972). Information control as a power source. *Sociology, 6,* 187–204.

Pheasant, S.T. (1991). *Ergonomics, work and health.* Gaithersburg, MD: Aspen.

Pickett, A.D. (1986). Drug testing: What are the rules? *Athletic Training, 21,* 331–336.

Planning facilities for athletics, physical education, and recreation. (1979). North Palm Beach, FL: The Athletic Institute.

Porter, M.M., & Porter, J.W. (1981). Electrical safety in the training room. *Athletic Training, 16*(4), 263–264.

Priest, S.L. (1989). *Understanding computer resources: A healthcare perspective.* Owings Mills, MD: National Health Publishing.

Randolph, W.A., & Posner, B.Z. (1988). What every manager needs to know about project management. *Sloan Management Review, 29*(4), 65–73.

Rankin, J.M. (1992). Financial resources for conducting athletic training programs in the collegiate and high school settings. *Journal of Athletic Training, 27,* 344–349.

Rankin, J.M., & Ingersoll, C. (1995). Athletic training management: Concepts and applications. St. Louis: Mosby.

Ray, R.R. (1990). An injury-free budget. *College Athletic Management, 2*(l), 42–45.

Ray, R.R. (1991a). Performance evaluation in athletic training: Perceptions of athletic trainers and their supervisors. *Dissertation Abstracts International, 51,* 5053. (Doctoral dissertation, Western Michigan University, 1990).

Ray, R.R. (1991b). Training room efficiency. *Athletic Business, 15*(l), 46–49.

Ray, R.R. (1995). An electronic daily injury report system. *Journal of Athletic Training, 30,* 180–181.

Ray, R. R. (1996). Create your own HMO. *Athletic Therapy Today. 1*(4), 11–12.

Ray, R.R. (1997). Technology in athletic therapy: Expectation or Hope? *Athletic Therapy Today. 2*(5), 5.

Ray, R.R., & Shire, T.L. (1986). An athletic training program in the computer age. *Athletic Training, 21*(3), 212–214.

Reilly, T. (1981). Ergonomic aspects of sport and recreation. *Canadian Journal of Applied Sport Science, 6*(1), 1–10.

Reinhardt, C. (1985). The state of performance appraisal: A literature review. *Human Resource Planning, 8*(2), 105–110.

Ribaric, R.F. (1980). Taping/storage table. *Athletic Training*, 15(1), 50.

Ribaric, R. (1982). The computer in sports medicine. *Athletic Training*, 17(4), 309.

Rowell, J.C. (1989). *Understanding medical insurance reimbursement: A step-by-step guide.* Oradell, NJ: Medical Economics.

Schneier, C.E., Beatty, R.W., & Baird, L.S. (1986). How to construct a successful performance appraisal system. *Training and Development Journal,* 40(4), 38–42.

Schneller, T., & Godwin, C. (1983). *Writing skills for nurses.* Reston, VA: Reston.

Scholey, M., & Hair, M. (1989). Back pain in physiotherapists involved in back care education. *Ergonomics*, 32(2), 179–190.

School Records. (1996, May). *Your School and the Law,* 26(5).

Scott, R.W. (1990). *Health care malpractice.* Thorofare, NJ: Slack.

Secor, M.R. (1984). Designing athletic training facilities or "Where do you want the outlets?" *Athletic Training,* 19(1), 19–21.

Settle, S.M., & Spigelmyer, S. (1984). *Product liability: A multibillion-dollar dilemma.* New York: American Management Association.

Sikula, A.F. (1976). *Personnel administration and human resources management.* New York: Wiley & Sons.

Smith, D.M. (1994). Pre-participation physical evaluations: Development of uniform guidelines. *Sports Medicine,* 18, 293–300.

Snider, S.W. (1982, January). Planning a new building? Consider design/build. *Athletic Purchasing and Facilities,* pp. 50–51.

Source book of health insurance data. (1998). Washington, DC: Health Insurance Association of America.

Standards of practice. (1987). Dallas: National Athletic Trainers Association.

Steers, R.M., & Porter, L.W. (1987). Motivation and work behavior (4th ed.). New York: McGraw-Hill.

Stein, J. (1996). Source book of health insurance data. Washington, DC: Health Insurance Association of America.

Steiner, G.A. (1979). *Strategic planning.* New York: The Free Press.

Stewart, D.L. (1993). Health care delivery system. In Stewart, D.L. & Abeln, S.H. (Eds.). *Documenting functional outcomes in physical therapy.* St. Louis: Mosby, pp. 1–31.

Stewart, D.L. & Abeln, S.H. (Eds.). *Documenting functional outcomes in physical therapy.* St. Louis: Mosby, pp. 135–174.

Stoner, J.A.F. (1982). *Management* (2nd ed.). Englewood Cliffs, NJ: Prentice Hall.

Synnott, W.R., & Gruber, W.H. (1981). *Information resource management.* New York: Wiley & Sons.

Tanner, D., & Tanner, L. (1987). *Supervision in education.* New York: Macmillan.

The Foundation Center Staff (1997). National guide to funding in health. New York: Author.

Theunissen, W. (1978). Planning facilities: The role of the program specialist. *Journal of Physical Education and Recreation,* 49(6), 27–29.

Thomas, K.W., & Kilmann, R.H. (1974). *The Thomas-Kilmann conflict mode instrument.* Tuxedo Park, NY: Xicom.

Thompson, R.A., & Sherman, R.T. (1993). *Helping athletes with eating disorders.* Champaign, IL: Human Kinetics.

Thorland, W. (1990). Drug detection. In *Substance abuse in sports: The realities.* Dubuque, IA: Kendall/Hunt, pp. 71–75.

Tropman, J.E. (1996). *Making meetings work: Achieving high quality group decisions.* Thousand Oaks, CA: Sage.

U.S. Small Business Administration (1980). *Job analysis, job specifications, and job descriptions.* Washington, DC: U.S. Government Printing Office.

U.S. Small Business Administration. (1980). *Business basics: Inventory management.* Washington, DC: U.S. Government Printing Office.

U. S. Small Business Administration. (1981). *Risk management and insurance.* Washington, DC: U.S. Government Printing Office.

Wadlington, W., Waltz, J.R., & Dworkin, R.B. (1980). *Law and medicine.* Mineola, NY: Foundation Press.

Want, J.H. (1986). Corporate mission. *Management Review, 75*(8), 46–50.

Weber, M. (1962). *Basic concepts in sociology* (H.P. Secher, Trans.). Secaucus, NJ: Citadell.

Wildavsky, A. (1975). *Budgeting: A comparative theory of budgetary processes.* Boston: Little, Brown.

Witkin, B.R., & Altschuld, J.W. (1995). *Planning and conducting needs assessments: A practical guide.* Thousand Oaks, CA: Sage.

Worthen, B.R., & Sanders, J.R. (1973). *Educational evaluation: Theory and practice.* Worthington, OH: Charles A. Jones.

Wright , B.J. (1983). *Automated purchasing: Key to new potential.* New York: American Management Association Membership Publication Division.

Yukl, G.A. (1981). *Leadership in organizations.* Englewood Cliffs, NJ: Prentice Hall.

INDEX

The letters *f* and *t* after page numbers indicate figures and tables, respectively.